THE MAZE OF FEAR

SECURITY AND MIGRATION AFTER 9/11

EDITED BY JOHN TIRMAN

SOCIAL SCIENCE RESEARCH COUNCIL

Withdrawn

THE NEW PRESS

NEW YORK
LONDON

The cover photograph is a Z® Backscatter X-ray image revealing illegal immigrants attempting to enter Southern Mexico from Guatemala in a truckload of bananas. The photograph is © 2004 by American Science and Engineering, Inc. (AS&E). Used with permission.

Published in the United States by The New Press, New York, 2004
Distributed by W. W. Norton & Company, Inc., New York

LIBRARY OF CONGRESS CATALOGING-IN-PUBLICATION DATA

The maze of fear : security and migration after 9/11 / John Tirman, editor.
p.   cm.
Includes bibliographical references and index.
ISBN 1-56584-916-7 (hc.) — ISBN 1-56584-906-X (pbk.)
1. Terrorism—United States.   2. September 11 Terrorist Attacks, 2001.
3. Emigration and immigration—United States.   4. Internal security—United States.
5. Security, International.   6. Globalization.   I. Tirman, John.

HV6432.M385   2004
363.32'0973—dc22   2004044899

The New Press was established in 1990 as a not-for-profit alternative to the large, commercial publishing houses currently dominating the book publishing industry. The New Press operates in the public interest rather than for private gain, and is committed to publishing, in innovative ways, works of educational, cultural, and community value that are often deemed insufficiently profitable.

The New Press
38 Greene Street, 4th floor
New York, NY 10013
www.thenewpress.com

Composition by dix!

Printed in Canada

2   4   6   8   10   9   7   5   3   1

CONTENTS

ACKNOWLEDGMENTS

This volume is the fourth in a series produced by the Social Science Research Council and published by The New Press. The series was created soon after the attacks of September 11, 2001, by SSRC president Craig Calhoun and The New Press editor André Schiffren, an exceptional collaboration attempting to grasp the broad significance of the 9/11 atrocities. The first three volumes are *Understanding September 11* (edited by Craig Calhoun, Paul Price, and Ashley Timmer); *Critical Views of September 11: Analyses from Around the World* (edited by Eric Hershberg and Kevin W. Moore), and *Bombs and Bandwidth: The Emerging Relationship Between IT and Security* (edited by Robert Latham). Each has its own perspective and draws on leading social scientists to grapple with the complexity, danger, and tragedy of 9/11 and its aftermath.

As editor of this fourth volume, I thank Craig Calhoun and André Schiffren for their perseverance in this important effort. I also thank my SSRC colleagues Paul Price, SSRC editor, and Josh DeWind, who heads the Program on International Migration, for their help, which has been skillfully applied to this volume in several different ways. My colleagues in the Program on Global Security and Cooperation—Itty Abraham, Margaret Schuppert, Petra Ticha, Veronica Raffo, and Karim Youssef—also deserve thanks. The book was made possible with the financial assistance of the William and Flora Hewlett Foundation and the John D. and Catherine T. MacArthur Foundation.

We began to plan this volume within weeks of the 9/11 attacks. As the substance of its contents evolved, we faced the inevitable difficulties of capturing a topic in flux. The ensuing eighteen months witnessed the toppling of the Taliban and fitful nation-building in Afghanistan; thousands of arrests and detentions of suspects in the United States, Europe, and elsewhere; new laws and executive edicts in Washington and other capitals to strengthen state responses; spikes of political violence and military reprisals worldwide; and the U.S. war against Saddam Hussein's regime in Iraq, among other events. To say that insightful analysis of such dynamic times is difficult would be to state the obvious. It is indeed a testament to all the volumes in this series—the first two of which were produced within weeks of 9/11—that such solid contributions to understanding the attacks, their origins, and their consequences could be assembled at all. To the authors of the following chapters, then, go particular thanks for thinking and writing under unusual circumstances. The essays in this volume—attempting to dissect these phenomena with respect to security, state responses, and migration—reflect, no doubt, the complexity, contradictions, and passions provoked by what we now call, with deceptive simplicity, "9/11."

—*John Tirman*
February 2004

THE MAZE OF FEAR

INTRODUCTION: THE MOVE
PEOPLE AND THE SECURITY OF

JOHN TIRMAN

A few weeks after the September 11 terrorist attacks on the World Trade Center and the Pentagon, I was walking home along a busy street in Washington, D.C., when a Lexus sedan pulled up and stopped a few feet away. I noticed it immediately because it was adorned with several American flag decals and an American flag on the dashboard along with two new baseball caps, one with the initials "NYPD" on it and the other with "NYFD." Even in the patriotic flush of the post-9/11 climate, this car was conspicuous. Two middle-aged men jumped out of the car to greet a third on the sidewalk; they were all well dressed in tailored suits. And then I noticed the final detail: they appeared to be Arabs, probably Arab Americans.

The brief scene stuck in my mind's eye because one could virtually unravel an entire drama behind it: an Arab American businessman and his family, frightened by the prospect of being swept up in recriminatory hysteria, opt for garish displays of American patriotism to ward off criticism, or worse. It signified many political and social currents in one vignette—that immigrant communities, particularly those from Muslim countries, were at risk, or, more ominously, that they posed a risk; that the nation's unity and identity were unassailable; and, perhaps most significant, that the durable shibboleth of America's love affair with immigrants had been betrayed.

That scene, replayed perhaps in a thousand different ways all over the United States, certainly signals a change in the way we view the relationship between migration and security. Much in international relations has been transformed by the September 11 atrocities and the aftermath. The perception of threat, the global realignment of allies and "evildoers," the stigmatizing of states harboring terrorists, the renewed concern about weapons of mass destruction, and the embrace of strong states are all apparent consequences, at least in the short term, among many others. Very high on this agenda is migration and its implications for global security.

The link stems from the profiles of the nineteen attackers in those four airplanes. All of them were in the United States on temporary visas, three of which had expired. All of them were from the Middle East, mostly Saudi and Egyptian,

, all were Muslim. As it became clear that this was the work of the al Qaeda network of Osama bin Laden, and the links to other acts of political violence were established, the migration-security dimension began to take shape. And a large shape it is: the previous attacks and network activities of al Qaeda and its allies included the World Trade Center bombing of 1993, the attacks on U.S. embassies in Tanzania and Kenya in 1998, and the attacks on a U.S. military base in Saudi Arabia and a U.S. Navy ship in Yemen. Soon al Qaeda cells were revealed to exist in Germany, Italy, Malaysia, Indonesia, and elsewhere. Money trails were leading to all corners of the globe. Training took place in several "failed states" and possibly in other "rogue" states. This was a worldwide operation, with no firm territorial or national base. Terrorism was, in short, a transnational security threat and, by its nature, was dependent on migration of people, weapons, information, and money.

After the September 11 attacks, the culprits of American vulnerability were widely identified as porous borders, generous entry policies, violations of the terms of entry, and the entry of immigrants from the Middle East more generally. Fortunately, the anxieties embedded in this new sense of vulnerability did not result in more than a few instances of violence against such immigrants. But the identification of the problems did quickly spur the government to tighten immigration policy. Within days, the Immigration and Naturalization Service (INS) expanded its powers to detain aliens. The Homeland Security Presidential Directive 2, "Combating Terrorism Through Immigration Policies," was issued by President Bush on October 29, 2001, and locked immigration and security together bureaucratically. The directive provided the platform for these federal agencies to work together to "deny entry into the United States of aliens associated with, suspected of being engaged in, or supporting terrorist activity; . . . [and] to locate, detain, prosecute, or deport any such aliens already present in the United States."

That same week, the USA Patriot Act was enacted by Congress and signed by the president. The act expanded the powers of the attorney general in particular to detain and prosecute aliens under a variety of provisions. (In the first year after the attacks, 1,250 men were so detained for many months.) The act, wrote Nancy Chang, senior litigation attorney of the Center for Constitutional Rights,

> deprives immigrants of their due process and First Amendment rights through two mechanisms that operate in tandem. First, Section 411 vastly expands the class of immigrants who are subject to removal on terrorism grounds through its broad definitions of the terms "terrorist activity," "engage in terrorist activity," and "terrorist organization." Second, Section 412 vastly expands the authority of the Attorney General to place immigrants he suspects are engaged in terrorist activities in detention while their removal proceedings are pending.

Political speech was specially targeted. An immigrant engaging in a peaceful political demonstration, for example, or giving money to an organization active in support of, say, Palestinian children, could be detained indefinitely and deported, or prosecuted and imprisoned. The broad and vague definitions of "terrorist" activity or organizations were particularly worrisome to civil rights experts. The point here, however, is that forging the new link between migration and security was a primary objective of the U.S. government, and it forcefully did so with alacrity in less than seven weeks.

A second set of responses, the global "war on terrorism" that began most dramatically with the bombing of Afghanistan on October 7, 2001, also reified the migration-security nexus. The al Qaeda bases in Afghanistan were the principal target. As became obvious through the ensuing military campaign, the al Qaeda fighters and the Taliban forces that also became targets of U.S. action were multinational militias moving with impunity across borders, particularly the mountainous divide between Pakistan and Afghanistan. The latter country, long besieged by outside forces, had been a petri dish for political militants from much of the Middle East, South Asia, and Central Asia, many of them bred in refugee camps. Al Qaeda itself was there out of convenience; none of the principals were Afghans, a few were Pakistanis. So this opening gambit in the war on terrorism was engaging an enemy that is by its very nature transnational, unfixed, and politically ephemeral.

The Taliban dissolved under pressure from U.S. bombers and fighters from rival tribes but apparently reconstituted itself in Pakistan. The al Qaeda members targeted by U.S. forces fought briefly and then fled to Pakistan and elsewhere. Meanwhile, police investigators throughout the world were uncovering al Qaeda cells, money-laundering operations, brief alliances with other criminal organizations, and other evidence of the exceptional geographic expanse of the network. Virtually all of this illegal activity, designed to support a large, dispersed network of political violence, was conducted by migrants, underscoring, along with the U.S. military and police campaign to destroy or disrupt their actions, the newly minted connection between security and migration, or, to use an unwieldly term, the "securitization of migration."

Migration was previously appreciated as having security implications, though such situations tended to be localized and outside the West. Consider, for example, the Kurdish insurgency in Turkey. The long struggle for Kurdish autonomy in southeast Turkey, led by the Kurdistan Workers' Party (PKK), was from 1984 to 1999 a bloody affair taking some 30,000 lives and leading the Turkish military to forcibly evict as many as one million Kurds from their villages. This set in motion a large influx of Kurds in Istanbul in particular and aided the rise of an Islamic political party, which twice won pluralities in parliamentary elections and sparked a crisis of secular governance. The PKK also operated for years from bases in Iraq and Syria, prompting cross-border raids by the Turkish military, creating a recurring source of tension between the two major factions among Kurds in northern Iraq, and spurring Ankara's opposition to U.S. plans to liberate Iraq because of the specter of another refugee crisis (which occurred in 1991–92) and the potential for renewed Kurdish militancy. Tens of thousands of Kurds migrated legally or illegally to Germany, Italy, Greece, and elsewhere, causing a variety of problems in those countries, including violent clashes spurred by PKK members in Germany against Turks who were labor recruits. The single factor of migration does not explain this cascade of effects, of course, but it is prominent and clearly connected to state and human security in Turkey and possibly elsewhere in the region and Europe.[1]

The Kurdish issue, while unique in its precise dimensions, is similar to other migration phenomena that clearly raised security concerns and responses. The large movement of Haitians in the early 1990s to escape poverty and repression became an acute national security issue for the U.S. government in 1994, when some 21,000 Haitians were interdicted and President Clinton, citing national security logic, threatened military intervention in Haiti to remove its military regime and to restore the democratically elected president. In the former Yugoslavia throughout the 1990s, forced migration became an objective of war, a grisly tool of ethnic cleansing, rousing the West to intervene decisively in Bosnia in 1995 and in Kosovo in 1999. In the aftermath of the 1994 Rwandan genocide, it was soon realized that the refugee camps in the Congo were becoming platforms for Hutu militancy, prompting (along with other factors) a civil war and intervention by outside states that kept the Congo roiled for years afterward. That was neither the first nor the last time "refugee-warriors" challenged their old regime or that of a host country. Fiona Terry of Medecins sans Frontieres points out that such militants have been active for five decades around the world, sometimes manipulated (or even created) by larger powers.[2] These refugee-warriors comprise a long list replete with instances of cross-border interventions—Afghans in Pakistan, Nicaraguans in Honduras, Palestinians in Lebanon, and so on—and legal haiku. Because refugees are protected by international law, host countries are drawn into the conflict, as are humanitarian relief groups and U.N. agencies that nonetheless are obliged to protect the nonwarriors displaced in camps that also serve as guerrilla bases. In fact, the incentives to cross borders in order to make war on the homeland regime are powerful.

The episodes of the migration-security nexus, as Terry and others point out, are hardly confined to the post–Cold War world. This nexus can be a useful lens to understand much of the history of colonialism. (Consider the migration of European-American "settlers" into the American West and the genocide of indigenous peoples that resulted.) This connection, however, has not been appreciated much by the theorists of migration nor the theorists of international relations. Some work in the early 1990s did address the link, perhaps most significantly by Myron Weiner, who sorted out five categories of how migration and security are intertwined: (1) when refugees and immigrants organize against their homeland regime, as Khomeini did from Paris in the 1970s; (2) when they pose a risk to the security of the host country; (3) when large influxes of migrants overwhelm the host country's language, customs, self-image, etc.; (4) when they create a social and economic threat to natives, particularly in employment; and (5) when immigrants are used as "weapons" of war, as when Saddam Hussein held foreigners hostage during the 1991 Gulf War. Of these, the social or human security aspects received the most attention.[3] Only now, after the September 11 attacks, does Weiner's second definition become the most prominent and urgent.

DOMESTIC SECURITY AND GLOBALIZATION

It was often opined in the aftermath of the September 11 attacks that the terrorist phenomenon is somehow a consequence of globalization, but exactly how that may be true was not fully articulated. Globalization carries several connotations with varying degrees of precision, but three of the most prominent have been attached to post-9/11 analysis. First is the reference to "cultural imperialism," which typically means the transmission of so-called American values through television, music, and other exports—the migration, one might say, of ideas, or at least popular entertainment. Because so many of these ideas defy traditional mores, they have created some resentment. Cultural globalization, says Stanley Hoffmann, "takes form in a renaissance of local cultures and languages as well as assaults against Western culture, which is denounced as an arrogant bearer of a secular, revolutionary ideology and a mask for U.S. hegemony."[4]

This perception of American dominance is key, apparently manifested by the other two, more tangible, dimensions of globalization. The second (and most central) aspect of globalization is the "marketization" of the economies of developing countries (and former communist countries)—with tendrils woven back and forth to the wealthy countries—and the actualizing policies thrust upon them by the G-7 and by the United States particularly. These policies have, among other consequences, drastically reduced social spending in the global south and have left great numbers of people on the outside looking in; the anger at seeing great wealth, sometimes corruptly gained, is perhaps most acutely felt by those who have useful skills and education but are still excluded. This phenomenon leads in some places to resentment and in others, to migration.

The third most prominent aspect of globalization is its essential supranationalism; in communications technologies, in the movement of capital, and in the ease of travel, this dimension, which braces the other two, accelerates the speed of social and economic change while making possible the kind of organization al Qaeda apparently is: dispersed, migratory, nonnational, financially opportunistic, and networked. "Technological networks," writes one analyst, "facilitate the operation of larger and more-dispersed social networks and can even act as a critical force multiplier." [5]

These characteristics of globalization come into play in several pertinent ways. Consider the borderlands of places like Afghanistan, Iraq, Congo, and West Africa, or the triple border joining Argentina, Brazil, and Paraguay. Most of these are beset by lawlessness or war or both; several are platforms for foreign militias of various kinds, and all have reputations as being porous to any kind of contraband. They are all associated with the movement of people and things across borders: migrations of greater or lesser illicitness; movement of people-*as*-things, traded like watches, drugs, or weapons; and movement of people as political agents, possibly guerrillas or terrorists. One can point to the forces of globalization as being a contributor to these essentially criminal zones: weakened or failed states; marginalized regions where crime always pays; easily conveyed worldwide demands for certain goods and services; largely unregulated transfers of money, and so on. These are the venues for much of the warfare we see today, and they may be the most obvious places where migration and (in)security are fused. Here, too, are the most questionable applications of traditional security mechanisms, as the United States soon discovered in all its "humanitarian" interventions of the 1990s as well as the in pursuit of al Qaeda in Afghanistan. It scarcely needs to be noted that to the extent the multiple effects of globalization have created or contributed to the underlying causes of weak states, criminalized borderlands, international networks of terrorists, etc., the "West" and particularly the United States have been instrumental in engendering this momentous security dilemma.

Of course, it was not in Afghanistan or Angola that the al Qaeda operatives launched their deadly attacks of September 11; it was not there that they learned how to fly jetliners or how to make their way to Logan, Newark, and Dulles airports, or how to integrate into American society just long enough to hatch their plans. These tasks were carried out in America. So the troubling migrations besetting U.S. antiterrorism policy today are not only those of the lawless borderlands in Central Asia, but also those taking place in the humdrum locales of visa application offices, INS checkpoints, airport passenger lists, etc.—the gigantic American border, which is not only lines on a map but a complex labyrinth of entry points, status, intention, and time. This puzzling vulnerability is what set the USA Patriot Act and like-minded measures in motion with only the faintest public quibble.

The official U.S. securitization of migration is set in a perplexing tangle of long borders, large-scale and welcomed labor migration, and sizable throngs of tourist and student visitors. Every year, about 31 million foreigners enter the United States, most of them legally under reciprocal visa waivers with twenty-nine countries. Some 8.5 million who are in the United States at any one time are unauthorized—i.e., those without such visa waivers, or those with visas or waivers who have overstayed their ninety-day period (as some of the 9/11 attackers did). At 200 U.S. consulates and embassies around the world, more than 1,000 consular officers issued 7.1 million visas in fiscal year 2000.[6] As several analysts have noted, the United States has had essentially open borders.

These sizable numbers are attributable in part to the need for migrant labor—both skilled for industries like information technology and semiskilled or un-skilled for work in, for example, agriculture. Much of what constituted pre-9/11 immigration policy in the United States and Europe revolved around labor is-sues. Labor migration was encouraged in various ways over time, even as con-cerns about immigrants displacing native workers mounted in times of economic downturns. Meanwhile, the number of student visas issued has grown almost fivefold in the last three decades, rising from 65,000 in 1971 to 315,000 in 2000, an increase partially endorsed, perhaps erroneously, on economic grounds.[7]

As a result of these long trends and traditions in American immigration, which to some degree mirror those of Western Europe, economics has tended to trump security as a policy consideration. To the extent security was considered at all, it was framed as a problem of "social" security—namely, of the challenges to natives' jobs, to the nation's cultural identity, to crime control, and the like. A re-cent assessment of the trade-offs between economic and social concerns con-cludes that "even among Western democratic states, where national identity is comprised at least in part of liberal notions of toleration and assimilation, per-ceived threats to societal sovereignty have created new objects of security"—the threat being migrant labor. Policy makers in the United States and Europe tended to make relatively minor adjustments in immigration policy, coupled with highly visible attempts to police borders to prevent illegal immigration. The latter, while not exactly cosmetic, has had a minor impact on overall numbers of immigrants. "Policies in the 1990s were not characterized by increasing closure across the board vis-à-vis migration, but rather, by the state's desire to finesse societal insecurities while concurrently maximizing economic gains. This was accomplished by shaping policy to address *fears* rather than *flows*." [8]

Immigration policies, whether in the United States or elsewhere, are reactions to migration that has already occurred in very large numbers. Scholars of international migration focus vividly on economic motivations as the underlying reason individuals and families leave their homes and communities and travel, sometimes great distances and at some peril, to seek material gain somewhere else. But that alone, arguably the main cause of human migration throughout history, does not explain the striking rise in migration in recent years. The current answer to the fundamental question for these migration theorists—Why do people migrate?—revolves around the current form of economic organization: worldwide marketization and its accompanying processes. This globalization is so pervasive that "seeking material gain elsewhere" falls far short of capturing the complexity of the phenomenon. As a leading scholar of migration, Douglas S. Massey, opens his discussion of a synthetic theory:

> International migration originates in the social, economic, cultural, and political transformations that accompany the penetration of capitalist markets into nonmarket and premarket societies. . . . [I]n the context of a globalizing economy, the entry of markets and capital-intensive production technologies into peripheral regions disrupts existing social and economic arrangements and brings about a displacement of people from customary livelihoods, creating a mobile population of workers who actively search for new ways of achieving economic sustenance. International migrants tend not to come from poor, isolated places that are disconnected from world markets, but from regions and nations that are undergoing rapid change and development as a result of their incorporation into global trade, information, and production networks. In the short run, therefore, international migration does not stem from a lack of economic development, but from development itself.[9]

How this movement then plays out is explained by demands for labor, by immigration policies and recruitment, by the creation of immigration vectors alongside other forms of connectivity, and so on. What is striking about this theoretical account, Massey notes, is the absence of the state as a key actor, as well as the state's central responsibility, security. Thus, as actions of states in the global arena is the central concern of international relations theory, it should come as no surprise that the intersection of the two fields has been minimal.[10] As this volume should make clear, however, the status of migrants and the phenomenon of migration and related processes are quite central to framing the challenges of security in the post-9/11 environment. But in some very important respects, we may be speaking about two different kinds of migrants.

Most studies of international migration concern people, families, and communities whose principal goals are to "achieve economic sustenance" and, as migrant communities grow in the new country, to replicate or adapt cultural and social patterns of living from the home country and community. They aren't, in short, interested in committing acts of terror. The September 11 attackers, by contrast, were not in the typical migratory flow, kept to themselves, were financially supported directly by al Qaeda itself, and had no interest in permanent or semipermanent residency and work. So we have two very different phenomena, and conflating them is to invite confusion. Parsing these differences is surely important in getting right the emerging immigration policies aimed at preventing terrorists from entering the country. But there are several other relevant links between security and migration that remain powerful and understudied. The first focuses on how these two different kinds of immigrants intersect. That is, to what extent is there a social base—active support groups—in any of the transit points of an international network of political violence that draws on migrant communities? Who are these groups and why are they supportive? How are they different from "law-abiding" immigrants who come from the same places? Is the support in money, as is alleged with respect to certain Islamic charities that have been identified as such, or in other forms? It is worth noting that the result of thousands of interviews, investigations, and detentions in the two years post-9/11 resulted in a handful of arrests and indictments in the United States against alleged terrorists and of those not a single conspiracy linking those who were charged with any al Qaeda plot in America was established. That does not mean a social base for al Qaeda does not exist in America, but it suggests that any such base is miniscule and probably not criminal in nature.

A second, and quite separate, link between security and migration concerns the paroxysms of sudden population movements impelled by wars that have secondary security effects in neighboring countries. Similarly, consider the more chronic but no less important refugee camps, incubators of discontent and violence, as noted earlier. Forced migrations and temporary settlements have a security dynamic of their own apart from whatever was the proximate cause of the displacement. This is not well understood, despite its significance for the management of complex humanitarian emergencies, in which the international community has over the last dozen years invested greatly, with uncertain results.

The practical, political consequence of seeing migration itself as a security issue is most clearly evident in the United States and its creation of the Department of Homeland Security (DHS) in late 2002. In part a response to partisan politics, the DHS nonetheless became a sizable bureaucracy overnight with a significant emphasis on controlling the borders and immigration policy in the service of military, or at least antiterrorist, security. The absorption into DHS of the INS, the Customs Service, and the Coast Guard was enough to signal this intent. The department was created virtually without dissent in Congress (the only fractious issue being whether DHS employees could be members of labor unions). It sustained in very concrete form the instant embrace of the security-migration link forged after 9/11 and embodied in the arrests, detentions, and legislation noted earlier. Within these agencies, moreover, a significant shift in mission was soon evident, particularly at INS, where the tightening of visa requirements became quite restrictive and for a time reduced immigration. It is likely that the DHS will become a political instrument, not unlike other security agencies, in which the department's resources and public face will reflect the political exigencies of the president and Congress—more or less alarmist, more or less tarnishing certain immigrant communities and noxious regimes, and so on. The parallels to the 1947 National Security Act—which created America's enormous military and intelligence bureaucracy to fight the Cold War—are potentially instructive: a security culture evolved that emphasized worst-case scenarios, embedded secrecy, monitored and occasionally harassed domestic dissenters, rewarded allies in Congress, and insisted on its primacy in U.S. governance. The similarities to the homeland security juggernaut are clear.

Nowadays the internal and migratory threats are paramount: the nefarious activities of diaspora communities and individuals within the United States will remain the province of the FBI and the Justice Department, but the activities of the two groups—the DHS and federal cops and lawyers—will go hand in hand. In all of this, then, the securitization of migration will become a more routine political genre. As long as globalization proceeds along its present lines, and the United States and its proxies aggressively pursue terrorists and rogue states—thereby creating more political refugees needing new homes—the pressure of potentially threatening migration on the United States will be quite pronounced and will keep the DHS a busy place enlivened by perpetual political tension.

THE CHALLENGE TO INTERNATIONAL RELATIONS

In the realm of international relations, the discourse about global security has been subsumed in the discourse about terrorism, and the discourse about terrorism has largely fixated on the transnational character of al Qaeda. Its nonstate attributes appeared as a sharp punctuation in years of argument about the relevance of the nation-state as the principal focus of activity and study (although it was the multinational corporation and global civil society that initially occasioned this argument). The origins of political violence, the political and security ramifications of religious extremism, the parameters of asymmetrical warfare, the significance of failed states, the futility of Cold War–era collective security approaches and doctrines—these among other topics came to the fore, taking account of the inescapable nature of the transnationalism of money, weapons, ideas, organization, and people.

Spurred by President Bush, the discourse shifted again to focus on the harbors of terrorists: first Afghanistan, then Iraq. The "hot pursuit" mission in Afghanistan, emphasized by bombing begun on October 7, 2001, to find Osama bin Laden and his cohort quickly became an effort to demolish the Taliban regime as such a harbor master. Surrounding this rather swift episode was a discussion about the origins of Afghanistan's failed state and the probability that it would once again provide sustenance to the dystopians if a serious, multilateral effort of state-building did not follow the B-52s. This reemergence of concern with the security implications of development remains tenuous, since attention to the Afghan project—which many feel is halfhearted, Kabul-centric, and skewed toward security over development—was soon overwhelmed by a new fixation on Iraq. This focus in part resulted from the ingrained habit of major powers like the United States to conceive of security threats as emanating from states: all the preparations, the technologies, and the legal mechanisms of war are shaped by this assumption. War against al Qaeda, once the Afghan operation was mainly completed, became a police operation (more successfully carried out in Europe than anywhere else, where many dozens of suspected terrorists—virtually all of them immigrants—were arrested) or a function of homeland security. While many al Qaeda suspects were rounded up, other aspects of the war were lackluster in performance. Tracing and significantly halting financial flows to and from al Qaeda proved quite difficult. Recruits to al Qaeda were reported to have increased in 2002. Attacks in Bali, Kenya, Saudi Arabia, and elsewhere indicated the terrorists' willingness and ability to hit "soft" targets. Pakistan and its border with Afghanistan remained parlous, as did other borderlands in the region. So the success of the "war on terrorism" was doubtful, and surely would remain doubtful for some years to come. However, a war against Afghanistan's Taliban and Iraq's Saddam Hussein were far more concrete ventures.

While the disintegration of the Taliban provided a model of sorts for the strategy of undoing a harbor master (even though it was a post hoc rationale for intervention), the attack on Iraq was pursued for reasons of which only one was framed as an element of strategy in the antiterrorist campaign. By early 2003, this rationale was becoming ever more prominent, perhaps as a political initiative to gain public support in Europe and America. The purported ties between

Hussein's regime and al Qaeda were rickety, but it occasioned the one clear reason why, for example, East European leaders joined the U.S. war effort: they cited the "nexus" of Iraq and terrorist organizations. Thus the link to the transnational perpetrators of terrorism and the Iraqi state was forged, at least as part of the way in which Iraq's evil was conceived in Washington. When an operational bond between Osama bin Laden and Saddam Hussein could not be established before or after the war, the speculative notion that the Iraqi regime would surely supply "al Qaeda–like" terrorists with weapons of mass destruction became one of the prime rationales for preemption just before the United States began bombing Baghdad on March 19, 2003.

There was another, more significant rationale undergirding the U.S. action, however, which speaks again to the migratory essence of terrorism. That was the assertion by some U.S. policy leaders that they intended to make Iraq a "model" for Arab democracy. Translated, this meant the United States would possess, in post-Saddam Iraq, a platform to discipline the recalcitrant region, forcing reform in the gulf monarchies, Syria, and possibly Iran, denying havens and support for anti-American or anti-Israeli causes, and disrupting the flows that support terrorism. (The grapevine in Washington had it that telephone intercepts on September 10, 2001, had established that Saudi elites were supporting bin Laden, and this in turn made the creation of a U.S. platform nearby all the more urgent.) This ambitious agenda, fortified by an escalation in doctrinal assertiveness worldwide, was another response to the transnational elusiveness of al Qaeda: drain the swamp, and the pests will die.

How far-reaching these actions are with respect to our theories of international relations will take some years to sort out. To some degree, the Bush administration is intensifying long-held attitudes and approaches: essentially unilateralist, military-oriented, and hegemonic. The standard "national interest" of protecting U.S. economic assets and prerogatives is located most obviously in Iraq's enormous oil reserves. Assertive nuclear doctrine and preemptive military intervention were tendencies of varying latency for many years. It is noteworthy that a number of prominent "realists"—John Mearsheimer, Stephen Walt, and Steven Van Evera, among others—lamented the obsession with Iraq in part because they believed Saddam did not pose a direct threat to U.S. national security and in part because it was a diversion from the actual threat, al Qaeda. But this school of thought must also take a few turns to integrate, theoretically, the imperative—not to say the difficulty—of coping with a nonstate network of migrants as a principal threat on the global stage. And, indeed, what is most novel about the action against Iraq is the rationale based on the assertion that non-

Iraqi terrorists posed a threat to the United States and were operating from Iraq with the regime's cooperation. This kind of novelty runs through the security-migration nexus; as Aristide Zolberg points out in a similar vein in the first volume of this series:

> The attack on the United States confirms what had already been evident from less spectacular manifestations of international terrorism: the growing importance of non-state actors in the contemporary world system. Nevertheless, American responses are being cast primarily within a classically Westphalian framework. . . . Not only does the elaboration of obstacles to international movement clash with the objectives of economic globalization, but globalization in turn provides negative feedback for national security, since it brings about greater population diversity. . . ."

The flip side of the "securitization of migration," then, is the international-relations dimension: the ways in which this priority—destroying havens, draining swamps, militarily confronting the network itself—becomes a defining feature of international relations and security, in theory and in practice.

THE MAZE OF FEAR

This volume is an attempt to raise questions about and provide perspectives on how the 9/11 aftermath has altered security calculations and how migration particularly has entered into this formula. The essays herein do not purport to lay out a new theory of the migration-security relationship, but rather intend to shed light on this emerging concept from the standpoint of academic thought and practitioner experience. Given all that has occurred in the months since 9/11, one expects the implications for international relations, migration, domestic security, and the theories explaining them to unravel for some years to come. Just as journalists like to claim they are producing the first draft of history, we in this volume may claim to be taking the first crack at the post-9/11 migration-security nexus. This effort takes many forms in its thirteen chapters.

We address several discrete but interrelated aspects of the emerging perception of threat posed by migration and related phenomena. The link between security and migration in a global milieu of hegemonic power is not entirely new, as Engseng Ho points out. Networks of Yemeni traders established on the periphery of the Indian Ocean were primary in resistance to British imperialism, an historical and social constellation that remains vital. In the contemporary setting, we can see that terrorists are able to use ordinary migration processes of long-standing utility to infiltrate the countries where they operate and attack. They use communications and financial networks that are also central to globalization. And, as Fiona Adamson makes clear, they apparently draw support from a social base in host countries that is typically within immigrant communities, which are more or less politicized and interconnected.

One recurring theme of this volume is that the "threat" implied in migration is significantly shaped by state responses: as noted, the security threat posed by al Qaeda is a difficult challenge in large part because it is nonstate, nonnational, nonterritorial, dispersed, and in motion. But the responsibility for protection and capture is nonetheless one of states and international organizations. Tracking and stopping financial flows, for example, is one such (difficult) task of states and international organizations—one that Thomas Biersteker explains and that has engaged him as a scholar and policy maven. The networks of terrorism are unsustainable without those resources, the movement of which may rely on globalized processes and immigration itself. Interdiction of money is one of the instruments states seem to have at their disposal, and they have employed it quickly. More broadly, states have responded by targeting the transnational co-religionists of al Qaeda indiscriminately—Muslim migrants and immigrant communities. In the United States, this has involved Islamic "charities" of various kinds, which brings into one antiterrorist strategy the diasporas or recent migrants, political activism, and transnational mechanisms of supporting militant organizations around the world.

Among civil-liberties specialists, the targeting of immigrants is contested, but the state has constitutional grounds for singling out immigrants, as legal scholar Peter Spiro shows. This state response has variously involved (in the United States and elsewhere) curtailment of rights (including migration itself) and the strengthening of political authority and institutions, in addition to pursuit by police and military action. The United States has targeted immigrants in past national crises, as historian Gary Gerstle demonstrates, and this also is occurring now in several allied regimes in Central Asia and elsewhere, and, to a lesser extent, in Europe—as explained in the chapters by Howard Adelman, Paula Newberg, and Mario Zucconi. It is noteworthy, and reflected in those chapters, that the threat of terrorism remains a source of political dissonance (in Canada and Europe), and, in Central Asia, a logic for greater authoritarianism that has only tenuous relevance to migration. Yet the strengthening of states to cope with the perceived threat of terrorism may itself contribute to the conditions and beliefs that promote transnational political violence and crime. For example, the United States, in targeting Iraq, used the rationale of Hussein's harboring terrorists, argues Stephen Schlesinger, possibly as a small bow to public perceptions of threat in a larger, unilateralist scheme to project hegemonic power. Overall, then, the role of the state in the response to terrorism and the consequent and secondary securitization of migration is pervasively enlarged, and we are able to begin to describe and analyze it.

The social dynamics stirred by state responses to 9/11 are gradually becoming visible. How immigrant Muslim communities in the United States are dealing with the targeting is varied, as Louise Cainkar describes, and this reaction has both positive and negative consequences. In some places, migrants and refugees have long been regarded as security problems, and this has now been exacerbated by 9/11, as several chapters note, but is most forthrightly illustrated by Imtiaz Ahmed in his description of the "stateless" peoples of South Asia, victims both of political delegitimation and the new emphasis on antiterrorism. The tensions driven by 9/11 are also affecting other related issues—such as the Israeli-Palestinian conflict—and this, as Yossi Shain argues, is having a spillover impact on Jewish-Muslim-Christian relations outside the region. But are such social dynamics properly understood as issues of international security or as the "securitization" of migration?

That, along with other questions, reflects the challenge posed by 9/11 and its aftermath; such questions are ones that international-relations theory is not wholly prepared to address. That is, migration as a security threat is not well accounted for in IR theory, just as migration theory itself does take account of security issues adequately. Jeffrey Checkel surveys the theoretical terrain in the closing chapter.

The vast enterprise of international migration involves countless risks and baffling complexity. Gradually, as the number of migrants—many escaping war—has mounted worldwide, the social scientists and advocates who try to grasp its scope and meaning have understood that the social and political dynamics of migration are multifarious, both for the people in motion and for those who are asked to provide them with a place to call home. This complexity and the anxieties that it inevitably stirs are like a "maze of fear," as our late colleague Arthur Helton put it. Helton, a distinguished lawyer and champion of migration reform who was killed in the terrorist bombing of U.N. headquarters in Iraq in August 2003, recognized how migration—itself a fearful venture—besets the hosts with fear as well. "Notions of decency and tolerance can quickly erode in the face of a community's fears and insecurity," he wrote in the on-line journal *openDemocracy* in January 2003. "Indeed, such pressures can ultimately cause severe damage to a system of world order."

By locating the many dimensions of this maze of fear, we expect that this volume can go partway toward redressing these lacunae in theory regarding the migration–security link. It is a collection of essays by intellectuals written mainly from the international relations and international security perspective. But identifying how and where migration has been put into play in the security arena is a fateful step in defining the relationship. And the list of examples is long: from lawless borders, roaming refugees, and politically active diasporas to rationales for military intervention, institutions, and law to the instrumentalities of terrorism. The new appreciation of how people in motion pose a threat—real or imagined—is likely to be a recurring and consequential theme of international relations for many years to come.

EMPIRE THROUGH DIASPORIC EYES: A VIEW FROM THE OTHER BOAT*

ENGSENG HO

There is something very characteristic of the indifference which we show towards this mighty phenomenon of the diffusion of our race and the expansion of our state. We seem, as it were, to have conquered and peopled half the world in a fit of absence of mind. . . . We constantly betray by our modes of speech that we do not reckon our colonies as really belonging to us.

—J.R. SEELEY, 1883[1]

And finally, be straight with the American people. Tell them the truth—and when you cannot tell them something, tell them you cannot tell them.

—DONALD RUMSFELD, U.S. SECRETARY OF DEFENSE[2]

IMPERIAL AMNESIA

In 1982, Eric Wolf published *Europe and the People Without History*[3] to identify and begin rectifying large gaps in anthropological knowledge. That project remains unfinished. In the years since September 11, 2001, the necessity of filling in some of these gaps has become urgent. The history of relations between Western powers and transnational Muslim communities in the Indian Ocean is one of them.[4] An anthropologically nuanced understanding of such communities as diasporas, thought in tandem with their continued relations with Western empires over five hundred years, lends a potentially useful perspective on a set of conflicts which is massively unfolding. Threatening to become the self-fulfilling prophecy of a clash of civilizations in popular discourse and political decision making, a phenomenon on this horrendous scale remains within the purview of anthropologists if one sees it as an instance of culture contact under conditions of global imperialism, unmitigated by colonial administration.

The distinction between imperialism and colonialism is critical. Talal Asad's *Anthropology and the Colonial Encounter*[5] launched anthropology on an auto-critique by noting that its quiet field sites were fields of colonial power, and its practitioners members of colonizing societies.[6] Colonialism refers to foreign presence in, possession of, and domination over bounded, local places. Today, the multisited ethnographies we increasingly pursue need to be analytically framed within a field of power which is transnational. The term imperialism refers to foreign[7] domination, without the necessity of presence or possession, over expansive, transnational spaces—and over many places. Within the purview of U.S. power, then, the appropriate term for this frame is not postcolonialism, but ongoing imperialism. The time may soon be upon us for a sequel to Asad's volume, now trained on American anthropology and the *imperial* encounter. While the terms globalization, neoliberalism, and late-liberalism may have been productive in probing the complexities of consent to contemporary transnational hegemony, they have been less attentive to its classical twin, coercion. While colonialism may be the past of British and French anthropology, imperialism is the long present of the American one. Thus the sense of urgency, again.

In what follows, I look at a series of such contacts through the eyes of a Muslim diaspora, as it were—a mobile people with a written history. The review suggests that what is new to this history is the unique nature of American power worldwide. In its global reach it is imperial, but in its disavowal of administration on the ground, it is anticolonial.

OCEANIC INTIMATES

For some years, I have been studying a diaspora of Arabs from Hadramawt, Yemen, across the Indian Ocean. In September 2001, I was reviewing British colonial files from the time of World War I, in which correspondence was taking place among British officials in Cairo, Jedda, Aden, Mukalla, Simla, Singapore, and Batavia discussing the movements and activities of Hadrami Arabs in these locations. The officials were careful to distinguish Hadrami Arabs who were on their side from those aligned with their rivals: the Germans, the Italians, the Ottoman Turks, and Muslims agitating for a pan-Islamic caliphate in South and Southeast Asia. Good Arabs were major landlords in Singapore, religious bureaucrats in Malaya, businessmen in Batavia, sultans in British South Arabia, enthusiasts of T.E. Lawrence's pro-Sharif policy in Arabia—many loyal British subjects. Bad Arabs were pan-Islamists: caliphate agitators in Java, India, and Ceylon; Ottoman agents in British South Arabia and Italian ones there and in Ethiopia-Somalia; fundraisers for the Yemeni imam among wealthy diasporic Hadramis in Singapore and Java. Good and bad Arabs were sometimes from the same far-flung Hadrami families. The intercolonial correspondence was important to formulating policy in two arenas: restricting travel for marked individuals across the Indian Ocean, and propaganda interventions in the newly international European and Arab presses. British officials needed to consult their counterparts in colonies elsewhere to cross-check information they were being fed by their Hadrami informers, who were themselves partisans in internal Hadrami disputes manipulating British fears for their own ends.[8] In the arc of coasts around the Indian Ocean, the British and the Hadrami Arabs were everywhere, and everywhere overlapping. A diaspora and an empire were locked in a tight embrace of intimacy and treachery, a relationship of mutual benefit, attraction, and aversion.

When the World Trade Center and the Pentagon were hit on September 11, my train of thought jumped tracks. The British were immediately supplanted by the Americans, while the Hadrami diaspora remained. In particular, the dual aspect of Osama bin Laden locked the pair of Western empire and Hadrami diaspora in place for me: he is at once a figure of revulsion and familiarity. Hadrami owners of the largest Saudi construction conglomerate, his family are on close terms with the ruling Saudi royal family,[9] and on familiar terms with the Bush presidential family.[10] Bin Laden visiting professorships are endowed at Oxford, as are fellowships at Harvard. As the events of September 11 unfolded, the peculiar mix of intimacy and treachery I had observed between the British empire and Hadrami diaspora continued to present itself to my eyes. Brzezinski's jihad trap for the Soviets in Afghanistan had come home to roost ("We now have the opportunity of giving to the USSR its Vietnam war.");[11] Americans were now bombing bases and fortified cave complexes they had built in that country partly with Bin Laden Group construction equipment. A succession of such observations made it clear to me that this whole tangled mess could be thought of productively in terms of a long-standing historical relationship between empire and diaspora. In contrast, globalization, poverty, and Islam vs. the West were floating concepts with which I could never see the way down to the ground of events. In Washington's eyes, the impassive face of evil transmogrified from Brezhnev's to bin Laden's. How did communism and Islamism become interchangeable? Why were attacks on American interests arrayed around the Indian Ocean? The question made me rethink my thoughts on empire and diaspora, and I did so by revisiting material I was familiar with, a history of relations between the two in the Indian Ocean. This essay presents the results of that investigation. It is a view of the imperial ship of state as seen from a smaller boat sailing the same seas.[12]

UNIVERSALIZING DIASPORAS

Twenty years ago, the word diaspora referred to Jews, and was spelled with a capital D. The more general meaning is of a people who were originally homogeneous, then became mobile.[13] Today, almost every ethnic group, country, or separatist movement has its diaspora. This is a notion of diaspora as a particularistic form of sociality. Let's call it the Jewish model—i.e., the notion of people who were originally homogeneous, then moved.[14] There has been an explosion of such diasporas.

There is another way of thinking about diasporas, however, by reversing the terms—meaning peoples who moved, and as they did so became homogenized into a unitary conception. Let's call this the British model. Recent work by British historians, such as David Armitage[15] argue that after the union of the Scottish and English crowns in 1707, a coherent notion of Britishness grew up across the Atlantic and was expressed most strongly first away from the homeland. Abroad, the notion of Britishness was understood in terms of belonging to an empire, a British empire. The concepts which informed this notion of empire—that it was commercial, maritime, Protestant, and free—were also concepts fundamental to the self-understanding of Britain as a nation.[16] The notion of a British empire abroad was central to bringing together the disparate groups and kingdoms of the homeland. If we think of the empire as a diaspora, then Scots, Irish, and Englishmen came to think of themselves as commonly British as they became mobile. In this sense, they moved, then became homogeneous.

This British model understands diaspora as a composite rather than homogeneous whole. Mobility is a process which reshapes the basic units of sociality. The British became an imperial people—that is to say, they became *a people* as they became *an empire:* Britannia ruled the waves. In the concatenation of a people and an empire, the British model of diaspora became a powerful one. Britishers do not land on the shores of other people's states to become ethnic minorities and particularistic lobbies. They create states: the United States, Canada, Australia, New Zealand, South Africa. When Greeks emigrated, they ipso facto left the city-state; when British people emigrated, they took the state with them.[17] There are very few such diasporas, for obvious reasons. In their very success, such diasporas may also take on universalist ambitions, accommodate other peoples, and become hard to identify as diasporas. The British overseas, even after severing ties with the motherland, continued seeing themselves in very similar ways across their diaspora. Specifically, their loyalties came to cluster around institutions, such as private property, free trade, Protestantism, a yeoman right to bear arms, equal access to law. While all this was seen as coming out of the tradition of the Freeborn Englishman, the elaboration of the tradition in this range of institutions ultimately served to deracinate it and open up countries dominated by the British diaspora, such as the United States, to Germans, Italians, and non-Europeans as well, over time.[18]

The British model is good to think with, because the Hadrami diaspora is akin to it in being a composite. Over the past half-millennium, there has been a continuous and vigorous movement of persons from Hadramawt to destinations throughout the Indian Ocean: East Africa, western India, the islands of Southeast Asia.[19] They are part of a broader flow of persons from Arabia and Persia, but a continuously visible part. The travelers are almost invariably men,[20] and they marry local women where they land. The offspring of such unions may assimilate into local society. But often they retain a mixed, creole identity and form whole new third communities, which are understood to be partly Arab, partly local, and fully Muslim. The Swahilis of East Africa and Mappilas of Malabar are thought to be such peoples. Before the twentieth century, most of the mobile Arabs from Hadramawt who were readily identifiable were descendants of the Muslim prophet Muhammad. Their movement became identified with a missionary purpose, of spreading the religion.

Thus, while the British diaspora took the form of an empire, the Hadrami diaspora took the form of a religious mission. In this, the Hadrami diaspora had vastly greater universalist ambitions than the British. It brought together not just peoples from the homeland but peoples in destinations throughout the Indian Ocean region as well. Here, Hadramis played a major role in the expansion of Islam, and conversion stories in the region often begin with the arrival of a Hadrami religious figure. In their marriages with local women, Hadramis and their offspring became Swahilis, Gujaratis, Malabaris, Malays, Javanese, Filipinos. They became natives everywhere.[21] At the same time, the men and their offspring continued to move throughout this oceanic space, for reasons of trade, study, family, pilgrimage, and politics.[22] Throughout this space, a Hadrami could travel and be put up by relatives, who might be Arab uncles married to foreign, local aunties. Many had wives in each port. In the arc of coasts around the Indian Ocean, then, a skein of networks arose in which people socialized with distant foreigners as kinsmen and as Muslims. Like the British model, movement in the Hadrami diaspora brought together hitherto separated peoples, though not in an empire, but in a religion instead. Like the Jewish model, they began as a homogeneous diaspora, but like the British, they ended up a composite one.

By religion, I mean not just a spiritual space, but a civil and political one as well. As the bearers of Islamic knowledge and prestige, the Hadramis were everywhere potential creators of public spaces and institutions such as mosques, courts, schools, and pilgrimage shrines. Thus, in Muslim states undergoing expansion, one witnesses the arrival of Hadrami religious figures, who often marry local princesses. Such alliances connected obscure backwaters to the transregional networks of the Indian Ocean, and were sought after by both local potentates and diasporic Hadramis. Some of these religious creators of public institutions became rulers of states in their own right.[23] Muslim Mindanao in present-day Philippines (from the fifteenth century), the Comoros Islands in East Africa and Aceh in Sumatra (from the seventeenth century), Pontianak and Siak in Borneo and Sumatra (from the eighteenth), Perlis in Malaya (from the twentieth century to the present)—all have had Hadrami sultans. As people who maintained communications with relatives in foreign countries over centuries, they were very useful as diplomats in their countries of domicile. For example, the separation of British Malaya from Dutch Indonesia (now enduring as the sovereign states Indonesia, Malaysia, and Singapore) in 1824, which drew the border down the Straits of Melaka and through the Riau islands, was brokered by Hadrami diplomats who had married into ruling families on all sides.[24] Today, they remain in the public light: the current foreign minister of Malaysia, Syed Hamid Albar, is of Hadrami descent, as are his two previous counterparts in Indonesia, Ali Alatas and Alwi Shihab. So are the king of Malaysia and the prime minister of independent Timor, Mari Alkatiri. Like the British in the Atlantic and the Pacific, the history of the Hadrami diaspora in the Indian Ocean region is interwoven with the history of state formation and trade competition. Moments of conflict and cooperation between Muslim and Western states are present in this history.

DOMESTICITY DISRUPTED: VASCO DA GAMA STILL

The great empires of Europe, through their colonies and spheres of influence, spread authority, order, and respect for the obligation of contract almost everywhere; and where their writs did not run, their frigates and gunboats navigated. Methods were rough, division of benefits was unfair, and freedom was not rated high among the priorities; but people, goods, and ideas moved around the world with less restraint than ever before and, perhaps, ever again.[25]

—DEAN ACHESON

In the fifteenth century, the Indian Ocean hosted a transregional network of peaceable trade and social exchange that was experienced by its diasporic natives as an extensive domestic realm. The transformation of that realm by the Portuguese into an arena of military and commercial geostrategy was to give religion and diaspora new meanings, in this first encounter with empires.

Across the Indian Ocean, a number of grand exchanges brought distant places into vital communication. Pepper, highly prized in Europe, was carried by Muslims from its source in Malabar to Cairo via the Red Sea, then from Alexandria across the Mediterranean to Europe by Venetians. The market for Gujarat's cloth stretched from Arabia to the Malay peninsula, and Cambay became a fulcrum for trade between Jedda and Malacca. The Cambay sultan kept in close contact with Jedda and Mecca, while Gujarati merchants frequented Malacca. From Cairo to Malacca, through Jedda, Aden, Shihr, Hormuz, Cambay, and Calicut, Indian Ocean trade was conducted by traders and sailors who formed the sort of creole, transnational, Muslim networks of which the Hadrami diaspora was a part. Southeast of Malacca, it stretched to the spice islands of the Moluccas and Timor.

Throughout, what provided a public representation of commonness was not a state, but the Shafi'i school of Islamic law coupled with Sufi practice, both furnishing a shared legal, ritual and educational culture and curriculum. East of Malacca, the trade with China was no longer in Muslim hands but carried on Chinese junks.

The arrival of the Portuguese and Spanish marked the advent of a truly global economy in the Indian Ocean region, linking the Pacific and the Atlantic.[26] As few European products were in demand, they brought silver from the Americas, mined by natives under duress, as their ticket for entry. It was a space in which Europeans came as newcomers to a preexisting Muslim world of port states, trading routes, and religious and kinship networks.[27]

From the European perspective, what was strange about this rich world of the Indian Ocean and its international economy was that no one state controlled it, or even had the idea to do so. The Portuguese, with the scientific geographers assembled by Prince Henry the Navigator, were the first to think of this ocean as a unity and to thereby dream up a systematic strategy to monopolize the means of violence within it.[28] Looking out from Lisbon, precious commodities such as pepper came directly through the hands of the Venetians, and behind them, their Muslim partners. A route around the Cape of Good Hope would cut out the Venetians, and beyond it, a series of strategic ports could control the seas and cut out the Muslims. Alfonso de Albuquerque realized the audacious plan in his lightning capture and garrisoning of Hormuz, Goa, and Malacca in the first decade of the sixteenth century. The Portuguese had brought a trading-post system of imperial garrisons pioneered by Venice and Genoa in the Mediterranean to the Indian Ocean. It remained incomplete, however, as Aden stood and the Red Sea thus remained open to Muslim shipping.[29]

A succession of European powers subsequently carried the geopolitical strategic project through: Dutch, French, English, American. Maritime empires came to dominate this space. The period in which this domination held, from the advent of the Portuguese in 1498 to the end of World War II in 1945 and Indian independence, has been called the Vasco da Gama Epoch by the Malabar-born Indian diplomat and historian K. N. Pannikar.[30]

What made this period distinctive was the new importance of state violence to markets, power to property, flag to trade, and their inseparability, as Dean Acheson cognized in his characterization of nineteenth-century European imperialism quoted earlier. Whether markets were free or not, power over the ocean itself needed to be monopolized. Portuguese and American views which cap this period at both ends share this assumption, and strategic security became an end in its own right, first among all goods. In other words, the stakes were raised to such a height that only the interchangeable languages of empire, civilization, and religion would be powerful enough—together—to match the unholy mix of money, might, and murder set in train when, in 1498, the Christian Vasco da Gama arrived in an Indian Calicut dominated by Muslim merchants under a Hindu sovereign. Religion in the Indian Ocean region would never be the same again once the medieval Crusades, that particular mix of universal religion with strategic politics, had come East.

And what of the Muslims in all this? The Indian Ocean had been called an "Arab Lake" by the early Europeans, but neither Arabs nor Muslims ever had a unitary state throughout the region, nor the ambition for one. What they did have was the network of trade, kinship, port-states, and religion that I've sketched out. This network contained potentials of great power, potentials which could be harnessed and actualized by a leader who had the transregional consciousness, connections, and imagination to convince others that they were capable of powerful actions, if only they would act in concert.

They were to act sporadically, and in concert only under the baton of phantom leaders who had mastered the secrets of ships, airplanes, and communications. It is no coincidence that these very vehicles of Western domination in commerce and warfare were to figure dramatically in Muslim responses to that domination.[31]

DIASPORA CONTRA EMPIRE

From the sixteenth century onward, a series of wars of resistance against European colonization erupted in various parts of this oceanic realm. At least four features of these wars are notable: (1) Direct colonization created widespread social dislocations, generating a groundswell of opposition locally; (2) Leaders of resistance were often members of the Hadrami diaspora or their scholarly associates, who, being already mobile and in correspondence across the ocean, incessantly crossed and frustrated imperial jurisdictions; (3) Spatially and temporally separate and unrelated events of European colonial penetration provoked responses which bore family resemblances to each other in Muslim communities from Malabar to Mindanao; (4) The combination of these factors resulted in wars that were protracted, lasting decades.

The most dramatic of these encounters involved Muslim Malabar and Aceh, suppliers of pepper—the pre-modern "black gold" sought after by Portuguese, Dutch, and Americans alike—to the world. The earliest American millionaires, operating out of Salem, Massachusetts, amassed their fortunes by going across the Pacific in the late eighteenth century to buy Acehnese pepper, bypassing Dutch blockades between Aceh and Malabar.[32]

In the thirty-year war of conquest launched by the Dutch against Aceh in Sumatra in the late nineteenth century, a Hadrami leader figured prominently. Born in Hadramawt, Yemen, in 1833, 'Abd al-Rahman b. Muhammad al-Zahir was taken to Malabar in India at the age of two, then educated in the Islamic sciences in Egypt and Mecca.[33] He returned to India as a young man, began trading between India and Arabia on his wealthy father's ship, the "Jeddul Manau," and got married in Malabar. He visited Turkey, Italy, Germany, and France, and was rumored to have met Napoleon. Like the mid-nineteenth century founders of the three Hadrami sultanates (Kathīrī, Qaʿayti, Kasādī), he commanded troops on feudal commission as *Jamadar* for the Nizam of Hyderabad.[34] But he was footloose, set up shop and villa in Calcutta as a successful goldsmith, shuttled between Bombay, Hyderabad, and Calicut, and found service with the westernizing sultan of Johor in Malaya. In 1864, he finally went to Aceh. There, his superiority in religious learning was quickly made apparent, and he became a leading jurist and administrator, marrying the sister of a senior minister, the widow of sultan Ali Iskandar Syah. He streamlined taxation and organized cooperative efforts to build large, central mosques and public works. He gained the ear of the sultan and became regent when the latter died, holding the reins of state in his hands.

When war broke out between the Dutch and the Acehnese, al-Zahir traveled to British Malaya as envoy of the Acehnese sultan, went on to Malabar in India where he visited with his wife, then to Jedda where he collected recommendations from the sharif of Mecca and other notables, then to Istanbul. He was received by the Ottomans as emissary of Aceh, decorated by the Ottoman ruler, and promised help against the Dutch. His presence stirred reports in the pan-Islamic press of Ottoman intervention in Aceh, creating consternation in European diplomatic circles. Ottoman help never quite materialized, but on his return trip he was now well received by Dutch and British consuls in Jedda, Singapore, and Penang. By involving the Ottomans and the British in the Acehnese war, he set up many new, international constraints on the Dutch. The British had their own reasons for getting involved, including arms sales and pepper purchases. When al-Zāhir finally returned to Aceh, he was lionized. He was received as a representative of the grand Ottoman Caliph, who to the Acehnese was the leader of the only Muslim empire in the modern world.[35] Al-Zāhir went on to lead the Acehnese in war against the Dutch.

As he moved around, al-Zāhir's sophisticated strategies of self-representation increased his stature. His visit to the governor of British Penang on horseback in full regalia created "a spectacle."[36] His expensive international diplomacy was financed by telegraphic transfers of Acehnese pepper profits. He was like a mirror which reflected the glory of the ever more powerful figures he met and was associated with. While on one level he moved in a very personal space of the Hadrami diaspora, visiting wives and relatives along the way, on another level he was able to harness and actualize potentials embedded in the larger Muslim networks of the Indian Ocean region. In his mobile actions, we may say that his masterful command of a whole diasporic repertoire of constituting a persona—routes, relatives, and representations—magnified a local conflict in Aceh to international proportions, making it larger and more protracted.

Al-Zāhir was not the first such figure in the Hadrami diaspora, nor was he the last. This model, of a confrontation between an empire and an Islamic community represented by a diasporic persona, provides a framework for thinking about the current confrontation between Osama bin Laden and the United States. Bin Laden is a member of the Hadrami diaspora. The geography of his operations, from East Africa to the Philippines, is an old venue for it. Wealth and mobility combine iconically in the family, in the ownership of airplanes and in travel in Europe. In his movements between Arabia, Sudan, and South Asia, he has been able to build his stature by associating with important states and causes. He has been able to harness great potential by expressing, in a religious idiom, notions of unity in an otherwise discombobulated congeries of Muslim states, societies, and causes. Like pepper-rich Aceh, another state endowed with a prized world commodity is involved—Saudi Arabia. Whether he is actually intermarried with Taliban leader Mullah Omar's family or not, the issue arises precisely because it is part of an old pattern.

Although the war in Afghanistan and beyond is of a scale and complexity that dwarfs all the previous confrontations between Muslims and Europeans led by Hadramis in the Indian Ocean area, the existence of this pattern, of moments of cooperation and conflict between diaspora and empire, gives us one way of thinking about relations between Muslims and Westerners. Specifically, alertness to historical precedent helps us think through the peculiar suddenness with which the stakes have been rhetorically ratcheted upward to the moral absolutes of a conflict between whole religions and civilizations, as has happened more than once before. In the Indian Ocean region, the notion of jihad as just war was articulated directly in response to the Portuguese depredations of the sixteenth century. It emerged out of diasporic Muslim circles. Its expression affords us one view of empire through diasporic eyes, in the earliest encounter. Before Aceh's confrontation with the Dutch, the Malabar coast of southwest India had already borne the brunt of imperial aggression. It is to Malabar that we will now turn.

JIHAD, LONG MEMORIES OF AN OLD BUSINESS

In the 1570s, a book was written in Malabar entitled *Gift of the Jihad Warriors in Matters Regarding the Portuguese.*[37] The author was Zayn al-Dīn al-Malibārī (or al-Mulaybārī, or al-Maʿbārī), a Malabar Muslim jurist associated with networks of Hadrami religious scholars.[38] The book catalogued Portuguese atrocities against Muslim communities in Malabar and elsewhere across the Indian Ocean sphere in great detail. Similar descriptions are given in Hadrami chronicles from the same period, recounting Portuguese atrocities in East Africa and Yemen.[39] Portuguese accounts of the events generally agree with them in substance but not judgment.

Al-Malibārī composed his book with the express purpose of mobilizing Muslims to take up arms against the Portuguese, and gifted it to Sultan ʿAlī ʿĀdil Shāh of Bijapur.[40] The first chapter makes a case for jihad, and sets out the religious and legal arguments:

> I have made this compilation out of the desire to have the people of faith fight against the slaves of the cross. Jihad against them is a religious obligation, on account of their entering the countries of the Muslims and harming them. I have called it *Gift of the Jihad Warriors in Matters Regarding the Portuguese*. In it I recount what has transpired of their vile deeds, relate the appearance of Islam in Malabar, and include a section setting forth the principles of jihad, the greatness of its rewards and the texts of revelation and tradition that call for it.[41]

As a jurist, al-Malibārī gives the anti-Portuguese struggle a specific legal basis in Islamic law, as a just war against those who would harm Muslims. But in making the case, he marshals ethnographic and historical arguments to paint a broader picture of Malabar society, of what it is that the Portuguese are attacking.[42] His account includes Brahmins and Nayars, carpenters and fisherfolk, caste relations, prohibitions against commensality, a range of phenomena familiar to anthropologists today. The ethnography maintains the perspective of an outsider describing local customs; the call for a just war is not a nativist anticolonialism. Neither is it simply religious warfare, for the threatened Malabaris are also non-Muslims, long-settled Christians, and Jews who fled persecution in Portugal. In al-Malibārī's depiction, Malabar society was a civic, commercial, urban realm, a string of cosmopolitan port cities with merchants of different religions engaged in peaceable long-distance trade.

His historical account of how this society developed articulates legends of the king Cheraman Perumal and his relationship with foreign peoples.[43] Under the influence of a group of Sufis, the king had conceived an affection for Islam and its prophet, divided his realm, and sailed for Arabia. He remained at the Hadrami port of Shihr for a long time, then fell ill. Before passing away, he gave written instructions to his companions to take back to Malabar. They subsequently returned, divided gardens and lands among chiefs, and built mosques in the towns of Calicut, Cranganore, Kanjercote, Quilon, and others. Congregations of Muslims settled around the mosques. Rulers dealt with the Muslims fairly, so their port cities attracted Muslim traders from all directions and prospered. Muslims submitted to the justice of non-Muslim rulers, and if a Muslim was executed, his body would be returned to the community for washing and burial. Al-Malibārī described the customs ('ādāt) peculiar to each community to show how they led to intercommunal reciprocities. Among Brahmins, strict rules of primogeniture meant that only eldest sons could marry, to avoid inheritance conflicts. Younger Brahmin sons thus consorted with women of the Nayar community, whose matrilineal and polyandrous customs allowed for such complementary arrangements. Rigidities of caste distinction, such as maintaining social-spatial distance, washing upon contact, and caste endogamy meant that individuals who transgressed strictures found themselves repudiated, left their communities, and if they were young boys or women, threatened with enslavement among strangers. To save themselves, they converted to Islam, as they did to Christianity also.

Al-Malibārī's Malabar Muslims were a community facing in two directions— on the one hand bound in multiple moral and legal relations with non-Muslim rulers and peoples over generations in Malabar, and on the other engaged in trade with distant places. It was precisely these creole Muslim networks that the Portuguese targeted as they established their forts across the Indian Ocean region in places like Hormuz, Muscat, Diu, Sumatra, Malacca, the Moluccas, Milapur, Nagapatam, Ceylon, and all the way to China.[44] In addition to plunder and murder, the Portuguese reserved for themselves trade in profitable items like pepper and ginger, thus ruining the Muslims in all departments.

In short, Portuguese colonial and imperial actions were destroying the multireligious, cosmopolitan societies of trading ports in Malabar and the diasporic Muslim networks across the Indian Ocean region which articulated with them. Vasco da Gama's epoch-setting journey in 1498 had gone from Lisbon to Calicut, the premier spice emporium of the mid-Indian Ocean, a joint operation of its non-Muslim ruler the Zamorin and Muslim merchants. As the Muslims were victims throughout the length and breadth of Portuguese ambitions, it is not surprising that Muslim scholars such as al-Malibārī were most aware of the imperial scope of those ambitions, and most resolute in resistance to them.

From that time onward, opposition to Portuguese, Dutch, and English colonial rule in Malabar has continually been formulated in religious terms of martyrdom, as Dale has shown.[45] Between 1836 and 1921, under British rule, thirty-two outbreaks of rebellion by Malabar Muslims were recorded. A majority of them were led by the Hadrami-Malabari scholar Sayyid Fadl. Sayyid Fadl was a third-generation Hadrami in Malabar, and came from a line of scholars and public figures. He was finally expelled by the British in 1852, went to Yemen and Mecca, and became an official of the Ottoman court in Istanbul. As Ottoman governor of Zufár in present-day Oman from 1875–79, he was to return as a threat to British dominance over the Aden-Bombay shipping route. He lived out the rest of his days at the Ottoman court of the pan-Islamist sultan Abdul Hamid the Second. It was this sultan who patronized the earliest modern political Muslims, such as Jamāl al-Dīn al-Afghānī, and declared himself the universal Caliph.[46]

When the caliphate was abolished by the Young Turks, movements were set up in India and Dutch Indonesia to reinstate it. As I've said, Gandhi aligned the Muslim caliphate movement in India with the larger anticolonial struggle, involving Muslims and Hindus on the same side. In Malabar, however, mobilization for the caliphate movement led directly to a major Muslim rebellion in 1921. Muslim clerics, including one of Sayyid Fadl's descendants, led the revolt, and the terms were familiar from the sixteenth- and nineteenth-century struggles. In its desperate phase in 1922, a number of suicide charges took place.[47] The issue of the caliphate was to reemerge in bin Laden's conflict with the United States, as we shall see later.

We have so far been using the terms diaspora and empire. Diasporas we know still exist and continue to multiply. But what about empire? I believe the term continues to be useful, even critical, in thinking about the United States today. How is the United States an empire? By comparison with the Portuguese, Dutch, or British, the United States enjoys a curious misrecognition of its place as a world power.

EMPIRE OR REPUBLIC? AN ANTICOLONIAL EMPIRE

The United States is an empire without colonies. This sounds anomalous because we have come to think of imperialism and colonialism as the same thing. Analytically, they are not. Colonialism is the occupation of territory by foreign settlers, soldiers, or administrators. Colonies are possessions of master societies, so master and subject populations answer to different laws. The relationship between owning and being property is generalized to two categories of persons, colonizer and colonized. Imperialism, in contrast, is the projection of political power across large spaces, to include other states, whatever the means: colonies, mercenaries, gunboats, missiles, client elites, proxy states, multilateral institutions, multinational alliances. No assumption of property need ground the imperial relationship, and influence rather than presence is what counts. Two colonies in an imperial space may have different significances: British Egypt in the 1890s was held as a means to a higher end—British India and its security. Merely comparing them as colonies (and postcolonies subsequently) obscures the connective and differential analysis demanded by the concept of empire. A brief characterization of European imperial history, and its American avatar, will help clarify what I mean by a noncolonial empire, or an anticolonial one.

The roles of conquest and commerce in the creation of European empires have varied over time, as have their ideological valences. A shift in ideological emphasis, from conquest to commerce, may be discerned in the half-millennium of European imperial experience. This was the thrust of eighteenth-century Enlightenment argument against empire, which Anthony Pagden has demonstrated with rare erudition.[48] The shift may be correlated with a military-industrial history in which *colonial occupation has been declining even as the projection of imperial power expanded apace.* Competitive imperialist expansion created a technological ratchet of military domination over ever thinner geographical media that increasingly approximated a smooth, frictionless plane of decreasing resistance: cavalry over flat plains; warships on the water of the oceans; aircraft in the air of the skies; and, potentially, new devices in the vacuum of outer space. This history can be thought of in three phases:

1. The first European empires, of the Americas, were established by complete settler colonization. Power was projected and maintained manually, by horses and populations on the ground. Britain, France, Spain, and Portugal rushed for and through the New World on this common basis. On the cusp of this expansion in the sixteenth century, Machiavelli observed that colonial settlements—which Rome always planted after foreign wars— were the surest way to make foreign conquest profitable and permanent rather than ruinous.[49] Territories and peoples were the private property of Europeans, to be worked. As interstate analogues to private property, colonies were economic and political monopolies held by imperial states against each other.

2. The second European empires, of Asia and Africa (especially from the nineteenth century onward), expanded via the projection of power on water, and on land was maintained by the demographically lighter colonization of company, army, and administration rather than a settler population.[50] While political territories were owned or monopolized by European states as colonies, peoples were free as labor. Ideas of civilization and commerce, in contrast to conquest and extraction, provided the ideological writ in this phase. These concepts ironically were derived from late-eighteenth-century Enlightenment critiques of the first European empires as monopolies that kept prices high and production low, retained colonies with novel standing armies and navies, and burdened home populations with the taxes to pay for them.[51] Free trade, celebrated by Montesquieu as "sweet commerce," would bind nations in peace, liberate capital to seek energetic producers whether in colony or metropolis, enlarge the markets that gave products value, and supplant the violence that held empires and their monopolies in place.[52]

3. In the third European empire, that of the United States, there is no formal colonization. Both political territories and peoples are free, owners of themselves. There is maximal projection of military power through sea and air space, a system of subordinate sovereign states, and multilateral institutions. Just as critiques of the first European empires underwrote those of the second, critiques of the second empires underwrote the third. The U.S. empire supplanted its predecessors at the end of WWII, when it pushed a devastated Europe to decolonize and supported independence movements against them. The idea of empire had dissolved in the minds of the British-Indian soldier[53] and the British politician confronting national reconstruction. It was a rare moment when American, British, and anti-British independence interests were aligned.[54] The ideological coin struck in this third European empire was independence, freedom, democracy for all—not a return to precolonial native despotisms, but progress in American-style anticolonial republicanism. While ideals of commerce and free trade from the previous phase continue to be pursued, a more temporally complex form of economic engagement is at stake: not universal exchange, but investment on a global scale.

As plantations, mines, factories, and debtors, new nation-states[55] are not property like colonies but are free agents with contractual obligations to investors, who are partners in their development. They need short-term help with balance of payments and currency stability, long-term help with infrastructure and human development, and attention forever as local guarantors of the regime of private property. Respectively, the IMF, World Bank and noncommunist independent governments, all constituted after WWII, were the institutions charged with furnishing the public goods of this new, noncolonial world for private investment. How these institutions, which did not exist before, came to be vitally interconnected so suddenly may be compactly seen through the eyes of Dean Acheson, who, in the service of the U.S. State Department from 1941 to 1953, styled himself "present at the Creation."[56] He wrote the World Bank's charter. The world of colonies, previously rushing headlong into independence, all of a sudden stopped and waited to be developed, as the "Third World." The language of development, which inherited the civilizing mission of colonialism, is one of investment—public and private, foreign and domestic. Ideologically, why could independent colonies not revert to the hunting bands, chiefdoms, kingdoms, and even empires of their glorious past? Absent the old European empires, the nation-state provided the only accountable, acceptable, and disciplinable custodian for investments from far away and for social welfare domestically. Nations were no longer dependent colonies owned by Europeans, nor the private privies of native kings, but free contractors with obligations to partners, including a newly enfranchised population with an escalating bill for social welfare. This was a persuasive argument for decolonization.

It is important to understand that U.S. anticolonialism is not simply a cloak for U.S. empire, but rather a language that informs the very representation of its imperial authority. It is a broad language of political self-understanding developed before its empire acquired world status. Its vocabulary becomes discernible at the conclusion of the Seven Years' War in 1763, when Britain decisively beat France in rivalry for North America and India,[57] and boosted its presence as a state in its American colonies.[58] A world-straddling government, imposing a standing army of 10,000 men financed by burgeoning state debt and new taxes, engendered among the American colonists a paranoid fear of a British government "conspiracy against the rights of humanity,"[59] whether they saw it in English Whig terms as monarchical advantage over commoners in the constitutional balance,[60] or in Florentine Machiavellian ones of imperial expansion threatening republican virtue.[61] In any case, rejection of their status as possessed colonies in the American revolution was understood as a repudiation of monarchy and empire *in defense* of the English constitutional balance between estates of society. At the outset, American anticolonialism was wedded to a belief in a legitimate constitution.[62] A free people were at liberty to own, but could not themselves *be,* property of the English government. The new British impositions were especially galling because the American citizen-militias and allied Native Americans had fought alongside the British to expel the French, and now felt betrayed in victory. Fortified by experience in actual interimperial combat, they now had the self-confidence to project a new, independent "third way" separate from imperial entanglements—as enunciated in Washington's farewell address—and achieved it through guerrilla warfare against a conventional army.[63]

By 1787, the U.S. federal constitution which was enacted was no longer for a society but a state. Sovereignty flowed from the people, who vested immense powers in their representatives. Those powers could not be turned against the people because they were parceled out among government branches which balanced each other. Theoretically, who the people were and what their virtues were no longer mattered; an internally balanced government could accommodate all interests. The federal constitution was thus a structure capable of "indefinite expansion,"[64] of being both republic and empire. What it could not be was colonial, as power and sovereignty were assumed to flow from the people.

As the United States expanded on the continent, it avoided colonialism by incorporating new territories and populations under the constitutional structure.[65] The annexation of the Northwest Territories set the precedent for what was basically temporary colonialism. Congress chose governors and judges from resident freeholders; a legislature formed as population increased, with statehood and full constitutional cover ultimately being granted. Initial colonial power in the form of congressional authority from above was ultimately supplanted by popular sovereignty from below, in the form of a republican state. Although built up by European settler colonization in the meantime, the final political form was not that of a colony owned by the United States, but the cellular addition of a free and willing republic. New territories, even conquered ones, were purchased by the federal government wholesale, as it were, and retailed to citizens freehold in fee simple. Thus the Union could be thought of as an expanding empire of freedom and legitimate property rather than of conquest and colonial possession.

Louisiana, with its large French population in New Orleans, modified the precedent, with initial, absolute colonial power in the hands of the president, officials from nonfreeholders, and a longer journey to statehood, largely because the application of the Constitution was not easily separated from its ethnic roots, as guaranteeing the freedom of an English (not French-rooted) people. When further territories were captured from Mexico in 1848, Daniel Webster challenged the sort of colonial, extraconstitutional limbo Louisiana had been through, arguing that either constitutional cover and statehood be granted immediately, or the territories be left separate.

As the United States expanded, the courts invented, or "discovered," ever new statuses for peoples and territories,[66] because the Constitution was fundamentally an internalist document, concerned to "secure the Blessings of Liberty to ourselves and our posterity" (U.S. Constitution, preamble), not to foreigners. When foreigners and their lands came into U.S. possession and rule, authority was granted now to Congress, now to the president. This indeterminacy became even more apparent when the United States assumed transoceanic control of the Philippines, Guam, Cuba, and Puerto Rico in 1898 from Spain and annexed Hawaii, resulting in a full-blown debate over whether the country should pursue imperial ambitions. Total incorporation or total separation are the only legally rigorous solutions provided for in the Constitution, as its republican axiom of the people's sovereignty makes it necessarily anticolonial. The United States had been colonial in its continental expansion from the point of view of Native Americans and Mexicans and at their expense, but colonialism became fully visible and acknowledged only with the undeniable appearance of possessions overseas.

THE IMPERIAL REPUBLIC ABROAD

American citizens cede immense powers to their representatives and government because constitutionally they can recall them, and because the branches of government balance each other. Peoples who came under U.S. colonial rule did not have representation, and more seriously did not have the full machinery of constitutional government to protect them. Since WWII, the categories and numbers of such persons have multiplied, to include those living outside of direct U.S. colonial rule but within the purview of its empire. Condemned to invisibility by the U.S. Constitution, they are subject to tyranny—in the classic Whig sense of domination by a powerful few, and in the U.S. constitutional sense of unchecked power of one branch of the U.S. government, often the executive, *with overseas organs*, whether it be the military, intelligence, or foreign service.

That constitutional invisibility of the foreign has translated into customary policy and practice within the executive, congressional, and judicial branches and the citizenry at large. In a recent example, federal judge Colleen Kollar-Kotelly ruled that foreign prisoners held at the U.S. Navy's Guantanamo air base were not covered by the U.S. Constitution because they were not on U.S. territory.[67] U.S. occupation of enemy Cuban land entails no legal encumbrance despite its possession in perpetuity on lease. While the courts have been creative in discovering in the Constitution new territorial statuses to justify U.S. government possessions overseas since 1898, they have oxymoronically denied that that same Constitution applies overseas. In consequence, the United States enjoys rights in those lands but owes no legally demandable obligation to foreigners there; it is a generalized right to enjoy one's own property in private. Without recourse to U.S. law, prisoners at Guantanamo are subject to the unchecked and therefore tyrannical power of the U.S. president. The judge's denial of their request for *habeas corpus* condemns them to invisibility in precise legal terms. There is a history of such judgments, and the reasoning can best be understood in the clear language of the earliest precedents.

In a test case over Puerto Rican tariffs a century ago, the U.S. Supreme Court ruled (in *Downes* v. *Bidwell*) to the effect that the Constitution suspended itself temporarily on the colonization of alien races, leaving Congress to its discretion. The judgment reads, in part:

> A false step at this time might be fatal to the development of what Chief Justice Marshall called the American Empire. Choice in some cases, the natural gravitation of small bodies toward large ones in others, the result of a successful war in still others, may bring about conditions which would render the annexation of distant possessions desirable. If those possessions are inhabited by alien races, differing from us in religion, customs, laws, methods of taxation and modes of thought, the administration of government and justice, according to Anglo-Saxon principles, may for a time be impossible . . . (182 U.S., 286f).[68]

Balanced against destroying the "American Empire," the court chose to suspend the liberty of alien races instead. Abroad, government could act unconstitutionally because the classic threat of arbitrary rule was posed to alien races, not to Anglo-Saxon Americans.[69] At the limits of historical precedent on the question of colonial rule abroad, the court retreated from a universal conception of natural freedom and a Madisonian Constitution blind to the qualities of citizens to one closer to the British-Italian, Harringtonian-Machiavellian spirit, which was embodied in constitutions[70] for the growth of large empires as the secure property of a *particular* free people, Anglo-Saxon Americans.[71] While temporary colonialism merely repeats the pattern of continental expansion, how long the temporary lasts hinges on whether the foreigners can be transformed into freeholding Americans—unlikely in the case of ten million Filipinos in 1902 and a few hundred Taliban prisoners in 2002.

By granting American politicians extraconstitutional power over foreigners, and by reelecting those politicians (such as McKinley's 1900 presidential victory on an imperialist platform), the judiciary and citizenry acquiesce to arbitrary rule abroad by branches of government for reasons they deem desirable. If such branches act abroad without fanfare or visibility, it is a convenience rather than an affront to the other parts of the republic (the judiciary and the citizenry), given their lack of authority and responsibility over external affairs. An invisible empire allows the republic to sustain its anticolonialist self-regard. Except for small groups of citizens attuned to the classical fear of empire abroad corrupting the republic at home, such as the Boston brahmins of the Anti-Imperialist League, the All-America Anti-Imperialist League of the Workers' (Communist) Party, and Jane Addams's Women's International League for Peace and Freedom, there developed, in the twentieth century, a "see no evil" attitude toward United States actions abroad. In such a domestic context, U.S. administrations developed a penchant for invisibility in foreign affairs when given the opportunity, and there were many.

REPRESENTING AUTHORITY: INVISIBILITY AS POLICY

KABUL, Afghanistan, July 28—American security guards in T-shirts and jeans, carrying large assault rifles, were prowling the president's office here this weekend. The first half-dozen members of an American security force were in place to guard President Hamid Karzai, working alongside their Afghan counterparts.[72]

—NEW YORK TIMES, JULY 29, 2002

T-shirts and jeans? The American imperialism that succeeded Britain's was markedly different in character. Features such as military occupation, colonial administration, and the dependent status of local sovereigns were all moved from the open, formal, acknowledged, public sphere to that of covert operations. In the American empire, there are no Indian durbars with Her Majesty's Governors in starched white tunics and feathered caps surrounded by colorful rajas and sultans. The ruling image, rather, is that of remote control—of invisibility, in fact. The passing of the baton is marked by the progress from gunboat diplomacy to aerial bombing. American involvement in another country's politics becomes visible, most often only when someone "messes up big time," and the military is called in for the duration of a crisis, which by definition is exceptional and short.

America does not formally recognize the existence of hierarchy in its relations with foreign sovereigns, unlike all previous empires. With no durbars, no younger brothers, no tribute gifts, America's friends are free to come and go— "You're with us or you're against us," as president George W. Bush reiterates. In this sense, America's subordinate countries are kept in a form of imperial concubinage.[73] Dominance, intimacy, and consequence flowing from the relationship remain unacknowledged. While previous empires dominated their colonies with pomp and ceremony, the American invention of "extraterritoriality" formalizes the idea that they are not really present. Extracted from China at the end of the 1839–42 Opium War, extraterritoriality demands that servicemen at U.S. bases abroad be not subject to the laws of their host lands, sartorial or otherwise.[74] Their presence is furtive, their absence fictive. Prowling about in their T-shirts and jeans, the Afghan president's American bodyguards could just as well be at home in North Carolina or Florida. As one of Sri Lanka's leaders is supposed to have said of his country's Tamil rebels: how can you conduct business with someone who doesn't have a telephone number? Many peoples around the world feel the same way about America.

Bernard Cohn has written that public representation of authority is key to the maintenance of rule. Why and how Indians should listen to Englishmen needs to be expressed in a language comprehensible to and usable by all parties. The British settled on a satisfactory language only after the mutiny of 1857–58, which shook colonial rule to its foundations. That violently traumatic event brought clarity of vision and representation. Henceforth, Indians were subjects of the British queen, and in 1877, the Imperial Assemblage announced her to be empress of India as well. In this durbar of durbars, all categories of Indians recognized by the British—rajas, landlords, editors, native gentlemen—participated in making her their empress, and in making themselves the kinds of public men[75] the British recognized them to be. Cohn writes that ". . . the goal of the assemblage was to make manifest and compelling the sociology of India,"[76] a disambiguated ruling hierarchy for an unruly jumble of castes and claims.[77]

In comparison, one is tempted to say that by not representing their rule, power, or influence, the Americans are misrepresenting their role, or practicing dissimulation, or hiding unpleasant things. We have discussed invisibility as a glaring feature of American imperialism abroad. But invisibility goes along with a host of related features that shrink the space and time of coercive action without sacrificing impact: the notion of a quick entry and exit in military adventures; surgical air strikes; occupation as temporary measure; the lack of hierarchy in relations with other nations; even the U.S. secretary of state's 2002 zip tour of Southeast Asia, barely passing a few hours in each capital despite the prime importance of signing them up for a major antiterrorism pact.[78] Seen together, these add up to a ruling sociology of international society which affirms that nations are free to choose their destinies and friends, that colonialism is illegitimate, and that American military action can be omniscient, devastating, and healing all at once, liberating nations hijacked by despotic states. T-shirts and jeans, in their now wholesome association with the sexual liberation of 1960s U.S. counterculture worldwide, metonymically signify and announce, rather than hide, the religious, political, social, and possibly sexual liberation of Afghanistan.[79] We can only conclude that invisibility is a form that the United States chooses as policy to represent its authority in the world.

TERRORISM AS SPECTACLE: HISTORY LESSONS

Spectacle is one answer to invisibility, and the filmic quality of the attack on New York in September 2001 has been much noted. While there has been no legally conclusive evidence so far that bin Laden was behind the World Trade Center and Pentagon attacks, the bombing of Afghanistan and bin Laden's TV appearances constitute an elaborate public dialogue (with wide audience response) open to interpretation. So what does bin Laden want? Or want to say?

First, he has a longstanding request, since the Gulf War, that American troops leave Saudi soil.[80] He has since extended that to Palestine, by proxy. This demand takes American anticolonial ideology at face value, and puts the United States on the horns of an ideological dilemma. If the United States is indeed anticolonial, what are its troops doing there? The U.S. reply is that they are there by invitation of the legitimately constituted government.[81] This brings us to the second point: In the videotape issued at the onset of the bombing of Afghanistan, bin Laden said: "What America tasted today is something of what we have tasted for decades. For eighty-some years, our community has tasted this humiliation and tasted this degradation . . . no one heard and no one answered . . . But when the sword came after eighty years to America, hypocrisy appeared and raised its head."[82] What is he referring to when he says eighty years?

If you convert the years of the Islamic calendar into Gregorian time, eighty years takes us back to 1924. This was the year in which the Ottoman universal caliphate was abolished by a Turkish parliament, an act that was followed in quick succession by Sharif Husayn's declaration of himself as Caliph, followed by his defeat at the hands of the Saudis, who took over custody of the holy cities of Mecca and Medina. Within the space of six months, eighty years ago, a modern Islamic empire was finally carved up by its European counterparts, and a tribal chief was installed in the stead of the universal Caliph as Custodian of the Two Holy Mosques.

While the eyes of the world were transfixed on U.S. action in Afghanistan, bin Laden was pointing toward Saudi Arabia. Once one makes that geographical adjustment, it becomes clear that the conflict is being couched as a historical one, and that bin Laden is saying: "Historicize!" He is saying that an imperial world is a tough neighborhood in which Muslims, bereft of an empire of their own, are fair game. Their local leaders such as the Saudis cannot protect them, yet cannot be deposed. Their political process is stuck. Bin Laden's immediate objective is, I think, Saudi Arabia, not the United States, which is simply a medial obstacle. Yet this view is not enough to comprehend the anger, paranoia, and audacity with which his demands are couched. Strange as it may seem, these sentiments echo revolutionary America after Britain's defeat of France in 1763 (discussed earlier), including the millenarian, chiliastic registers—absolute morality inveighing against absolute corruption.[83] Bin Laden and the "Afghan Arabs" returned from helping the Americans defeat the Soviets in Afghanistan only to find the now-unchecked Americans garrisoning their country in the early 1990s.[84] Their militia success against one imperial power and sense of betrayal by the other fuel their guerrilla campaigns against the United States from this time onward. But the United States was not simply a colonial occupier or an imperial power, but one newly freed of a restraining counterpart worldwide, as the British seemed to the Americans after 1763. Whether bin Laden wants to establish a Muslim empire, be Caliph, or simply keep America's imperial reach at bay is secondary. What is clear is that this is a vision for some "third way," deluded or not, between and beyond Soviet-U.S. imperial rivalry. And it has struck a chord across not only the Muslim world but Latin America and France as well.[85]

The abolition of what the South Asians call Khilafat, the universal Caliph, was one of the two main issues which kept British intelligence busy worldwide post-WWI. The other was international communism. Today, web pages have sprung up celebrating the Internet as the authentic means by which a world Muslim Caliph can be democratically elected. Pakistanis in Britain are among the strongest proponents. The first one I saw had two nominations: Mullah Omar and bin Laden, and called for more, including other attractive characters such as Dr. Mahathir Mohamed, prime minister of Malaysia.

The parallels with the past are striking.[86] Bin Laden's video response to the bombing of Afghanistan—"eighty years"—made reference to one historical event: the demise of the universal Muslim Caliphate. His view of the conflict with the United States, in my reading, draws on this history of conflict between European empires and the universalizing Muslim Hadrami diaspora in the Indian Ocean region, starting with the Portuguese. The response, suicide as martyrdom in the face of overwhelming odds, has recurred during critical phases and has had theoretical formulation since the 1570s in al-Malibārī's sixteenth-century text. It is worth mentioning here the remarkable fact that al-Malibārī had also complained of "countless forms of oppression and viciousness . . . over more than eighty years." [87] Since then, another text, the *Hikayat Prang Sabi,* celebrating martyrdom in the Aceh struggle against the Dutch, emerged during the Dutch-Aceh war in the late nineteenth century. Further east, in Muslim Philippines, it inspired similar action against Spanish—and American—suppression of independence struggles.[88]

In the present, as in the past, a single individual, skilled in navigating the waters shared by diaspora and empire, is able to gain great influence, internationalizing a conflict that was otherwise confined to colonial corners of imperial geography.

The most striking parallel with the past is the geography of it. Though the Ottoman empire never really went past the Red Sea, the idea of a universal Muslim empire fired imaginations in the populous British India[89] and the Dutch East Indies (present-day Indonesia), among other places. Gandhi aligned it with India's anticolonial struggle in 1919, and this marked the beginning of the end for the British in India.[90] It is notable that the attacks on U.S. interests associated with bin Laden have not taken place in the Middle East but around the Indian Ocean: Indonesia, Tanzania, Kenya, Somalia, and Aden in Yemen.

These geographical parallels mean that, viewed in South and Southeast Asia, the events unfolding on the TV screen have deep historical resonances. Huge fireballs and warriors on horses are screen visuals familiar from the epic tales regularly beamed by government TV stations on religious and national anniversaries.

History as spectacle. The cycle of bombing fireworks in Afghanistan and replays of the September 11 drama, interspersed with bin Laden's al-Jazeera appearances, speaking the romantic, classical Arabic of the epics in measured cadences and gesturing sporadically with a long index finger, had the eerily didactic quality of history lessons, now updated with Americans woven into the story. The empire which represents its authority in the mode of invisibility unwittingly contributed the spectacle of its massive presence to the programming. Indeed, the spectacle of the September 11 attacks themselves had challenged the invisibility of its authority.

The instances of conflict between diaspora and empire I've mentioned—Malabar in the 1570s against the Portuguese; 1840s and 1921 against the British; Aceh at the end of the nineteenth century against the Dutch; bin Laden at the end of the twentieth century against America[91]—have all surfaced when a very mobile, religious, cosmopolitan, and entrepreneurial member of the Hadrami diaspora managed to rouse wider Muslim sentiment against the European empire on the back of local anticolonial struggles.

The logic of this history and this argument forces us to look from the Hadrami diaspora and its latest figure, Osama bin Laden, to his opponent, the United States. It forces us to think of the United States as an empire, but one with a completely unique and new form. It is an empire without colonies. We do not understand the full ramifications of such a phenomenon, but one can already see that there are aspects of it which are extremely dangerous and need to be seriously thought about.

The issue of imperial power is what links the United States and the Muslim world today. On the one side you have an empire not knowing that it is one; on the other you have a non-empire knowing full well that it is not one.

IMPERIAL POLLUTION, A NEW WORLD DISORDER

Empires create messes all over the place. Empires with colonial administrations have the machinery in place to clean up those messes. The United States, as an empire without colonial administration, does not clean up after itself. As George W. Bush says, "We are not into nation building." Thus the debris proliferates. Bin Laden's growing network feeds off that expanding detritus. But the problem of imperial debris goes beyond the United States. In addition to the Middle East, Bin Laden's recruits and supporters come from southern Philippines, Chechnya, Afghanistan, Azerbaijan, and Xinjiang. These are all Muslim trouble spots, trouble spots because they are on the borders between non-Muslim empires present and past: Spanish, British, Chinese, Soviet, American. These are precisely the regions which experienced centuries of imperial violence without the benefits of colonial administration. While Afghanistan used to divide the empires ranged on all sides, after September 11 it united them against itself: Russia, China, and America found common cause against the Taliban. This configuration was an ironic, transient coincidence, but one that generates the feeling among those who identify with them of being universally put upon. In the words of Sufi Muhammad, who organized thousands of armed Pakistanis to enter the fray in Afghanistan: "This is a strange occasion of world history. For the first time, all the anti-Islamic forces are united against Islam."[92] The cycle of terrorist attack and imperial response—passenger planes as manually guided missiles vs. remote-control aerial munitions—deepens the well of recruitment from peripheral to mainline Muslim populations. This is explosive beyond Afghanistan.

The only body in the world officially charged to clean up this sort of mess is the UN. This Nobel Peace Prize winner seldom delights at the prospect of playing proxy colonial administration. Its bureaucratic hands are full and it does not have a tax base, nor a standing army. What is the United States to make of the cheers for bin Laden? Are the natives actually ganging up, or is it just the sound of spectators clapping, never mind what they think? How is the United States to respond?

Is it conceivable for the United States to be neither imperial nor colonial, relinquishing its global military arm, cutting loose all proxy states, trusting in free trade and God to equilibrate all markets and level all inequalities?[93] Or is the opposite—full-scale colonization—the inevitable answer?[94] Ever more attuned to the burdens of domination than the liberals, American conservatives have staked out the poles between which their newspapers editorialize and their government lurches—Pat Buchanan's "America First" isolationism on one side,[95] and Kristol and Kagan's "benevolent global hegemony" on the other.[96]

Damned if you do and damned if you don't, flip-flopping between isolationism and nation-building abroad, two priorities at least are clear for the U.S. government: internal securitization of the U.S. population itself, and increased investment in methodologies of invisibility abroad. Remote-control bombers fly ever higher out of sight[97] while military advisors disappear into the Filipino jungles,[98] Yemeni mountains,[99] and Georgian gorges.[100] As invisibility continues to be the method of choice for dealing with the dominated, imperial concubinage will doubtless continue to spawn political bastards who will behave as such. Over the longer term, the increasingly shrill language of "failed states," "weapons of mass destruction," and even "human rights" prepares public opinion for an ambitious redrawing of political maps. These terms are becoming cudgels, like "slavery" in the nineteenth century, with which Britain went around opening the doors of native states, and the northern United States conquered and liberated the South.

WHY A DIASPORIC PERSPECTIVE?
MANIFEST DESTINY OCCULTED

Political opinions aside, American anthropologists are professionally affected by the scale of the conflict. The "war on terrorism" amounts to a worldwide war, in which the field sites of many anthropologists are subject to militarization, especially by "culturally sensitive" U.S. "special operations forces." In addition to the usual rigors of fieldwork abroad, anthropologists associated with the United States—like journalists, diplomats, company employees, tourists, and others—are also potential targets of violence for the unknown duration of this invisible war. Practical responses will have to be worked out by individuals and their institutions. As for an intellectual one, contemporary postcolonial theory is inadequate here because the geographical dimensions of the conflict are beyond its ken. A broader perspective is needed, and a diasporic one may be a good starting point.

The weakness of postcolonial theory comes from its roots in postindependence revisions of colonial history. Concerned to write history from the point of view of the colonized native, revisionist historians willy-nilly aligned themselves with the nationalist agendas of the new states. This locked discussion of colonialism and its consequences into a fundamental dualism, which postcolonial theories retain: West/East, colonizer/colonized, foreigner/native, self/other, white/black, master/slave. A Hegelian Frantz Fanon serves as touchstone. As the dual was generated on the axis of power inequality between colonizer and colonized, the struggle for national self-determination that sought to reverse the inequality revolved around the same axis, thereby keeping the dual in place. Because this dual is the nationalist point of view, focused on wresting a piece of land from colonizers who are (by nationalist definition) foreigners, its appreciation of geography is parochial when compared to that of colonizer, for most colonial powers were not just colonial; they were imperial in extent and outlook. When viewed from the imperial center, the many colonies that fired nationalist dreams and became so many postcolonial states were merely parts of a single empire. Thus, while nationalist dreams and strategies were narrowly terrestrial, imperial ones were expansively maritime and aerial.[101] That remains the case today.[102]

Whereas postcolonial theory is predominantly dual, imperialism has always been plural with respect to places and parties involved.[103] An appreciation of its plural nature is crucial to understanding unauthorized ideological crosscurrents, such as communism and pan-Islamism, which flowed with alarming speed across empires at the beginning of the twentieth century. The subversives who peopled such movements were mobile cosmopolitans whose agendas were presumably extraterritorial. They were often members of diasporic groups such as Jews, Armenians, Greeks, Arabs, Chinese, and Indians, found across imperial domains in more innocuous dress as "trading minorities" and indentured labor. One could not deal with them as one could provincial nationalist independence fighters, for their geographical mobility often meant crossing imperial and departmental jurisdictions, stretching the capacity of empire for political intelligence. Nor were they imperial equals one could treat on the customary terms. A phrase common in British official writing from the period is *imperium in imperio*.[104] It pointed to an inferior, subaltern entity that was nevertheless diasporic, cosmopolitan, and sophisticated like empire itself, and enough so to represent a potential threat to the mother-empire—a threat growing within the belly of empire itself.

The internationalization of anticolonial struggle has hung like a specter over the Western empires since the end of the nineteenth century. This was the fantasy W.E.B. DuBois savored in his fictive *Dark Princess,* in which the problem of the color line becomes embodied in an international conspiracy of colored peoples—Blacks, Indians, Japanese, Arabs—against white domination.[105] It remained a fiction. Race never rose to the challenge of internationalism. Communism and Islamism did. Internationalization of anticolonialism achieved what a spatially less ambitious push could not: anti-imperialism, a clear view of the beast, the full elephant of empire instead of merely one of its four colony-legs touched by the blind. Geography is key. Peoples native to old diasporas have geographical sensibilities as large as whole empires; possessed of folklore, ritual, and literature, their cultural memories reach back even further. It is an expansive intelligence of this sort, I believe, that has now taken up arms against its geographical equal, the American empire.

The earlier conflicts in Malabar and Aceh that I described were anticolonial in the sense of being localized. The territory under contention was also the site of violent conflict. The current conflict between bin Laden and the United States is different. While the territory under contention—Saudi Arabia—is localized, the site of conflict is not. The territory under contention cannot quite be the site of conflict because it is under the tight control of a proxy state housing U.S. troops.[106] At some point after the Gulf War, a choice was made to enlarge the terrain of struggle from an anticolonial to an anti-imperial one.[107] That is what makes the strategy terrorist in U.S. eyes. U.S. embassies and soldiers—and later, civilians—became targets worldwide. Anti-imperialist terror is now potentially everywhere—both where the United States does and does not have presence, both mimicking and mocking imperial omniscience, with its invisibility, remote-control operatives, spectacular surgical strikes, and quick exit strategy up to heaven beyond retaliation. This globalization of the conflict acknowledges the imperial terms of engagement, and takes the true measure of imperial reach in its strategy and its self-representation.

DISPLACEMENT, DIASPORA MOBILIZATION, AND TRANSNATIONAL CYCLES OF POLITICAL VIOLENCE

FIONA ADAMSON

INTRODUCTION

The attacks of September 11, 2001, and the emergence of al Qaeda as a major security concern for the United States, brought to the fore a set of transnational dynamics and relationships that have not received significant attention from either international security studies or international migration studies. Scholars of international security have traditionally focused on violent conflict as something that occurs either between or within states. The migration studies literature, on the other hand, has examined global migration flows and local or national forms of immigrant incorporation and political participation, but has paid scant attention to how migration flows impact on the international security environment. In the wake of 9/11, however, there is increasing concern regarding the perceived nexus between migration and national security. In this context, it is useful to examine current developments in a historical and comparative context by studying how migration-based networks and diaspora populations impact on the broader international security environment.

The origins of, and the strategies employed by, transnationally organized "networks from below" can only be understood within a broader geopolitical context. This point is alluded to in the Ho and Ahmed chapters in this volume. Certainly, a full analysis of the relationship that exists between transnationally organized contentious politics "from below" and the geopolitics "from above" is beyond the scope of this chapter. Nevertheless, examining common patterns and processes in the relationship that exists between displacement, migration, and exile on the one hand and the emergence of transnationally organized contentious politics and cycles of political violence on the other hand is a useful starting point. Processes of displacement always occur within a broader geopolitical context—in other words, they are part of cycles of political violence that are embedded within sets of interactions and relationships that occur at the level of the international system.

The international system, as Tirman and Adelman point out in this volume, is increasingly defined by processes of globalization that lead to the intertwining of migration and security in both theory and practice. Rather than positing a direct relationship between globalization, processes of displacement, and the emergence of transnational contentious politics, however, this chapter focuses on one specific dimension of broader cycles of political violence: the role played by political entrepreneurs in diaspora mobilization, and the politicization of transnational constituencies of displaced populations. Processes of displacement and dislocation resulting from a lack of economic opportunities, political repression, or the presence of violent conflict, have long served as impetuses for individuals and groups to exit their homelands in search of greater opportunities and, in many instances, to use the new opportunities as resources to effect political change in either their countries of origin or in the larger order of the international states system. Violence has not always played a role in the political movements that emerge from these cycles of displacement, migration, and exile, but it has done so in a significant enough number of cases to warrant investigation.

In the rest of this chapter, I analyze how processes of displacement and migration form the foundation for the transnational politics of diaspora mobilization, and examine the impact that the politics of diaspora mobilization have had on the international security environment. I do so in the following manner: First, I point to studies that have demonstrated the significance of diasporas and migration networks to our understanding of cycles of political violence. I then analyze how the experiences of exile and boundary-crossing can be catalysts for the emergence of new political categories, identities, and ideologies that are then deployed by political entrepreneurs as mobilizing devices. I examine the funding sources and financial resources that are drawn upon by nonstate political entrepreneurs during processes of mobilization, then discuss the organizational basis of transnational movements that are formed by processes of diaspora mobilization. I discuss how strategies of political violence are drawn upon as tools during processes of political mobilization and how, likewise, the process of political mobilization itself can be used as a means of promoting destabilizing cycles of political violence in a target country or in the international system as a whole. Finally, I conclude with comments regarding the directions in which policy-relevant research in this area should be conducted in the future.

DIASPORAS AND CYCLES OF VIOLENT CONFLICT

Recent studies of civil wars have shown a correlation between the existence of a significant diaspora population and the probability of recurrent violence in a state that has already experienced violent conflict—a finding that points to diasporas as playing a significant role as intervening variables in ongoing cycles of political violence. According to a World Bank study, even though countries with no or insignificant diasporas experience a 6 percent chance of the recurrence of violent conflict, the probability of renewed violence goes up to 36 percent in countries that have unusually large diasporas abroad. The author of the report from which this finding is taken adds that "diasporas appear to make life for those left behind much more dangerous in post-conflict situations."[1] Other studies have reached similar conclusions regarding the role that diasporas play in conflicts. A Rand Corporation survey of sources of external support in contemporary insurgencies noted that one of the major changes in the international security environment has been the increased importance of nonstate actors in general, and diasporas in particular, as funders of armed insurgency organizations.[2] Benedict Anderson argues that diasporas are increasingly marked by a politics of "long-distance nationalism" that he describes as:

> . . . a serious politics that is at the same time radically unaccountable. The participant rarely pays taxes in the country in which he does his politics: he is not answerable to his judicial system . . . he need not fear prison, torture or death, nor need his immediate family. But, well and safely positioned in the First World, he can send money and guns, circulate propaganda, and build intercontinental computer information circuits, all of which can have incalculable consequences in the zones of their ultimate destinations. . . . That same metropole that marginalizes and stigmatizes [the migrant] also allows him to play, in a flash, on the other side of the planet, national hero.[3]

Similarly, a number of other scholars have pointed to the ideational and material impacts of diasporas in conflicts during the 1990s, particularly in the Balkans, where, according to the Independent International Commission on Kosovo, "It was the Kosovar Albanians in the Diaspora who became the most radicalized part of the Kosovar Albanian community and were to create the KLA."[4]

Despite the quantitative and qualitative evidence of the significance that diaspora networks can play in cycles of political violence, there have been few studies that have traced the process by which this occurs. Furthermore, there has been almost no attention to how diaspora mobilization activities fit into broader cycles of political violence in the international security environment. The very definition of diaspora has historically been associated with a dispersal of a people resulting from a cataclysmic event.[5] More recently, diaporas have come to be viewed less as naturalized entities and more as transnational identity constructions that emerge through political practice and that characterize a variety of migration processes.[6] With the possible exception of the migration of highly skilled labor, however, most forms of migration involve some history of violence, repression, or dislocation. This includes economic and labor migration in addition to the migration of refugees and political asylum seekers. Economic and labor migrants can be the product of large-scale dislocations, economic repression, and structural violence that in many ways parallel the experiences of political ref ugees and asylum seekers.[7]

Episodes of transnationalized contention originating in diaspora communities are often articulated as responses or counterclaims arising from past or ongoing instances of displacement, repression, or marginalization. Diaspora-based episodes of contention, therefore, are one component of ongoing cycles of political violence that also include the very conditions that lead to processes of displacement—processes that, in effect, produce a potentially new political entity. An example of this can be seen in the emergence of the transnational Algerian nationalist movement that eventually led to the founding of the *Front de Libération Nationale* (FLN) in 1954. The early movement, which originated in immigrant communities in Paris in the 1920s, was articulated as a response to the massive displacement and outmigration that had occurred due to patterns of French colonization and European settlement in North Africa.[8] Another example is the transnational Kurdish nationalist movement, and the Kurdistan Workers' Party (PKK), which operated in Europe during the 1980s and 1990s, drawing on the sense of economic and political dislocation that was prevalent among economic immigrants as well as political asylum seekers and refugees from southeastern Anatolia, who settled in Germany and other European states. Both of these groups had suffered experiences of dislocation from southeastern Anatolia, whether through processes of economic or political marginalization and repression. The politicization of the Sikh diaspora and the emergence of transnational strategies of violence and militancy emerged out of a context of violence and displacement in the Punjab and has been sustained through visual representations of torture and repression on the Internet and in other materials that are distributed throughout the diaspora.[9]

Observations regarding the role that diasporas play in violent conflicts usually begin with the assumption of an already politicized and reified diaspora, and then proceed to describe the activities of this transnational collectivity and the impact of these activities in conflict situations. Yet the emergence of mobilized and politicized diaspora networks—or even the existence of a collective political identification with a particular diaspora—is dependent on processes of political mobilization carried out by political entrepreneurs. The mobilization of diaspora networks by political entrepreneurs, and the emergence of political or financial support for strategies of violence in the diaspora, depends on their ability to produce categories, identifications, and ideologies that link memories, perceptions, or lived experiences of forced dislocation, displacement, marginalization, or repression with strategies of political action that are designed to mount a challenge to the political status quo. The process of the political mobilization of diaspora populations is therefore dependent on the ability of political entrepreneurs—in the form of dissidents, activists, intellectuals, and émigrés—to effectively design strategies that address the political and economic grievances of populations of the displaced (and descendents of the displaced) who have had to leave their homeland for lack of economic and political opportunity. Personal or political grievances that surround processes of displacement can be activated, diverted, channeled, and harnessed to the purposes of a transnational political movement through a well-constructed and articulated political ideology.[10]

BORDER-CROSSING, EXILE, AND THE EMERGENCE OF NEW MOBILIZING IDEOLOGIES AND CATEGORIES

Processes of displacement, migration, and exile from a so-called homeland produce constituencies that are defined, to greater or lesser extents, by experiences of marginalization in relation to the political status quo in both their country of origin and their country of destination—indeed, by the experience of a degree of marginalization within the international system as a whole.[11] The transnational networks that are formed by such processes of displacement and migration, therefore, constitute potential constituencies and bases of political support for those political entrepreneurs who can successfully articulate identity categories and political ideologies that speak to the experiences of displacement and marginalization. In other words, the task of the political entrepreneur engaged in the transnational mobilization of diaspora networks is to construct or deploy ideologies and categories that can be used to create new political groups out of existing social networks. As Michael Mann writes:

> An ideology will emerge as a powerful, autonomous movement when it can put together in a single explanation and organization a number of aspects of existence that have hitherto been marginal, interstitial to the dominant institutions of power.[12]

The experience of liminality and marginality can be transformed into the articulation of new categories that are catalysts for political change. Exile, migration, and boundary-crossing from one political system to another all serve as impetuses for the creation of new categories and discourses, since these activities expose an individual to novel social and political conditions and thus allow for a reinterpretation of what might have been viewed previously as a naturalized state of existence. Edward Said has described the relationship between the process of exile and the emergence of new forms and categories that can be used in the process of political critique in the following manner:

> [B]ecause the exile sees things both in terms of what has been left behind and what is actual here and now, there is a double perspective that never sees things in isolation. Every scene or situation in the new country necessarily draws on its counterpart in the old country. Intellectually, this means that an idea or experience is always counterposed with another, therefore making them both appear in a sometimes new and unpredictable light.[13]

A key aspect of diaspora mobilization is therefore the utilization by political entrepreneurs of categories or political ideologies that can be used to frame the experiences of those who have subjectively experienced dislocation and marginalization, so as to stimulate, in Charles Tilly's words, "the process by which a group goes from being a passive collection of individuals to an active participant in [international] public life."[14]

One of the most widespread categories or political ideologies used to create a sense of "groupness" out of a "passive collection of individuals" in modern times has been nationalism. Nationalism has been particularly successful as a mobilizing category due to what Benedict Anderson describes as its "modular character."[15] The utility of nationalism as a political category is that it combines a universalist imperative—the linking of cultural groupings to demarcated territorial spaces—with the flexibility to incorporate an infinitely wide range of cultural, linguistic, and symbolic artifacts as mobilizing instruments. Many of the great nationalist movements have had their origins in exile. Mahatma Gandhi, for example, studied in London, and his first major political project was to found the Natal Indian Congress in South Africa in 1894, which was established to fight discrimination against Indian traders, before becoming one of the leading figures of Indian nationalism. Ho Chi Minh studied in France and was a founding member of the French Communist Party before establishing his nationalist-communist revolutionary movement in Vietnam.[16] Many historical instances of *nationalist* mobilization have therefore actually started as instances of *transnational* mobilization, involving diaspora populations and emerging from experiences of either personal or collective exile and dislocation.

Like a number of nationalist movements, contemporary Islamist movements have also been shaped by experiences of exile, emigration, and boundary-crossing. The prominent Egyptian Islamist figure Sayyid Qutb, for example, whose writings are said to have been a source of inspiration for Osama bin Laden, became radicalized and politicized during a stay in the United States between 1948 and 1950. Ayatollah Khomeini, of course, produced his writings and teachings from exile in France before returning triumphantly to revolutionary Iran in 1979. Exile has also historically played a crucial role in the emergence of new bases of political power in Afghanistan, which was especially the case during the Soviet occupation, in which Pakistan became the place for the emergence of the Mujahidin opposition.[17] Political entrepreneurs associated with radicalized Islamist groups, some of which have links with al Qaeda, have used the ideology of radical Islamism to recruit disaffected members of Muslim immigrant communities in Europe and elsewhere. One of the interesting areas of investigation for understanding contemporary patterns of diaspora mobilization is the extent to which new religious and cultural categories are replacing nationalism as tools of political mobilization since the end of the Cold War.[18]

Exiles and émigrés armed with a newly articulated ideology or politicized identity category, in combination with dispersed communities of immigrants, refugees, or the displaced, create the possibility of the emergence of a transnational political constituency or politicized diaspora population. The first step in this process is for political entrepreneurs to draw upon emerging categories, discourses, and symbols and to use them in a way that can tie together dispersed social networks under a single category, thereby converting them into activated and politicized networks that can be drawn upon by political entrepreneurs in the pursuit of a political goal. Tilly, referring to the work of Harrison White, notes that there are two components to creating a sense of collective identity. The first consists of a *category,* which contains "people all of whom recognize their common characteristic, and whom everyone else recognizes as having that characteristic." The second consists of *networks* of people who are linked to one another. "A set of individuals is a group to the extent that it comprises both a category and a network."[19] In the context of ongoing processes of globalization it is increasingly possible, as noted by Tirman and Checkel in this volume, for transnational networks to emerge as salient collective identities in contemporary international society. The emergence of new categories, and the process of mobilization by political entrepreneurs who draw on available technologies, helps to explain how such transnational collective identities come into being.

FUNDING TRANSNATIONAL MOBILIZATION: RESOURCE EXTRACTION IN A GLOBAL ECONOMY

The emergence of transnationally organized political movements relies not just on processes of identity formation and politicization, but also on the ability of political entrepreneurs to generate material resources. Across a wide variety of cases of diaspora mobilization, the generation of material resources for a political struggle has included the following elements: fund-raising and taxation of activated transnational networks and political constituencies; informal sources, such as unreported labor remittances, gray economy networks and international organized crime; and other miscellaneous sources, such as states or individual donors, in addition to the harnessing of skilled and unskilled labor in the form of recruits for the movement.[20]

One means by which political entrepreneurs engaged in mobilization processes harness dispersed resources is by tapping into material resource bases available within the transnational networks they have activated and mobilized. Mobilized transnational networks such as diaspora networks can be tapped through voluntary donations, taxes, and/or coercion. This has been a common strategy of transnational mobilization in the past and is of increasing significance to the understanding of the dynamics of contemporary conflicts. Between 1916 and 1921, for example, nearly 800,000 Irish Americans joined nationalist organizations, contributing over $10 million to Sinn Fein and the Irish Republican Army (IRA) in the cause of Irish independence from Great Britain.[21] In the early 1970s Irish Americans supplied at least half of the Irish Republican Army's total budget via the organization Irish Northern Aid (Noraid), which was based in New York and had ninety-two chapters in the United States, with a paid membership of 5,000.[22]

The Liberation Tigers of Tamil Eelam (LTTE) of Sri Lanka has one of the most effective contemporary transnational fund-raising organizations. Their $50 million annual budget is acquired through a combination of direct donations by Tamil migrant communities, money skimmed off from the budgets of Tamil NGOs (nongovernmental organizations), human smuggling operations, and Tamil-run businesses. Tamil diaspora communities in the United Kingdom, Canada, and Australia are estimated to provide $1.5 million a month via donations and informal taxes.[23] The transnational fund-raising techniques of al Qaeda—which include the use of informal networks; legitimate businesses, such as the honey trade; criminal enterprises, such as the drug trade; and global donations and money skimmed from charity organizations—follow a common pattern of transnational resource mobilization that is familiar to students of diaspora mobilization.

In addition to direct financial contributions by politicized transnational networks, political entrepreneurs tap into a number of other transnational flows as sources of revenue for their political projects. These include labor remittances, transnational gray-economy networks, and transnational networks of organized crime. The transnational flow of labor remittances is estimated to be at least $75 billion annually.[24] Depending on how remittances are channeled, they can contribute to a wide variety of economic and political outcomes. For example, labor remittances have played an important role in postconflict reconstruction within El Salvador, and they have contributed significantly to the economic growth of countries such as Ghana.[25] Remittances can also be harnessed to other political ends and can be mobilized by political entrepreneurs to empower new groups in society. Labor remittances from workers in Gulf states in the Middle East have, for example, played a determinative role in funding radical Islamist networks in Egypt and the Philippines and in helping to bring a fundamentalist Islamist movement to power in the Sudan.[26]

Global revenues from transnational organized crime have been estimated to be as high as $1 trillion annually—the size of the entire U.S. federal budget in 1993. Drug smuggling alone generates approximately $500 billion per year, which is more than the annual global trade in oil.[27] Trafficking in humans brings in approximately $9 billion in revenues annually, with more than 4 million people smuggled across borders every year.[28] Organized crime networks often define themselves on the basis of ethnicity or nationality, a form of social capital that can be drawn upon to generate resource-rich transnational economic networks, which in turn are drawn upon by political entrepreneurs.[29] Countless examples exist of the role that networks of organized crime play in funding localized conflicts: the illegal trade in diamonds has played a key role in the conflict in Sierra Leone; the Armed Revolutionary Forces of Colombia (FARC) relies heavily on drug trafficking as a source of funding; the LTTE engages in human smuggling to raise money for its political struggle.[30]

MacGaffey and Bazenguissa-Ganga note that "Globalization is generally thought of in terms of multinational companies and the changing relations between nation-states and peoples as they become enmeshed in the world economy, [but a study of transnational informal economic networks] focuses instead on individuals operating at the interstices of these larger entities, and on how they manage to take advantage of the way the world economy now works."[31] Transnational economic networks are usually also social networks, in that they rely heavily on personal relations between members rather than on formal or impersonal organizational structures. The opportunities for transnational mobilization of economic resources via organized crime or informal structures have increased greatly with changes in communication and transportation technologies, the emergence of a global financial infrastructure, and increased flows of licit trade between states.

THE ORGANIZATIONAL BASIS OF MOBILIZATION: TRANSNATIONAL NETWORKS AND STRUCTURES

Both political scientists and students of migration have focused on political participation as occurring within the arena of the state. Yet despite the primacy of the state—or perhaps because of the failure of the state in some regards—other

organizational structures have traditionally commanded the loyalties of constituencies as well as provided these constituencies with valuable services in exchange. These services include not just a sense of membership and belonging,
but also a number of functions, such as education, welfare, security and protection, and other social services that have traditionally been associated with the
state. Political entrepreneurs engaged in the process of mobilizing and politiciz-
ing a diaspora population set out to create transnationally organized structures
that can harness the political energies of displaced populations and compete
with state institutions for obtaining loyalties and providing of services.

An emerging literature on transnational networks and transnational relations
has begun to examine the logic of transnationally organized networks and movements, such as those of human rights organizations, environmental groups, and
other nongovernmental organizations.[32] Yet this literature has focused overwhelmingly on Western-based transnational organizations that espouse liberal
political causes. It has largely ignored ethnic and religious organizations or other
transnationally configured political movements that may resemble the organizational form of the transnational networks of liberal activists yet differ in their political goals and everyday activities.

Similar to international NGOs that are organized according to local branches
and networks, transnationally organized nonstate political movements are organized into branches and cell structures, depending heavily on existing social networks and personal ties. Such organizations have long existed in organized
religions, for example, whether it be the Catholic church or Sufi orders during
the Ottoman Empire. In many regards, such transnationally organized networks
predate the state as a locus of political participation, loyalties, and affinities. Yet
contemporary political science has largely discounted participation in such organizations as "political participation," instead relegating such participation to
the realm of "civil society." This misses the fact that many transnationally organized movements may operate as quasi-states in that they have a geopolitical
agenda rather than simply a social or cultural agenda, and/or view themselves as
directly challenging the interests and identities of existing state elites in either the
home or host state. Thus, active participation in such organizations goes beyond
membership in civil society organizations and can be viewed as a direct competi-
tor to participation in existing state institutions.

Domestic social movements engage in a variety of activities, such as framing,
coalition building, lobbying, and agenda setting, at the domestic level in order to
make claims against state authorities in their attempt to change the status quo.
Transnational mobilization involves many of these same activities, yet within a
very different and unevenly institutionalized context. Like domestic political en-

trepreneurs, transnational political entrepreneurs attempt to frame their demands in ways that will mobilize political support, build coalitions, lobby powerful actors, and engage in agenda-setting activities that shift the terms of debate at various "sites of power" around the international system.[33] In short, political entrepreneurs who mobilize at the level of the international system use many of the same techniques as domestic political entrepreneurs, yet the lack of a centralized institutional infrastructure in the international system means that entrepreneurs need to engage in strategies that will harness dispersed sources of political power, for which network organizational structures are well suited.

In addition to the strategic use of discursive frameworks, media outlets, and information, nonstate actors can also choose to strategically deploy violence as a means of mobilizing political support. Terrorism, often referred to as a "weapon of the weak," is deployed by groups to gain media attention and visibility, which is the first step in gaining "name recognition" within the international community.[34] Terrorism, writes Hoffman, "is designed to create power where there is none or to consolidate power where there is very little. Through the publicity generated by their violence, terrorists seek to obtain the leverage, influence and power they otherwise lack to effect political change on either a local or an international scale."[35] History has proven terrorism to be a successful strategy at times in gaining legitimacy and recognition from the international community. Even if the actual acts of terrorism are universally condemned by actors in the international community, they can stimulate media coverage of an issue and provide an opening for the political wing of an organization to ask the public to consider the legitimacy of its cause as separate from the tactics with which the cause is being promoted.

"Legitimacy" is an intangible and difficult-to-measure quality that has been largely ignored in the literature on international politics.[36] Yet it is a crucial concept to an understanding of the dynamics of transnational mobilization by relatively powerless nonstate actors. Gaining widespread legitimacy in the international system as the sole representative of a people, state, nation, or cause can compensate for a lack of material resources and other conventional measures of power. Gaining legitimacy and official recognition is both a goal in and of itself, as a well as a means to an end. Attaining legitimacy on the international stage opens up new avenues for the mobilization of resources and offers actors new opportunities for attaining their political goals. The intangible quality of legitimacy is what separates a terrorist from a freedom fighter and transforms a rebel into a statesperson or an opposition movement into a regime. It was not a change in the material capacities of Yasser Arafat and the Palestinian Liberation Organization (PLO) or Nelson Mandela and the African National Congress (ANC) that transformed the two from outlaws into recognized leaders on the world stage; rather, it was a change in their *status* from illegitimate to legitimate actors.

CONCLUSION: BREAKING TRANSNATIONAL CYCLES OF POLITICAL VIOLENCE

I have argued so far that the mobilization and politicization of dispersed communities of displaced or dislocated populations by nonstate political entrepreneurs comprises a distinctive political phenomenon that has received little attention in the field of political science, and that has ongoing consequences for levels of international security and stability. In cycles of political violence, diaspora mobilization by political entrepreneurs plays the role of an "intervening variable" between the processes of displacement, dislocation and uprooting of populations, and the politicized responses that can include forms of contentious politics and political violence.

Displacement of populations may occur within the context of physical violence, such as armed conflict, or structural violence, such as political or economic repression. Violence, however, often plays a crucial role as well in the process of mobilizing populations that have been displaced or have historical memories of displacement. All too often, for example, tactics of extortion, forced taxation, and extraction of resources via networks of organized crime play important roles in generating resources for transnationally organized nonstate opposition movements. Likewise, in the process of forging a collective identity, strategies of violence and coercion that are used as means of enforcing loyalty are common, meaning that communities of the displaced are not only vulnerable to the violence of state actors, but also to the violence of non-state political entrepreneurs.

Diaspora politicization and diaspora mobilization may be viewed by their participants as legitimate responses to prior exposure to displacement, marginalization, and political violence. At the same time, however, processes of diaspora politicization help to fuel ongoing cycles of political violence in the international system as a whole. This occurs both through the emergence of transgressive contentious politics that include tactics of political violence, as well as through the direct material and political support of campaigns of political violence as a means of attempting to effect change at either the local or systemic levels.[37]

The question remains as to how to address the consequences of diaspora mobilization and diaspora politicization in ways that ameliorate their security impacts and in ways that contribute to enhanced levels of international security. While the purpose of this chapter is not to provide specific policy recommendations, I will conclude with three directions in which policy-relevant research should be directed in the future. The first concerns the origins of displacement and dislocation, which stem from what I have referred to elsewhere as the "unevenly institutionalized" character of the international system, in which severe disparities in levels of economic and political development around the globe contribute to the actual or structural violence that leads to the emergence of dislocated and displaced populations who are then open to politicization and mobilization by nonstate political entrepreneurs.[38] Addressing the root causes of dislocation and displacement—i.e., low levels of economic development, violent conflicts in weak states, and political repression and human rights abuses by autocratic regimes—are important priorities in and of themselves. Additionally, however, such tasks should be viewed not only as humanitarian issues but as issues that are integral to the overall security and stability of the international system. Through processes of displacement, dislocation, and subsequent politicization and mobilization of displaced populations, the cycles of violence which are produced by economic exclusion, political repression, and marginalization become transnationalized and reembedded in transnational networks that span the globe—part of a larger process of what Ahmed, in this volume, refers to as "subaltern globalization"—thus affecting the security interests of even the most powerful states in the international system.

The second area in which policy-relevant research needs to be undertaken is in the area of the political participation of displaced populations and diasporas. Because political science has equated political participation with participation in formal state institutions, it has devoted much less time to understanding the dynamics of participation in informal institutions and processes, such as occurs during processes of diaspora mobilization. This is true even in the literature, in migration studies that have focused overwhelmingly on formal questions of citizenship, voting patterns, and integration into receiving country political systems, as opposed to studying participation in informal institutions, including transnational organizations and networks. There is an underlying assumption in most of the literature that immigrant political participation is zero-sum—in other words, that incorporation into national political structures and institutions somehow precludes participation in informal or transnational networks. While further research needs to be done in this area, anecdotal evidence seems to indicate that this is not necessarily the case. The most avid supporters of the nineteenth-century Fenian movement in the United States were Irish immigrants in the Union army, with the Republican Party acting as the institutional basis for the creation of Fenian cells and organizations within the Irish immigrant community in the United States.[39] Collier's study of the influence of diaspora populations on the course of violent conflicts looks specifically at diaspora populations in the United States as being correlated with higher levels of recurring violence in the "home country"—despite the fact that the United States is generally viewed in the literature as having a relatively open and accessible political system that encourages participation and incorporation of immigrant populations into the political system.[40]

Finally, the third area that requires further research concerns the types of institutions at the international level that can help to ameliorate the security externalities produced by the transnational mobilization of dispersed populations. The post–World War II infrastructure of international institutions was established as a means of managing conflict and facilitating cooperation between sovereign and unitary state actors that were equal in theory, if not in practice. However, the institutional infrastructure that we have inherited assumes that states represent the sum of the aspirations of their own populations and societies and, based on that assumption, has had difficulty in responding to instances of conflict between state institutions and social forces that emerge at the level of the international system, whether in the form of networks of human rights and humanitarian NGOs or in the form of transnationally organized political movements that derive their support from displaced populations, stateless peoples, or constituencies that are marginalized within the current geopolitical order. Constructing an architecture of global governance that can be used by nonstate actors and transnational networks to articulate claims and to channel grievances—i.e., to engage directly in forms of politics at the level of the international system by drawing on effective institutional structures rather than strategies of violence—is an important component of ensuring that any strategy for countering terrorism not only increases the disincentives for the use of strategies of violence and terror as political tools by nonstate actors, but also provides effective alternatives to violence in the form of institutionalized channels and formal procedures for voicing grievances, channeling claims, and effecting political change.

THE RETURN OF THE STATE? FINANCIAL REREGULATION IN THE PURSUIT OF NATIONAL SECURITY AFTER SEPTEMBER 11*

THOMAS J. BIERSTEKER WITH PETER ROMANIUK

The middle half of the twentieth century—roughly spanning the period from the mid-1920s through the mid-1970s—was a period of profound growth and expansion of the state. It was the era of the national security state, the welfare state, experimentation with national planning, and the vigorous defense of national currencies. It was a period of recovery from the collapse of laissez-faire capitalism and profound national mobilizations for war (first for World War II and later for the Cold War). Harold Lasswell warned Americans in 1940 about the danger of the growth of a "garrison state,"[1] and there was a secular expansion of the state's role in the economy throughout the entire period.

The final quarter of the century, by contrast, was an era of unremitting challenge to the state, and in particular to the state's role in the economy. Spurred on by technological changes, dramatic increases in cross-border transactions, and an ideological turn toward the market, greater openness, and liberalization, the state was bureaucratized, transnationalized, and transgovernmentalized "until it has virtually ceased to exist as an analytic construct."[2] Globalization eventually became the watchword of the day, both for advocates and opponents of the new phenomenon. Within the academy, state-centered analyses were on the decline, and within policy discussions, new actors and conceptual framings were increasingly in vogue.

The attacks of September 11, 2001, changed all of this, at least at the outset. The immediate response of the United States was to close its borders with Canada and Mexico, in effect imposing on itself a costly embargo, "a successful blockade of the U.S. economy."[3] Civil liberties were curtailed, domestic surveillance increased, military spending increased dramatically, and a new cabinet-level Department of Homeland Security was created. Even though the terrorist attacks emanated from a nonstate, transnational, complexly networked actor, the U.S. government framed its immediate responses in traditional statist terms and had difficulty coming up with any contigency plans that were not state-based.

The Bush administration's approach was defined early during one of its first National Security Council meetings following the attacks. As Bob Woodward reported from his interviews with President George W. Bush, the administration defined its doctrine to counter terror around the idea of holding to account those states that harbor, feed, or house terrorist groups.[4]

This was a profoundly statist response. States would be held accountable for the actions of terrorist groups operating from their territorial domains. The logic was simple and straightforward. If you strengthen the coercive and regulatory capacities of the state, you will reduce the ability of transnational terrorist networks to operate. As subsequent developments have shown, the administration that came to power criticizing the nation-building policies of its predecessor was quick to adopt *state*-building projects of its own. Priority has been given to intelligence sharing between states and to bolstering the core instruments of the coercive apparatus of the state—particularly the police and the military. However, its state-building efforts are also evident in the approach it has taken to counter terrorist financing.

In a departure from the unilateralist tendency established in many other spheres of activity, the Bush administration has pursued a relatively multilateral approach when it comes to the issue of terrorist financing. It has utilized the United Nations and other international institutions (the Financial Action Task Force [FATF], the International Monetary Fund [IMF], and the World Bank among others) to support a multilateral framework to counter terrorism by degrading the access of terrorist organizations to financial support for their activities. Most significant to date in terms of scope are the multilateral activities that have been undertaken under the auspices of the United Nations Counter Terrorism Committee (CTC). The pages that follow describe the significance of some of these new activities and address what we know to date about the depth and breadth of these ongoing efforts. The sustainability of these efforts (that ultimately have to be implemented by states in order to be effective), and some of the legal issues, problems, and challenges that have emerged to date (or are likely to emerge in the not too distant future) from efforts to harmonize state policy in this arena will also be reviewed. We conclude with some reflections on the "return of the state" for contemporary global governance.

I. MULTILATERAL EFFORTS TO COUNTER TERRORIST FINANCING BEFORE SEPTEMBER 11, 2001

Prior to the attacks of September 11, there was no coordinated, global, multilateral effort to suppress or constrain the financing of acts of terrorism, and "the existing prescriptions were woefully inadequate in dealing with the multi-dimensional nature of the challenge."[5] There were important efforts underway within the UN to strengthen the Convention for the Suppression of the Financing of Terrorism adopted in December 1999, but they came in the wake of twenty years of financial market liberalization and financial deregulation across the globe. The principal concerns of most analysts and policy practitioners during this period were first, how to institutionalize the liberalization process, and second, how to figure out ways to address recurring problems of financial market volatility and/or fragility (as indicated by the 1994 peso crisis, the 1997 Asian financial crisis, and the 1999 financial crises in Brazil and Russia). When compared with the pattern of domestic financial regulation and national financial and currency controls in place in most countries from the late 1930s through the 1970s, a dramatic transformation of the global financial system had taken place in the last quarter of the twentieth century.

During the course of the 1990s, however, there were two important institutional innovations counter to the general global trends toward financial deregulation and liberalization. One was the Financial Action Task Force process to combat money laundering and another was the effort to reform multilateral sanctions, initiated within the UN Security Council, particularly with the adoption of targeted financial sanctions.[6] Both of these efforts entailed a partial reregulation of the global financial system, and both of them have been drawn upon in recent efforts to curb terrorist financing. The FATF campaign against money laundering was first launched at a G-7 summit in 1989, but it is a process that has gained momentum in recent years with its list of forty measures that states should implement, its highly visible public naming and shaming of offshore financial havens (for illegal drug money, flight capital, and tax evasion), and its persistent insistence that minimal bank supervision rules and know-your-client procedures be introduced throughout the world. The movement toward targeted financial sanctions (as an alternative to the imposition of comprehensive sanctions) was first initiated within the UN Security Council but gained momentum under Swiss leadership in the Interlaken Process meetings held in 1998 and 1999. The general effort to target sanctions emerged as a response to the ineffectiveness and humanitarian consequences of comprehensive sanctions directed against Iraq during the 1990s. As we shall see, both of these initiatives—the FATF and the targeting of financial sanctions by the UN—have played an important role in the multilateral effort to freeze and suppress the raising, holding, and movement of terrorist funds.

II. MULTILATERAL EFFORTS TO COUNTER TERRORIST FINANCING AFTER SEPTEMBER 11, 2001

Immediately following the September 11 attacks, the Bush Administration told the American public that it would not mount a traditional effort in the "war" against terrorism. It also indicated that the campaign would be a protracted affair, and that it would need to invoke nontraditional methods, institutions, and resources, including an effort to freeze and suppress both the raising and the movement of funds that could be used to support the acts of global terrorists. The USA Patriot Act, passed in fall 2001, contained a number of provisions related to U.S. unilateral measures to disrupt terrorist financial networks, but the Bush administration also realized that it could not act alone on this issue, and it has supported efforts within the UN and other multilateral institutions.

The UN Security Council acted decisively one day after the attacks, on September 12, 2001, adopting resolution 1368 (2001), which established a legal basis for further action against global terrorism. The resolution invoked Article 51 of the UN Charter, recognizing the inherent right of self-defense, essentially legitimating subsequent U.S. military action in Afghanistan against the perpetrators of the September 11 attacks. With the passage of UN Security Council resolutions 1373 on September 28, 2001, and 1377 on November 12, 2001, the Security Council expressed its clear willingness to do something about terrorist access to financial support. As Jamaican Ambassador Curtis Ward has argued, "[T]here was no lack of political will and the Council achieved unanimity on its chosen course of action."[7]

Much of the content of resolution 1373 deals with blocking or suppressing the financing of terrorist groups. The resolution calls for criminalizing active or passive support for terrorists, the expeditious freezing of funds, the sharing of operational information by member states, and the provision of technical assistance to enhance multilateral cooperation in this area. The resolution also established an innovative process to implement the terms of the resolutions under the guidance of the Counter Terrorism Committee (CTC). Chairs of UN Security Council committees can be decisive in determining their effectiveness, and the appointment of U.K. Ambassador Sir Jeremy Greenstock as the initial chair to head the CTC, combined with the presence of genuine political will to do something about terrorist financing, have proven essential for institutional innovation in this area.

Among the most innovative aspects of resolution 1373 is its reporting process. Paragraph 6 of the resolution specifies that states should report on what actions they have taken to implement the resolution. The monitoring process established by the CTC also suggests that there should be greater consistency in, and transparency of, reporting on implementation, based on specific questions posed and guidelines established by the committee.[8] Member states are requested to file written reports on their implementation of the resolution, following a common set of questions posed by the CTC. Following review of those reports, ambassadors can be called before the committee for clarification of key points in their reports, which are addressed in the next installment of the reporting process. Every country report submitted to the committee is made publicly available at the UN's web site,[9] although member states do have the opportunity to ensure the confidentiality of sensitive information. There is much more transparency in the CTC process than has been present in UN Security Council sanctions committees in the past, and as the final document from the Stockholm Process on Implementing Targeted Sanctions suggests, "Some important precedents have been established that could be drawn upon in future UN Security Council resolutions targeting sanctions." [10]

The CTC process recognizes that many states may require technical and financial assistance in implementing the requirements of the resolution. Paragraph 13 of resolution 1377 invites states to seek assistance with implementation if they need it. Paragraph 11 of the same resolution calls on member states to assist each other in implementing the resolution fully, while Paragraph 14 invites the CTC to explore ways states can be assisted by international, regional, and subregional organizations. The CTC process also suggests a potential menu of choices available to help in identifying sources of financial support to assist the implementation by critically located states lacking administrative capacity and the means to provide it: a directory of sources of support, offers of bilateral assistance from those members willing to provide it, and the provision of multilateral donor community support.

Finally, resolutions 1373 and 1377 recommend that states be encouraged to appoint a central contact point for implementation in their capitals. The CTC has published a directory of contact points, updates it at regular intervals, and encourages all states to make use of the directory for contacts on matters related to implementation of resolutions directed toward terrorist financing (recognizing that cost or personnel requirements can often be an inhibiting factor).

Thus, with regard to its reporting and monitoring system, offers of assistance, identification of contact points, and insistence on transparency, the CTC has provided a model of institutional innovation for dealing with terrorist financing that has been drawn upon by the committee established pursuant to UN Security Council resolution 1267 responsible for listing terrorists and terrorist organizations and is likely to be drawn upon for future UN targeted sanctions efforts. At the same time, the UN has not been alone in the effort to construct a multilateral, networked response to the financing of global terrorism. The FATF has proposed eight special recommendations on terrorist financing as a supplement to its forty recommendations on money laundering,[11] the World Bank and IMF have jointly begun to explore how best to design global standards for anti–money laundering efforts and for combating the financing of terrorism, and the Wolfsberg group of private sector financial institutions has developed its own guidelines on the suppression of the financing of terrorism.[12]

III. A PRELIMINARY ASSESSMENT OF THE EFFECTIVENESS OF THE UN'S CTC MEASURES

It is too soon to say definitively how effective the UN's innovative measures directed against the financing of global terrorism have been. However, a research team at Brown University's Watson Institute for International Studies has been investigating the extent to which countries across the globe are actually doing something about implementing the sweeping counterterrorist measures. The Targeting Terrorist Finances Project (TTFP) has identified four different phases of the terrorist financing process: raising funds, holding funds, moving or transferring funds, and dispersing funds to commit terrorist acts. The project is investigating degrees of implementation of the counterterrorism effort in each of these four areas by examining the reports of different countries and evaluating them according to the degree of implementation, ranging from "the policy is under review or consideration" to "new legislation criminalizing the financing of terrorism has been promulgated," "assistance with implementation has been requested," "administrative infrastructure to implement counterterrorism measures has been identified, established, and given new resources to regulate this area" to "there is substantial evidence of compliance" (i.e., banks and institutions involved in financial transactions have received notice; they have established or modified internal procedures; they have begun to use name-recognition software; terrorist assets have been identified), and "there is evidence of enforcement" (i.e., assets have been frozen and/or prosecutions pursued and penalties imposed for noncompliance).

Based on a preliminary assessment of the data available to date (primarily from an examination of the reports received from countries in Europe, North America, the Middle East, and Asia), there is evidence to suggest that the CTC process is making real progress. With regard to reporting, all of the member states of the United Nations have filed reports on their compliance with counterterrorist resolutions to the CTC.[13] This, in itself, is an extraordinary achievement and includes reports received from both Iraq and North Korea. Most states have filed more than one report, and the majority of the reports submitted follow the detailed structure laid out by the committee. In a briefing prepared to evaluate the CTC process, Walter Gehr, one of the members of the group of experts convened by the UN, observed that "the overwhelming majority of the reports follow the structure of UN Security Council resolution 1373." [14] He continues that country reports that do not follow the structure of the resolution tend to lack substance. Similarly, from a review of the reports received to date, Ambassador Curtis Ward, the CTC's advisor on technical assistance, has concluded that every state has had to adopt new legislation in order to meet fully all of the requirements of resolution 1373. [15]

There is also evidence that both the quality of reporting and the progress on criminalizing terrorist financing have improved over time. In the first round of reports submitted to the CTC in late 2001 and early 2002, many states argued that they already had sufficient legal instruments to criminalize the funding of terrorist activity and many were using anti–money laundering legislation to meet their legal obligations to criminalize terrorist financing. During the dialogue between states and the CTC prior to the second round of reports, members of the CTC (and their expert advisors) have been able to bring to member states' attention the critical difference between anti–money laundering legislation and terrorist financing. As Gehr argues, "[T]he crucial difference between money laundering and the financing of terrorism is that moneys used to fund terrorist activities are not necessarily illegal. Assets and profits acquired by legitimate means and even declared to tax authorities can be used to finance terrorist acts, too." [16] Reviews of some of the second-round reports to the CTC (all of which were due to be submitted to the CTC by December 31, 2002) suggest that as the dialogue between member states and the CTC has proceeded, states are beginning to move beyond reliance on anti–money laundering legislation to promulgate new laws specific to terrorist finances.

As described earlier, UN Security Council resolution 1377 invites states to seek assistance with implementation and calls on member states to assist each other to implement the resolution fully. Ambassador Curtis Ward suggests, "Forty-seven states indicated in their first reports that they needed assistance to implement resolution. This number has grown to fifty-five, as more states reach a clearer understanding of what is expected of them." [17] According to Ward, the greatest needs for assistance appear to be in drafting antiterrorism law and in developing banking and financial law and regulations.

With regard to legal changes, most countries have shown progress on criminalizing either the willful collection of funds for terrorism and/or providing a legal basis for freezing the funds of terrorist groups and individuals. New legislation has either been adopted or is formally under review in most countries. Anti–money laundering rules have been tightened in Europe and the Middle East (though not as much in Asia), and, as indicated earlier, more countries are beginning to recognize—quite possibly from the CTC policy dialogues—that anti–money laundering regulations may not be sufficient to suppress terrorist financing. Most countries have signed international conventions on terrorism, and progress is visible in this regard in nearly all countries when their first and second reports are compared. To date, only the United States and the European Union have developed their own lists of groups and individuals legally identified as terrorists, while most other countries rely instead on the lists provided by the UN.

Concerning the establishment of an administrative infrastructure to implement counterterrorism measures, the CTC has appointed an assistance team to dispatch information about common standards and best practices, and it has established a Directory of Assistance on its web site. Ninety-one states have utilized this resource to date, and Ward reports that CTC assistance teams, in bilateral consultations with different states, evaluate gaps in administrative capacity and facilitate assistance from willing donors.[18] Most countries have identified an implementing agency or intra-governmental mechanism for administering controls on terrorist financing, and nearly all have identified central contact points for the CTC.

In the area of compliance, banks and financial institutions have been notified about new regulations in most countries, though this is generally less evident in some major markets in Asia to date. Most countries have also imposed new reporting requirements on financial institutions, though formal audits have been used less frequently. EU members tend to be the most prone to conducting audits, investigating charitable organizations, and pursuing special measures for high-risk (offshore) centers under their jurisdiction. The U.S., the UAE, Pakistan, and Hong Kong have introduced new measures for the regulation of informal money-transfer systems, or *hawalas.*

Finally, with regard to enforcement, a preliminary investigation of the reports submitted by member states to the CTC shows that little information is given regarding actual funds frozen, although U.S. government sources report nearly $140 million has been frozen as of early 2004. Reporting states may mention investigations pursued or underway, but few have new evidence of concrete success. Many assert that their financial systems are not susceptible to misuse by terrorists and suggest that they already comply with resolution 1373 by virtue of existing anti–money laundering legislation.

Of the $125 million in assets of terrorist organizations blocked to date, $34.3 million has been frozen by the United States and $90.7 million by other countries (approximately $24 million by Switzerland, $11.9 million by the U.K., $5.5 million by Saudi Arabia, and an undisclosed amount by the UAE). Nearly all of this was frozen or blocked in the first few months immediately following September 11, 2001. Prosecutions have been pursued, especially in the United States, Germany, and Indonesia but few have resulted in the freezing of additional funds. There is virtually no evidence of the suspension of any banking licenses.

In its parallel multilateral effort, the FATF reports that more than 120 countries in the world have participated in one of its self-assessment processes to compare their current practices against FATF standards embodied in its eight special recommendations on terrorist financing. It uses these self-assessments to identify countries for priority technical assistance from the World Bank, IMF, and the UN.

To summarize, there have been important changes in state policy introduced throughout the world, from Europe and Russia to traditional offshore locations such as Bahrain and Hong Kong. There also have been important expressions of a global willingness to do something about terrorist finances, even if material progress to date has been relatively slow.

IV. LEGAL ISSUES, PROBLEMS, AND CHALLENGES

Just how sustainable are these efforts? Are we witnessing the establishment of a basis for the return of financial reregulation by the state across the globe? There are two principal central sets of issues, problems, and/or challenges that have emerged to date from the multilateral effort to freeze terrorist finances: (1) issues surrounding the listing of individuals and organizations accused of supporting terrorists financially, and (2) legal problems and challenges stemming from the lack of parallel implementation of policy in different legal jurisdictions. Either or both of these sets of issues could prevent the effort from going very far and/or from being consolidated, despite the contemporary enthusiasm for state building in this area.

A. LISTING

1. Who is listed?

One of the central challenges associated with freezing terrorist finances is deciding whom to list. Identifying the core leaders of terrorist organizations is often possible, but intelligence about their aliases and key supporters (or front organizations) can be extremely difficult to uncover. Coordination of intelligence gathering from different national agencies is often difficult, as is agreement on evidentiary standards across different national jurisdictions. Furthermore, commonly used names and the different methods of transliteration used by different intelligence agencies can lead to errors of listing innocent individuals.

Experience with efforts to target financial sanctions has demonstrated that it is important that the domestic agencies engaged in international efforts to combat global terrorism provide as much identifying information as possible about the targets of UN Security Council resolutions and domestic enabling legislation. At a minimum, there should be an effort to include the full name, any known or likely aliases, date of birth, and complete address of any member of a global terrorist organization, as well as details about potential front companies or institutions used by the terrorist organization. The Office of Foreign Asset Control of the U.S. Treasury has long maintained lists of specially designated nationals (SDNs), narcotics traffickers (SDNTs), and terrorists (SDTs). The recently created lists of specially designated global terrorists (SDGTs) and terrorist organizations are more detailed and comprehensive, but they still lack adequate detail about many of the names included on them. Without this level of information, it is difficult for financial institutions to know precisely which accounts and transactions should be investigated.

In an important development in November 2002, the UN's 1267 Committee (the committee responsible for the operational listing of members of the Taliban and the al Qaeda organization) issued guidelines for both the listing and delisting of names. The committee guidelines state that proposed additions to the list "include, to the extent possible, a narrative description of the information that forms the basis or justification for taking action," as well as "relevant and specific information to facilitate their identification by competent authorities: For individuals: name, date of birth, place of birth, nationality, aliases, residence, passport or travel document number. . . ." [19]

Providing more identifying information about potential targets requires enhanced multilateral cooperation, including the sharing and coordination of sensitive intelligence information. Intelligence coordination is especially important for identifying potential abuses of the *hawala* system, since it is not as susceptible to electronic surveillance as the formal banking system. However, intelligence agencies are apparently not willing to provide information on all potential targets. For example, Ali Qaed Sunian al-Harithi (aka Abu Ali) was important enough to assassinate with a predator drone in the Yemeni desert but was not included on *any* of the official lists of suspected terrorists—not the lists of the EU, the UN, or the United States. According to former U.S. officials involved in monitoring terrorist financing, the lists are designed to identify who does the banking for the terrorist networks, and the goal of listing is often to take out a node in the financial network rather than penalize directly those who commit terrorist acts. The listing process can be used as a preventive mechanism. Sometimes the goal is to block potential movements of funds that could support a terrorist act. Sometimes a name is deliberately left off the published list in order to watch the movement of funds in and out of a monitored account for subsequent intelligence purposes.

2. Whose list is authoritative?

Beyond the difficulty of determining which names should be listed is the challenge of determining whose list is authoritative. Historically, in the case of UN Security Council resolutions targeting financial sanctions, the United States provided most of the intelligence for the UN list. The United States gathered information from its intelligence services, and its list was disseminated to U.S. financial institutions by the Office of Foreign Asset Control (OFAC) of the U.S. Treasury Department. The U.S. list would be sent to the Europeans, who might choose to delete a few names and add several of their own. However, the differential capability (and intensity of interest about most sanctions) between the United States and Europe meant that the listing process provided an illustration of the operational practice of U.S. hegemony.

More recently, during the later stages of targeted sanctions against the Milosevic regime in the former Yugoslavia and especially in the aftermath of targeted financial sanctions against the Taliban and al Qaeda, the European Union has invested more time and effort in developing lists of its own. Nevertheless, the U.S. list continues to be far more expansive and detailed than the lists prepared by the EU. U.S. domestic legislation permits it to maintain a long, consolidated list through which it implements all measures. This approach differs from that of the EU, which regularly updates its regulations to reflect the numerous additions and deletions of UN sanctions committees but maintains a more modest counterterrorism list in implementing UN Security Council resolutions.

The lists maintained by the UN lie somewhere between the U.S. and EU lists in length and detail, although recent changes in listing procedures announced by the 1267 Committee should bring the UN lists closer to those of the United States. For most states, the lists maintained by the relevant sanctions committees of the UN have the most legitimacy, but the fact that there can be only a partial consensus on the list of targeted individuals or organizations across different jurisdictions (United States, EU, UN) creates parallel enforcement problems.

In the specific case of al Qaeda, the first use of targeting focused on the Taliban regime and was imposed by UN Security Council resolution 1267 (1999). Although there was a delay in developing a list of targeted persons immediately after the passage of the resolution, the Sanctions Committee eventually circulated a list. With the adoption of UN Security Council resolution 1333 (2000), the mandate of the Sanctions Committee was extended beyond the Taliban to include, "Usama bin Laden and individuals or entities associated with him as designated by the Committee, including those in the Al-Qaida organization" (para. 8[c]). From that point onward, until September 11, 2001, the work of the 1267 Committee focused on the selection and preparation of a team of monitors to be stationed on Afghanistan's borders, with the aim of improving the effectiveness of the sanctions. That initiative was called off following the attacks of September 11.

With the passage of UN Security Council resolution 1390 (2002), the scope of the 1267 Sanctions Committee was broadened once more to include, "Usama bin Laden, members of the Al-Qaida organization and the Taliban and other individuals, groups, undertakings and entities associated with them" (para. 2). The mandate of the 1267 Committee, whose listing designations are mandatory for member states, differs from the UN's counterterrorism measures under resolution 1373. The 1267 Committee maintains the tactical list of names, while the CTC charts the strategic response to terrorist financing.

3. Falsely listed individuals or organizations

Since individuals can be listed erroneously, it is important that procedures be established to enable them to petition for the removal of their names from the list. This issue was first taken up in the report on the Interlaken Process produced by the Watson Institute for International Studies. The Bonn-Berlin Working Group on Travel and Aviation-Related Bans also addressed the right of targeted individuals to contest being listed, and recommended that falsely listed individuals be allowed to petition the chair of the relevant sanctions committee directly on the basis that their listing is unfounded or that they have changed their behavior.[20] It is not clear where the burden of proof should reside—with the appropriate UN committee or the listed individual—and decision-making authority for the listing by the United States or the EU appears to be located in the Treasury Department or the European Commission, respectively.

More recently, following the passage of UN Security Council resolution 1390, the 1267 Committee established a procedure—the first of its kind—for those wrongly listed to petition for removal of their names from the list. The procedure allows a petitioner (individual or group) to petition the government of their country of citizenship or residence to request a review of their case. It is incumbent upon the petitioner to provide justification for their request. The petitioned government is asked to review the information, and if it wishes, it can approach the government[s] that originally requested the listing bilaterally to seek information and hold consultations on the case in the hope that member states will be able to resolve the matter between them. Where that is not possible, the committee may decide whether to delist, by consensus—in effect operating with a unit veto system. The details of the delisting procedures are spelled out in the guidelines released by the 1267 Committee on November 7, 2002.

This issue has important human rights implications, as evidenced by the legal suit filed in the European Court of Justice by Swedish citizens of Somali origin over the listing of the Barakat International Foundation in Stockholm. In the final analysis, it is important to establish procedures for appeal and potential removal of the names of individuals and institutions wrongly designated as being associated with the financing of terrorism. As the Council on Foreign Relations task force on terrorist financing recommended, "[L]egitimate disquiet in some quarters concerning the potential for due process violations associated with the inaccurate listing of targeted individuals can retard progress in global efforts. Since the full sharing of sensitive intelligence information is unlikely, the establishment of such procedures will take such concerns "off of the agenda" and prevent them from being used as an excuse for ineffective implementation." [21]

B. CHALLENGES OF PARALLEL IMPLEMENTATION

1. Legal frameworks

Because private-sector financial institutions are on the front lines of efforts to block terrorist finances, they need to be protected in domestic law from potential claims arising from their compliance with UN Security Council resolutions and other enabling legislation. If they are not provided with this legal protection, the freezing of funds could cause a financial institution to be in violation of its fundamental obligations to its customers. This concern can be readily addressed by the inclusion of a "nonliability" provision in enabling resolutions or legislation, calling on states to implement the intent of the resolution "notwithstanding the existence of any rights or obligations conferred or imposed by any other international agreement or contract, license, or permit." Ironically, most states do not have laws on the books that automatically enable them to apply national measures to give effect to decisions called for in UN Security Council resolutions. Only about twenty states (including the United Kingdom and the United States) have such legislation in place, and this has been a priority of international efforts to coordinate policies on targeted sanctions—both financial sanctions and arms embargoes. This priority has most recently been highlighted in the final report from the Stockholm Process on Implementing Targeted Sanctions.[22] If some kind of legal protection is absent in some legal jurisdictions, harmonized, global implementation will break down, and there will be important loopholes in the system.

2. Differing definitions

Given the fact that terrorism is a global problem and that responses to it require multilateral cooperation, clarity and consistency of definition and interpretation across different state legal jurisdictions are vital. Different definitions of what is an "asset"—as in efforts to block "funds" only rather than transactions involving "income bearing assets"—have led to inconsistent implementation of targeted financial sanctions between Europe and the United States in the past. This created unnecessary loopholes for potential sanctions violators (particularly potential "sanctions havens") and would provide the same for terrorist organizations. The clarity of the language used in UN Security Council resolutions and in national enabling legislation became a principal focus of the two Interlaken meetings and produced consensual definitions of terms such as "funds and other financial resources," "owned and controlled directly or indirectly," "to freeze," "financial services," and "assets." These are definitions that can and should be utilized in contemporary efforts to combat global terrorism. The UN Convention on Terrorism only defines three terms: "funds," "state facility," and "proceeds," but it is important to note that the 1267 committee has defined "economic resources" consistent with the convention's definition of "funds."

3. Administrative practices and efficiency of regulatory institutions

While broad-based multilateral cooperation is necessary for an effective global effort to combat terrorism, the experience with targeting financial sanctions has shown that most countries lack an adequate administrative capacity to implement UN Security Council resolutions effectively. The international effort to pursue sanctions reform has tried to identify "best practices" at the national level for both targeted financial sanctions and arms embargoes. There are also efforts underway to utilize sanctions assistance missions, technical assistance at the regional level, financial support for those most directly affected by compliance with sanctions resolutions, secondary sanctions, mutual evaluations, "naming and shaming," transgovernmental cooperation, and private-sector initiatives to ensure that there is broad multilateral participation in targeted sanctions efforts. Given the urgency of the threat posed by global terrorist organizations, there is a pressing need for dissemination of "best practices" to offshore financial centers and to the countries most likely to be transit points for terrorist funds. Again, inconsistent (or nonexistent) administrative implementation creates potential havens for terrorist funds. A networked global threat requires a networked global response.

4. Differing institutional capacity of financial institutions

The computer technology that enables global terrorist networks to exploit financial market globalization and move funds instantaneously across the globe can also be employed against them. Financial institutions throughout the world can be encouraged to utilize one of the many "name recognition" software programs already widely available on the market. This software could help them to determine—electronically and instantaneously—whether they are holding the accounts of any individuals or organizations identified as global terrorists. It is very difficult to search accounts and identify names and aliases without some kind of software assistance. Until recently, only the largest U.S.-based banks made routine use of name recognition software to comply with targeted financial sanctions resolutions. Neither smaller regional U.S. banks nor most major financial institutions in Europe and Japan have made use of this technology. Among the few European exceptions have been Deutsche Bank and Lloyds Bank, and a number of Australian banks are currently reviewing possible name recognition programs. Beyond its utility in identifying transactions involving individuals on the list, a new generation of the technology could be deployed to identify patterns of suspicious transactions that deviate from common norms in the frequency, size, or destination of transactions. Indeed, it was an individual observation of this kind of deviation from normal patterns of transactions that led a Boston-based bank employee to raise questions about suspicious transactions involving the al-Barakat organization. However, the use of computerized surveillance technology raises important, and legitimate, concerns about the potential violation of fundamental civil liberties. New norms need to be developed that establish both limits on the evasion of privacy and procedures for petition for removal from erroneous inclusion on the list of terrorists.

5. Retroactive reporting

The processes of targeting terrorist finances and targeting financial sanctions are essentially similar in many important respects. Both efforts entail the identification of a targeted list of names and corporate (or institutional) entities, both require extensive multilateral coordination to be successful, and both rely on the cooperation and participation of private-sector financial institutions for effective implementation. Efforts to target financial sanctions suggest that UN Security Council resolutions or national enabling legislation to block or freeze the assets of terrorist organizations should authorize financial institutions to trace funds retroactively. Requiring states to report on the movement of funds within their jurisdictions in a parallel manner for a specified period *prior to* efforts to freeze or block the movement of terrorist funds could generate valuable information about the location and movement of financial assets attempting to flee a jurisdiction. Thus, even if the funds cannot be trapped, they can be traced, enabling monitoring of the assets if and when they attempt to reenter the global financial system. This could prove vital for intelligence gathering purposes. The identification of funds in this manner also enables the potential "naming and shaming" of havens for the assets of global terrorist organizations, as the FATF has done with regard to havens for money laundering. Financial institutions across different national jurisdictions need to have parallel authority to report retroactively.

V. CONCLUSION: THE RETURN OF THE STATE?

September 11 prompted a virtual sea change in the tolerance for financial reregulation across the globe. The UN Counter Terrorism Committee has played a critical role in advancing the global effort to suppress and freeze terrorist finances and to harmonize state regulatory policies. While terrorist groups' access to finance can never be halted entirely, it can be disrupted, forced into other channels, and more generally degraded in important respects. The multilateral effort to trace the financial flows of terrorist groups can also assist with other forms of intelligence gathering operations and help illuminate details of the operations of global terrorist networks.

Whether the relative sea change that was initiated immediately after September 11 can be sustained, however, remains to be seen. As suggested earlier, it is likely to face continuing legal challenges related to listing and is also likely to be hampered by sovereign claims for exception that inevitably produce inconsistency in implementation across different state jurisdictions. A certain degree of difference across national jurisdictions can be healthy because it provides a basis for policy innovation and experimentation. As suggested earlier, however, too much variation can undercut the creation of a global networked response to the kind of global network that al Qaeda has benefited from in the past and the networked threat that it continues to pose. Finally, the further we get away from the security concern that drove the initial impetus to state reregulation of finance, the more the costs of compliance for private-sector financial institutions may begin to become an obstacle to the effective implementation of policies in this area. Up to this point, the private financial sector has shown a strong willingness to comply with the new regulatory effort.

The Council on Foreign Relations task force report on terrorist financing concluded cautiously in October 2002 that "U.S. efforts to curtail the financing of terrorism are impeded . . . by a lack of political will among U.S. allies."[23] This contributed to vigorous debate about the extent to which key allies such as the Kingdom of Saudi Arabia were committed to efforts to freeze and suppress terrorist financing, particularly after it was discovered in November 2002 that charitable donations from members of the royal family associated with the Saudi Arabian embassy in Washington, D.C., ended up in the bank accounts of some of the terrorists who committed the attacks of September 11.

Although the jury is still out, the global effort to target terrorist finances could indicate a growing acceptance, once again, of regulation—or state building—in the financial area. It is part of a more general effort to strengthen the capacity of the state to provide a bulwark against the threat from global terrorism. While it potentially poses threats to the free movement of capital and to some civil liberties, it also has the potential for creating positive externalities and long-term benefits in related issue areas, from drug trafficking to tax evasion. Indeed, initial reticence at the highest levels in many states may be countered by the emergence of transgovernmental networks of regulatory authorities who have been meeting routinely on some of these issues for years, by the enhancement of tax and internal revenue agencies' abilities to limit tax evasion and improve drug interdiction efforts, and by interest in the anti–money laundering efforts of the FATF. It could even contribute to a nascent form of global governance in a critically important arena.

9/11: INSINUATING CONSTITUTIONAL AND INTERNATIONAL NORMS*

PETER J. SPIRO

As September 11 looms a little smaller in the imagination, there is the possibility of a less alarmist perspective on its significance. In the immediate wake of the attacks, there was well-founded anxiety that the enormity of the episode and the war talk that followed would result in the significant curtailment of civil liberties, and particularly of the rights of aliens. The historical precedents pointed in that direction, and some proposals, seriously taken, would indeed have constituted a serious setback to individual rights. But the more extreme fears have not been realized. Although elements of the government's response to the events of 9/11 have been rights-restrictive, the overall resiliency of rights protections has perhaps been more remarkable.

This chapter explores, with tentative brevity, three possible explanations for why the early predictions of rights reversals have not transpired. First, it may be that however horrific the attacks, they did not in fact constitute so serious a threat as to warrant—as a matter of policy—the severe curtailment of rights. A second explanation highlights a largely extrajudicial dynamic in which the restriction of civil liberties was defeated as inconsistent with constitutional norms. Finally, the international community and international law appear to have played a significant role in restraining the government from a more serious assault on civil liberties. Geopolitical dominance and the magnitude of the security threat notwithstanding, the United States—like it or not—is being brought into the ambit of international norms.

THE RIGHTS SCORECARD

The September 11 attacks generated a new security discourse. They also provoked a parallel campaign to protect individual rights in the face of antiterrorism efforts. The civil liberties community condemned the government's response to 9/11 as a major assault on individual rights.

This vigilance is well founded. The antiterrorist security agenda has rights implications at every turn. The potential threat has been grave, especially with respect to the rights of aliens. The most significant legislative response to the attacks, the USA Patriot Act, expands domestic law enforcement authority in important respects. Three individuals (two of them U.S. citizens) have been apprehended in the United States and detained without charge as "enemy combatants," denied access to counsel and any form of legal process. The rounding up and incommunicado detention of several hundred aliens on minor immigration or criminal charges posed significant liberty concerns.[1] The president authorized the establishment of military tribunals for noncitizens with virtually no provision for procedural protection of the accused.[2] The military tribunal option has not been formally rejected. Congress enacted legislation allowing for the detention of aliens certified as terrorists, and significantly expanding the definition of terrorism for immigration purposes.[3] Thousands of others have been subjected to special registration requirements imposed only on young male aliens holding Middle Eastern nationalities.

On the other hand, the damage to civil rights has been mitigated, and may ultimately prove minimal. The Patriot legislation is unexceptional in many respects, for example, updating surveillance authority to address such new information technologies as voice mail. More controversial provisions are subject to a four-year sunset, if they are not repealed or amended before then, and the act does not single out noncitizens for differential treatment in most respects. Detention of aliens certified as terrorists is limited to seven days, after which the U.S. attorney general must commence removal proceedings or lodge criminal charges, failing which the alien must be released.[4] The detention of aliens by other cause has been undertaken on preexisting authority, and few from the initial roundup remain in custody. Immigration authorities have made little use of the expanded definition of terrorist activity.[5] Although the military tribunals remain an option, especially for those in detention at Guantanamo Bay, it is possible that in the end no military tribunals will be deployed. Whatever civil liberties concerns persist, they are a far cry from such historical anti-alien episodes as the Japanese internment or the Palmer raids, often invoked in the early days after September 11.[6]

THERE ARE WARS AND THERE ARE "WARS"

The factual context of the events has plainly facilitated the government's relative restraint. If this had been real war, in the sense of massed armies hurling themselves against each other in a clear conflict of peoples, the setback to civil liberties would have been far more serious. In this sense, the citation of Japanese internment as a possible result of 9/11 presented a false precedent. So long as the attacks were limited to those on September 11, and insofar as the attacks did not evidence a conflict between Americans and some other society, the situation did not demand the significant curtailment of individual freedoms.[7] In other words, this wasn't "war," and the less than extreme enforcement response simply reflected that. To the extent that rights have been suppressed, it has been in the same peripheral way that rights have been suppressed as part of the "war" on drugs and crime generally. The adversary here is more like a shadowy criminal syndicate than an ethnic, religious, or national community; although all of the terrorists may be Muslims, it has been clear from the top that few Muslims are terrorists. If, on the other hand, we now faced continuing casualties, conscription, ration books, and a clearly defined "enemy," the reversal of individual freedoms would have been pronounced.

This take on the facts—characterizing the response as "war" in the metaphoric sense only—is necessary to an account in which rights reversals have been limited. But it doesn't suffice to explain the restraint. It seems clear that if the executive branch had been enabled to act unilaterally, it would have adopted far more intrusive measures in September 11's wake. Initial legislative proposals from the Bush administration would have authorized the attorney general to remove any alien certified as a terrorist, with no review of either the certification or the removal. The detentions and the executive order authorizing the establishment of military tribunals, both undertaken without legislative participation (or indeed any advance notice), also evidence the administration's inclination to consider civil liberties as an afterthought. In the end, the attacks may not have required a war footing, but given its druthers, the administration would have assumed one.

CONSTITUTIONAL FRONT LINES

The executive branch has ultimately been constrained by domestic and international actors working to vindicate domestic constitutional and international norms respectively. In the domestic political context, various constitutionally relevant entities have resisted the curtailment of civil liberties. Congress, most notably, refused to accept executive branch requests for significantly expanded enforcement powers. The USA Patriot Act accepted only a limited subset of original administration demands; it is hard not to describe it as anything other than watered-down. Congress has used committee hearings to highlight questionable executive branch practices undertaken on existing authority, such as the roundup detentions. Some of this resistance from the legislative branch has been framed in constitutional terms; that is, Congress has denied demands for expanded enforcement powers on the grounds that the expansion would violate constitutional norms, as conceived by the legislative branch.[8] Congressional resistance has been echoed among the elite opinion makers, including editorialists at such major papers as the *New York Times* and *Washington Post,* as well as among legal and other academics. More than 150 state and local jurisdictions have passed resolutions condemning the USA Patriot Act. Most of this opposition to expanded authority has come from the left, but significant elements on the right also rejected the request for additional enforcement authority.[9]

This interbranch and public interplay has been of constitutional consequence. The episode has evidenced and defined constitutional norms, and the result has been characterized in large part by their successful enforcement. As now accepted by most constitutional theorists, the courts are not essential to the interpretation of constitutional standards; the Constitution lives outside of judicial decisions.[10] Events following 9/11 present an example of this extrajudicial constitutional dynamic. (As a general matter, episodes implicating foreign relations, where the courts have often demurred under the political question and other jurisdictional doctrines, are particularly useful in demonstrating the efficacy and evolution of constitutional norms beyond the courts.)[11] September 11 was, of course, in many respects unprecedented; never had the homeland suffered such an attack, nor confronted the specter of a faceless, insidious adversary. That left the constitutional parameters of the response unclear, at least in the immediate wake of the attacks; if one conceives of the episode as a new "case," its resolution was not foreordained, at least not on the margins. Subsequent developments made clear that the threat was not a mortal one. That clarification narrowed the constitutional playing field; wholesale suspension of civil liberties was never a real danger, in, say, a Civil War sense. But the constitutional constancy of some proposed responses was not so easily dismissed.

Among those closer questions were ones involving the treatment of aliens in immigration proceedings. Constitutional constraints as set by the Supreme Court have been minimal. Under the plenary power doctrine, the Court has ceded almost all its standard powers of review of immigration decision making by the political branches; this is evident in decisions studded with references to their peculiar competencies in matters involving national security and foreign relations.[12] Even as it appears to be beating a retreat from plenary power premises (most notably in its 2001 decisions in the *Nguyen* and *Zadvydas* cases),[13] the Court has constructed hatches through which cases involving core national security concerns can escape.[14] Against that doctrinal backdrop, it takes no great leap to see the Court upholding virtually any immigration measure adopted in the aftermath of September 11. Even so fairly extreme a proposal as that initially vetted by the administration, under which even permanent resident aliens could have been deported without review if certified as terrorist,[15] would likely have been upheld by the Court, another in the long line of cases in which perceived threats to the national security trump any claim of individual right. Taken as the law, court-made doctrine posed an improbable barrier to the curtailment of alien rights; in the end, however, no such judicial barrier was necessary to stave off the basic challenge.

This is not to diminish the value of judicial review to protect against arbitrary action in particular cases. The courts can police the boundaries of constitutional rectitude with greater precision and alacrity than can the political branches, and there will be many issues at the margins where the courts will expand the scope of individual rights. Nor is this to defend the plenary power doctrine, an artifact of another era. Plenary power and the enormity of attacks notwithstanding, some lower federal courts have shown surprising fortitude in constraining, or attempting to constrain, various elements of the antiterrorist response.[16] But this judicial activity has been second order, pointing again to the possibility that the Constitution can be sustained by institutions other than the courts, and that aliens, even as deprived of direct voice in the polity, can find their rights largely vindicated by political branch action, or at least vindicated more than the courts would require. As a matter of domestic constitutional function, events following 9/11 tested the system and showed it (mostly) to work.[17]

Others would disagree, of course. There has been a steady drumbeat, most heard from progressive elements, that the response to September 11 has cut to the core of constitutional rights. The extremity of these characterizations may owe more to political strategy than accurate description. It seems hard to deny, to the extent that we have witnessed civil liberties reversals in the wake of September 11, even significant ones, that they have not been nearly as severe as initially feared. Isolating possible agents of restraint thus becomes a useful undertaking. Second, the mere fact of such characterizations, and of mobilized advocacy against rights-infringing responses, is itself constitutionally consequential and evidentiary, especially when set in historical relief. Such constitutionally grounded opposition to antiterrorism measures reflects a constitutional discourse in which security concerns no longer represent a constitutional trump. There have surely been abuses of individual rights in the wake of September 11. But important players in the constitutional dynamic have mounted a vigorous and for the most part successful defense of constitutional liberties, as framed in the pre-attack context.

So the protection of basic civil liberties here can be seen through a domestic lens, in the dynamic interplay of domestic constitutional actors. It was understood by Congress and opinion makers that the situation did not warrant severe curtailment of civil liberties, and those actors were able successfully to bury executive branch initiatives that would have been rights-destructive.

INTERNATIONAL LAW, INTERNATIONAL WILL, AND INTERNATIONAL POWER

But this domestic focus cannot fully explain the result. International actors and international law has also been consequential to the resolution of rights-related issues. Indeed, it is this aspect of the legal implications of 9/11 that may in historical relief emerge most significant. If international law proves irresistible in this core security context, then it is likely to prove irresistible in other contexts as well. The observation is consistent with other trends concerning the relationship of U.S. law and policy to international law and decision making. Notwithstanding the bluster of an administration whose culture is deeply antagonistic to international institutions,[18] the United States is coming to find itself in a position where the costs of noncompliance with international law outweigh the benefits of asserting full sovereign discretion.

Most telling here is the treatment of noncitizen detainees outside the immigration process. Early on, the Bush administration formally authorized the establishment of military tribunals to prosecute noncitizens for terrorism and related activity. The order itself allowed for significant departures from standard criminal due process protections, even as diluted in the context of military justice.[19]

No tribunal has yet been constituted under the order. The administration notably rejected the option in initiating prosecution of the alleged twentieth hijacker under normal procedures in federal district court. That decision made clear that tribunals would not be deployed against aliens present in the United States. There is the remaining possibility that tribunals will be constituted to prosecute some of the al Qaeda and Taliban detainees at Guantanamo Bay. If so, the tribunals will operate with procedures not dramatically removed from those used in military justice.[20] In the end, the tribunals may not be deployed at all.

Given an unencumbered choice here, prosecutors would likely have opted for a tribunal in the Moussaoui case and would put them to work in the Guantanamo cases. The question then is what is acting as the agent of restraint. As stated earlier, some of these agents are domestic. Some members of Congress have criticized the tribunal innovation, especially the administration's failure to consult with Congress, much less secure its approval,[21] before issuing the order. To a greater degree, editorialists scorned the initial authorization of the tribunal option.[22] But the domestic response here has been more variable than it has been with administration demands for broadened enforcement powers. Congress has made no institutional pronouncement against the tribunals,[23] and the legislature would not likely obstruct their use against the Guantanamo prisoners. A significant mainstream academic component (including most notably law professors Lawrence Tribe[24] and Ruth Wedgwood[25]) have lent their qualified support to the tribunal concept,[26] and the use of tribunals would enjoy strong doctrinal support in the *Ex parte Quirin* decision.[27] The American public strongly supports the tribunal option;[28] few Americans would take to the streets in response to tribunal prosecutions of al Qaeda and Taliban detainees. Even the editorialists now appear to accept some use of the tribunals, with the adoption of procedural rules significantly constraining of tribunal prosecutions.[29] If, then, we looked at the question as a matter of purely domestic norms, we would expect the government to make at least some use of the tribunals.[30]

And yet the tribunals may not be constituted, and the posture of international community may be determinative on the question. International opposition to the tribunals (and to the terms of the Guantanamo detention generally) has been intense. European public opinion and the major international human rights groups have been particularly vocal in condemning the tribunal option.[31] Much of this opposition has been framed in terms of international law; that is, the U.S. conduct is condemned not just as bad policy, but as illegal.[32]

Of course, in the past, international sentiment that U.S. action was inconsistent with international law did not make it consequential (the mining of the Nicaraguan harbors and the related American withdrawal from the limited compulsory jurisdiction of the International Court of Justice provide notable examples from recent history). One cannot, as with at least some domestic actors, assume that international actors will be able to dictate their positions, and, if not, that those positions are meaningful. Where alleged lawbreakers face few costs for noncompliance, one can question whether in fact they are breaking the law. The widespread noncompliance with various formal international norms during the Cold War era explains in part why international law suffered so long in the American legal community as not being "law" at all. That mentality persists, not the least among major players in the Bush administration, which has rhetorically made good on its unilateralist campaign pledges, and on some issues—such as the Second Amendment attack on a proposed international small-arms-control regime[33]—it has aggressively followed through with action. In the face of this normative hostility, Bush administration practice supplies a controlled context in which to apply an interest-based test to U.S. compliance with international law.

BRINGING THE HEGEMON TO HEEL

In some contexts the United States will be able to resist the imposition of international norms. But there are others in which eventual submission appears inevitable. The military tribunals issue may be one where, notwithstanding an open contempt for international opinion, the United States may have to buckle under. There are three possible mechanisms for the imposition of international norms on the United States in this context: first, where other states have terrorism suspects in custody and make conditional their rendition to the United States; second, where other states make forms of important cooperation conditional on U.S. disposition of the suspects; and third, where the reputational costs of proceeding pose other significant costs to U.S. interests.

In the first case, international capacity to dictate is most obvious but also infrequently available. He who has the bodies can call the shots. The Europeans are resorting with increasing frequency to this device in the death penalty context, in the wake of the 1989 *Soering* decision from the European Court of Human Rights, under which it was found a violation of the European Human Rights Convention to extradite an individual to the United States if he might face not only a death sentence but (as is invariably the case) an extended stay on death row before execution.[34] Since *Soering,* extraditions in capital cases have been made conditional on U.S. agreement not to pursue the death penalty. The same is occurring in the post-9/11 context,[35] with the twist that extraditions are likely to include the additional condition that those extradited not face prosecution in military tribunals. Spain has already announced this policy with respect to suspected al Qaeda operatives in its custody.[36] In this context, U.S. authorities have no choice but to accept the European position, assuming an interest in rendition. Of course, the mechanism is available only when the foreign country has in custody terrorism suspects wanted by U.S. authorities.

Second, European and other governments are in a position to condition their cooperation on terrorism in such areas as intelligence sharing on a U.S. decision to abjure the tribunals. The immediate U.S. response to 9/11 may have been essentially unilateral, with only token international forces participating in the military operations in Afghanistan. But it is clear that effective preemptive action against terrorist organizations must be multilateral. Too much groundwork for terrorist attacks can be laid outside the target country's borders (as was true with 9/11 itself, for which significant planning was undertaken in Germany). In this respect, the United States needs something from other governments. If those governments care enough about the military tribunal and other related issues, they are in a position to extract behavioral changes from the United States. The added value of the tribunals may be in a higher confidence of conviction as an incident of procedures that are more flexible than in an ordinary federal criminal prosecution. But that added value may not outweigh the downside of qualified European cooperation in the fight against terrorism.[37]

The apparent U.S. retreat from bringing British national detainees in Guantanamo before military tribunals would seem to underscore that constraint. In July 2003, the Bush administration identified six detainees, two of them British, as eligible for tribunal proceedings. The prospect provoked broad-based condemnation in Britain and created a serious political headache for British Prime Minister Tony Blair, already embattled for his support of the U.S. invasion of Iraq. British authorities protested the possible prosecutions, extracting specific assurances from the Bush administration regarding the use of the death penalty and leaving open the possibility that the planned prosecutions would quietly be abandoned. British arguments against the tribunal were draped in the mantle of human rights and international law. The leverage here was clear: if the United States proceeded with the tribunal prosecutions, they risked the unwavering support of a loyal partner in the post-9/11 context, too steep a cost for the marginal returns of flexible tribunal procedures. And in stepping back from its contemplated tribunal prosecution of the British detainees, the United States further compromised the tribunals as an option in other cases, insofar as other states work to win similar concessions for their detainee nationals.

Finally, there is the less easily measured fallout from general public and transnational NGO condemnation of the tribunal option. To the extent that this opposition is fierce, it can translate into the foreign governmental policies highlighted earlier; governments facing transnational opposition to cooperation with U.S. authorities are obviously less likely to undertake it. But there is a more direct impact on the perceived international legitimacy of U.S. prosecution of suspected terrorists. On the one hand, the immediate American interest is to put terrorists behind bars, and the tribunal option facilitates that objective. On the other, the implications of perceived illegitimacy could be serious.[38] The credibility of future antiterrorist strategies and responses would be undermined. Terrorists imprisoned by the commissions might be more easily glorified, possibly contributing to the destabilization of various friendly Arab regimes whose hold on power may already be tenuous. In this legitimacy game, the position of key NGOs is critical.[39] With such groups as Amnesty International, the Lawyers Committee for Human Rights, and the International Commission of Jurists opposing tribunal prosecutions as inconsistent with international human rights,[40] the administration would start on the defensive were it to take the tribunal route.

The marginal gain in exploiting relaxed tribunal procedures might not be worth the hit taken in other quarters.

This international positioning already helps to explain the relatively exacting procedural rules imposed on the tribunals in regulations following the initial sketchlike executive order. If the government does not in the end deploy the tribunals, the international community will have likely tipped the balance against them. Of course, international views will not always be determinative, in somewhat the same way that nonjudicial perceptions of constitutional norms will not always be effectively enforced. An example of this in a 9/11 context involves the application of the Geneva prisoners-of-war convention to the Guantanamo detainees. Although there appears to be some basic consensus that POW status should itself be determined by some judicial-type entity, the administration unilaterally declared the convention inapplicable to both al Qaeda and Taliban detainees without a significant international backlash. The administration arguments were stronger here, however, than with respect to the tribunals, and the consequences of the decision (relating mostly to conditions of confinement) less significant. The invasion of Iraq, of course, similarly demonstrates the capacity of the United States to defy the conceptions of other actors on questions of international legality. But neither example disproves the salience of international law to U.S. decision making. It is highly unlikely, for example, that in the face of international rejection of the grounds for the invasion that the United States will undertake "preemptive" action against other states. That the costs of illegitimacy can be borne in some contexts will not make them bearable in others. As in the domestic law context, imperfect enforcement of legal norms does not undermine their ultimate status as such.

PLAYING OUT THE TRIUMPH OF INTERNATIONAL LAW

One must also qualify this account with the rather obvious caution that the episode is still unfolding and that its ending could deviate from the storyline here suggested. After having been derailed in the immediate wake of the post-attack detentions, the tribunal option appears to have been revived.[41] If deployed selectively against senior al Qaeda operatives (with respect to whose prosecution a strong argument for secret proceedings might be made), European and other governments might demur. This development, however, wouldn't be inconsistent with the insinuation of international norms; it would, rather, be reflective of the substance of those norms.[42]

Perhaps the more significant remaining test would be posed by what is emerging, either by default or by design, as the Bush administration's alternative to prosecution (whether by military tribunal or through the ordinary instruments of criminal justice) or release—namely, the possibility of indefinite detention without charge. This option is now being openly vetted, with an accompanying legal justification that the laws of war permit detention until the cessation of hostilities, hostilities here comprising the long-haul fight against terrorism.[43] International concern regarding the detentions is likely to accelerate on the time line[44] at the same time that domestic actors are unlikely to mobilize on the issue.[45]

International pressure is beginning to show affirmative results. The United States has agreed to release three juveniles whose detention had been highlighted by rights groups. At least eight friendly states, including Britain, Russia, Pakistan, and Spain, have lodged diplomatic protests regarding the continued detention of their nationals at Guantanamo, prompting a cabinet-level fracas within the administration. Opposition from other international quarters will intensify. It is not implausible that sustained international pressure—and associated costs—will result in the release or prosecution of substantial numbers of the Guantanamo contingent. If so, it would further demonstrate how the aftermath of September 11 has both reflected and advanced the efficacy of international norms.

The events of September 11 were exceptional, but there are some broader lessons here for less exceptional situations. On the domestic side, 9/11 evidences that alien rights can be at least partially vindicated outside the judicial process. But that possibility has already been established in other contexts. So it may be a new international dynamic that proves the more interesting development. If international actors are able to cabin U.S. discretion in this core security context, they will surely be in a position to do it elsewhere. Other developments are pointing in this direction as well. Where 9/11 might at first have been feared an obstacle to the advancement of international law and institutions, it may emerge an accelerant. Parallel developments are found in the consular convention cases and with respect to the continued application of the death penalty by some U.S. states. As other battles are engaged in such contexts as international environmental law, criminal law, humanitarian law, and on other human rights issues, 9/11 may point to an multilateralist future, whether by choice or not, for the United States as for everyone else.

THE IMMIGRANT AS THREAT TO AMERICAN SECURITY: A HISTORICAL PERSPECTIVE

GARY GERSTLE

For most of its history, America has been remarkably open to immigrants from most parts of the world. So many have come—more than fifty million in the last one hundred and twenty years alone—that the very history of America is incomprehensible without a consideration of who these immigrants were and what manner of life they made in their new home. Oscar Handlin, a pioneer in the field of immigration history, captured this truth in his Pulitzer Prize–winning 1951 book, *The Uprooted: The Epic Story of the Great Migrations That Made the American People.* "Once I thought to write a history of the immigrants in America," he wrote. "Then I discovered that the immigrants were American history."[1] From the seventeenth-century Pilgrims to the nineteenth-century Germans to the late-twentieth-century Cubans, immigrants and their children have left their mark on virtually every period and aspect of American history: as workers and revolutionaries, entrepreneurs and inventors, scholars and artists, entertainers and politicians, journalists and reformers. Americans have lavished praise on many individual immigrants and their offspring, including the Puritan John Winthrop, the farmer Hector St. John Crevècoeur, the industrialist Andrew Carnegie, the reformer Lillian Wald, the filmmaker Frank Capra, the labor leaders Walther Reuther and Cesar Chavez, and Chief of Staff and Secretary of State Colin Powell.[2]

But Americans, at a variety of moments, have also feared immigrants and lashed out at specific groups of newcomers who were thought to imperil the nation's present or future. Those singled out for attack have included the Irish and Chinese in the nineteenth century, Germans in World War I, foreign-born radicals and the groups allegedly nourishing them (Jews and Italians) in the 1920s, Mexicans in the 1930s, and Japanese in World War II. Extensive literature exists on each of these episodes of anti-immigrant agitation but few attempts have been made, especially in the last twenty years, to compare these episodes with each other and to understand their similarities and differences.[3] Little effort has been made as well to explain how, when, and why mild or inchoate anti-immigrant sentiments, which are almost always present, metamorphose into coherent and powerful crusades that seek to deprive immigrants of their civil liberties, personal safety, and sometimes even the right to live in America.[4] Undertaking this kind of inquiry seems especially important in light of the events of September 11, 2001, and the ongoing fear that current immigrant populations are harboring or supporting terrorists intent on striking against the American people, their leaders, and their institutions. What can history tell us about how Americans of past generations identified subversiveness among immigrants, the legitimacy of such accusations, and the consequences of policies adopted to counter the threats that immigrants were thought to pose? Can previous responses to fears of immigrant subversion illuminate how we will, or should, respond today? This essay will attempt to answer these and related questions.

The essay has three parts. The first attempts to group into four general categories immigrant behaviors and identities that historically Americans have labeled subversive. The second examines several situations in which Americans became obsessed with particular groups of immigrants and took action. The third attempts to situate the current fear about the threat that immigrants pose into the previously developed historical context.

I. THREATS OF IMMIGRANT SUBVERSION: A TYPOLOGY

While a cumulative list of the specific ways in which immigrants "threatened" America in the past would occupy many pages, it is possible to identify in only a few four generic kinds of "subversive" behavior and identities that immigrants were commonly accused of embodying: religious, political, economic, and racial. This typological exercise requires us first to understand not what kind of threat immigrants really posed but how the "protectors" of America constructed that threat in their own minds. It requires us, in other words, to see the immigrants as those whom historians have labeled "nativists" saw them. Nativists are those who believe that America belongs to its native population (usually meaning its white native population) and that the country's welfare is threatened by the presence, beliefs, and actions of the foreign-born. In some cases, it will be obvious that what past generations of nativists considered threatening and subversive was nothing of the sort; in other cases, we will have to undertake careful analysis to disentangle the real from the perceived threat.

FEAR OF RELIGIOUS SUBVERSION

At its origins, and for much of its history, the United States wanted to be a Protestant country. That meant not only that Protestants of all varieties would be able to worship free of interference from the state (or some state-endorsed religious establishment). It meant as well that the country should do everything in its power to create a society in which Catholicism, and more specifically, papal influence, would have no purchase. This fear of Rome is difficult for twenty-first-century Americans to understand because it is no longer a motive force in our politics or immigration policy. But, for most of our history, the Catholic Church's theology, liturgy, and rituals, its life-and-death struggle with European Protestants, its sheer international size and power, and the control that it was thought to exercise over rank-and-file Catholics alarmed American Protestants. Catholicism was depicted not only as the enemy of God but as the enemy of republicanism. To Protestant Americans, the Church stood for monarchy, aristocracy, and other reactionary forces that America was seeking to escape. Where the pope "ruled," Protestants charged, "the people" most certainly did not. And, thus, Catholic influence had to be resisted, even eradicated.[5]

The Catholic group in America that bore the brunt of American Protestant fury were the Irish, who, when they arrived in the 1830s and 1840s, constituted the first mass immigration of Catholics to America. Fleeing an Ireland devastated by colonial rule and famine, these Irish immigrants were largely destitute; they had few skills, little access to good jobs, and not much familiarity with urban living. Many native Protestants viewed them as an urban underclass, cut off from "American" values and traditions, their assimilation to their new land blocked by what these Protestants took to be a fanatical and unholy devotion to the Catholic Church. America's first mass nativist movement, the Know-Nothings, arose in the 1840s and 1850s in reaction to the "Irish peril." The Know-Nothings stirred up anti-Irish sentiment and sparked vigilante attacks by Protestant gangs on Irish neighborhoods, Catholic schools, and even, in some cases, Catholic churches themselves. In their more "respectable" moments, the Know-Nothings organized politically to end Irish immigration, to remove the children of Irish Catholic immigrants from parochial schools so that they could be educated in a proper Protestant environment, and to bar immigrants from holding public office and, in some cases, from voting.[6]

The politics of sectionalism and the outbreak of the Civil War sent the Know-Nothings into eclipse and also provided opportunities for Irish immigrants to demonstrate their loyalty to the Union, to rise in the social order, and to gain more respectability for their Catholic ways. But, even so, the religiously-motivated discrimination Irish Catholics had experienced in the antebellum era persisted for another hundred years. As late as 1928, the Republicans defeated the Democratic Irish Catholic nominee for president, Al Smith, by arousing anxiety about the threat that a Catholic president would pose to the United States. And even in 1960, another Democratic hopeful and Irish Catholic, John F. Kennedy, had to appear before a group of Protestant ministers in Houston to prove to their satisfaction that his election would not make the Vatican the ruler of Washington.[7]

It is easy for us to critique our forebears for their small-minded and intolerant hostility to Catholicism. But before we congratulate ourselves on our current broad-mindeness, we should note that we are once again living in an intensely religious age more akin to the nineteenth century than to the twentieth, and that, in this current age, many Americans are once again talking about the threat that a foreign religion, in this case Islam, poses to American values, traditions, and security. Thus, the early history of Irish Catholics in America may have more relevance to current problems than we might at first have imagined, in particular in terms of how American society as a whole is reacting to the presence of millions of Muslims in its midst.

FEAR OF POLITICAL SUBVERSION

The second kind of threat that immigrants were thought to pose was political. If America wanted to be a Protestant country, it also wanted to be a republic, one in which the people ruled. A republic had to guarantee not only popular sovereignty, but political and economic liberty for its citizens. In the late eighteenth and early nineteenth centuries, America was virtually unique among the nations of the world in its republicanism, and its creators feared that this system of politics would not last long, giving way to monarchy, aristocracy, or democracy (then pejoratively equated with mob rule). Republicanism, it was believed, depended on citizens who were fierce in defense of their independence and liberty and abundantly endowed with virtue. Citizens had to resist the temptations of excessive wealth and power. Those Americans who saw themselves as the guardians of their country's republican inheritance kept a close eye on immigrants who, especially in the nineteenth century, might not comprehend republicanism's value or fragility. In this respect, the antebellum fear of Irish Catholics was not just religiously grounded but politically grounded as well: could these immigrants, who owed so deep an allegiance to Rome, be counted on to embrace and defend American republican and libertarian principles? Would not their subservience to the monarchical pope incline them to favor authoritarian forms of secular rule in America?[8]

By the late nineteenth and early twentieth centuries, the threat to American republicanism was thought to emanate as much from the revolutionary left, comprising the followers of Marx, Proudhon, Bakunin, and Lenin, as from the Catholic right. Significant numbers of these leftists had come to the United States as immigrants: from France, Germany, Finland, Russia, the Balkans, Italy, Mexico, Cuba, and elsewhere. Many participated in continent-spanning international networks—some, such as those of the anarchists, were similar to al Qaeda in their decentralized character and in their refusal to put allegiance to any nation ahead of their loyalty to their revolutionary cause. Many also were contemptuous of American political principles and the state that embodied them. A few were saboteurs and terrorists. They contributed to roiling class conflicts and aroused fears that America, as a result of their agency, would soon be gripped by proletarian revolution. To many Americans, such a revolution incarnated the threat that republicans had discerned in democracy in the eighteenth century—mob rule, violence, contempt for individual liberties and private property. Should it occur in the United States, American republicanism would be subverted in the most profound sense, a denouement that helps to explain the extraordinary hostility of so many Americans to anarchism, socialism, and communism, and the large-scale violations of civil liberties that would be justified to eliminate those revolutionary movements from American soil.[9]

Sometimes the charge that immigrants posed a political threat was leveled at entire populations of immigrants and not just the comparatively small groups of agitators who resided within them. This happened in the 1920s, when many native-born Americans argued that Jewish and Italian immigration to America had to be stopped altogether, because the communities they formed here bred Bolsheviks and anarchists. It also happened in World War I and World War II, when all immigrants who had come from an enemy's land—Germany in the first instance, Japan in the second—were tarred with the charge of disloyalty. An immigrant group would not always be stigmatized in this way—it happened to Germans in World War I but not in World War II—making it necessary for us to explain the circumstances in which this kind of charge took root (a topic that will be taken up in a subsequent section).

FEAR OF ECONOMIC SUBVERSION

The third kind of threat that immigrants were thought to pose was economic. Most immigrants came to America to work. The heaviest immigration occurred during economic upturns, when labor demands were acute. But immigrant flows could never be perfectly synchronized with the business cycle. It took time for news of economic downturns to reach foreign shores. And even those immigrants who came during boom years might experience a depression a year or two after they arrived, their presence then swelling a labor surplus and no longer filling a labor need. The scarcity of jobs during downturns meant rising unemployment, falling wages, and the inability of wage earners to support their families. It is hardly surprising that, in such circumstances, native-born Americans often accused immigrants of causing unemployment and depressing wages, and called on their labor leaders and political representatives to curtail further immigration. Virtually every immigrant group that has come to America has been, at one time or another, the target of these accusations and demands: the Irish in the 1840s and 1850s, the Chinese in the 1870s and 1880s, the "New Immigrants" from eastern and southern Europe in the early decades of the twentieth century, and the Mexicans in the 1930s and 1990s.[10]

FEAR OF RACIAL SUBVERSION

The fourth kind of threat that immigrants were thought to pose was racial: the belief that some immigrants belonged to racially inferior groups unsuitable for American life. Racism, of course, was a defining feature of the American republic from the moment of its creation and remained so for one hundred and fifty years. Though the Constitution outlawed slavery in 1865, its Supreme Court interpreters failed to put it squarely on the side of racial equality until the 1950s and 1960s. In 1790, the first Congress passed a law stipulating that to be eligible for naturalization, an immigrant had to be both free and white. In 1870, Congress amended this law to permit the naturalization of black immigrants, but the law continued to bar the naturalization of most east and south Asian immigrants until 1952. From the earliest days of the republic, many Americans justified their hostility toward immigrants by arguing that certain groups simply did not—and would never—possess the intelligence, character, independence, and regard for republicanism that the country demanded of its citizens. By the 1840s and 1850s groups such as the Irish and the Mexicans (whom the United States was fighting in Texas) were being compared unfavorably to the racially "superior" Anglo-Saxons, who had allegedly first brought liberty to England in the Middle Ages and then brought even greater liberty to America in the seventeenth and eighteenth centuries.[11]

Nineteenth-century romantic nationalists in England and America idealized these Anglo-Saxons as part of their effort to locate the greatness of their nations in the special genius of a people who were thought to form both nations' cores. These early romantic nationalists had not yet fully developed the racial implications of their Anglo-Saxonism; that task would be left to their Social Darwinist successors of the late nineteenth century. By that time, the shapers of both educated and popular opinion were attempting to measure the "racial character" of each of the world's peoples and to arrange these peoples in a hierarchy of racial aptitude. Intelligence, honor, virtue, sobriety, and capacity for self-government became traits that were thought to inhere in some groups more than others.

Those groups that possessed these traits in abundance—invariably western and northern Europeans who were labeled Anglo-Saxon, Nordic, or Caucasian— ended up on top of racial hierarchies and those groups thought to lack them— principally blacks, "Orientals," and "brown" peoples such as the Indians and Mexicans—ended up on the bottom. Diverse groups emanating from eastern and southern Europe—Italians, Poles, Jews, Greeks, and so on—were precariously poised on the middle rungs of these hierarchies, higher than blacks, Asians, and Indians but lower than the Anglo-Saxons, whose status, more often than not, was judged not to be in reach. Even the Irish came in for some racial drubbing, especially in popular cartoons that depicted them as monkeys or as black.[12]

In this climate, immigration restrictionists and eugenicists began arguing that it was the obligation of the United States to maximize the number of racially superior immigrants and to minimize the number of racially inferior ones. Absent that kind of policy, America as a land of liberty, popular sovereignty, and economic strength would cease to exist. This racially motivated restriction campaign emerged in the 1880s when Congress passed the Chinese Exclusion Act, the first of a series of laws that barred most Chinese from emigrating to the United States for a period of sixty years. It continued in 1907 with the Gentleman's Agreement with Japan, which ended mass Japanese emigration to the United States, and it climaxed in 1924 when, in addition to all east and south Asians, most people from eastern and southern Europe, the Near East, and Africa were barred from entering America. Racism defined American immigration policy, a phenomenon that would not end until the 1960s.

II. THREATS OF IMMIGRANT SUBVERSION: CASES

Occasionally, any one of the four kinds of subversive behaviors that immigrants were accused of embodying—religious, political, economic, and racial—could generate an anti-immigrant crusade on its own. But more commonly the greatest obsessions with the threats posed by immigrants and the most sustained movements against them occurred in instances where two or more kinds of subversive behavior were believed to be reinforcing each other. Thus, the Know-Nothings, who conducted the most determined campaign against the Irish, charged these immigrants with religious *and* political subversion. The campaign against Chinese immigrants arose in the West not just because Chinese workers were thought to be competing with American workers but also because the Chinese were alleged to be racially incapable of striving for decent standards of work and pay.[13] The indiscriminate attacks on German Americans in World War I for their alleged political subversiveness depended on the transformation of the once-honored German immigrant into the racially feared "Hun." And the draconian campaigns against eastern and southern Europeans after World War I and against Japanese immigrants and their offspring in World War II rested on the charge that their disloyalty was grounded in a racial character that chronically predisposed these groups to subversion.

The greatest civil libertarian peril we face today, in handling the terrorist threat, is probably a similar kind of merger of different kinds of subversive charges, in which the protectors of America construe the threat as residing not simply in terrorist bands that want to destroy America but in Arab or Muslim peoples whose racial or religious character is thought to be antithetical to American cultural values and political principles.

To illuminate these points further, I will discuss three different cases of alleged immigrant subversion and responses to them: the Germans in World War I; the Red Scare and eastern and southern Europeans after World War I; and the Japanese in World War II. Each of these cases of alleged subversion occurred in war or near-war situations; considered together, they offer the best historical framework within which to understand the current "War on Terror."

GERMANS IN WORLD WAR I

The Germans form one of the most interesting historical cases of immigrants charged with subversion because of their high status prior to World War I. In the late nineteenth and early twentieth centuries, they ranked among the most economically successful of immigrants. They developed a reputation for cultural accomplishment, founding centers for learning and the arts in their communities. They also drew praise for the family-oriented and wholesome character of their popular culture. German immigrants did not, of course, escape all suspicion. A substantial minority were Catholics who experienced the general anti-Catholic prejudices of the era. A significant number were socialists who, for a time, dominated radical political organization in the United States. Germans also tended to be avowedly pluralist in their cultural politics, proclaiming that they would cultivate their German language and traditions, newspapers and schools, in the United States. This proud and public display of Germanness generated an undercurrent of anxiety among many native-born Americans who expected all immigrants to shed their "Old World" habits and to embrace American culture completely.[14]

To mobilize a fractious American population for war in 1916 and 1917, Woodrow Wilson's administration first exhorted Americans to rally around the country's ideals of freedom, democracy, and self-determination, and to view the war as a crusade to bring these beliefs to the peoples of Europe. But when that effort failed to produce the requisite social harmony and war enthusiasm, the government's campaign for unity turned harsh, now intent on punishing those who were slow to demonstrate their allegiance and loyalty. In the most far-reaching restriction on free speech enacted since 1798, Congress passed the Espionage and Sedition Acts in 1917 and 1918, empowering the government to prosecute aliens and citizens for writing or uttering any statement that could be construed by government attorneys as profaning the flag, the Constitution, or the military.[15]

The Germans were especially vulnerable to this government loyalty campaign. On the eve of war, they still constituted the largest immigrant group in America—four million strong. If one were to add to that total the number of immigrants who had come from some part of the Austro-Hungarian Empire—Germany's ally—that figure doubled to eight million. Any government would have been worried about those numbers; even if the numbers of loyalists to the kaiser or the Austrian emperor among those eight millions was infinitesimally small, they could still have formed a subversive force large enough to harm American security.[16] The government might have made every effort to focus its security campaign on those Germans who could be identified as truly subversive. That would have meant exposing and arresting actual agents of the German government and putting under careful surveillance those who were outspoken in their support of German war aims and the kaiser. It would have meant, additionally, resisting the temptation to arrest or punish those German immigrants who were simply fond of their Old World culture or who opposed America's entry into war because they believed that a victory by either side would bring no benefit to working men or women. And it would have meant refusing to ostracize individuals whose only subversive act was the possession of German ancestry.

Instead of making such distinctions, the government began to regard (and racialize) all Germans as "Huns." This epithet tied modern-day Germans to the barbaric tribes who had emerged from Europe's forests a millennium and a half earlier to devastate European civilization and plunge the continent into the Dark Ages. The latter-day Huns, like their forebears, were brutish and apelike men who did not understand the meaning of compassion, mercy, restraint, or democracy. The Committee on Public Information, the American government agency charged with arousing popular support for the war, spread images of the "German as beast" in posters it plastered everywhere. It tied the German army's atrocities against the Belgian people to the subhuman character of the German people. It encouraged the public to see anti-German movies, such as *The Prussian Cur* and *The Beast of Berlin*.[17]

Unleashing an anti-German hysteria justified the government's campaign to arrest thousands of German and Austrian immigrants whom it suspected of subversion. Congress, meanwhile, passed the Trading With the Enemy Act, which required German-language publications (as well as other foreign-language publications) to submit all war-related stories to post office censors for approval. It also passed the Volstead Act, prohibiting the manufacture and distribution of alcohol, at least in part because of the belief that the German American brewers who controlled the beer industry would ply loyal Americans with alcohol and thus weaken their will to fight.

At the popular level, and at the level of state and local governments, German Americans became the objects of popular hatred. Boston's city government banned performances of Beethoven's symphonies and the German-born conductor of the Boston Symphony Orchestra was forced to resign. Although Americans would not give up the German foods they had grown to love, they would no longer call them by their German names. Sauerkraut was rechristened "liberty cabbage," hamburgers became "liberty sandwiches." Libraries removed works of German literature from their shelves, and politicians urged school districts to prohibit the teaching of the German language. Patriotic school boards in Lima, Ohio, and elsewhere actually burned German-language books in their districts.

German Americans risked being fired from work, losing their businesses, and being assaulted on the street. Even before Prohibition went into effect, German American brewers found it difficult to sell their beer and thus to keep their enterprises afloat. A St. Louis mob lynched an innocent German immigrant whom they suspected of subversion. After only twenty-five minutes of deliberation, a St. Louis jury acquitted the mob leaders, who had brazenly defended their crime as an act of patriotism.

These sorts of experiences devastated the once-proud German American community. Its members began hiding their ethnic identity, changing their names, speaking German only in the privacy of their own homes, and celebrating their holidays out of the public eye. While the physical assaults on individual Germans, the violation of their civil liberties, and the racialization of Germans as Huns stopped soon after the armistice was signed in November 1918, many German Americans would take far longer to recover from the shame and vulnerability they experienced in 1917 and 1918. Many would never again celebrate their Germanness in public; quite a few abandoned their heritage entirely, choosing to assimilate into a white Protestant culture or, if they were Catholic, into an Irish American culture. It can be argued that this assimilatory process would have happened anyway, as second and third generation German Americans succeeded the immigrants in their communities and saw less reason to maintain Old World language and culture. But had not the war intervened, this process would have unfolded more slowly and unevenly than it did.[18] So thoroughly did Germans assimilate that twenty-five years after World War I ended, important Americans such as Dwight D. Eisenhower and Walter Reuther would not be known or thought about as German Americans. They were simply, and 100 percent, American.

It is a measure of the assimilative capacities of American society that members of a group who had been so despised in the 1910s could reach the highest levels of government and labor movement power only a generation later. The fear of Germans subsided so completely that already by 1924, when the United States was putting its immigration restriction system into place, the government gave Germany one of its largest and most coveted quotas. The quickness of this about-face only served to underscore how bizarre and shameful the indiscriminate assaults on the German American population in World War I had been.

THE RED SCARE AND IMMIGRATION RESTRICTION, 1919–1924

The patriotic emotions whipped up by the government and private patriotic groups during World War I carried over into the postwar period, focusing primarily on political radicals as the chief threat to American security. Suspicion of political radicals had emerged during the war itself, especially once the principal radical organizations, the Socialist Party and the Industrial Workers of the World, declared themselves to be opponents of the war. This suspicion grew when the Bolsheviks took power in St. Petersburg in November 1917, withdrew Russia from the war, and called on workers everywhere, including those in the United States, to fight capitalist power rather than the armies of the Central Powers. The Bolshevik Revolution stirred considerable interest in the United States, not only among radicals, about two-thirds of whom would soon leave the Socialist Party to form two Communist parties, but also among hundreds of thousands of American workers, many of whom had emigrated from Russia or countries proximate to Russia in Eastern Europe. Most of these immigrants never became socialists or Communists, but they were stirred by the dream, embodied by the Bolshevik Revolution, that workers could successfully revolt against their capitalist masters and thus transform the conditions of their labor.

Labor militancy among American workers had risen during the war itself and intensified once the war ended. In January 1919 a general strike paralyzed the city of Seattle when 60,000 workers walked off their jobs. By August, walkouts had been staged by 400,000 coal miners, 120,000 textile workers, 50,000 garment workers, and 300,000 steelworkers. Altogether, four million workers—one-fifth of the nation's manufacturing workforce—went on strike in 1919. This reality of massive labor unrest, combined with the fear that this unrest would enable Bolshevik sympathizers to stage a revolution in the United States, forms the essential background to the Red Scare of 1919.[19]

The trigger for the Red Scare occurred on April 28 and 29, 1919, when mail bombs arrived at the office of Mayor Ole Hanson in Seattle and the home of former U.S. Senator Thomas W. Hardwick in Atlanta. The bomb meant for Hanson did not explode, but the one for Hardwick did, blowing off the hands of the maid who opened the package and seriously burning Hardwick's wife. On April 30, a clerk in the New York City Parcel Post Division discovered sixteen more bombs that had been set aside in his office because they contained insufficient postage. Another eighteen bombs already traveling through the mail were then intercepted before they could reach their recipients. Altogether thirty-six mail bombs were identified, targeted either at capitalists, such as John D. Rockefeller and J.P. Morgan, or at government officials who had been deemed "class enemies." Nor was this episode the last to involve explosives: on June 2, 1919, bombs exploded within the same hour at the homes of manufacturers and government officials in eight different cities on the East Coast.

One of these June 2 bombs was meant to destroy Attorney General A. Mitchell Palmer's home in Washington, D.C., but the device exploded prematurely, blowing up the bomb thrower on the steps leading up to Palmer's abode. Enough of the man's body was recovered to identify him as an Italian immigrant from Philadelphia. That he was an anarchist seemed confirmed by a pamphlet found near the door to Palmer's house. It contained these words: "There will have to be bloodshed; we will not dodge; there will have to be murder; we will kill . . . there will have to be destruction; we will destroy. . . . We are ready to do anything and everything to suppress the capitalist class. . . . The ANARCHIST FIGHTERS." [20]

Radicals charged that the June 2 bombings had been executed and the pamphlet planted by those who wanted to discredit the left and whip the American people into an antiradical frenzy. To support their case, they pointed to the fact that the government, despite massive manhunts, failed to arrest or to bring to trial a single person accused of making or planting the bombs. More likely, however, the bombs were the work of anarchists, some of whom espoused violence as the only way to upend capitalist power. The terrorist streak in anarchism had first surfaced in the United States in the late nineteenth century, causing injury or death to Americans—to workers and police involved in the Haymarket protest of 1886; to Henry Clay Frick, Andrew Carnegie's right-hand man, wounded by the anarchist Alexander Berkman in 1892; and to President William McKinley, assassinated by anarchist Leon Czolgosz in 1901. But, while many anarchists defended the use of violence as a matter of principle, very few of them engaged in it themselves. The bombings of 1919 were probably the work of a small, clandestine group of anarchist terrorists. Not only were the prominent anarchists of the period, such as Emma Goldman, uninvolved in these acts; they probably did not know themselves the identities of the perpetrators.

Anarchism was a decentralized movement, its adherents organized into many different cells and groups, often acting independently of each other. Adding further to the complexity of the situation, the two larger and more influential wings of radicalism in 1919, the socialists and the Communists, had repudiated assassinations as legitimate techniques of class struggle.[21]

These different attitudes toward violence among the various radical groups and within the anarchist movement itself, however, made little impression on either government authorities or the public in large. The bombings of the spring of 1919, combined with the year's labor unrest, convinced most Americans that a Bolshevik-style revolution was unfolding in the United States and that every measure had to be taken to stop it. Suspicion fell most heavily on communities of immigrants, especially those that had originated in eastern and southern Europe and who were thought to be vulnerable to Bolshevik propaganda. These immigrants, predominantly Catholic, Christian Orthodox, and Jewish, had never possessed the social prestige enjoyed by the Germans prior to World War I. In the language of the time, they were "new immigrants," a pejorative shorthand for those newcomers whose religion, politics, customs, personal hygiene, racial "fitness," and capacity for self-government did not match the standard expected of American citizens or set by such "old immigrant" groups as the Germans and the Swedes. These new immigrants were easy targets for charges of subversion and treachery.[22]

Attorney General Palmer and state law enforcement authorities struck against the new immigrant "Reds" in November 1919, arresting 750 aliens in New York and deporting 249 of them a month later. Most of these aliens were immigrants from Russia or other countries in eastern Europe. On January 2, 1920, the authorities struck again, arresting more than 4,000 suspected radicals in thirty-three cities spread across twenty-three states. Meant to expose the extent of revolutionary activity, these raids netted exactly three pistols, no rifles, no explosives, and no plans for insurrection. Nevertheless, those arrested were jailed for weeks and, in some cases, for months without being charged with a crime and often under harsh conditions. Of these, 591 would be deported by the spring of 1920 and the rest would be released.[23]

In some respects, the Red Scare of 1919–1920 ebbed rather quickly. The cases of those aliens arrested during the scare were largely resolved within six months. Congress refused to give Palmer and his energetic young assistant, J. Edgar

Hoover, the peacetime sedition law they needed in order to prosecute native-born radicals.[24] Moreover, significant opposition to Attorney General Palmer's methods had already surfaced among federal judges, who began ruling, as early as January 1920, that evidence gathered in illegal seizures of papers could not be used in criminal proceedings. By April, Assistant Secretary of Labor Louis Post, in charge of immigration control, had thrown out hundreds of warrants issued by Palmer and released almost half of those arrested on January 2. Threatened with impeachment by Congress for his "leniency," Post demanded and received a congressional hearing, during which he convinced his accusers that the attorney general's office had violated the civil liberties of hundreds of innocent individuals. These hearings diminished Attorney General Palmer's prestige. Palmer then discredited himself altogether when the radical violence he had predicted for May 1, 1920, failed to materialize. By the summer of 1920, the Red Scare had largely subsided.[25]

The effects of the Red Scare lingered in two ways, however. First, the raids and arrests had decimated the Communist left, reducing its membership from 70,000 to 16,000 in 1920 alone. By 1927, that number stood at a paltry 8,000.[26] Reliable figures on anarchist membership do not exist, but there can be little doubt that the arrests and deportations of 1919–1920, combined with the seven-year ordeal of Nicola Sacco and Bartolomeo Vanzetti, Italian anarchists convicted of murdering a Brockton, Massachusetts, paymaster in 1920 and executed in 1927, damaged the anarchist movement.[27] Other radical movements, including the Socialist Party and the Industrial Workers of the World, also would suffer from the calumny that the Red Scare had heaped on all "Red" ideologies.

Second, the Red Scare lingered in the attempt by federal authorities to target entire groups of "new immigrants" for their alleged role in nurturing radicals. Bolshevik sympathy probably was stronger among Jewish immigrants, most of whom had fled the tyranny of czarist Russia and celebrated the czar's fall, than among any other single immigrant group; anarchism drew a disproportionate number of its immigrant supporters from the Italian community. In both cases, the numbers of Bolsheviks and anarchists constituted only a small percentage of the total immigrant Jewish and Italian populations living in the United States. Many government authorities, however, refused to make this distinction. Increasingly, they treated Italians as constitutionally hot-tempered and prone to criminality and violence, and Jews as parasitic, immoral, yet clever—precisely the qualities that had allegedly allowed a small "Judeo-Bolshevik" clique in Russia to seize power and embark on a program of world revolution. Because these qualities were thought to be inborn, no amount of exposure to the ennobling

American environment would erode them. The political subversion of Jews and Italians was now thought to rest on these two groups' racial character.[28]

Once the problem was defined in this way, the only solution was to bar such groups from coming to the United States, which Congress did, first in emergency legislation in 1921 and then as a permanent measure in 1924. The 1924 legislation established an immigration quota for each of the world's nations pegged at 2 percent of that nation's population present in the United States in 1890. At that date, very few Jewish, Italian, or other "new immigrants" resided in the United States, guaranteeing that those groups' post-1924 quotas would be small. Indeed, those quotas reduced immigration from eastern and southern Europe to a trickle, from a prewar annual average of 738,000 to only 18,439, a 97 percent decrease.[29]

Racialist language permeated discussions of the 1924 immigration restriction legislation when it was being discussed on the House and Senate floors. For example, Congressman Fred S. Purnell of Indiana (Republican) declared: "There is little or no similarity between the clear-thinking, self-governing stocks that sired the American people and this stream of irresponsible and broken wreckage that is pouring into the lifeblood of America the social and political diseases of the Old World." Ira G. Hershey of Maine (Republican) alleged that all eastern and southern European revolutionaries—"soviets and the socialists and the bolshevists, the radicals and anarchists"—were "mixed bloods" who would mongrelize America, sapping it of its morality and good sense. America's salvation from the Bolsheviks, degeneracy, and other evils, declared Congressman R.E.L. Allen of West Virginia (Democrat), lay in "purifying and keeping pure the blood of America."[30] The legislation favored by these racial purists passed both houses of Congress by overwhelming margins, and kept most eastern and southern European immigrants out of the United States for the next forty years. Among other things, it made the admission of eastern European Jews fleeing the Holocaust virtually impossible. In such ways did the effects of the Red Scare endure.

Japanese in World War II

No group that had voluntarily emigrated to the United States suffered what 120,000 West Coast Japanese Americans experienced for almost three years in the 1940s: imprisonment by the government in ten "relocation centers" in California, Arizona, Utah, Wyoming, Colorado, and Arkansas. Next to the slavery and the confinement of Native American populations on reservations, this policy arguably constituted the worst violation of civil liberties in American history. President Roosevelt signed Executive Order 9066 authorizing the removal of people deemed dangerous from "military areas" on February 19, 1942. Though Japanese Americans were not actually named in this order, they were its targets. The general roundup began in March 1942. The government made no distinction between those Japanese Americans who were likely to be subversives and those who were not, or even between those who were immigrant aliens and those who were native-born citizens. All were told to sell their homes, businesses, and the possessions that they could not personally carry with them. Once stripped of their material wealth and belongings, they were transported by the U.S. Army to sixteen assembly centers. By May, they were distributed to the ten camps. These camps were, in fact, federal prisons. Barbed wire surrounded them and armed guards patrolled their perimeters. No one was permitted to leave or enter without permission. Beginning in late 1943, some Japanese Americans who signed loyalty oaths were allowed to leave the camps to work in cities or agricultural regions of the Midwest or to serve in the U.S. military. By early 1945, those who had passed loyalty tests were permitted to return to the West Coast and many did. But 18,000 who failed them were held until 1946.[31]

It is not surprising, of course, that Americans feared the Japanese in the aftermath of Pearl Harbor. The December 7, 1941, attack was the most devastating assault by a foreign power on American territory since the War of 1812. Incredulity and fear only mounted in the months after December 7, especially as the Japanese military, sweeping through the Southeast Asian colonies of Great Britain, the Netherlands, France, and the United States, demonstrated that the ease of its victory at Pearl Harbor had been no fluke. Americans began to wonder whether Japanese nationals and their descendants living in Hawaii—158,000 strong— had assisted the Japanese military in its surprise attack. But such concerns did not necessarily lead to the conclusion that all Japanese Americans in Hawaii or on the mainland had to be rounded up. Indeed, no government agency would ever attempt to round up the entire Japanese population in Hawaii; and, initially, the federal government did not even attempt such a roundup on the mainland. Rather, in the days following Pearl Harbor, the Department of Justice and the Federal Bureau of Investigation deployed the techniques they had developed to deal with the Germans in World War I and the anarchists and Communists in 1919: they arrested 12,000 immigrants from Japan, Germany, and Italy whom they suspected of political subversion. Only 2,000 of those arrested were Japanese Americans, signaling that these governmental institutions had not yet singled out the Japanese.[32]

By the standards of World War I and the Red Scare (and of the Radical Islamicist Scare of 2001), the arrest of 12,000 was itself staggering. The FBI, under the command of J. Edgar Hoover, believed that this extensive dragnet had snared most pro-Axis political subversives and thus ensured the internal security of the United States. Continued surveillance netted another 3,000 suspects by October 1943. Of the cumulative 15,000 detained in this way, 5,705 were interned in camps administered by the Border Patrol, and the rest were released.[33] A roundup of alleged political subversives of this magnitude had never occurred in America before, and the laws and techniques used to accomplish it established precedents for future programs of surveillance and arrest, including the anticommunist campaign of the late 1940s and early 1950s. Only in comparison to the mass evacuation and incarceration of 120,000 West Coast Japanese Americans does the scope and intensity of this other sweep begin to seem tame.

The program of Japanese internment resulted from pressure that politically powerful groups of white Americans in the western states and military authorities stationed there were able to exert on the federal government. Declaring that the sabotage of key military installations and perhaps even a Japanese military invasion on the West Coast were imminent, these groups demanded the immediate and mass evacuation of the area's Japanese American population. For a few weeks, Attorney General Francis Biddle resisted these demands. But, by February, the internment arguments had carried the day, and FDR signed Executive Order 9066 after barely a moment of reflection.

The allegations made by white westerners and the Western Defense Command were grounded not in reality but in fifty years of racist stereotypes about the Japanese. These stereotypes ascribed a variety of negative and threatening qualities to the Japanese race: its members were too clannish to assimilate to American life; they possessed the mentality of a herd, readily submitting to emperors and strongmen and unable either to cultivate their own individualism or appreciate the importance of self-government; they labored like beasts of burden, working themselves, their wives, and their children to the bone. Not only did such habits of work undermine Japanese family life but they also subverted the wages, hours, and working conditions that "American" workingmen had fought so hard to attain. Finally, the Japanese were accused of being inscrutable and unknowable, possessing an "Oriental-like" habit of stealth and subversion. The combination of their stealth and hard work, white Americans feared, endowed these people with superhuman qualities that might enable them to conquer the white race militarily and economically. Because these qualities were thought to be racial in origin, they could never be shed. The Japanese could never become true Americans.[34]

White Americans had expressed their hostility to the Japanese as early as 1907, when their protests had compelled President Theodore Roosevelt to ban most Japanese immigration to the United States. In 1913, California passed an

Alien Land Law, prohibiting Japanese and other Asian aliens from owning property in the state. In 1924, the Immigration Restriction Act barred all Japanese immigrants from coming to the United States.[35] The treatment of Japanese Americans after Pearl Harbor drew directly on this history of racial stereotyping and exclusion. General John L. DeWitt, the commander of the Western Defense Command in 1942, was simply reciting an oft-repeated slur of the era when he declared, "A Jap's a Jap." In his report urging internment, DeWitt argued that "the Japanese race is an enemy race and while many second and third generation Japanese born on United States soil, possessed of United States citizenship, have become 'Americanized,' the racial strains are undiluted." [36] Fears of racial subversion had joined fears of political subversion with profound consequences both for Japanese Americans and America itself.

Significantly, the government in World War II ordered no mass evacuation or incarceration of the German American or Italian American populations. Of course, it would have been much harder to execute such a policy since those groups numbered in the millions, not the hundreds of thousands. The Japanese Americans in Hawaii themselves escaped mass incarceration because, at 35 percent of the Hawaiian population, they were simply too vital to the local economy to be locked away in prisons. But the arguments about expediency can only be carried so far. Had the Germans and the Italians numbered in the hundreds of thousands, it is still unlikely that they would have been rounded up *en masse*.[37]

This is true even though a good case could have been made, in the 1940s, that Germans posed a greater internal security risk than did the Japanese. Not only was the German American Bund a dangerous pro-Nazi organization that, in size and influence, had no pro-emperor counterpart in the Japanese American population, but the German military possessed an ability to strike the mainland United States that the Japanese military lacked. German submarines regularly prowled the Atlantic coastline of the United States in ways that Japanese subs did not do in the Pacific. The German military actually executed, on New York's Long Island, what American alarmists on the West Coast falsely charged the Japanese military with planning to do in California: debark saboteurs from submarines to blow up key American army, munitions, and communications facilities.[38] And yet despite the evidence pointing to the greater danger to East Coast America posed by the Germans, fears of subversion and sabotage focused almost entirely on the Japanese on the West Coast.

Those fears might have subsided sooner had critical government intelligence been allowed to surface and influence the deliberations of the Supreme Court when it began considering the constitutionality of internment in 1943. The U.S. Solicitor General's office had in its possession at that time a detailed report assembled by the Office of Naval Intelligence arguing that the Japanese population on the West Coast posed no loyalty threat to the United States and that its incarceration was therefore not a military necessity. But the Solicitor General suppressed the report, making it impossible for any of the Supreme Court justices to review it. We cannot know how that report might have affected the internal deliberations of the Court, but it would have made it possible for those justices, such as Frank Murphy, who were disturbed by the policy of internment, to challenge the stigmatization of the Japanese as an "enemy race" capable of extraordinary treachery.[39]

The Germans and Italians escaped the worst effects of the government's anti-subversion campaign because they were no longer racially suspect. In their case, fear of political subversion was not compounded by the fear of racial subversion. That U.S. authorities and public opinion no longer construed the German and Italian populations as racially threatening can be interpreted as evidence that egalitarian sentiments had made progress against racist ones since the 1910s and 1920s. And yet the treatment of Japanese Americans reveals how far the United States still had to go in ridding itself of its racist habits.[40]

III. USING THE PAST TO ILLUMINATE THE PRESENT

The historical record instructs us that war or near-war situations often put immigrants at risk, especially if those immigrants have come from a part of the world or belong to a race or religion perceived to be the enemy of the United States. Fears of internal subversion during wartime are probably inevitable. Governments are charged with protecting the nation they represent and the people who comprise it. In wartime, governments will usually demand and receive authority to pursue subversives that, in republican or democratic polities, they would not be given in peacetime. In most wartime situations, governments will have to discharge their responsibilities to provide security while possessing imperfect information about the sources and likelihood of subversive acts. The lack of adequate information does not usually lead to caution but to overreach in the form of indiscriminate violations of civil liberties that would not be tolerated during peacetime. Immigrant groups associated through nationality, race, or religion with America's enemy have been especially vulnerable to government overreach. Marked as different, they are easily construed as dangerous.

Such groups are commonly accused of wanting to aid our enemies and thus to subvert the political integrity of the United States. But, in the first half of the twentieth century, those groups that suffered the most—the Germans in World War I, the southern and eastern Europeans during the Red Scare, and the Japanese in World War II—were those whose political subversion was thought to be grounded in another kind of subversion, most commonly that of race. It may be difficult for us to comprehend that Germans and eastern and southern Europeans—groups who today are considered to be white—were once stigmatized as something other than or less than white, but such accusations were made in the early decades of the twentieth century. Leveling the charge of racial subversion imperiled an entire group, for the tendency to political subversion could now be construed as inhering in any individual born into that group. This joining of political subversion to racial subversion suited the needs of those Americans trying to arouse hysteria as well as those of government officials who could now relieve themselves of the difficult task of distinguishing between actual subversives and those who were innocent.

An evaluation of current government efforts to provide security to America in the ongoing "War on Terror" allows us to say that, in some respects, we have learned from past experiences. While Arabs and/or Muslim terrorists are considered to be the chief threat to American security, no attempt is being made to eradicate from American society all aspects of Islamic or Arab culture, a policy that governments and private citizens pursued against German culture in World War I. To the contrary, public and private organizations have understood the urgency of learning more about Arab and Muslim civilizations, past and present, and have undertaken projects in schools, universities, and interfaith assemblies to do just that. Nor is any attempt being made to round up all Arab or Muslim Americans as was undertaken against the Japanese in World War II. While many Americans have verbally abused or physically attacked individual Arabs and Muslims since September 2001, the highest public authorities have refused to condone such popular prejudice and vigilantism. President George W. Bush has made it clear in ways that Woodrow Wilson and Franklin Roosevelt never did that it is simply not acceptable to stigmatize an entire racial, cultural, or religious group because of the small number of terrorists and enemies who reside in its ranks.

In other respects, however, we may not yet have learned the lessons of the past well enough. The anti-Red campaign of 1919–1920 is the episode in American history that most closely resembles the current War on (Islamic) Terror, and paying close attention to the similarities will reveal the danger America runs of repeating past mistakes. Both campaigns crystallized around terrorist acts—mail bombs sent to the homes of "class enemies" in the first case, airplanes turned into bombs and directed toward buildings (and their inhabitants) that symbolized American power in the second. Both acts were the work of revolutionists who were willing to sacrifice anything, including their lives, to achieve their aims (though the revolutionists of 1919 did not celebrate the killing of innocent civilians the way that the revolutionists of 2001 did). The terrorists in both instances belonged to small cells that were virtually impossible for outsiders to penetrate but that drew support from global networks of supporters. Both acts of terrorism occasioned frenzied roundups by U.S. government authorities of thousands of immigrant suspects who were held for a long time, often without access to bail, attorneys, or decent conditions. Both of these roundups yielded remarkably little information about those who had been involved in terrorist acts while spreading fear in America at large about those populations of immigrants with whom the terrorists shared a nationality or religion. In the 1920s, as we have seen, this fear led to the racialized stigmatization of entire groups of immigrants and the decision to bar them from the United States.

This has begun to happen in regard to Arab or Muslim immigrants, not through a blanket immigration restriction act of the sort passed by Congress in the 1920s but through a series of administrative acts by federal authorities. Several months after September 11, 2001, the government asked five thousand men from Middle Eastern and Muslim countries to "volunteer" for interviews with immigration officials; some of these interviews have triggered deportations. About the same time, the Immigration and Naturalization Service (INS) ordered public and private universities to provide it with information about their Middle Eastern and Muslim students. Hundreds, perhaps of thousands, of university students from Middle Eastern countries have already dropped out of school and gone home, and applications from prospective new students have plummeted. In February 2003, the INS began registering and fingerprinting 44,000 immigrants from specified Arab and Islamic countries. A federal noose has tightened around Muslim and Arab immigration, giving the government the ability to choke it off altogether. It took five years after the Red Scare of 1919 to install a punitive and racialized system of immigration restriction. We may well have another one in place by the time we reach the fifth anniversary of September 11.[41]

Whether we do or not will depend on whether the charge of political subversion leveled at Muslim terrorists becomes compounded by the charge of racial or religious subversion. The charge of racial subversion would be leveled at Arabs, who would be depicted as harboring a racial affinity for terror. The charge of religious subversion would be leveled at Muslims, who would be accused of adhering to a faith fundamentally hostile to the political ideals that Americans hold most dear and exercising a grip among its adherents so strong that no one who is exposed to it can escape its grasp. The precedent for religious subversion accusations lies in the charges made against Catholicism in the nineteenth century. Those who charged Catholicism with putting America in mortal danger stressed, as critics of Islam do today, its incompatibility with democracy and its lack of regard for individual rights and liberties. No Muslim figure parallels that of the pope, since Islam is a decentralized religion, but the charge that Muslims prefer to live in theocracies, autocratic polities controlled by clerics, is similar to the allegation that American Protestants made against Catholics one hundred and fifty years ago.

The defense against stigmatizing entire groups as threats to America lies in the willingness of Americans to insist that charges of political subversion be separated from those of racial or religious subversion, and that the arrest, prosecution, and deportation of individuals be limited to those whose actions, separated from a consideration of race and religion, can be shown to be subversive. Attorney General Palmer was partially stymied in his anti-Red campaign because judges and government officials had the courage to take a stand against his methods. The postwar Red Scare also brought into being the American Civil Liberties Union, an organization committed to fighting illegal campaigns to strip individual Americans and aliens of their rights. The ACLU still exists and has mounted vigorous protests since 2001 against the surveillance and prosecution of Arab and Muslim individuals that exceed the authority vested in the government by the Constitution. Its work draws support from a large number of other groups, ranging from the U.S. Civil Rights Commission to an array of ethnic and racial antidiscrimination organizations larger and more influential than those that existed in 1920. But the counterparts of the judges and government officials who, in 1920, did so much to thwart Attorney General Palmer seem to be in short supply today.[42] And even that robust anti-Palmer opposition, it must be said, did little to stop the campaign for racialized immigration restriction that came on the Red Scare's heels.

In times of war or near war, it is not easy to resist demands for unity, conformity, and homogeneity. And yet, the record of the twentieth century reminds us how important it is for private citizens and public officials to be vigilant in defense of constitutional rights and to resist the temptation to stigmatize entire immigrant groups as threats to the American republic.

GOVERNANCE, IMMIGRATION POLICY, AND SECURITY: CANADA AND THE UNITED STATES POST-9/11

HOWARD ADELMAN

"Before September 11, the conventional wisdom had been that globalization was fast making war obsolete; after September 11, the conventional wisdom was that globalization was making war an all but permanent and inescapable part of life in the twenty-first century," says A.J. Bacevich.[1] Terror itself was not altogether new. The World Trade Center had been attacked almost a decade earlier. The American embassies in Kenya and Tanzania had been bombed. The USS *Cole* had been attacked and disabled.

What was new was mass murder and destruction on American soil by a hidden overseas enemy that had infiltrated the United States. The Weinberger-Powell doctrine of limited objectives with clearly defined outcomes carried out by overwhelming force was set aside for a long-term sustained conflict with no exit strategy or clear precedents for military deployment. The soon to be renamed Operation Infinite Justice was launched as Operation Enduring Freedom. The new Bush doctrine, enunciated by the president with surprising eloquence before a joint session of Congress on September 20, 2001, defined the new war against "terror" and evil as a moral one in terms of the defense of freedom and global, not simply American, democratic values.

The paradoxes became more acute. The war was to be fought in the name of "greater openness," but of markets and the movement of goods, *not* greater openness in the movement of peoples. Though America no longer had a defensive perimeter and its arena of military operations encompassed the whole globe, in the name of home security American borders were now to be sealed in a way that they had never been previously, including the longest undefended border in the world, the demarcation boundary between Canada and the United States. Globalization was more clearly than ever before a euphemism for an American-directed and dominated economic system to which the al Qaeda terrorists were just the most extreme and malignant opponents. It was difficult to separate the war for freedom, liberty, and democracy from the acquisitive interests of American capital.

As a result, instead of making globalization and transnationalism[2] congruent, they were set against each other. Transnational members with links to specific Arab and Islamic countries became objects of suspicion. More generally, the freedom of Americans and of American capital had to trump the freedom and choices of non-American individuals, particularly immigrants—freedoms that they had forged for themselves in their choices, networks, and priorities. These were now to be subordinated to the American imperial thrust. Refugees initially appeared to be the biggest losers as efforts now focused on sending the homeless home and inhibiting their right to move and choose even further.

Transnationals from these Arab and Islamic countries entering the United States from Canada would feel the impact most acutely, but so would Canada as a whole. This chapter explores the contradictory effects of the new era of American moral globalism on Canadian security and immigration policies. It also turned the longest undefended border in the world into a security barrier as Americans after 9/11, at least initially, viewed that porous border as one source of their problems.

BACKGROUND

The beginning of American interest in the security of the Canadian border actually had its origins when the World Trade Center bombers of 1993 appeared to have used forged Canadian immigration papers to gain access to the United States. The interest was reinforced after U.S. customs officials captured Ahmed Ressam in December 1999 trying to enter the United States with a carload of explosives as he tried to cross into Washington State on a ferry from Victoria, British Columbia, with a plan to bomb Los Angeles International Airport. However, pre-9/11, the concern seemed to be more with Canadian laxity on organized crime than on lax security concerning potential terrorists. A year later, a December 2000 headline read, "President Clinton singles out Canadian immigration policies for making it easier for international gangs to conduct illegal activity in the U.S."[3] As Doris Meissner, former commissioner of the U.S. Immigration and Naturalization Service (INS), wrote, "Immigration as a threat to national security was not at or near the top of anyone's list."[4]

Just before 9/11, Mexican president Vincente Fox met with George Bush to declare that integrating and harmonizing the migration issue was a top priority for his country, a view that President Bush endorsed. This was at the same time that a meeting with Canadian immigration officials to discuss coordination and integration with respect to border issues was cancelled by the United States. Harmonization with Canada was indeed not a priority.

The radical shift in emphasis from the Mexican to the Canadian border took place only after 9/11. For example, in the October 4, 2001, edition of the *New York Times,* Sam Howe Verhovek contrasted the former focus on preventing people from wading across the Rio Grande or hiking across the scorching desert that borders the United States and Mexico with the new focus on securing the border between Canada and the United States against terrorists. In contrast to pre-9/11, George Bush on October 29, 2001, ordered his officials to begin harmonizing customs and immigration policies with those of Canada as well as Mexico to ensure "maximum possible compatibility of immigration, customs and visa policies."[5]

Three options were available: a common immigration regime, a common security perimeter, or a defended border. Americans really wanted the second option. They wanted to harmonize security around both countries. However, they initially thought that it would also be necessary to harmonize immigration and refugee policies in order to accomplish that task. Allan Thompson of the *Toronto Star* reported that Canada and the United States were edging toward establishing a common security perimeter by establishing joint screening procedures to stop security threats at the source.[6] His interpretation of government policy was wrong, however. All Immigration Minister Elinor Caplan had said was that "We need to be able to develop a network where we share information overseas so that we can better protect our continent" in implementing a common objective, "stopping those who pose any kind of security threat from coming to Canada or the United States to begin with." Caplan insisted that Canada/U.S. discussions stop short of harmonizing all policies and focus instead on information sharing.[7] "Let there not be any misunderstanding. Canadian laws will be made right here in the Canadian Parliament," Caplan said. However, she had not interpreted the initial American thrust correctly: "This directive from the President of the United States to his people is completely consistent with what our approach has been and that is to share information, not to stop people from coming." The prime minister and other ministers became very skittish even about the phrase "security perimeter," especially since it was initially identified with immigration and refugee policy harmonization.[8]

Paul Cellucci, the U.S. ambassador to Canada, became the most vocal proponent who initially was interpreted as urging the two countries to harmonize their immigration and refugee laws. However, he was misinterpreted. As he clarified himself: "As people come from overseas, we want to have these common security efforts, and the compatibility on security efforts would be helpful. But I don't think anyone is saying you have to have exactly the same immigration policies."[9] One year later, Cellucci's views did not alter one iota. However, his language did.

Instead of speaking of harmonizing policies or establishing a common security perimeter, he now spoke of creating a "zone of confidence." [10]

Belatedly, Canadian legislators expressed support for such a move. The Foreign Affairs and International Trade committee of the House of Commons drafted a report at the end of 2002 entitled, "Partners in North America: Advancing Canada's Relations with the United States and Mexico," suggesting efforts in the past had been reactive rather than proactive and incoherent rather than coherent. The report advocated establishing a North American security perimeter and customs union both to recover Canada's diminished diplomatic status and to enhance Canadian/American diplomatic, trade, and security integration. [11] However, unilateral measures were well underway that would make any effort at creating a common security perimeter much more difficult.

THREE OPTIONS—THE SAFE THIRD COUNTRY AGREEMENT

A discussion of a common security perimeter around Canada and the United States connected to the harmonization of Canadian/American immigration and refugee policies became one of the options after the disastrous events of September 11, 2001. It stressed shifting jurisdiction over immigration and refugees to a transstate level in response to alleged fears that Canada's refugee system was serving as an entry point for terrorists to use Canada as a base for attacking the United States. [12] The issue of governance [13] came to the fore as proposals were made for superstate agencies to assume a significant role and authority in dealing with nonstate actors—immigrants, refugees, and terrorists as well as tourists and business and professional travelers. The alternative second option of a common security perimeter in which immigration and refugee policies would only be harmonized if security was an issue was not clearly proffered until the third option—each country taking care of its own security, cooperating as necessary and desired—became the dominant model.

The Safe Third Country provision was the only legislated effort to harmonize immigration and refugee policies, and it specifically focused on refugees. For many refugees, Canada offers a number of advantages, such as providing virtually immediate access to employment as opposed to waiting six months in the United States. Further, under Canadian asylum procedures, refugees have a 4 to 5 percent better chance of being accepted, largely because the rules governing hearings in Canada give the benefit of the doubt to refugees instead of simply balancing the evidence, as in the United States. However, Canada has far fewer direct flights from abroad and a very stringent overseas interdiction program.

For many refugees, it is much easier to get to Canada by passing through the United States.

The Safe Third Country option had long been present in Canadian legislation with the intention of transfering jurisdictional responsibility for at least 40 percent of refugee claimants in Canada to the United States. After all, only 200 potential claimants traveled from Canada to the United States while well over ten thousand traveled the other way. Prior to 9/11, Canada had been unsuccessful in getting American cooperation on the issue. However, on December 3, 2001, Canada and the United States signed a "Joint Statement of Cooperation on Border Security and Regional Migration Issues" that included a commitment to work toward a Safe Third Country agreement that would significantly reduce or bar access to Canada for refugee claimants passing through the United States. The agreement stated that "We plan to develop the capacity to share such information and to begin discussions on a safe third-country exception to the right to apply for asylum. Such an arrangement would limit the access of asylum seekers, under appropriate circumstances, to the system of only one of the two countries." This provision requires that if claimants passed through a country where they were entitled to make a refugee claim, then they would not be allowed to make a claim in the country of arrival; instead, the refugee would be sent back to the earlier country to make his or her claim. On the same day that Canada's new immigration legislation went into effect, on June 8, 2002, Canada and the United States signed the agreement in principle and initialed a final text of the agreement on August 30, 2002. The Canadian government finally tabled the new regulations of the Safe Third Country provisions providing for the return of refugee claimants entering Canada from the United States on October 25, 2002[14] and introduced the requisite implementation legislation at the beginning of December 2002. Meanwhile, the United States passed its complementary legislation, signed the new agreement into law in December 2002, and began to put into effect its new regulations for implementing its part of the agreement.

The new Safe Third Country regime was expected to have two immediate impacts. First, the number of refugee claimants entering Canada would be reduced by at least one-third, a reduction on top of the already declining numbers of refugee claimants entering Canada.[15] The number making claims in the United States would be increased absolutely by between 10,000 and 12,000.[16]

Secondly, critics in both the United States and Canada not only argued that the new measures reduced access to protection for refugees by diverting part of the influx of refugees into Canada to the United States without enhancing security,[17] they even claimed that the measures would increase rather than diminish the challenge to border controls, requiring enhanced security between Canada and the United States. In other words, the first legislated bilateral arrangement connecting security and refugees would lead to strengthening security barriers *between* the two countries rather than establishing a common security and refugee regime for the two countries. At the same time, it would add to the security burden of the United States as it reduced that of Canada, for the United States would now be responsible for security checks of over 10,000 additional claimants.

In the only real legislated effort to employ option one—harmonizing Canadian and American refugee policy—Canada benefited and the security burden on the United States was enhanced.

U.S. UNILATERALISM

Failing to make progress on a common security perimeter, with or without immigration policy harmonization, the Americans focused on strengthening the border between the two countries. President Bush announced a plan to create a new border security agency in which the U.S. Border Patrol, which had been part of the immigration service, would be merged with the Customs Service, now a part of the Treasury Department, and both placed under the Justice Department. Merging the beleaguered U.S. Immigration and Naturalization Service and the Customs Service into a single agency was intended to tighten border security in response to the September 11 attacks. The initial plan called for consolidation to make it easier for the federal government to oversee the nation's borders, limit border crossings in response to specific threats, and cut out bureaucratic hurdles and wasteful spending by federal agencies with overlapping functions. The clear victory of the Republicans in the midterm elections allowed Bush to have his way. The consolidated Department of Homeland Security was established in November 2002. Instead of opting for a larger transstate security regime, the administration broke up and strengthened the border system without realistically assessing whether such efforts would have any real impact on screening out would-be attackers while not slowing down the approximately 500 million people, over one million trucks, and over two million railway cars that cross the American border each year.

This was but one of many new unilateral American practices that had a direct impact on Canadians in general. It had a much greater impact on specific groups of hyphenated Canadians and landed immigrants. In November 2002, Canada protested the new restrictions imposed by the U.S. State Department on Canadian citizens born in Iran, Iraq, Libya, Sudan, or Syria, as well as the extra special measures for Canadians born in Pakistan, Saudi Arabia, and Yemen; these Canadians were to be subject to photographing and fingerprinting on entering the United States, and sometimes much worse.[18] When Canada issued a public travel advisory[19] suggesting that Canadian citizens born in any of those countries reconsider traveling to the United States, the automatic application of this provision was withdrawn. However, when the Americans announced that this provision would still apply to landed immigrants in Canada from those countries, these landed immigrants did not receive the same Canadian government high-level intervention and eventual public lobbying against the provision. Quite the reverse! On Wednesday, November 6, 2002, the Canadian prime minister, Jean Chretien, said, "If they do not have a Canadian passport, it's no longer my problem. It's their problem. Let them become Canadian citizens, and we will protect them."[20] Further, right after Canada's foreign minister, Bill Graham, had announced in the House of Commons that the United States would not apply these enhanced security measures to Canadian citizens, journalist Victor Malarek detailed the delays of Ms. Tehrani-Ami, a Canadian born in Iran who was traveling with her Canadian-born husband to a conference in the United States.[21] In spite of the Canadian announcement that the United States had withdrawn the application of this "security" measure to citizens, these press stories documented that this provision continued to be applied to Canadian citizens from these countries.[22]

Further, new U.S. rules[23] also required landed immigrants to Canada from almost fifty Commonwealth countries to obtain visitor visas at a cost of $100 to enter the United States.[24] Ambassador Cellucci defended the visa proposal, arguing that the United States was simply standardizing entry requirements for all citizens of certain countries. "If you have a citizenship from a Commonwealth country, the rules will essentially be the same as if you live in that Commonwealth country, because that is your country."[25] Contrary to the statements of the prime minister, Immigration Minister Denis Coderre attacked the proposed U.S. rules on visas and depicted the special attention to landed immigrants from specified countries as "racial profiling." He promised to raise the issue with U.S. officials.

U.S. Attorney General John Ashcroft, speaking at a news conference in Niagara Falls, New York, on November 7, 2002,[26] insisted that Canadians were not exempt from the tough new American screening rules at the border. At the same time, he promised that Canadians crossing into the United States would not automatically be fingerprinted, photographed, and interviewed based on their place of birth. For Ashcroft, these measures did not amount to ethnic profiling.

Following the Republican victory in the midterm elections, the American Senate passed the Homeland Security bill by a vote of 52–47.[27] Canada moved to all-out damage control. On December 5, 2002, the first anniversary of the thirty-point border security agreement, Deputy Prime Minister John Manley,[28] whose relationship with U.S. Homeland Security Secretary Tom Ridge is warm and productive, hosted Ridge for dinner at the Canadian embassy in Washington. Honey works. Ridge assured Canadians that the requirements of new border security measures would not damage the two nations' important connections.[29] Manley was more blunt. He told Canadians that they would just have to get used to tough American scrutiny when crossing the border into the United States.[30] The U.S. homeland security legislation, creating both the largest reorganization of government in over half a century and a huge government department, in fact raised the wall between Canada and the United States rather than creating a common security perimeter.

CANADIAN MEASURES

As the United States unilaterally enhanced security *between* Canada and the United States[31] even as Canadians balked,[32] Canada made a number of moves (regarded by American officials and even many Canadians as half-hearted)[33] to allay American suspicions about Canada being used as a base for terrorists.[34]

EDUCATIONAL MEASURES

In order to disabuse both the Canadian public and Americans that Canada was a source of terror, especially given its refugee system, the Standing Committee on Citizenship and Immigration of the Canadian House of Commons reported on the effects of 9/11 on border and immigration issues. The report, entitled *Hands Across the Border* (henceforth *Hands*) and subtitled *Working Together at our Shared Border and Abroad to Ensure Safety, Security and Efficiency*, with an additional subtitle: *Co-operation, Co-ordination and Partnerships*,[35] noted that just because immigration and border security were being examined together, that fact should not be taken to imply that immigrants or refugees pose a particular risk to Canada. Chapter two of the report went on to say that "Evidence to date indicates that the attacks of September 11th were largely orchestrated and carried out by a group of people who entered the United States legally," and had nothing to do with individuals attempting to enter Canada to win status as refugees.[36]

The opposition parties in the House of Commons generally endorsed the *Hands* report. The Progressive Conservative/Democratic Representative Caucus fully endorsed the argument of *Hands* that the conjunction of refugee and security issues was fallacious. Even the official opposition Canadian Alliance Party, widely and erroneously perceived as an anti-immigration party, affirmed its support for both immigrants and genuine refugees. "The Official Opposition will continue to work with the government to maintain Canada as a nation that welcomes immigrants, and is a country that accepts its internationally fair share of genuine refugees." However, the Canadian Alliance qualified its overall endorsement of the report with the following criticism: "Capacity creates its own demand, for where there is a weakness it will be exploited. The 'refugee system' continues to be exploited by non-refugees and is a grave security concern." In other words, in both the media and among *some* parliamentarians, refugees were focused upon when the security issue came up.

BORDER ENFORCEMENT

Efforts initially were made in the Canadian media to show that the refugee and security issues were *not* conjoined. At the same time, Canada was depicted as being vigilant with suspects. Bill Schiller cited the case of Ary Hussein, who came to Canada to file a refugee claim. He ditched his papers before landing at Pearson airport and landed behind bars after confessing to having once participated in a kidnapping.[37] Besides Ary Hussein, a half-dozen other Middle Eastern people were detained in 2001: Palestinians Mohammed Al Muttan, age nineteen and thirty-five-year-old Ribhi Jamel Sheikha (subsequently released) on September 27, 2001; Hisham Essa, an Egyptian detained August 2 trying to cross from Windsor into the United States at Detroit while hidden in the back of a truck; Mohammed El Shafey, another Egyptian subsequently deported after living in Canada illegally for four years; Ziyad Hussein, a Palestinian with a Jordanian passport detained September 22, 2001, at Pearson when an immigration official did not believe his story that he had come to attend a trade show but wanted to remain in Canada or go to the United States where he has family; and a Palestinian woman from Syria, Reema Nakhleh. The fact is, one of these individuals was detained pre-911 and the others would have been handled the same way if 9/11 had not happened.[38]

Though detailed analysis suggests a discrepancy between America's declared policy (and especially the rhetoric used to justify that policy) and actual practice,[39] America was far more vigorous in its efforts to undercut terrorist cells in that country. Over 2,000 were detained in the United States since 9/11 under the Foreign Intelligence Surveillance Act of 1978, an act that allowed the government to seal warrants of those detained for national security reasons permanently with a judge's consent. Men arrested were allegedly kept from their attorneys and confined in jails without proper food or protection. In contrast to the United States, Canadian civil libertarians only had to be exercised about those detained at the border, and the number of even alleged abuses could be counted on the fingers of one hand.

There is far more to enforcement, however, than simply border checks of individuals. There are two components of enforcement measures: a sign system for identification of legitimacy (e.g., passports, visas, identification cards) and a signal system to detect irregularities (intelligence, monitoring, and inspection). The sign system is undermined by the forging and theft of passports, corruption used to buy visas, and the absence of a system of identity cards prevalent in continental Europe. On September 27, 2001, a report released by Canadian immigration officials indicated that 2,200 misuses of passports occurred between 1998 and 2000. These misuses included altering passports fraudulently, using stolen passports, borrowing passports, and obtaining legitimate passports illegally, the favorite method. Bertoliny Eugene, described in the press as an enterprising student, testified at Ressam's trial that he had obtained five other passports 'easily' in addition to the one he supplied Ressam, and only received $300 for each of them. Another supplier also testified that passports were very easy to obtain and that he sold them for $800 each. I have no evidence that this situation has been improved.

Other areas of cooperation and coordination between the two countries include intelligence and law-enforcement coordination, visa screening abroad, preclearance of flights abroad, and the sharing of passenger information before planes arrive at an airport. On the bureaucratic front, there has been progress in cooperation in all these areas. One important area of coordination is the intent to work toward a common list of countries exempt from visa requirements. A day after Canada and the United States signed a joint border and immigration accord on December 4, 2001, Canada imposed visa requirements on the following countries: Dominica, Grenada, Kiribati, Nauru, Tuvalu, Vanuatu—six small island states[40]—as well as Zimbabwe and Hungary. Although a small percentage of Roma (also called Gypsies) have been accepted as refugees, Hungary was included because Roma from Hungary continually arrive in Canada to become refugee claimants. However, a majority of Zimbabweans who reach Canada to make a refugee claim are successful even though the introduction of a visa requirement has already deterred many Zimbabweans from arriving, many of whom may well be genuine refugees. Hungary and Zimbabwe were among the top ten countries producing claimants between January and September of 2001.[41] Though these measures would do something to reduce the refugee intake into Canada, they seemed to have little to do with security concerns. Further, even with the addition of those eight countries, the Canadian list of countries exempt from visa requirements is still over 50 percent larger than the American one.

DOMESTIC MEASURES

Canada did not seem to be taking extraordinary steps to check for the supporting systems for terrorists using charitable organizations. In fact, the Canadian government sometimes bent over backward to demonstrate that Arabs and Muslims were *not* being targeted. The government went further. In spite of Hezbollah and Hamas openly declaring their responsibility for terrorist attacks, and the Canadian Security Intelligence Service (CSIS) branding both as terrorist organizations,[42] the Canadian government delayed delisting them as charitable organizations, let alone freezing their assets in Canada, until, in response to public pressure, Hamas[43] and several other charities were delisted. The government argued, correctly, that these organizations have worthwhile charitable functions. However, it never refuted the widespread evidence that the charitable fundraising of these organizations had been used as fronts for recruitment and for raising money for militant and political activities. Initially, Bill Graham, the Canadian foreign minister, refused, in spite of public pressure, to list Hezbollah as an illegal terrorist organization[44] in spite of widespread allegations that Imad Mugniyah[45] directed a terrorist cell and/or network in Canada.[46] Further, Fawzi Ayoub (alias Mohammed Mustafa Ayub, or Abu Abbas), a Canadian citizen who immigrated to Canada from Lebanon in 1988, has been held in an Israel jail accused of being a senior Hezbollah militant and a trained explosives expert who planned sophisticated terrorist attacks on Israel using a forged U.S. passport.[47] There were others: a Syrian-born Canadian whom the United States deported back to Syria without formally consulting Canada, a Kuwait-born Canadian captured in Oman and now held at Guantanamo Bay. Nevertheless, none of these were refugees. Each of them held Canadian citizenship.

The Canadian government avoided looking closely at Canadian citizens and Arab organizations (though Canadian agencies had no such reluctance) that might pose security threats, but finally took action after considerable pressure. Hezbollah was eventually made illegal.

LEGISLATION

Other than greater bureaucratic cooperation on some fronts, Canadian border measures seemed little different prior to 9/11. Where different, they seemed to have more to do with reducing the refugee intake than enhancing security. Canadian domestic measures against charitable organizations supporting terrorism moved with alacrity. If educational measures were hyped to establish Canadian innocence of complicity, Canadian new legislative measures seemed more forceful. The House of Commons report, *Refugee Protection and Border Security:*

Striking a Balance, was tabled in the House of Commons in March 2000. Bill C-11: The Immigration and Refugee Protection Act contained clauses related to refugees and security issues, such as provisions for condensing the security certificate protection procedure. These clauses were drafted before 9/11, though the bill received Royal Assent on November 1, 2001, to come into force in June 2002. Thus, in Canada, the Immigration and Refugee Protection Act already evinced a significant concern with security. The same could be said of the United States. The *Krouse-Perla Report* to the American Congress on terrorism and recognition technology was tabled on June 18, 2001, almost three months before 9/11. It specifically referred to refugees as potential terrorists.

Though this appeared to be carrying forward what had already been planned, new elements were added in response to the radically changed environment after 9/11; the legislature seemed determined to pass legislation that would have a direct impact on reducing terror. In the fall of 2001 in the aftermath of 9/11, Parliament passed into law "An Act to amend the Criminal Code, the Official Secrets Act, the Canada Evidence Act, the Proceeds of Crime (Money Laundering) Act and other Acts, and to enact measures respecting the registration of charities, in order to combat terrorism." Part 1 of the bill amended the criminal code to implement international conventions related to terrorism, to create offenses related to terrorism, including the financing of terrorism and the participation, facilitation, and carrying out of terrorist activities, and to provide a means by which property belonging to terrorist groups, or property linked to terrorist activities, can be seized, restrained, and forfeited. After passage of the bill, the cabinet approved new regulations freezing the assets of twenty-two groups and individuals with links to Middle Eastern terrorism. Part 2 transformed the Official Secrets Act into the Security of Information Act to address threats of espionage by foreign powers and terrorist groups, as well as economic espionage and coercive activities against émigré communities in Canada. It also created new offenses to counter intelligence-gathering activities by foreign powers and terrorist groups, including the unauthorized communication of special operational information. In contrast to all these provisions that raised the possibility of infringements on human rights, Part 1 also provided for the deletion of hate propaganda from public web sites and created an offense relating to damage to property associated with religious worship.

Part 3 contained the provisions that truly frightened civil libertarians. These amendments to the Canada Evidence Act were criticized extensively by human rights lawyers and organizations because they obligated parties in legal proceedings to notify the attorney general of Canada if they anticipated the disclosure of sensitive information, the disclosure of which could be injurious to international relations, national defense, or security. Moreover, it gave the attorney general powers to assume carriage of a prosecution and to prohibit the disclosure of information in connection with a proceeding for the purpose of protecting international relations, national defense, or security. Part 4 updated a previous act and renamed it the Proceeds of Crime (Money Laundering) and Terrorist Financing Act, which provided for assisting law enforcement and investigative agencies in the detection and deterrence of the financing of terrorist activities, facilitating the investigation and prosecution of terrorist activity financing offenses, and improving Canada's ability to cooperate internationally in the fight against terrorism. Part 5 amended a number of other acts to strengthen the security apparatus of the Canadian government, while Part 6 enacted the Charities Registration (Security Information) Act, and amended the Income Tax Act to prevent those who support terrorist or related activities from enjoying the tax privileges granted to registered charities.

In addition, the Public Safety Act, passed in the post 9/11 period, includes in Part 9 amendments to the current Immigration Act as a way of implementing some of the provisions before Bill C-42 came into effect. These include provisions for stopping a refugee proceeding if a claimant is discovered to be a member of an inadmissible class or under a removal order. According to a Transport Canada backgrounder on the bill, under the amendments, refugee determination proceedings before the Immigration and Refugee Board (IRB) can be suspended or terminated if there are reasonable grounds to believe that the claimant is a terrorist, senior official of a government engaged in terrorism, or a war criminal. The changes also implement the requirement for airlines to provide information on passengers before arrival and for penalties for those engaged in trafficking or assisting illegal entrants. The bill provides stiff increases in penalties for those who engage in human trafficking and smuggling; those convicted face fines of up to $1 million and/or prison sentences for life. Aggravating factors can be considered in sentencing, such as whether the offense was undertaken for profit or in association with a criminal organization, and whether it resulted in bodily harm or degrading treatment.

Much of this legislation was criticized because it seemed to undercut much of the Privacy Act (1980-81-82-83, c. 111, Sch. Ii) intended to protect the privacy of individuals with respect to personal information about themselves held by a government institution and to restrict access to that information. In Article 1 of the Privacy Act, a government institution can only collect personal information *directly* from the individual to whom it relates, unless otherwise authorized by that individual or under subsection 8(2). Article 2 requires a government institution to inform any individual from whom the institution collects personal information of the purpose for which the information is being collected. The new legislation takes the position that the laws that protect the privacy of citizens also hinder law enforcement. Human rights defenders argued that the new laws that enhance law enforcement infringe on rights of privacy. For example, information under previous laws could not be shared between Revenue Canada (the department that collected income tax and the information on the income tax filing forms) and the RCMP without administrative warrant.

The expansion of law-enforcement powers to arrest, detain, and force those arrested to talk, and other initiatives, all challenge the core tenets of civil liberties and the restrictions to police powers at the core of our conception of democracy.[48] However, although Canada witnessed a great deal of formal movement in law, there were few changes in practice.[49]

COURTS

The NGO refugee support groups were just as exercised about the actions of the Supreme Court of Canada as over legislation. Why? After all, in the Suresh case,[50] the Supreme Court of Canada overruled on January 11, 2002, the decision of the Lower and Federal Appeal Court denying Manickavasagam Suresh, a Convention refugee from Sri Lanka, landed immigrant status. In 1995 Suresh was turned down on security grounds and deportation was initiated based on the opinion of the Canadian Security Intelligence Service (CSIS) that he was a member and fund-raiser of the Liberation Tigers of Tamil Eelam (LTTE), an organization alleged to be engaged in terrorist activity in Sri Lanka. However, the court decision was made on a technicality: Suresh had not been provided with a copy of the immigration officer's memorandum, nor with an opportunity to respond to it orally or in writing.

Although the request for appeal was accepted and the department was ordered to rehear the case on the grounds of procedural concerns, the government won on the key issues. The Court held that the Immigration Act was constitutional provided that the minister exercised her discretion in accordance with the act, and that the right to life, liberty, and security and freedoms of expression and association were not violated. Engagement in acts of violence was not protected by the freedom of expression and freedom of association safeguards of the charter. The phrase "danger to the security of Canada" and the term "terrorism" were not perceived by the Court as unconstitutionally vague. Procedural protections did apply when a refugee established a *prima facie* case that there was a risk of torture on deportation, a threshold that Suresh met. Thus, although the Court ruled that Suresh had been denied the required procedural safeguards and should have been provided with the material upon which the minister based her decision and an opportunity to respond in writing, the Court also held that a discretionary decision in this sphere may only be set aside if it is patently unreasonable in the sense that it was made arbitrarily or in bad faith, cannot be supported on the evidence, or the minister failed to consider the appropriate factors. Likewise, the minister's decision on whether a refugee faces a substantial risk of torture upon deportation should be overturned only if it is not supported on the evidence or fails to consider the appropriate factors. The court should not reweigh the factors or interfere merely because it would have come to a different conclusion. So as long as the minister follows the procedural instructions, Suresh is likely to be deported on the next round. The Court strengthened the hands of the bureaucracy's right to report.

The media response to the ruling was even more interesting. For example, the *Vancouver Sun* of January 14, 2002 applauded the ruling for loosening the "deportation knot" in determining that refugees facing torture can be deported in exceptional circumstances; the pattern of the Court placing obstacles in the way of the government had been reversed. Presciently, the editorial also opined that the length of the refugee determination process was a security threat in itself.

In the case of Mansour Ahani,[51] the issue was more straightforward and the case is really a footnote to that of *Suresh*. The appellant was a citizen of Iran who entered Canada on October 14, 1991 and was granted Convention refugee status based on his fear of persecution due to his political opinions and membership in a particular social group. However, the CSIS suspected that Ahani was a member of the Iranian Ministry of Intelligence Security (MOIS), which sponsors a wide range of terrorist activities, including the assassination of political dissidents worldwide. CSIS also believed that Ahani received specialized training in the MOIS that qualified him as an assassin. Ahani was contacted by an Iranian intelligence official, allegedly a commander of the MOIS, whom he met in Zurich, Switzerland, traveling on a false passport. Both traveled separately, and met again in Fermignano, Italy, apparently home to a number of Iranian dissidents. Ahani returned to Switzerland, then traveled to Istanbul, Turkey, where he obtained another false passport and returned to Canada. Upon his return to Canada, Ahani met with CSIS agents. CSIS alleges that during those meetings, Ahani admitted that his military training was part of his recruitment into the MOIS, and that the intelligence officer he met in Europe was a previous associate.

The minister of Citizenship and Immigration filed a security certificate (s. 40.1) with the Federal Court Trial Division, alleging that Ahani was a member of the inadmissible classes described in the antiterrorism provisions of the Immigration Act [ss. 19(1)(*e*)(iii), 19(1)(*e*)(iv)(C), 19(1)(*f*)(ii), 19(1)(*f*)(iii)(B), and 19(1)(*g*)]. Ahani was arrested under s. 40.1(2)(*b*) of the Act and has remained in custody ever since. The Court determined that Ahani had not cleared the evidentiary threshold required to access the s. 7 protection guaranteed by the Canadian Charter of Rights and Freedoms. Further, as in the case of *Suresh,* the provisions allowing the minister of Citizenship and Immigration to deport a refugee for membership in a terrorist organization were determined not to unjustifiably infringe Charter rights of freedom of expression and association because the appellant failed to make a *prima facie* case that there was a substantial risk of torture upon deportation. Unlike *Suresh,* the minister provided ample evidence in the record to support the discretionary decision that the appellant constituted a danger to the security of Canada. The minister's decision was found to be reasonable, and no error was committed that required the intervention of the court.

The third case was that of Muhammad Zeki Muhammad Mahjoub, who was allegedly in imminent risk of being forcibly returned to Egypt by the Canadian authorities, where he would be at grave risk of torture and an unfair trial as well as subject to other serious human rights violations. The Egyptian government claimed he was part of the leadership in exile of the armed Islamist group Tali'at al-Fatah (Vanguard of the Conquest); he was so charged and was sentenced in absentia in April 1999 to fifteen years' imprisonment by the Supreme Military Court. Mahjoub has been in custody in Canada since June 2000 under a ministerial security certificate in which Mahjoub was named as a threat to Canada and detained pending possible deportation. In spite of the *Suresh* ruling, or perhaps as much in response to it, the NGO refugee support community remained totally at odds with the government in the tension between human rights protection and security concerns.

PUBLIC OPINION AND ECONOMICS—TOWARD A COMMON SECURITY PERIMETER

There are countervailing forces moving Canada toward a common security perimeter with the United States. Immediately after 9/11, public opinion seemed to indicate great sensitivity to the security issue. In the United States, the security issue was initially identified with immigrants and refugees. Though the 9/11 terrorists evidently entered the United States legally as visa students and not as immigrants or even refugee claimants, and a few had resided there for some years, according to a nationwide poll in the United States, two-thirds of those polled (68 percent) believed that enforcement of immigration laws and the border had been too lax. They believed that not enough was being done to control the border and vet prospective immigrants, thus allowing terrorists to enter the country easily. In the media, both in the United States and Canada, the weak-link thesis often focused on Canada.[52]

Initially, a poll conducted for the Council for Canadian Unity indicated that the support for reduced immigration rose immediately after 9/11 from 29 percent to 45 percent. However, an even larger percentage, 80 percent according to Léger Marketing, demanded stricter controls over immigration. This perception shifted as time went on. In an Ipsos-Reid Poll (May 10, 2002), although three-quarters (77 percent) of Americans believed that potential terrorists slipped into the United States through Canada, interestingly enough the blame was no longer placed on Canada. The majority (72 percent) of Americans blamed U.S. immigration and border security. Even more Canadians than Americans (81 percent) believed that potential terrorists slipped into the United States from Canada. More Canadians than Americans blamed Canada. Further, although a slim majority (52 percent) of Canadians disputed allegations that Canada had become a terrorist "haven," only 42 percent specifically blamed Canada's Immigration and Refugee rules, far fewer than the Americans who blamed their own border security apparatus. Thirty-two percent of Canadians believed that the most blame should be on U.S. immigration and border security, though 20 percent indicated that blame for these incidents lie on both sides of the forty-ninth parallel.

The big issue in Canada came to be its economic relationship with the United States and not the fear of terrorists. Business leaders experienced this most acutely. A key finding from week 1 of the *Financial Post*/Chamber of Commerce/CIBC Survey of CEOs and business leaders found that business leaders agreed that a common perimeter was essential for the Canadian economy (October 26, 2001). The overwhelming majority was convinced that it is at least somewhat essential (17 percent), if not very essential (36 percent) or extremely essential (38 percent) for the Canadian government to harmonize with U.S. rules and practices. Eighty-five percent supported making changes to create a joint North American security perimeter and 70 percent supported joint border posts staffed by Canada and U.S. officials instead of the existing separate Canadian and American posts.

Thus, if the antiterrorist legislation raised the ire and fears of civil libertarians, the lack of action by Canada raised much greater fears in the economic sector of the civil society, not so much because of the effect of the terrorism, but because of how the American response impacted the Canadian economy. Before 9/11, anxious Canadians and barely interested Americans had been moving to integrate their economies even more than they had been. Other than the outpouring of sympathy for Americans, post-911 effects were most acutely felt at the long delays at border points for both people and goods. The pressure to enhance border harmonization to ease the obstacles to the free flow of goods, services, and trustworthy people between Canada and the United States had never been greater, and seemed far more important to most Canadians than the security issue itself.[53] As a headline in the *Globe and Mail* screamed: "Waits at U.S. Border Hurting Economy, B.C. Premier Says."[54] The *National Post* added, "Perimeter Will Save Trade: CEOs—74% Say We Need Common Security Rules as Worries Mount Over Access to Key Market."[55]

The economic sector tried to make sure that the Canadian/U.S. border played a minimal role in interfering with the transport of goods and the movement of citizens across the border. This concern was evident in the smart-border declaration signed by Foreign Minister John Manley and Tom Ridge, the U.S. director of Homeland Security, that included provisions for the long-standing efforts of Canada to create joint customs preclearance for commercial cargos and jointly operated customs facilities at remote border points that are not examined in this paper.

The real effort, however, was being expended elsewhere. Instead of making the free flow of goods and services across the border easier, reinforced security measures were being implemented along the border dividing Canada and the United States. What was once the longest undefended border was becoming a security barrier. As United States Border Patrol official, Robert Finley, chief agent for a nearly 500-mile stretch of the United States–Canadian border from the Continental Divide in Montana to North Dakota, was quoted in an article by Sam Howe Verhovek in the October 4, 2001 *New York Times* as saying, "There are all kinds of means to get across the prairie illegally. People use bicycles here; they drive in on snowmobiles. They come over by horseback." The result was that a border that previously had very few guards was manned; agent numbers along the border initially were tripled (from 300 to 900 in contrast to the 8,000 American agents along the U.S.–Mexican border) to close up the open prairie and to step up security checks at busy border crossings, with enormous resultant delays. By March 2002, there were 6,000 trained and armed agents assigned to the American side, a thirtyfold increase and scheduled to grow even larger. In November 2002, barriers were being erected at otherwise unguarded roads in remote areas of New Brunswick, where the border sometimes ran through a town.[56] The longest undefended border had become very defended indeed.

This contrasts with the previous emphasis under NAFTA (the North American Free Trade Agreement) on making the border as unobtrusive as possible, to create what the Canadian Minister of National Revenue in 1996, David Anderson, dubbed "a hassle-free border for honest travelers and businesses" to facilitate the world's largest bilateral trade, reportedly now at $420 billion a year. The installation of retinal recognition imagery to facilitate the fast movement of those who cross the border frequently is being planned, but has still not been launched. However, even as moves are implemented directed at facilitating faster movement of goods and people, the priority has focused on tighter security *between* the two countries.

SEEKING AN EXPLANATION

Three options were available to deal with the conjunction of security and immigration issues. Harmonization of immigration and refugee policy was one. In that sphere, the Safe Third Country Agreement was passed and has been implemented. It simply shifted almost half of Canada's refugee asylum problem (and the security issues related thereto) to the United States. A second option entailed developing a common security perimeter. This idea was tripped up, however, when it was confused with the integration model that assaulted Canadian nationalistic sensibilities. A combination of understandable urgency and an American gung ho approach led to separate and complementary unilateral measures that simply strengthened the security measures *between* the two countries that leave in place significant obstacles to developing a common security perimeter even though it is far more efficient and effective to check a very small proportion of those entering either Canada or the United States (both countries still have to do that) than to check all the people and goods traveling between the two countries.

Why was this least desirable outcome the result? Further, why was a fuller harmonization option not even seriously considered given that globalization,[57] reinforced by regional security issues, reduces the capacity of nation-states to have an independent immigration and refugee policy? In response to globalization and the need to develop regional security arrangements, higher (as well as lower) levels of shared jurisdiction—otherwise called multilevel governance—have to be developed and incorporated into domestic law to deal with immigration and refugee issues.

The overarching tension between the issue of governance within the context of enhanced globalization was countered by the desire of a state—Canada—to exercise sovereignty. Canada's choices were also impacted by the unilateral action of a megapower within the context of an emerging new imperial model. Canadians take shelter under and play a minor role in the American security umbrella while Canada defines its foreign policy in terms of a human security agenda in which Canada plays a lead role internationally on a multilateral stage. Thus,

Canadian foreign policy founded on multilateralism is at odds with American policy in which multilateralism is used only if it reinforces American interests and goals.

In addition to globalization and American military global power, Canadian sovereignty, in particular the desire to guard Canada's economic sovereignty, vies with bilateral economic integration. Given that 87 percent of Canadian trade is now with the United States, there is a drive to make sure that the Canada/U.S. border plays a minimal role in interfering with the transport of goods and the movement of citizens across the same border. However, the model of economic bilateral economic integration has always been at odds with an alternative model of economic subordination in which the economic interests of the imperial power always trump if economic integration threatens imperial dominance.

Canadian foreign and economic policy is torn among competing forces—a floundering state-centered conception, a bilateral one that puts primary stress on Canada/U.S. relations as equal partners, a multilateral one in which Canada plays an independent and, indeed, leading role on the world stage, but in a radically different way than America, or one that bows to the dominance of the imperial center. Different nonstate actors pose the major challenge to each of the alternative paths. Tension exists between the physical protection of Canadian citizens and their economic enhancement and two competing concerns—the protection of refugees and the protection of the citizens of the imperial power.

It should be no surprise that it is on the frontier of the ideal and the real, on the boundary between the private ideal and the public reality, that the physical border of the nation-state serves as the line on which the contradictions of the modern system become most apparent. The modern sovereign state vested power in its members as a collectivity and promised to protect its members as individuals. The system would only work within a global system of states where each individual was a member of a democratic state dedicated to the protection of the rights of its citizens. That meant that at the interstices of the system in which democratic states interacted with states not governed by a sovereign people where individual rights were not protected, individuals who fled such states could demand in principle the protection of states that were governed by such principles. As they increasingly did so, and as dissenters rallied to an alternative and reactionary transcendental global ideal under the banner of the radical Islamists, two perceived threats to the security of individuals within democratic states emerged. It is no surprise that the threat from terrorists and the threat of refugees claiming rights protection at the border were merged as the major threat to the security of the modern state. Instead of the boundary between internal reason and public rational space, between sovereign democratic states and authoritarian ones, serving as the launch pad for the expanding modernity's importation of a transcendental ideal, the border served to expose the bankruptcy of the contradictions between the ideal and the real. Fear, not rational debate, concerns with security and survival and not self-legislating moral agents, determined that coercive power rather than reason would adjudicate these problems. The treatment of refugees became the litmus test and early-warning indicator of the new emerging imperial order in combat with its transcendental religious challengers.[58]

The framework of tensions can be represented as follows:

Governance:	Global	vs	Sovereign State	vs	Mega-State
Protection:	Refugees	vs	Citizens	vs	Americans
Economics:	Integration	vs	Autonomy	vs	Subordination
Security:	Human	vs	State	vs	Empire
Impacts					
Foreign Policy:	Multilateral	vs	Bilateral	vs	Unilateral
Impactors					
Nonstate Actors:	Antiglobalization NGOs	vs	Human Rights NGOs	vs	Global Terrorists

CONCLUSION

Immigration and refugee policy has not been harmonized between Canada and the United States. Nor are there any indications that they will be. But neither has a common security perimeter been developed. The state sector—in particular, the bureaucracy—has been expanded at the expense of the role of substate actors, NGOs, and superstate institutions. Further, that bureaucracy has grown but it has fragmented as well.[59] In fact, all elements of governance have fragmented both with respect to the relations between various parts of the state sector as well as between the state and different elements in the civil society. The legislative foundation for reconciling security and immigration is in disarray. The courts have reinforced the role of bureaucracy, but the bureaucracy has an even larger challenge while it has itself become divided. There is little sign that the governments of the United States and Canada have in the works proposals to develop a multilevel system of governance in response to the challenges of reconciling human rights with security concerns.

The bottom line: Refugee protection has declined with little evidence of significantly enhanced security for Canadian citizens. Instead of transstate agreements to enhance protection of refugees, bilateral agreements shift the burden of protection from Canada to the United States with an agreement to enhance security measures. Though, in reality there was little security threat coming from the refugee entry system, the enhanced efforts to beef up security have been largely unilateral with little movement in the direction of transborder measures. Contrary to all the early talk about harmonization of refugee and immigration policy or even the more modest goal of creating a common security perimeter, the major changes enhance United States unilateral measures to secure the Canadian/U.S. border.[60] And what has been introduced has been at the cost of Canadian citizens or landed immigrants born in specific countries in the Middle or Far East. The interests of the imperial center have trumped any global perspectives under the presumed argument that America after 9/11 has woken from a ten-year sleep to once again discover that the world is a tough neighborhood in which America had better watch out for its own interests first and foremost. So much for the human security agenda of Canada! In the face of hidden and gathering danger rather than a clear and present one, America is now determined to get its enemies. In what George Bush accurately first described as a crusade, a term later abandoned lest it alienate Muslims, refugees and Canadian foreign policy can and have been sacrificed. At the same time, Canadian restrictionism is allowed to grow and both countries are losers.

PRAETORIAN PASSAGES:
CENTRAL ASIA AT THE EDGE OF WAR

PAULA R. NEWBERG

Beware of festering inner wounds, for inner wounds surface in the end. Distress no one insofar as you are able, for one cry of anguish can upset the whole world.

—ZAHIRUDDIN MUHAMMAD BABUR, *BABURNAMA*[1]

Among its provocative conjectures for 2003, the *Economist* predicted that central Asia's long-entrenched autocracies are bound to change. "Passions are stirring," it noted, and the region's five states "are all ripe for a sudden change, either to better governments or to ones that are even worse."[2] Its forecast is slightly off-center: conventional wisdom suggests that the global antiterrorism campaign would reinforce the rule of the already powerful, not create conditions for their passing. (It proffered this familiar argument about Pakistan's wearisome, frozen governance.) But the implications for central Asia are intriguing and enticing: that pressure from the western-led antiterrorism coalition, critical to political survival in central Asia, can have the effect variously of supporting aging dictators, confining their agendas, or even opening the political arena. Such projections reverse usual analyses of alliance politics: idealists are inclined to argue that the ambitions of the international coalition, and especially the United States, are essentially imperial; realists of the *Economist*'s sort suggest that even empires can tolerate a bit of uncertainty and leave open the possibility of political change.

The global antiterrorism campaign conducted in the shadow of Afghanistan's devastating wars has reempowered central Asian leaders who frequently veer toward the retrogressive. It therefore may seem counterintuitive to imagine political progress in central Asia as an outcome of the coalition antiterror campaign. After all, Afghanistan has struggled through decades of proxy wars and internecine fighting against odds set by its praetorian neighbors, and in turn, has defined central and south Asia's security environment for decades. But, as the *Economist*'s forecast implies, it is possible to imagine a more interesting central Asia, defined less by continual war and more by efforts to end it, a region literally re-formed in the space created by Afghanistan's reconstruction. This could come about in at least two ways. On the one hand, by altering traditional patterns of trade, investment, migration, and development, it is possible to think about

Afghanistan's recovery as a first step in the political recovery and liberalization of Afghanistan's neighbors.[3] On the other hand, looking beyond the immediate needs of the antiterrorism campaign and thinking imaginatively about real security across the region, the western-led coalition could alter radically the behavior of states from the Caspian Sea to Calcutta and in so doing, change some of the burdensome assumptions about nation-states that have so often led Asia to war. In both instances, the ancillary effects of the international antiterrorism campaign could, under these circumstances, override liberal objections to the international antiterrorism campaign by opening political opportunity among Afghanistan's neighbors.

It is also possible, of course, to imagine worse scenarios for central Asia, as failed or imploding states, increasing violent societies or countries embedded in perilous stagnation. But current events make it hard to jump too far ahead of the limits of war. Two years after the Bonn Agreement opened the door for a new government in Afghanistan, that country is caught among incompatible, competing demands that are extremely difficult to mediate. Coalition forces still wage war against the remnants of al Qaeda, the Taliban, and warlords who resist the rule of central government. Scarcity, deprivation, and the relative absence of economic opportunity mute the ambitions of the Afghan government and equally limit economic development among its neighbors. And the prerequisites for serious political reform in the states bordering Afghanistan are not only still incomplete, but in some states their absence contributes to a climate of pervasive fear and insecurity as well.

INTERSECTING EMPIRES

Today's central Asia descends from thousands of years of grand migrations, conquest, and state building. Contemporary central Asia lies—politically, economically, strategically, and geographically—at the heart of Eurasia's first empires. From Mongolia and China to Hungary, central Asia's migrating conquerors became dynasts of great reckoning, and turned Eurasia into a global economic force. Mongol armies, taxation systems, and bureaucracies made it possible to conquer vast nomadic steppes and settled agrarian lands and, in so doing, maintain the world's largest land empire.[4] Imperial intersections created the structures for the modern era: the Delhi sultanates set the stage for Afghanistan's interactions with the Indian subcontinent, the Moghal empire organized the great migrations of peoples and religions that joined north India to central Asia, and the British fixed the foundations of modern states in south Asia through a deft combination of military force and adroit administration. Later, the Soviet empire assembled a patchwork of states as an overlay on the political ecology of the Moghals, Marxist nationalities and language policies, and Russian-based realpolitik.

Afghanistan's past three decades of war have been prosecuted on a political map borne of these intersecting empires. Although many modern observers look at the anti-Soviet war of the 1980s and the anarchic forces unleashed in its aftermath as a replay of the Great Game between Russia and England in the nineteenth century,[5] the roots of contemporary conflict lie as significantly in the making of earlier empires, and particularly in the rule of the Moghals. Indeed, the dimensions of Afghanistan's late twentieth-century wars spanned almost precisely the contours of Babur's sixteenth-century domain. This was the landscape on which the Durrani and Ghilzai tribes conquered Afghanistan itself and made it possible for Mohammed Abdur Rahman Khan to unify the Afghan state in the nineteenth century. The ties and displacements that defined empire, as well as the resentments of conquest from the Moghal period, became the fault lines of today's politics.

Central and south Asia are not tied by a natural political economy, as romantics might argue, as much as by political relationships spawned in imperial economies. But the Cold War sliced the region in two. The independence of India and Pakistan in 1947 arrived with the Cold War, and with it the mutual inaccessibility of central and south Asia. Afghanistan, the historical crossroads between the two regions, became the focus of superpower competition, and with Pakistan and Iran, choreographed security and assistance relationships with the United States that anchored west Asia during the early Cold War period.[6]

Nevertheless, the borders between and among these countries remained perilously insecure. In Baluchistan—like Kurdistan, spread across many borders, with tribal loyalties more potent than national allegiance—antistate rebellions were spawned in Pakistan, Afghanistan, and Iran during the 1970s. The Baloch insurgency in Pakistan was put down by Zia ul Haq, the same military officer who as army chief later displaced civilian rule and led Pakistan through the anti-Soviet war in Afghanistan. The Durand Line between Afghanistan and Pakistan, set by the British and persistently contested by Afghanistan, demarcated a zone of mutual vulnerability where Pukhtun border tribes, rather than state functionaries, continued to exercise power even after Pakistan's independence. The writ of the state there is still more formal than real. In 2001, the same border tribes were important interlocutors as Afghanistan and Pakistan sought to stabilize a relationship bitterly torn by Pakistan's support for the Taliban. Only in 2002 did Pakistan's military government accede to U.S. demands to enforce a security cordon in these Taliban-supporting areas; it encountered virulent opposition, both to specific policies and more generally to central government prerogatives. The enforcement of border controls (and the contentious problem of hot pursuit provoked by the international coalition) proved potent in elections in 2002 that brought Islamist parties to power in Baluchistan and the Northwest Frontier Province.[7]

Afghanistan's northern borders have proved fertile political proving grounds as well. During the Soviet period, central Asia's socialist republics were subsidized by Moscow as eastern and southern buffer states. Old ties were cut: Uzbek and Tajik majority areas were separated by the Afghan border, it became almost impossible to trespass the mountain passes between Kashmir and central Asia, and Afghanistan became a literal buffer between the Soviet Union and the West. A psychology of separation, emphasized by central Asia's remoteness from Moscow and a version of the iron curtain to the south, was compounded by continuing war in Afghanistan. And although India and Pakistan believed that the independence of central Asian states in 1991 would foster an era of active trade and revive social relations that had been cut decades before, the Afghanistan war was an obstacle to these ambitions as well.

In 1991, the newly endowed political independence of central Asia's five states, the possibility of political change in Iran, and the brief renewal of civilian leadership in Pakistan seemed optimistically to presage a new era at the heart of Asia. Anarchy, war, and the rise of the Taliban movement in Afghanistan, however, prevented stability and prosperity, reinforced praetorian habits among the region's leaders, and magnified the region's inherited security threats into global terrors. The Tajikistan civil war and civil unrest in Uzbekistan found convenient footholds among Afghanistan's fighting factions: at times, it was difficult to determine in which direction central Asia's security threats were migrating, and toward whom. With the rise of the Taliban in the 1990s, however, Tajik- and Uzbek-backed factions renewed their claims to central leadership, and their critical cooperation in the international coalition offered them the opportunity to regain power in Kabul in the autumn of 2001.

WARS OF MANY HUES

The Soviet intervention in Afghanistan in late 1979 followed a period of instability within southwest Asia and in Afghanistan itself. The downfall of the Afghan monarchy and its Communist successor government, the cultivation by Pakistan of an Islamist Afghan opposition, the Iranian revolution and the Teheran hostage crisis, war between Iran and Iraq, the *coup d'etat* that brought military rule to Pakistan after only a few years of civilian government, the downfall of India's prime

minister and ruling party: the accumulation of these events, each multiply determined, led to a profound security crisis across Asia's southern and western flanks.
Each element of crisis reflected discontent in the region's varied domestic politics; each also influenced, and was influenced by, the region's changing economic
role. Given the long-term strategic importance of Pakistan and Iran, the war in
Afghanistan seemed a smaller, local affair until the United States determined to
use it as a way to bring down the Soviet Union. Once that decision was made, the
security map of the region was, in effect, redrawn. Chipping away at the under-
belly of the Soviet Union—the center of an "arc of crisis"—the United States and
its allies used the whole of Afghanistan as the front line, and brought down the
Soviet state.[8]

When the last Soviet troops departed Afghanistan in 1989, many foreign observers assumed that war had ended. Afghans knew better. The problems that
provoked civil strife in the 1960s and 1970s—disputes about the reach of the
Afghan state, its modernizing ideologies and changing foreign policies—were re-
visited on Afghanistan in the wake of the anti-Soviet war.[9] Competing parties
and leaders, all with foreign patrons, took after each other and ultimately wore
down the Communist government and then one another. Between the Geneva
Accords in 1988 and the advent of the Taliban movement in late 1994, claimants
to Afghan leadership managed to destroy almost everything that had not already
perished during the anti-Soviet war.

In the same period, Afghanistan's neighbors, competitors, former patrons,
and future interlocutors rethought their assumptions about regional security.
The results were neither consistent nor heart-warming. Afghanistan's immediate
neighbors and most important intermediaries viewed the failed Afghan state as
the source of lethal contagions like narcotics and arms, a pass-through for parallel economies, a barrier to commercial progress, the victim of foreign ambitions,
and a partner for evolving transnational nonstate and antistate actors. As the Taliban movement gained strength and territory, Afghanistan began to define insecurity for the region.

In large measure, the region's profound disquiet emerged from two kinds of
migration. First, war in Afghanistan produced the world's largest refugee population. Millions of Afghans moved to the border areas of Pakistan and Iran, and
millions more passed through on their way to Europe, Australia, and the United
States. Refugee camps helped to create a cross-border community that was reinforced by war itself. After the Geneva Accords, local populations in Pakistan and
Iran objected to the size and tenure of refugee populations, arguing that the original reasons for granting safe haven during the Soviet intervention had long
ceased to have meaning. Over time, heads of households would cultivate lands

and fight seasonally while their families remained in exile. Trading, transport, and labor markets followed suit. Afghanistan's borders—and thus, Pakistan's and Iran's, and to a lesser degree, central Asia's—softened, creating economic opportunity in the midst of war, but threatening border security at the same time. By the time of the Geneva Accords in 1988, southwest Asia's mobile population had created a transactional economy that eluded formal boundary regulation to survive, and perhaps even profit from, the exigencies of continued war. State authorities helped sustain this political economy, even as they periodically closed and opened the border, but normal state-to-state intercourse was threatened nonetheless.

Second, ideological groups involved in Afghanistan's war became—and were ultimately perceived to become—independent threats to neighboring states and regional stability. During the anti-Soviet war, the Western-led coalition had made common cause with a wide range of supporters. Exiled Afghan Islamist opposition groups were joined with transnational religious parties, through which massive funds where channeled through the 1980s and 1990s and beyond. Their respective agendas merged to some degree, and turned southwest Asia into fertile ground for radical recruits who were patronized by state actors, including Pakistan's intelligence and armed services. Others turned militancy into a strategic, antistate objective and found willing supporters in refugee camps and among traders who profited from lawless conditions. As a result, dispersed, competing armed groups trespassed and populated the Afghan/Pakistan and Afghan/Iran borders. They found a focus in the Taliban movement in the mid-1990s in Afghanistan,[10] in Pakistan's militantly Sunni Sipah-i-Sahaba, in the Harkat-ul-Ansar (later Harkat ul Mujahideen) in Kashmir, and later, a variety of groups operating along Afghanistan's borders with Tajikistan and Uzbekistan. Each worked with a specific agenda; all required similarly porous environments in which to operate.

The political and social contexts in which these groups functioned and evolved were (and are) complex and varied. Each state in the region has contended with a variety of movements and organizations specific to its own circumstances. Some turned violent, as happened in Tajikistan and Afghanistan, but others did not. Some ideologically oriented groups, like the pan-Islamic Hizbut Tahrir, have long been intent on reshaping the international state system and restoring the caliphate; the ambitions of others, like the Taliban movement, evolved from the local to the global. Others still, including several political parties in Pakistan and Uzbekistan, remain interested primarily in redistributing local power, and the many-hued spectrum of Islamist groups challenged traditional politics in Pakistan and Afghanistan, and more recently, in central Asia.

As insurgents and irredentists continued to take advantage of political weaknesses across the region, central Asia's leaders were engaged in multipronged, and occasionally incompatible efforts to shore up their own power. They compromised with Afghanistan's warlords, while also seeking to stem illicit trades; built up trade barriers among themselves while allowing unregulated trade with Afghanistan; and responded to external threats by strengthening their hands at home. By the mid-1990s, central Asia, like Pakistan, was finding it difficult to control its borders, encourage economic growth, or maintain the rule of law. In particular, Central Asia's republics moved quickly to quell disturbances as they arose—whether as explicit challenges to political authority or in response to specific policies—rather than absorbing dissent and encouraging pluralism.

These responses to volatility were not particularly original. Nearby Pakistan spent decades responding awkwardly and heavy-handedly to the twin threats of spillover from Afghanistan and domestic instability. Pakistan's alliance with the West had been riddled with problems, particularly after the Soviet army left Afghanistan in 1989, and its faltering relationships to the West had profoundly weakened its political society. Indeed, the praetorian problematic of Pakistan—in which military-led foreign policies helped to unravel domestic governance, erode the country's relationship to the global economy, and contribute to instability in Afghanistan—is an object lesson to all of Pakistan's neighbors and diplomatic partners. It is also a study in the contradictions of superpower diplomacy: the old-fashioned alliance demands of the United States weighed heavily on Pakistan's governance by favoring a strong military, even as the United States and others pushed rhetorically for Pakistan to civilianize and democratize.[11] Although Pakistan's polity and society suffered from many other inheritances, including a cumbersome constitutional structure often at odds with its class-divided society, its army's strategic, economic, and ideological prerogatives have severely weakened the country's capacity to grow and develop. In its efforts to find common cause with the West while cementing the rule of its leaders, Central Asia—at once stubborn, fragile, blustering, and uncertain—set out to replicate Pakistan's experience rather than improve on it.

SECURITY, DEMOCRACY, DIPLOMACY

Even before September 2001, it was clear that the antistate movements cycling through central and south Asia were not just local phenomena, but increasingly essential elements of the international state system.[12] Transnational groups were able to use international political, financial, and administrative systems to support global political and terrorist activities that threatened Afghanistan, its neighbors, and the rest of the world. When President George Bush used the phrase "terrorisms of global reach" in a speech to the U.S. Congress, he coined a term and accompanying concept for central and south Asia. He pointed not only to the international phenomenon of terrorism, but also to the phenomenon of local conflicts that could be sustained through the unintentional lacunae of international finance, reach deeply across the globe, and return to threaten countries like Afghanistan, Pakistan, and central Asia. The worst fears of the region—expressed with urgency and frequency by its leaders from the moment that foreign recruits joined the anti-Soviet cause in the mid-1980s—became broad, deep security threats for the world at large.

Until the autumn of 2001, many of these problems were viewed as limited and Afghanistan-centric rather than as regional or global burdens. Even the job of seeking peace in Afghanistan was sidelined as world attention moved elsewhere. But for central Asia's governments, Afghanistan's conflicts were a tragic, looming inheritance. Their independence was accompanied by the downfall of the Communist government in Kabul and the beginning of Afghanistan's anarchy; their efforts to join the global economy were burdened by the rise of the Taliban (with whom they were ideologically at odds), the continuing obstacle of Afghanistan in the region, and the emerging corruptions that narcotics and armaments trades imposed on their own economies and societies; and their security was compromised, over and again, by external war and internal instability. From the mid-1990s, even as most states in the region reinforced transitions from command to capitalist economies, the region was seized by vulnerabilities that it blamed increasingly on Afghanistan.

But its responses to these problems betrayed old-fashioned praetorian sensibilities. Central Asia's border states tried, at one and the same time, to contain Afghanistan's conflicts, separate their own antistate oppositions from the contagion of the Taliban, petition the international community to solve Afghanistan, maintain their involvement in the conflict itself by picking sides and supplying weapons, and preserve high barriers among their economies and societies. Even with regular, if constrained, elections (except in Turkmenistan, which doesn't hold them at all), every state in the region did its best to suppress internal conflicts, contain political opposition, and retain a central role for the army, police, and intelligence in the state apparatus. Every threat was cause, or excuse, for recentralizing authority and in this way, the transition clock kept turning backward.

Until September 2001, few central Asian states had persuaded the West that their security dilemmas justified domestic political repression. As political reforms languished or regressed and human rights protections waned, the region found itself on a downward diplomatic slide. Central Asia's dictators, led by Uzbekistan's president Islam Karimov, insisted that the region's security problems were radically misunderstood, and that Asia's future stability was at risk.

In the autumn of 2001, the West changed its mind. In order to prosecute a quick war in Afghanistan and preclude unhappy surprises in the hinterlands, the United States–led coalition inducted central Asia's southern flank—Uzbekistan, Kyrgyzstan, and Tajikistan. Military-to-military agreements, financial assistance, and political support became the new staples of diplomatic exchange. Perhaps most important, particularly to Uzbekistan, the United States and its partners decided to acknowledge publicly that central Asia's security threats were real. In so doing, the international coalition was echoing policies for which Zbigniew Brzezinski and others had called in the mid-1980s, when so many U.S. allies were classic praetorians: constructing an alliance of "linchpin states"—in this case, to counter terrorism rather than Communism—to which commitments for long-term security could be made.[13] And as happened elsewhere in the 1980s, foreign assistance to authoritarian states, especially to build up internal security as defined by those autocrats, can easily upset domestic politics and heighten rather than lessen internal security.

These similarities are overshadowed by differences. Communism may have seemed ubiquitous in the 1970s and 1980s, but international terrorism is far more diffused. Its causes, methods, activities, and consequences call into play complex phenomena whose trajectories are not fully understood; with military assistance, this group of relatively weak and inexperienced linchpins—each with complex relationships to transborder groups—can at best encircle a small number of comparatively small terrorist-supporting actors that are difficult to isolate, target, or remove. The best that some of central Asia's autocrats seek may turn out to be far less than what the international coalition and the broader international community desire, or need. Uzbekistan, for example, measures the success of the global antiterrorism campaign in two related ways: by the extent to which its government's hand in dealing with domestic opposition groups is strengthened, and the degree to which the international coalition recognizes and supports its security demands. The two are related, but do not always converge. If the Uzbek government strengthens civic governance—as it began to do, tentatively, in 2002—then security across the country is likely to be enhanced. If, on the other hand, the government uses its new security to stifle opposition—as it also did in 2002—domestic instability is likely to rise and Uzbekistan's value to the international coalition can quickly diminish.

These are not new sensibilities, but they are new to central Asia. Central Asia's value in the Soviet Union was its ability to maintain traditional stability in extremely sensitive locations. To central Asia's leaders, as to most praetorians, stability precludes change. But international alliances easily founder when collective security is not sustained by individual states, and security itself is increasingly defined by the assent of the governed rather than the dictates of leaders. Twenty years ago, when the United States sought to renew its relationship with Pakistan in order to fight in Afghanistan, bolstering security at the cost of limiting rights was commonplace and, to those in power on both sides of the alliance, acceptable. Although the United States and its coalition partners now know better than to excuse the purposeful abuse of rights, they still treat Pakistan as a hard, risky case. Because they underestimate democratic alternatives and accede to the virtual blackmail of Pakistan's nuclear establishment, the United States and others have consistently helped praetorians maintain control of the state. At times, this has meant helping Islamist groups who, in turn, have risked the security of the Pakistani state and worse, the rest of the world.

This is a hard lesson to learn, but for this reason, combating terrorism elsewhere cannot proceed solely on the basis of expedience. To support the coalition, for example, the United States undertook formal agreements with Uzbekistan and Kyrgyzstan to encourage democratic transition and respect for the rule of law. These commitments are stronger in rhetoric than they are in practice and the accepted benchmarks for democratization are not clearly demarcated; certainly, both central Asian governments have stretched the limits of compliance with these promises, and they will find themselves hard pressed to conform their praetorian inclinations and policies to democracy. Nonetheless, antiterrorism action is now linked to political liberalization in new ways in central Asia, and this fact alone is likely to encourage those striving toward political change.

Few observers would suggest that decisions taken in the days following the destruction of the World Trade Center and the Pentagon, and those preceding the coalition bombing campaign in Afghanistan, were premised on the nuances of democratization theory. Today's aging autocrats are unlikely to envision the breadth and depth of political and economic change needed to sustain serious democratic transition and ultimately, to correct a fallible state system as yet unresponsive to civic needs. However, if the international coalition can provide the foundation on which deep, rather than habitually superficial, security can be built—then the campaign against terrorism of global reach will take on new dimensions in central Asia and potentially help to improve the security environment across an even broader region. This is surely not the primary objective of today's antiterrorist campaign—to eradicate the elusive but pervasive violent movements that seek to displace the state system—but it does support its secondary goal of reforming international security to prevent further antistate violence. Those seeking an even newer world order to correct our fallible and often unresponsive state system will find intermediary reform too small and incomplete. For those in central Asia seeking relief from violence, war, and insecurity, however, this first step may resemble a revolution.

MIGRATION AND SECURITY AS AN ISSUE IN U.S.-EUROPEAN RELATIONS

MARIO ZUCCONI

1. INTRODUCTION

The attack of September 11, 2001, shocked the United States of America into an altogether new era of its foreign and security policy. And the shock waves of the attack against New York and Washington, D.C., were felt right away—as they continue to be felt at present—at the global level. To present-day America, the terrorist attack was a totally new experience: a deadly, military action well inside its territory (while massively attacked in December 1941, Hawaii is in the middle of the Pacific Ocean, and as far from California as it is close to Japan) and against some very important symbols of American power. Americans experienced for the first time what the Europeans were all too well accustomed to in their contemporary history: with the last massive war in their territory in the middle of the twentieth century, with the systematic bombing of each other's capitals during that World War, and with the enormous numbers of civilian casualties. Indeed, even after the end of the Cold War and as late as 1999, the Europeans experienced again the chain of war, destruction, refugees, and delayed necessary interventions in their continent.

A provider of security to the European and other allies during the Cold War, the United States found itself very much in need for help in different forms for its own security after it was attacked.[1] Among others, in a decision on September 12, 2001, that nobody on either side of the Atlantic would have thought possible in 1949 or later, the North Atlantic Council (NATO's governing body) responded collectively to the terrorist attack against the United States by invoking, for the first time in the alliance's history, Article 5 of the Washington Treaty. Thus both allies and newer partners in security matters lined up behind the United States in an exceptional display of solidarity and practical support.[2] Other countries around the world either expressed genuine concern or felt compelled to show solidarity. And for a while it looked like new bases for international cooperation in security matters were being created—a fact especially important due to the complexity of the struggle against international terrorism. However, despite all the bilateral and multilateral diplomatic activity stirred by the attack against the United States, major difficulties in bringing about a cohesive, collective approach to some major issues of world affairs and to the very struggle against international terrorism were to surface as time went by.

2. SECURITY AT THE BORDERS

One area that appeared immediately to be central in the cooperation especially among allied countries in the common fight against international terrorism related to the movement of people across international borders. In this area, the complexity and dynamics mentioned above were to bring to the surface unavoidable differences and preexisting separate conditioning—conditioning that was to prevail over the need and ability to create new, collective norms.

The terrorists who attacked with deadly effectiveness New York and Washington, D.C. on September 11 were foreigners, had entered the country with regular visas, and had typically overstayed their visa permits. Moreover, they were originally from Muslim countries. After September 11 it became commonplace to establish a relationship between that new sort of international terrorism and globalization, and especially the greatly intensified movement of people across borders. But now, in a country accustomed to relying on two oceans (people crossing over from Mexico are the exception), where 30 million people who legally enter the country every year are foreigners, and where $1.35 trillion of imports are processed yearly, the events of September 11 dramatically put the problem of the foreigners, of freight entering the country, and of transportation in a new security setting.[3] The United States has since long been and is at present the place of residence of the largest group of international migrants in the world (foreigners residing in a country for longer than a year): 25 million.[4]

The demand coming from Washington to support its struggle against international terrorism, to coordinate immigration policies, and to participate in the building of a safe international environment was most intense from the very beginning. It was directed both at traditional allies, such as the members of NATO and of its extended institutions, as well as at more contingent ones, such as Russia, Pakistan, India, and others. In particular with regard to the European allies, a major dimension of that demand for cooperation was in the area of migration policies. However, besides an inevitable policy-transfer effect (airport security, etc.), the consequences on European policies, and especially on the common behavior of the European Union countries, were complex and not necessarily moving in synchronism with developments in the United States and with the new requirements of American homeland security.

In the EU member states, strengthening of border controls was, on the whole, more limited than in the United States. Even more modest were changes with regard to legislation related to foreigners present in the different countries. Above all, the overall issue of migration flows had become for Western Europe a central security issue many years ago.

While it was part of a strong, overall, multicausal increase of foreigners moving toward the Western industrialized countries (the 36 million international migrants of 1986–87 in the United States, Canada, Australia, United Kingdom, France, and Germany, a decade later had become 46 million, with a 28 percent increase),[5] the relevance of the issue in particular to the Western European countries peaked in the first half of the 1990s and especially in connection with the war in Bosnia-Herzegovina. The long-term causes begin with demographic changes in the Western European countries such as the problem of falling fertility rates that make imported labor needed both for production and for feeding pension funds. There was a general shortage of workers in regions of strong economic growth (Bavaria, Northern Italy, etc.). Then, in the early phases of the Bosnia conflict and in a short period of time, over a million of the people who left their homes there because of the war reached Western Europe. United Nations figures for asylum seekers in EU member states rose from 397,027 in 1990 to 511,184 in 1991, and 672,381 in 1992, before declining to 516,710 in 1993 and to 300,000 in 1994. The figures then fell to an average of about 250,000 per year from 1995 on (with a peak again in 1999 due to the Kosovo crisis).[6]

The impact of this flow of war refugees was most dramatic in the case of Germany: over 400,000 people entered the country in the early years of the Bosnia conflict. What added weight to this development was that the pressure (logistical, financial, cultural, etc.) brought about by the Bosnian refugees, in the years after 1992, combined with the enormous pressure of the absorption of former East Germany and the pressure of immigrants—most often illegal—from countries of the former Soviet bloc. Besides the strains produced on resources, such combined pressure of immigrants, refugees, and the unemployed East Germans created very serious tensions, reprisals against older immigrants (Turkish nationals in Germany), and a scary expansion of rightist, xenophobic political formations. During those years, Germany established treaties and agreements with Russia, Romania, Poland, and other countries concerning the possibility of, and modalities for, sending back illegal immigrants.

In Italy, in the same period of time, the pressure came from across the Adriatic and especially from a failing state there—Albania. The pressures related to population movements in those years were a major motor of the evolution of the foreign policies of the individual European countries. That was, once again, the case of Germany, with its bilateral treaties (often inclusive of important financial commitments), and it was also the case of Italy, with its military initiative (Alba mission) aimed to assure some degree of stability in Albania and to control the departure of migrants to Italy. Those pressures even developed into a central factor that shaped the policies of those countries with regard to the successive crises in the Balkans. Germany rushed to take advantage of the Dayton Accords in late 1995 and sent back tens of thousands of refugees after that development, despite the fact that many could not go back to their places of origins in what was now the territory assigned to the rival ethnic group. Moreover, in the late 1990s, like other countries Germany tended to favor independence for Kosovo in the expectation that such a policy would stem the flow of people leaving that troubled region.

The immigration and refugee problems had thus turned into major security issues—and issues that shaped in a significant manner the foreign policies themselves—for the Western European countries and for the European Union itself long before September 11. Those were issues that created plenty of strains at the domestic level, among the EU countries and between them and the adjacent countries. With Turkey, migration policies became part of the conditions for accession into the European Union. Conditionality related to migration flows was more often applied in bilateral agreements with countries on the eastern and southern shores of the Mediterranean. In Austria, Germany, Italy, and France in particular there were political parties that successfully exploited the growing xenophobia and anxieties produced by the increased demographic pressures of those years.

One factor that needs to be kept in mind in discussing the political relevance of those movements of people is the considerable size of unauthorized migration into the Western European countries—much increasing in the 1990s. Official estimations of unauthorized migrants in France were as high as 500,000 at the end of the decade. In 1998 alone, the German authorities apprehended 40,000 illegal immigrants after they had crossed the border especially with the eastern countries. For Italy the estimated figure of unauthorized migrants was half that of France (but unofficial estimations are much higher).[7] Two important features are related in particular to illegal immigration. It is a phenomenon as often related to other forms of illegal smuggling and trafficking as to mafias. And that phenomenon finds most often strong logistic support (staging areas of illegal trafficking, etc.) in failed states, or weak states with low levels of control over the territory by the authorities.[8] Also important is the vicious circle of the strengthening of control over unauthorized border crossings by smugglers and traffickers and the more limited access being established by Western European governments for asylum seekers. As a result, asylum seekers attempting to reach those countries increasingly have found themselves with little choice but to turn to traffickers. That, in turn, increasingly intermixed their arrival with that of unauthorized economic migrants and with plenty of other illegal trafficking.[9]

If September 11 was to create a demand from Washington concerning immigration policy coordination and related intelligence sharing, much of what the Western European countries were to produce in that direction had been underway already before the attacks. That is the case of the negotiations related to the creation of a large data-bank collecting information about all visa applicants. The aim of the bank's creators was to improve the ability to trace immigrant individuals the authorities wanted to reach for some reason. Likewise, already under discussion in September 2001 was the creation of a custom guards system common to all the EU member states.

Clearly, September 11 further loaded domestic systems and interstate relations already fraught with tensions. However, the point here to stress is that as the attack on the United States in the end compelled that country to further strengthen its own individual defenses, the European countries had already moved in the same direction in the late 1990s as a consequence of the demographic and political pressures discussed earlier. Most meaningful in this respect is the progressive attempt—and in part failure—to "communitarize" migration policies among the EU member states during the 1990s.

Coming from a tradition of competition among them for the most useful immigrants (even competing among them in offering most advantageous agreements to sender countries), starting in the mid-1980s the EU member states began to discuss about how to deal collectively with migration issues. Following up on the suggestion of an area of free circulation of people contained in the European Single Act of 1986, the Schengen Convention (1990) created a new borderless space of European states and forced them, as a consequence, to look together at the problem of the "external" borders. This process found in the Amsterdam Treaty (1996) its broader strategic framework and then at the Tampere European Council (October 1999) for the first time a common approach to immigration and asylum policies was attempted. However, the enthusiasm proved to be short-lived and the planned assessment at the Leaken Council, in December 2001, indicated that, if there was any movement, it was increasingly in the opposite direction than institutionalisation of those policies. Tampere had probably contributed, already by itself, to mobilizing resistance. Moreover, in parallel with Tampere, beginning in the fall of 1999 political change took place in a number of European member states with the coming into power of political parties that often made restrictive immigration policies—and at times truly xenophobic programs—as their basis for political legitimation. That was especially the case of Austria and, shortly afterward, of Italy, but also of the Netherlands, France, and Portugal.[10] Attempts were also made directly by the European Commission to coordinate immigration policies. Now, however, in the changed political context, the individual states' parliaments had again much of the initiative.

To sum up, in the European countries the dynamics of demographic pressures, greatly increased during the 1990s, and of the related political responses were the overwhelming, conditioning factor in shaping policy reforms both before and after September 11. And if the terrorist attack against the United States further strengthened those ongoing dynamics, some officials in European capitals offered the suggestion that the Schengen system should be dismantled. However, a report readied by the European Commission clearly indicated the compatibility of the old rules with new security requirements.

An area related to terrorism and migration in which the events in the United States may have had a more important impact and speeded up change is that of European political refugees. In August 2002, France for the first time extradited to Italy a convicted Red Brigade terrorist (condemned to twenty-two years in jail for first-degree murder) and agreed to open negotiations with the Italian government about what to do with other convicted terrorists that, during three decades, have taken refuge in France. In addition to that, in the most recent years, Paris changed its policy of giving sanctuary to Basque terrorists and in fact turned a number of them over to Spanish authorities.

What unquestionably changed in Western Europe with the terrorist attack in the United States was the atmosphere of the debate on migratory movements and immigration issues in Western Europe. Thus, in Italy, September 11 contributed to that debate because it allowed some to advocate criminalizing the whole of clandestine immigrants (as indicated, a very substantial proportion of immigration into Europe). In Italy, where the pressure to allow large flows of immigrants came especially from the labor-hungry North, the archbishop of Bologna warned about the difficulty of integrating people with Islamic backgrounds. The leader of the xenophobic Northern League (part of the coalition government that came to power in June 2001) argued about the need to let in solely individuals coming from a Christian background.

Finally, and in a different fashion, September 11 had a direct, immediate impact on the intelligence cooperation between the two sides of the Atlantic with regard to the presence of terrorists and to their movements from one country to the other. Despite a simplified relationship established between the terrorist attack against the United States and a generic "clash of civilizations," the origin of that type of terrorism seems much more complex to explain and even hard to relate directly to strong religious and regional self-identification. Zacarias Moussaoui, arrested in the United States while getting flight training only weeks before the attack against New York and Washington, was born in France to a nonobservant mother. As a young adult he moved to the United Kingdom and got his religious education while attending the Brixton mosque (attended also by other Islamic extremists). Many of the fighters captured in Afghanistan and terrorists who had been trained there had originally gone there from Western European countries. Some were nationals of the United Kingdom or France. It is the conclusion of a recent, in-depth study on this phenomenon that "the Islamic militants implicated with the networks accused of terrorism are perfect products of Westernisation and globalisation." [11] It is also striking that they are all migrants.

3. MAIN GENERAL CONDITIONS IN THE STRUGGLE AGAINST TERRORISM

Better monitoring of Islamic migrants who cross the border into EU countries or the United States only scratches—at best—the surface of the problem of the origin and moving around of al Qaeda–type terrorists. In the centrality acquired by such an issue after September 11, much of the attention has been focused on the perpetrators and much of the remedy suggested has been concentrated on cooperation in directly uncovering terrorist groups. The suggestion here is that much more attention should be given to the context of international politics and of individual countries' policies within which international terrorism finds ways to move and grow and that, in this respect, major differences hamper the ability of the United States and Western European countries to work effectively together.

In contrast to the formal rules of international law established with regard to the right to resort to war and the very management of war, international terrorism creeps through areas of unregulated international behavior and through the sovereign space of the individual state. It thrives whenever unstable conditions hamper the possibility for strengthening international cooperation. Finally, international terrorism takes advantage of human mobility and the information revolution that characterize present day globalization. The state, and especially its participation in the creation of more advanced international norms, is a central mechanism to enhance the fight against international terrorism.

While doubtless there are subnational terrorist organizations spread around it, the world is subdivided into territorial jurisdictions, that is, the states—and those states, as indicated, must be the prime targets of political initiatives aimed at making the fight against international terrorism more effective.

That is, the fight against terrorism starts from the broadening of international consensus around rules that may even break the taboo of national sovereignty in the international order and build better arrangements for collective security. Present-day terrorists live—often overtly—in states (they are not eighteenth-century pirates taking sanctuary in remote islands in the Caribbean Sea or off the Southeast Asian coasts). Al Qaeda activities were traced in twenty different countries after September 11—Germany, Japan, Italy, and other Western countries included. The hijackers of September 11 received money from al Qaeda paymasters through traceable banking channels. They received flight training inside the United States. Two of the hijackers bought their plane tickets with credit cards issued in the United States to their names. At times, specific countries were subjected to punishment for their cooperation or for sponsoring terrorism. The Afghanistan of the Taliban regime is the latest and most important example. However, modern, decentralized international terrorism cannot be defeated with cruise missiles and other smart ammunition *directed at a single,* internationally marginalized "rogue" state.

Individual states, well integrated in the international community, may have reasons for sponsoring, enabling, or simply tolerating terrorist activities. And even states with a strong record of internationally cooperative behavior, such as the Western democracies, may at times claim sovereignty concerning activities that other Western countries consider to be terrorist activities, such as in the case of Italian Red Brigade terrorists who were offered sanctuary by France. Such was also the case of the help offered by Greece to the Kurdistan Workers' Party in its armed struggle in Turkey, or, until recently, of France in relationship to Spain, or even, not too far in the past, of the United States, from which the IRA of Northern Ireland drew private financial resources. And those just mentioned are all countries that also participate in the same tight institutional settings—that is, the European Union and NATO. What to a country is support of terrorism to another can simply be space left to a domestic special interest with some political influence.

September 11 put international terrorism at center stage. But September 11 also came at a moment of deep confusion about how to further collective, international rules and make international order progress. Meaningfully, one of the earliest initiatives in Washington after the terrorist attack was the decision to pay the overdue dues to the United Nations. At the center of the fight against terrorism is the possibility of broadening the international consensus about new, often rather intrusive rules of international behavior. To some extent, the problem of what we consider terrorist activities may reflect the spaces left unregulated in the policies of states that have international relevance. As the U.S. leadership set out to do after September 11, the international consensus on new rules needs to be pursued, built, and even bought by the use of political compromises and, if needed, the application of leverages. It also needs to be built around rules that are, as much as possible, general; and by working out solutions to the main international problems and regional conflicts that otherwise produce divisive alignment of the different countries on either sides of the conflict.

Even agreeing on a definition of who should be labeled as terrorists—and even after September 11—has proved much too hard. Such an agreement is difficult even solely among Western allied countries. With a dozen UN Security Council resolutions issued after September 11, legal experts talk today of a "robust legal framework" for dealing with terrorist activities internationally. However, a broadly accepted agreement on a definition of terrorism remains to this date an unaccomplished objective. And of course, a definition of terrorism is the prerequisite of any possible operative decision based on international law.

Here is where ongoing conflicts and developments on the international scene get in the way. The seventh session of the Comprehensive Global Convention Against International Terrorism, in early 2002, failed to reach such an agreement due to the rekindling of the Palestinian uprising in the occupied territories. The old notion that liberation wars should not be included in terrorist activities was dusted off in this case. And, while in the case of the Palestinian-Israeli dispute the main dividing line is with the Arab and Islamic countries, who resist defining Palestinian extremists as terrorists, there are profound differences even among the Western allied countries. Thus, the thirteen Palestinian extremists that took refuge in the Church of the Nativity in 2002 were accused of terrorism by Israel, and then Israeli foreign minister Shimon Peres promised he would ask for extradition, while the European countries that were going to accept them made clear that they had no pending charges against them.

And here comes the second general condition—and the most difficult to fulfill—related to the fight against international terrorism. For, the building of consensus cannot be limited to the opposition to terrorist activities. The rallying of that consensus is directly proportional to the ability of the main international actors to address grievances internationally and create international stability. Terrorism is nothing but an asymmetric instrument of influence relied upon by individuals, groups, and states to compensate for very high asymmetries of power. That success in the fight against terrorism requires solving important regional conflicts may sound obvious—or outrightly irresponsible given the urgency of the fight against terrorism. Still, even more obvious is the observation that the long-term success in that struggle has as an *unavoidable condition*—the ability to address some, especially important regional conflicts and to create a healthier international environment. As a recent study documented and argued, the al Qaeda–type terrorists have no direct relationship with the Arab-Israeli conflict.[12] Still, such a conflict feeds support for the terrorists in the Islamic countries, creates difficulties even for pro-Western, "moderate" regimes, and makes those regimes reach compromises with the very extremist groups from which the terrorists that attacked the United States came.

In addition to other regimes, such as the Saudi one, Mubarak's Egypt offers a good example of that problem. For, in recent years, the Egyptian government found it convenient not to repress decisively the Jihad movement in the country in the expectation of avoiding the kind of terrorist attack it suffered until 1998. It also acquiesced in some of the Egyptian Islamic Jihad's demands regarding implementation of the *shari'a*. The Egyptian Islamic Jihad's leaders Ayman al-Zawahiri and Muhammad Atef (the latter killed in the bombing in Afghanistan), are believed by investigators to be the ones who masterminded the attacks of September 11.[13] And in the last few years the Egyptian government has even released from prison a number of members of that movement in the country.

In such a context of uncontrolled regional conflicts and of ambivalence toward the terrorists in many countries, it is illusory to imagine that terrorism can be stopped at the border (no matter how indispensable it is also to better guard those borders). Terrorism is much too rooted in and related to a wealth of other political phenomena and situations. It is much too connected with economic interdependence, human mobility, migration flows, and the information revolution. And the borders of the United States or of the European countries can check only a very limited amount of that mobility and political interdependence. Once again, it is useful to stress here that the al Qaeda terrorists used the increased human mobility and migration flows not only to attack the United States—they were also a "product" of migration in Western industrialized countries, as Olivier Roy stresses in his recent *Islam Mondialisé*, with reference to the second-generation al Qaeda terrorists (those who attacked the United States). They had scant connection with their countries of origin; at times they were even born in the countries of family immigration and re-Islamized in those host countries.

Because of the new level of migration flows, of economic interdependence, and information, the problems of faraway regions are felt politically right away also within the most developed Western countries. And, in such a context, that fight against international terrorism is a highly complex and multifaceted struggle which requires statesmanship, steady international cooperation, and great investment of political and economic resources.

4. A PROBLEMATIC LEADERSHIP IN THE FIGHT AGAINST INTERNATIONAL TERRORISM

The cooperation especially among the most capable international actors is indispensable for long-term success in the fight against terrorism. And the leadership and the demand for cooperation coming from Washington is today central in that common endeavor. Here, however, things have turned out to be increasingly complex, especially in comparison with the earliest phase after September 11. As in the case of policies related to migration and border crossing, also in the case of the broader foreign policies, some national or regional dynamics have tended to prevail over the ability to establish a new, solid, collective approach.

There was plenty of disagreement with Washington, especially in the EU capitals from the very beginning of the presidency of George W. Bush. It was the declaration of the "death" of the Kyoto agreement and then the refusal to participate in the International Criminal Court. Those decisions, and other ones such as the withdrawal from the Anti-Ballistic Missile Treaty, drew charges of U.S. unilateralism. Then there was unanimous support offered to the United States in Western Europe, as in other regions, after September 11. However, subsequently things became more complex as the demand for cooperation coming from Washington evolved.

Understandably the attack by Islamic terrorists against New York and Washington drastically changed the domestic bases of U.S. foreign policy. The missiles deployed by Moscow in Cuba in 1962 were a hypothetical threat and one that the Americans learned about from their leaders. In 2001, civilian Americans were hit directly while they were going about their regular, daily lives. That attack changed the main focus of the country's foreign policy. "Homeland security" became the central front and the outstanding objective of U.S. security policies. Policies such as those related to the Arab-Israeli dispute, to regulating the price of oil, to coercing Saddam Hussein became directly related to the security of the U.S. citizens on American soil.

Most importantly, the attack against U.S. civilians had an overwhelming impact on the very foreign policy decision-making process. That meant, as indicated earlier, that international issues that were until September 11 rather remote for the American public became directly related to the physical security of the country. Moreover, it meant that now, in the foreign policy realm, politicians could find issues of immediate, overriding importance to the public and on which to base their own political legitimation. This, as indicated later, had most important consequences with regard to the ability of Washington to rally international support around its own policies.

With the midterm elections looming in the summer of 2002, President Bush bet on the results of polls that gave international terrorism as the priority concern of most Americans—and thus went on to defeat the Democrats, who were instead, and more traditionally, counting on bad economic news for a success.[14] Keeping the country mobilized—with Saddam Hussein and Iraq as more palpable villains than ghostly bin Laden and al Qaeda—proved a successful way of keeping up the rate of approval. However, while that is part of an unavoidable evolution of the foreign-policy decision-making in the United States after September 11, the political opportunities the administration can catch in that evolution poorly relate to an ability to create long-term stability—especially when such a strategy moves in parallel with an inability to keep the Israeli-Palestinian dispute on a negotiation track—and to lead other influential countries to commit and invest in that direction.

Besides the political problems provoked and the hypocritical and instrumental consensus at times gathered, the recent, obsessive focus on Iraq is detrimental to the attention needed to be paid other international issues more clearly related to the struggle against terrorism.[15] Such is the case of the U.S. disengagement from the Balkans admittedly speeded up by that new policy focus.

In the recent past, commitment from the United States, the EU, and other multilateral organizations helped local authorities to strengthen immigration controls and check trade routes. They enacted legislation capable, in the overall, of making those countries less hospitable to terrorists.[16] Despite those measures, lax border controls, weak law enforcement, and, at times, corrupt border officials still make places such as Bosnia, Kosovo, Macedonia (FYROM), Montenegro, and Albania preferential routes for drug, arms, and human trafficking. Eighty percent of the heroin reaching Western Europe comes that way. The same routes are often used by terrorists to travel to Western Europe unnoticed. And profits from such illegal activities are attractive for terrorists who want to finance operations abroad.

Apart from the Taliban's Afghanistan, the Balkans were proved to have given sanctuary to al Qaeda operatives much more solidly than Saddam's Iraq. Not too long ago, Washington itself was accusing the Kosovo Liberation Army of accepting financial help from bin Laden. In 1998, U.S. officials warned about a possible attack against the U.S. Embassy in Tirana by terrorist cells based in Albania. And terrorist networks there were then also uncovered because of the solicitation and help of Italian and German intelligence and authorities.

Not that Washington doesn't gather in general consensus around its policies. Rather, the more it announces it wants to tackle right away broad issues such as "evil" countries in the world and shows itself ready to take care of the whole problem by itself, the more it creates, on the one hand, opportunistic, cost-free consent and, on the other, room for hiding neglect and international irresponsibility behind an abstract reading of international legality. And this is a far cry from the solid, responsible, collective consensus needed at present around new norms and a collective effort for acting effectively in the struggle against international terrorism.

WAR AGAINST HAVENS FOR TERRORISM: EXAMINING A NEW PRESIDENTIAL DOCTRINE

STEPHEN SCHLESINGER

A pervading unilateralist impulse emanated from the White House from the moment former Texas governor George W. Bush ascended to the presidency in January 2001. Despite his very limited background in foreign affairs, Mr. Bush brought with him to Washington some basic affirmations about where America should be going in the world and why its past conduct under President Clinton, in his view, had been deplorable. By and large, George W. Bush believed that, while America should remain "humble," it should look out for itself because, under the Clinton administration, it had not always done so. Instead, U.S. global authority had deteriorated because Clinton had too often deferred to multilateral solutions to the detriment of our national interests, had weakened our military, and had incautiously apologized too regularly for past American foreign policy mistakes. Bush's abiding intention as chief executive was to reverse Clinton's course.

More than anything else, Bush wanted the United States, as the most powerful land on earth, to advance American interests around the globe using whatever assets, forces, or diplomacy were needed and employing whatever means were required. This meant, first, no longer compromising our interests on behalf of other nations; second, enhancing our military power so that no other country would ever threaten us or out-arm us again; and third, bringing retrograde regimes into the democratic community of nations by statesmanlike persuasion or, if necessary, military means. To accomplish its goals, though, Washington might on some occasions act alone. If the United States had to undertake unilateral operations, it would do so unembarrassed by its strength, unconstrained by outmoded treaties, and unbowed by adverse public opinion.

THE ASSERTION OF STATE POWER AS GLOBAL UNILATERALISM

The unilateralist approach became evident in the first nine months of the administration. Bush at that time sought most energetically to erase the stain of

Clinton's multilateralism. Within two months of assuming office, for example, he renounced the Kyoto Protocol on global warming—even though the United States accounts for 25 percent of worldwide greenhouse gases. Bush argued that the pact was fatally flawed because it allowed developing nations an exemption from emission reduction targets and placed too much of the clean-up burden on industrial nations. That, he asserted, would prove immensely costly to the American economy. He claimed that he could instead propose a credible alternative for cutting gas emissions by 18 percent over ten years, which, so far, he has not pursued. Also early on in his term he made clear his opposition to the International Criminal Court. He contended it would lead to politically motivated prosecutions of American soldiers and U.S. leaders—even though the drafters of the juridical covenant had included strict provisions allowing nations to prosecute their own citizens. In 2002, he publicly disowned the signature assenting to the agreement inscribed by Clinton.

Fulfilling another campaign promise, Bush said in 2001 he would pull out of the Anti-Ballistic Missile Treaty because he claimed it interfered with the development of America's Star Wars program. He made good on that vow in mid-2002. In the summer of 2001, he also sent U.S. diplomats to block a proposal to enhance the 1972 treaty banning the production of biological weapons, a pact that the United States had ratified at that time. The change would have added on to it a monitoring and verification system. The Bush representatives argued that such an arrangement was unenforceable and would, in any case, give foreign inspectors access to the trade secrets of American biotechnology companies. Bush's opposition forced postponement of the talks. That same summer, Bush emissaries weakened key provisions of a draft UN accord to curb illicit small-arms traffic that could restrict some civilian gun ownership in America. They contended it would interfere with the right of our citizens to bear arms. The United Nations accepted a watered-down version of the pact. Finally, at the insistence of American antiabortion groups, the State Department in late 2001 unilaterally cut off all U.S. assistance to foreign private organizations providing legal abortion services, counseling, and referrals.

Simultaneously, Bush's State Department, Defense Department, and National Security Council also made every effort to demean, discard, or block any and every global accord stretching back for the last two decades. The agreements ranged from the START 2 treaty reducing nuclear weapons, which Bush's father negotiated, to the United Nations Convention on the Laws of the Seas, which 133 nations ratified; from the Biodiversity Convention supported by 168 states, to the Nuclear Test Ban Treaty that the UN General Assembly adopted 158 to 3 in 1996 and which Republicans in the U.S. Senate defeated during the Clinton Administration in 1999. Also included were the 1997 convention banning antipersonnel land mines, the Conventions on the Rights of the Child, the Convention on Discrimination Against Women, and the Nunn-Lugar initiative that helped dismantle Russia's weapons of mass destruction but which required a boost in funding by Congress. In addition, George Bush boycotted the August 2002 UN World Summit on Sustainable Development, held in South Africa and attended by most other leaders of the world.

These rebukes to the international legal and social community, however, were but a foreshadowing of the new administration's most muscular outburst following the horrific terrorist attacks of September 11. That catastrophe at first led Bush to reverse, at least temporarily, the single-minded course of his first year in office and rally a coalition of democratic nations around a campaign to track down, attack, and defeat the al Qaeda and Taliban forces in Afghanistan. But, within months of this action, members of the Bush strategic planning team were already considering ways for the United States to take measures on its own against all rogue nations that potentially possessed weapons of mass destruction. The reasoning was expressed by the State Department's policy planning director, Richard Haass: "Sovereignty entails obligations. One is not to massacre your own people. Another is not to support terrorism in any way. If a government fails to meet these obligations, then it forfeits some of the normal advantages of sovereignty, including the right to be left alone inside your own territory. Other governments, including the United States, gain the right to intervene. In the case of terrorism, this can even lead to a right of preventive, or pre-emptory, self-defense."[1] This approach gradually developed into a plan by the United States to support preemptive military strikes. The policy became known publicly in fits and starts through a series of speeches that President Bush delivered after the World Trade Center attacks.

PREEMPTION AGAINST HARBORS OF TERRORISM

Beginning with his September 2001 address to Congress, Bush stated the case that any nations harboring terrorists would be fair game for American troops. He issued a challenge to the nations of the world that "you are either with us or against us" in this effort. Four months later, Bush enunciated a more specific terrorist threat in his State of the Union speech, a so-called "axis of evil" as embodied in three nations—North Korea, Iraq, and Iran. The United States, he contended, would now have to take major responsibility for dismantling the weaponry of those renegade countries. Five months later, in a talk at West Point, Bush for the first time spelled out in full detail a doctrine of American preemption. As he told the cadets: "Our security will require all Americans . . . to be ready for preemptive action when necessary to defend our liberty and to defend our lives." He went on to say, "If we wait for threats to fully materialize, we will have waited too long," and, finally, "We must take the battle to the enemy, disrupt his plans, and confront the worst threats before they emerge."

In taking this position, Bush disowned the past geopolitical strategies that had guided America for almost sixty years—developed during the Truman and Eisenhower administrations in the 1940s and 1950s—dismissing as inadequate or antiquated the concepts of deterrence and containment. Deterrence, which promises a devastating military retaliation against any nation that attacks America, he now claimed, would have no impact on shadowy terrorist networks that have no nation or peoples to defend. And containment, he said, would not constrain unbalanced dictators with weapons of mass destruction from passing their arsenals along to terrorist allies. With this new kind of threat, in short, we could no longer count on our foes to send out the kind of classic warning signals that can be handled by deterrence or containment. Hence the United States had to prepare for a different sort of conflict. Bush said that consequently the United States would no longer respect the principle of absolute state sovereignty, meaning we would cross borders at will to achieve America's national security, subordinating the security of every other nation to our own. In 1999, UN secretary general Kofi Annan told the organization that it should, on occasion, override a country's sovereignty in humanitarian emergencies; he never mentioned a rationale based on eliminating weapons of mass destruction.

By September 20, 2002, Bush elevated his thinking to official doctrine when he offered to Congress a thirty-three-page policy document, "The National Security Strategy of the United States." It spelled out his administration's full agenda on global security. While Bush made some obeisance to multilateralism, primarily he wrote of a "distinctly American internationalism" that will now have to deal with failing states rather than with conquering ones through new tactics. One of them he called "counter-proliferation"—the dismantling of fearsome foreign weapons in outlaw states while simultaneously building up U.S. missile defense systems. Bush said in this document that, as a part of this overall strategy, America could no longer permit "any foreign power to catch up with the huge lead the United States has opened up since the fall of the Soviet Union more than a decade ago." Washington's new policy under Bush, in short, seemed to be one of military supremacy over the entire earth—an endeavor more ambitious than that sought by an ancient Rome that merely confined itself to the Mediterranean and Europe, or even by a nineteenth-century Great Britain, which claimed only a fifth of the globe.

In his first two years, Bush backed up his openly aggressive posture with a series of significant moves to enhance the American military. First, he boosted U.S. defense spending 13 percent in the 2003 budget, the largest increase since the Reagan era. In military spending, the United States currently outspends more than the next fifteen industrialized nations combined, and, as the world spends about $800 billion a year for defense today, America accounts for almost half of that. Under the Bush proposal, the United States would take an even larger share of that global budget. In a Nuclear Posture Review released in January 2002, Bush embraced the notion of "offensive deterrence," whereby as president he would consider authorizing during a conventional war the use of specially constructed nuclear missiles to penetrate underground bunkers. Bush also indicated he might even order resumption of nuclear testing—a first for a U.S. President since the era of President Kennedy.[2]

In furtherance of his fight against terrorism, Bush dispatched American special forces to various countries to combat terrorism—including Yemen, the Philippines, Georgia, Pakistan, Colombia, and many of the former states of the Soviet Union. By the fall of 2002, the Bush administration had constructed, renovated, or added onto military facilities in Kyrgyzstan, Afghanistan, Pakistan, Bulgaria, Uzbekistan, Turkey, Bahrain, Saudi Arabia, Qatar, Kuwait, and Oman; had planned training missions, including some placement of U.S. forces on an open-ended basis, in Georgia, Djibouti, and the Philippines; had won airfield landing rights in Kazakhstan; and had undertaken major military exercises that involved thousands of American soldiers in India, Jordan, and Kuwait. In addition, the Pentagon stockpiled thousands of tons of military equipment in Middle Eastern and Persian Gulf states, including Jordan, Israel, Qatar, and Kuwait.[3]

Meanwhile, Bush extended his preemption doctrine to America's domestic scene. He permitted the roundup of hundreds of Arabs in the United States, mainly on immigration violations, as "material witnesses" to terrorism, detaining some indefinitely and putting many of them through secret deportation hearings. He arrested several American citizens on the grounds they were "enemy combatants," holding them without outlining any charges and preventing them from seeing lawyers or getting judicial review. He proposed setting up military tribunals to try some suspects in a way that would have precluded independent juridical examination and possibly would have allowed them to be condemned to death in secret. His attorney general asserted the right to listen in on private conversations between alleged terrorists and their lawyers. Bush pushed the USA Patriot Act through Congress, allowing him to designate any organization or individuals as terrorists, to freeze all of their assets, and to criminalize anyone giving them money irrespective of their intent. Under Section 802 of the act, surveillance was even authorized in cases where domestic activities "appear to be intended to influence the policy of a government by intimidation or coercion. . . ." Bush curtailed the Freedom of Information Act to protect "national security secrets." He set up a so-called TIPs program, asking Americans to spy on each other. He demanded that the 1878 Posse Comitatus Act be amended to allow soldiers rather than merely police to make civilian arrests. He asked scientists not to publish information about their research lest it fall into the wrong hands. He insisted that the FBI investigate members of the intelligence oversight committees in Congress for leaking information. And his defense secretary tried to allow American Special Forces to infiltrate allied countries without their prior knowledge to hunt al Qaeda operatives.

In early 2002, Bush announced a crusade against the man he deemed as the most dangerous leader among the so-called axis of evil countries, Saddam Hussein. He made an impassioned appeal to the American people for undertaking a preemptive attack on Baghdad to rid the world of the Iraqi tyrant. He said he was basing his power to act in this case on his inherent powers as president as well as on earlier UN resolutions enacted against Iraq during the Gulf War of 1991. As Bush began to ratchet up the campaign, however, he drew criticism from many quarters—within his own Republican ranks, from some opposition Democrats, and particularly from overseas allies.

The core argument of this opposition was that the United States had succeeded for eleven years or so in containing Iraq, had deterred Saddam Hussein from invading his neighbors, had stopped him from building a nuclear bomb, had prevented his transfers of weaponry to terrorists (unlikely in any case because such arsenals might well be turned against him), so now it wasn't clear why Washington should abandon such a policy and start a war rather than stick with containment until Hussein died or his regime collapsed. Containment was, after all, a strategy the United States had successfully used against the Soviet Union, a far more dangerous adversary. Containment had already weakened Hussein's army, eroded the potency of his chemical and biological stockpiles, and shifted about 40 percent of his land from the dictator's grasp into enclaves patrolled by American bombers. Bush officials countered, nonetheless, that they believed the embargo was too porous.

Other skeptics about the Bush policy argued that, quite apart from whether containment was working or not, preemptive action was flatly against international law and constituted aggression, especially when that action was actually "preventative" in character—that is, it would happen before a country actually became threatening. Preventative strikes had, one recalls, triggered both World War I and World War II. Indeed, the reasoning behind the creation of the United

Nations itself was to preclude nations from attacking other countries based merely on a fear of an attack or on the supposition of some possible harm at a future time. Article 51 of the United Nations Charter permitted a country to go into battle against another without first seeking approval from the UN Security Council only when it was the victim of an "armed attack" or when it was under the direct and immediate threat of a military invasion. Only then could a state invoke the right of self-defense against an aggressor. Israel had cited this provision to justify its surprise attacks in 1967 against Egypt, Jordan, and Syria, when it saw Arab troops massing ominously along its borders. But, these critics contended, the United States was not yet facing in Iraq an instantaneous, overwhelming threat that left no choices of means or time for deliberation. Iraq might, in brief, be a long-term hazard, of which Washington should properly be wary. But any U.S. intervention when Iraq was quiescent and nonthreatening would amount to an act of preventive war.

As a result of these and related arguments, the Bush administration went to considerable lengths to demonstrate the threat emanating from Iraq. The first was the purported threat from weapons of mass destruction, the most frequently cited excuse for preemption, though one for which there was no "smoking gun" before, and for ten months following the invasion. The second was the link to terrorists—indeed, not Iraqi terrorists, but those of other Islamic countries hiding in Iraq. As Colin Powell put it in his dramatic February 5, 2003, presentation before the UN Security Council, there existed a "sinister nexus between Iraq and the al Qaeda terrorist network, a nexus that combines classic terrorist organizations and modern methods of murder." He cited Saddam's past support of Palestinian terrorists, as well as the alleged actions of Abu Musab al-Zarqawi, a Palestinian working with Osama bin Laden and allegedly directing operations across the Middle East from Baghdad. "Ambition and hatred are enough to bring Iraq and al Qaeda together, enough so al Qaeda could learn how to build more sophisticated bombs and learn how to forge documents, and enough so that al Qaeda could turn to Iraq for help in acquiring expertise on weapons of mass destruction," Powell declared. He then summed up the Bush doctrine in a dramatic flourish underscoring the need for preemption: "When we confront a regime that harbors ambitions for regional domination, hides weapons of mass destruction, and provides haven and active support for terrorists, we are not confronting the past; we are confronting the present. And unless we act, we are confronting an even more frightening future."

Here, then, was the most direct statement linking transnational networks of political violence and a new U.S. doctrine to unseat regimes that might provide support, even passive support, to these migratory threats. The Bush doctrine, as applied to Iraq, *had* to include the terrorist threat—and one that was by its nature transnational—in order to be credible and to justify the case for self-defense by projecting military power into a sovereign state. Powell's was not a convincing performance, but it was a necessary one.

After the war, as the rationales for preemption appeared ever weaker, the administration repeatedly conflated Iraq's old regime, the postwar violence besetting the U.S. occupation forces, and the anti-terrorism campaign occasioned by the September 11 attacks. As Bush put it in an address to the nation in September 2003, "the war on terror [is] a lengthy war, a different kind of war, fought on many fronts in many places. Iraq is now the central front." As a number of commentators said at the time, the preemption itself created the unruly conditions— including signs of ethnic strife—in which various politically violent groups could thrive. To a striking extent, this was precisely what "realists" had warned of during the preamble to war, demonstrating again how extreme were Bush's doctrine and implementation.

PREVENTIVE WAR AS DEFENSE AGAINST TERRORISTS

Between 1800 and 1934, the American military had intervened many times— almost 180 times—mostly in Central and South America, often for legitimate reasons of saving Americans from harm, but also on some occasions preventively, to collect debts and overthrow hostile anti-U.S. regimes. America secretly spawned covert CIA operations in Iran in 1953, in Guatemala in 1954, in Indonesia in 1956, and in other trouble spots well into the 1970s and 1980s that were decidedly preventative in nature—few of which brought about the felicitous results America sought. But—at least on a public level—in that postwar period, the United States did inveigh against such unilateral forms of warfare. Indeed, at one especially hot time during the most frightening crisis of the Cold War, the 1962 Cuban Missile Crisis, the United States had an opportunity to launch a preemptive attack on Havana to wipe out the Russian missiles, but declined to do so. The Kennedy administration believed such a precipitous move by the United States would violate international law, appear as cowardly as the Japanese sneak attack on Pearl Harbor, and tarnish America's democratic values. And when it did finally decide to impose a quarantine on Cuba, Washington acted under the U.N. Charter Article 51, which allows regional bodies, in this case the Organization of American States, to take action in self-defense in the face of imminent peril. Finally, it should be noted that one of the most deeply conservative Republican presidents of modern times, Ronald Reagan, condemned Israel for its preventative destruction of Iraq's nuclear facilities in 1981 as a violation of the UN Charter.

More ominously, though, any example America was likely to set in regard to preventative forays could prove contagious for other nations. If the United States could act preventatively, why then could not every other nation in the world take similar liberties? Why shouldn't India invade Pakistan or China overrun Taiwan? In addition, once such a policy gained standing, would it not trigger arms races all over the globe, as every country would have an incentive to buy more weapons to protect itself against possible preventive wars? Some, indeed, might even initiate their own preemptive incursions to forestall surprise attacks. All of these consequences would spell the doom of the over 350 years of state-to-state diplomacy starting with the Westphalian Settlement in Europe in 1648 that recognized the sovereignty of the nation-state as the basis of world order. It would lead to the collapse of the United Nations, since the entire structure of that body's collective security would be destroyed. In short, this new paradigm could shift the world away from the stable system of the past half-century that had required states to operate within international law toward a lawless world dominated by raw power, shifting alliances, and rival power blocs in Asia, Africa, and Europe. It would precipitate the very anarchy that it claimed it wished to eliminate.

The last, perhaps most self-deceptive feature about preventive war is one that is often forgotten: it is based on the fundamental illusion that it is possible to foresee what is to come. As historians are wont to tell their students, history does not follow a logical path. It has a distressing habit of outwitting all certitudes. As the English historian Sir Herbert Butterfield once wrote: "The hardest strokes of heaven fall in history upon those who imagine that they can control things in a sovereign manner, playing providence not only for themselves but for the future—reaching out into the future with the wrong kind of farsightedness, and gambling on a lot of risky calculations in which there must never be a single mistake.[4]" Or, as Michael Duffey in *Time* magazine has suggested: "Bush's preemptive doctrine assumes that we may never have all the intelligence, we may be able to make only educated guesses about our enemies' arsenals and intentions, and we'll need to rely on wisps and warnings and our guts." Preemption can become a delusion of terrible consequence.[5]

Finally, this caution is underscored by the available alternatives. A state that feels imperiled by a possible threat of mass destruction can always go to the international community and ask for assistance. A country can, for example, request the U.N. General Assembly to strengthen the global treaties that are designed to control biological, chemical, and nuclear weapons, including such accords as the nuclear nonproliferation agreement and the various pacts designed to mitigate the perils of chemical and biological weapons. If such efforts fail, or outlaw nations remain unwilling to comply, there are recourses to more potent UN enforcement measures through the United Nations Security Council—for example, sanctions against an offending state, embargoes, seizures of assets abroad, or, in extreme cases, military involvement. Indeed, action against Libya's terrorism became effective with such a combination of constraints and disincentives, not the military action of 1986, which yielded only more terrorism.

TERRORISM AND HEGEMONY

All of this, though, seems to be of little interest to Bush strategists. It is clear that this administration sees preemptive action as leading to larger stakes. President Bush and his foreign policy entourage, almost since they took over the White House, and especially since September 11, have become persuaded that employing preemptive strikes around the globe advances a U.S. plan to expand the "zone of democracy" and reshape the entire world security system. As Bush put it in his West Point speech: the United States has "the best chance since the rise of the nation-state in the seventeenth century to build a world where the great powers compete in peace instead of prepare for war." And in that same talk, Bush vowed that "America has, and intends to keep, military strengths beyond challenge, thereby making the destabilizing arms race of other eras pointless and limiting rivalries to trade and other pursuits of peace." Shortly after the destruction of the World Trade Center, National Security Advisor Condoleezza Rice offered a blueprint along these lines: "I really think this period is analogous to 1945–1947 in that the events . . . started shifting the tectonic plates in international politics. And it's important to try to seize on that and position American interests and institutions before they harden again."[6]

With such pronouncements, Bush and his team have immediately raised the question of what new institutions they envisage for the planet, and concomitantly how they intend to convince the rest of the peoples on earth to go along with their vision. So far, they have remained mum on major plans for a new global order. While they seem ready to replace most of the existing commitments of prior American administrations, as evidenced by their hostility to existing global treaties, their replacement proposals appear to boil down to the view that the United States should alone take the leading role in the world in deciding the globe's fate by its sheer wits, superior intelligence, and outsized muscle. In effect, they are saying to the inhabitants of earth, "Trust us," instead of, "We'll work with you." This approach should not come as a surprise. Not only has the new president almost from the start signaled he would act unabashedly in America's self-interest, Condoleezza Rice remarked almost casually early in 2000, it is not "isolationist to suggest that the United States has a special role in the world and should not adhere to every international convention and agreement that someone thinks to propose."[7]

The Bush administration continued to publicly support several ratified non-proliferation treaties dealing with nuclear, biological, and chemical weaponry. These included: the Missile Technology Control Regime, an informal arrangement among twenty-nine countries to prevent the export of technologies for delivering nuclear warheads and weapons of mass destruction; the Chemical Weapons Convention, which bans chemical weapons and provides for inspections of chemical factories; the Non-Proliferation Treaty, which seeks to prevent the spread of nuclear weapons to countries that do not have them, and which has 182 signatories; the Australia Group, an informal arrangement of thirty-three countries to prevent the export of biological and chemical weapons; and the Biological Weapons Convention, which prohibits the development, production, or possession of biological weapons. Bush, in June 2002, also secured an agreement with the G-8 nations, pledging an American contribution of $10 billion over ten years, to prevent the spread of weapons of mass destruction.[8] But, as Richard Haass, the State Department's policy planning chief, has noted, this was part of Bush's "a la carte multilateralism" approach to international affairs.

The one treaty Bush negotiated of any consequence—the so-called Moscow Treaty with Russia in May 2002—was designed to reduce nuclear warheads on both sides to 1,700–2,200. But this, critics contend, is a sham pact that allows the United States to continue holding onto its nuclear arsenal and permits both Washington and Moscow to violate Article VI of the Nuclear Non-Proliferation Treaty, which obligates all nuclear powers to disarm. The deal allows each side to eliminate warheads at any pace they wish and, most significantly, does not force them to destroy any of their missiles. Instead they are allowed to stockpile, warehouse, or store them (thereby increasing the chances they might be stolen). The only time the United States actually has to reduce its weapons is on a single day at the very end of the ten-year agreement—on December 31, 2012. Even then, the American reduction needs only to last for that sole twenty-four-hour period. Thereafter the United States can quickly restore its full complement of warheads. There is a provision, too, allowing withdrawal at any time if a three-month notification is given. But even after withdrawal, or after the end of the treaty period in 2012 (absent any extension), the two governments can return to any level of warheads they desire. Further, there is no effort to ban land-based missiles with multiple warheads or the 10,000 or so tactical nuclear weapons that both sides reportedly together possess. As one Bush official stated to the *New York Times:*

"What we have now agreed to do under the treaty is what we wanted to do anyway. That's our kind of treaty."[9]

Some analysts today see the overall Bush geopolitical thrust as an attempt "to parlay its momentary power advantages into a world order in which it runs the show," according to international relations theorist John Ikenberry. Or, as *International Herald Tribune* columnist William Pfaff suggested, "Their utopianism is their belief that American domination of international society is history's natural conclusion—since, as President George W. Bush himself recently said at West Point, America is the 'single surviving model of human progress.'" Pfaff summed up: "This is their version of American Manifest Destiny. Its authors themselves describe it as a tough version of Wilsonianism, created in the higher interest of all." Fundamentally, this version of foreign affairs is an outgrowth of a viewpoint that we live in a Hobbesian universe, in which no nation can be ruled out as a possible adversary, international laws are unreliable, and military power exercised by a single nation alone can bring order and sustain democratic systems. This is an extreme form of American exceptionalism. But, as *New Yorker* columnist Hendrik Hertzberg has observed: "The Bush vision is in the end a profoundly pessimistic one, and, as such, more than a little un-American. It is, among other things, a vision of perpetual war."[10]

The salient dangers of such an overweening approach are manifold. The primary one—historically the most perilous—is that other nations eventually will resent the primary power and create alliances against it. America's kind of domination can itself spur further terrorism and breed disorder rather than bring order. And, in any case, predominance of power alone has proven in the past to be unable to run the planet. America or any other great power always needs other countries to help keep the peace. The major oddity about the Bush policy, though, is that it shows such scant knowledge of its own country's postwar history: over the past sixty or so years, it is the very intricate and integrative obligations and legal frameworks, forged mainly by the United States and its allies, that have led to global stability and worldwide prosperity and have essentially eliminated world war. "The United States," as John Ikenberry has written, "made its power safe for the world, and in return the world agreed to live within the U.S. system. . . . The result has been the most stable and prosperous international system in world history." Bush's maneuvers—his reassertion of the strong American state over and above the value of global cooperation—now threaten to disrupt, if not shatter, all of these achievements.[11]

In the end, even the most ideological state will have to adjust to the realities of life. Bush can't control every single event, global public discontent is growing, and pragmatic considerations cannot be avoided. Finally, because he wants to be reelected, Bush will now have to compromise to survive politically. On Iraq, for example, Bush, under intense criticism from allies and domestic constituencies, ultimately conceded that he needed to obtain prior authorization from Congress and from the United Nations before he could undertake an invasion of that country (even while preserving his right to act if neither body approved of his decision). He once opposed nation building; now he is going forward with it in Afghanistan and Iraq. He once hinted he might withdraw American peacekeeping troops from Kosovo and Bosnia, yet in office, changed his mind and kept American soldiers at their posts. He said that he would not talk with North Korea, a member of the "axis of evil," but since authorized discussions under pressure from regional allies. In the first year of his administration, he stayed out of the Middle East; but after the escalating and bloody conflicts in the region, he reasserted America's peace-brokering role in the Israel-Palestine dispute. He once inveighed against foreign aid and international bailouts, but after attending the Monterrey Conference in Mexico, he increased U.S. assistance abroad, and, following the possible collapse of Brazil in mid-2002, he authorized a $30 billion rescue loan for that country.

Bush is not retreating from his unilateralist course, however, as the Iraq war itself demonstrates. This is in spite of what Columbia professor Simon Schama, among others, has written—that since September 11, "in place of the luxury of isolation, Americans have no option but to accept the necessity of connection. . . . If Americans are, for the foreseeable future, fated to live inside, rather than alongside, the imperfect, dangerous world, they are also likely to experience a greater, rather than lesser, share of its ancient woes and misfortunes. The worst thing to do would be to treat such adversity as might come their way as if it were some sort of violation of American exceptionalism, when it is, in fact, the result of it. Perhaps, in any case, there are worse things than bidding farewell to the fond illusion that Americans would remain forever exempt from the ways of the world, calamities included." Put another way, in the words of Thomas Jefferson over 200 years ago in the Declaration of Independence, America must show "a decent respect to the opinions of mankind." [12]

Terrorism has, indeed, altered the equation of how today we see ourselves as residents of this country. It has made every responsible official reconsider what we must do to defend our citizenry against further predatory assaults. Two great oceans, the Atlantic and the Pacific, once provided the United States a haven of security against outside adversaries. Neither the First World War nor the Second World War touched the United States in any serious way. But the unprecedented attacks of September 11, 2001, showed America now how vulnerable it was to lethal outside assaults. This reality has shaken the country to its roots. Our government is still reacting in ways that are being judged and evaluated; we can't fully assess their meaning at this time. We remain a nation traveling down uncertain pathways. Hence, we must keep a careful watch over where we go. But we must hold to the credo that the surest vision for American foreign policy in a fractious and troubled world is to pursue law and consent, not a Pax Americana.

GLOBALIZATION, LOW-INTENSITY CONFLICT, AND PROTRACTED STATELESSNESS/REFUGEEHOOD: *THE PLIGHT OF THE ROHINGYAS*

IMTIAZ AHMED

September 11 has been an eye-opener for many. Let me share my experience. When I first met Selim (obviously not his real name) I had no clue that I was meeting a Rohingya. I got a call from him the night before and found him eager to meet me the very next day. This was, incidentally, a year or two before 9/11. The meeting was brief but precise. The discussion went like this:

> *"Do you know that I am a Rohingya?"*
> "Not really."
> *"Do you know anything about us?"*
> "A little."
> *"How little?"*
> "Well, your traditional home is in the Arakan, and you have been driven out by the Myanmar military government several times into Bangladesh. And now, save 21,000, all of you have gone back to the Arakan."
> *"Did you know that we are still stateless people, and the Myanmar government has refused to recognize us as citizens since 1948?"*
> "Well, yes, I heard something about that."
> *"Do you think the people of Bangladesh know that?"*
> "I doubt it."
> *"Do you think the people of this region know that?"*
> "I doubt it."
> *"Do you think the world knows about our plight, about our statelessness?"*
> "I doubt it."
> *"Well, I have no doubts. No one knows anything about us. No one cares about us. Is this living? Have you any idea how difficult it is for a stateless person to live in this world, and that again for over fifty years, practically from birth to death?"*
> "What do you want me to do?"
> *"Write about us, speak about us. The younger generation is becoming violent every day. They don't want to live like this. They want to change things. If nothing is done soon, it will be difficult to stop their rage!"*

Selim left as he came, unnoticed but in appearance slightly disturbed. I must confess that I was moved by his plea and saw merit in his argument. But then, when the world came to know about the Rohingyas' "rage," albeit in bits and pieces, I never thought that it would be in relation to 9/11, or more precisely, in relation to the aftermath of 9/11. Soon after the U.S. military got rid of the Taliban they came to know that some Rohingya "fighters" had made their way into Afghanistan and were trained by the Taliban.[1] Rohingyas in Afghanistan: how could that happen? How did they manage to cross 1,500 miles and that again, just to train themselves militarily? Who was paying for them? What weapons were they using? Were Bangladeshis culpable in their flight to Kabul? Or, were they helped by the Indians and Pakistanis to cross their respective borders and then managed to arrive in Afghanistan via the land routes? Or, did they come via some Middle Eastern countries, shipped and smuggled by a global network of traffickers? Are we then witnessing newer global networks or a newer globalization beyond trade, investment, and production?

In experiential terms, the scenario seems to suggest a complex relationship between the Rohingyas, Bangladeshis, Indians, Pakistanis, Arabs, Afghans, and now even the Americans. The list of people could be extended further. If we take the weapons in the hands of the Rohingya "fighters" (invariably all having illegal small arms), the relationship possibly would include the Europeans, the Chinese, or even the North Koreans—that is, as makers of these weapons. But more important a group of relatively "unknown people," engaged in a conflict that is in military jargon "low-intensity," found themselves categorized and tarnished overnight. The "plight" that they have been experiencing since birth became further entrenched, and this time not only nationally but also regionally and globally. If this requires reconceptualizing the relationship between globalization and low-intensity conflict (LIC) then there is all the more reason that the life and living of stateless people or refugees, as they have practically turned out to be,[2] are reconceptualized as well.

Two contentions are critical here. First globalization (understood here more in the economic sense) tends to *devalue* and *marginalize* conflicts (civil, political, and even national) if such conflicts have little or nothing to do with its reproduction. A conflict is otherwise graduated to "low-intensity" not so much for its lack of *intensity* (with respect to casualty, military involvement, cost of war, etc.) as for its relationship or lack of it with the globalized world. Second, insofar as LIC is devalued and marginalized, the resolution of LIC, including the refugee situation or, as in some cases, the statelessness, arising out of it also tends to be *marginal* and *ad hoc.* As a result, the refugees or stateless people end up in a state of *protracted refugeehood.* But then, protracted refugeehood creates space for the refugees to get connected to what can be best labeled as *subaltern globalization*—that is, with forces and networks resisting (economic) globalization and also, more interestingly, with the globally organized "dubious groups" "shadowy activities." I will have more to say about this issue shortly.

LIC and subsequently protracted refugeehood in the age of globalization is otherwise set to increase the suffering of the marginalized population, but then the latter makes effective use of globalization, often of the "subaltern" variant, to redress its plight. The current fate of the stateless Rohingyas and the frightening prospect it holds is but only one of the numerous cases worldwide. Before taking up the case of the Rohingyas, let me examine the multiple formations and understandings of globalization, explaining mainly the complex formation of subaltern globalization and how it is attractive to those who benefit almost little to nothing from the more formalized structure of economic globalization.

THE MULTIVERSITY OF GLOBALIZATION

Globalization, mainly because of its birth from a complex combination of multiple interactions, has given rise to a *multiversity,* or multiple universes, of knowledge and practices. Three precise modes could easily be identified. First is *economic globalization,* the second is *reverse globalization,* and the third is *subaltern globalization.* A closer exposition will make them clear.

ECONOMIC GLOBALIZATION

This has also been referred to as *globalization from the top* or *above.*[3] Its meaning has been best captured by an OECD publication which, while crediting the term to Theodore Levitt, who first used it in 1985 in his book *The Globalization of Markets,* sees globalization as "a seamless or borderless, global economy." More concretely, it is informed by precise sets of economic activities with precise characteristics on a world scale.

There exists a subtle difference between the "internationalization of economy" and "globalization" according to this perspective. While the former primarily refers to the internationalization of *trade* and later on the internationalization of *finance* and *investment,* each coming in the wake of precise historical moments of capitalism, globalization refers to the complex combination of all these but more importantly one that is inclusive of a thoroughly transformed *production* structure. The latter can be best described as the organization and development of a *denationalized* form of production.

That is, multinational, or, rather, transnational companies, now *collect* resources in several countries, *process* them in another several countries, and finally *export* the finished products to the rest of the world. A fully finished product, therefore, no longer has one single birthmark; it has multiple birthmarks since several countries have produced it. A Compaq computer, in that sense, is no longer entirely American, nor is a Toyota car fully Japanese. The final product of both these items will have components made in several countries of the world. Put differently, unlike the previous internationalization of things, in the globalization phase of capitalism the thing itself is the product of the international or global market. In this newer configuration, the nonstate enterprises are often more critical than the state-oriented or state enterprises in the reproduction of capitalism. But then, this is only one mode with a precise layer of activities that has come to fashion globalization.

REVERSE GLOBALIZATION

The second meaning of globalization is very much intrinsic to the developing country's craze for modernity, principally the organization of the (postcolonial) nation-state in the image of the modern "Western" state. In some respects this has been well described by Nirad C. Chaudhuri as early as 1926 when he, while referring to "a clash of civilization" between the East and West, sarcastically noted that "the real cultural role of the [colonized Indians] is to assimilate *the ways of Europe*."[4] This is indeed a subtle way of viewing globalization from the standpoint of those who are at the receiving end and are not the pacesetters and real gainers of the global economy. The meaning here is as cultural and intellectual, as it is economic, with the global economy remaining intrinsically related to globalization.

Put differently, if OECD's definition could be referred to as economic globalization, the modernist aspirations of the developing or less developed countries could be referred to as *reverse globalization*. The global reach of Bollywood (India's film industry) and Indian restaurants are good examples of reverse globalization, where the nonstate forces of the East or the South are no less critical in channelizing the development of the (culturally and intellectually colonized) less developed or developing countries.

SUBALTERN GLOBALIZATION

There is yet another type of interaction informing and reproducing globalization. This is a complex mode and therefore requires greater care in its exposition. Critics have already referred to the mushrooming of global networks *resisting* economic globalization, refering to the globally organized resistance movements as "globalization from below." As Brecher pointed out:

> Just as the corporate and political elites are reaching across national borders to further their agendas, people at the grassroots are connecting their struggles around the world to impose their needs and interests on the global economy. Globalization from above is generating worldwide movement of resistance: globalization from below.[5]

This is substantially different from the mode that has been referred to as *reverse globalization*. The latter has a precise economic dimension arising mainly out of cultural and intellectual domination, whereas globalization from below, as suggested by Brecher (2000), refers mainly to the "resistance movements" against economic globalization. More concretely, globalization from below includes a diverse group of people—environmentalists, NGOs, religious groups, small farmers, labor unions (incidentally of both the developed and developing countries), women's movements, consumerists, African debt relief campaigners, anti-sweatshop activists, and the like, all one way or another either critical of or directly suffering from and struggling against the impact of economic globalization. Here the forces of the seemingly disempowered nonstate have creatively joined hands to overcome the exploitation of the empowered nonstate, i.e., the forces of economic globalization. The subaltern nature of the resistance movements, particularly the networking, can hardly be minimized.

But then, there is a further subaltern variant to the whole notion of globalization from below. This refers to the deepening of relationship between and among the "dubious groups" and "shadowy activities" ranging from smuggling of goods and people and illicit production and trading of small arms, to money laundering, narco-production and trading, terrorism, and the like, across and beyond national, ethnic, racial, and even religious affiliations. The subalterns, particularly the poverty-ridden and marginalized populations, become easy targets of such groups and activities, but more important the state of being itself becomes a factor for certain groups of (relatively well off) people to rally support and even clandestinely work for their cause. A protracted nature of poverty and marginality and a lack of substantive global concern also push them to seek informal or even criminal means to reproduce their lives or redress the situation. The complex networking at this level and in combination with the resistance movements against economic globalization could be best referred to as *subaltern globalization*. Here the subalterns, including their ardent supporters and sympathizers, are no less creative and empowered when it comes to organizing and reproducing their activities at the global level, often by challenging the overly empowered forces of economic globalization.

Two things are worth pointing out here. First is the subtle connivance of the state machineries with the dubious forces in reproducing subaltern globalization. According to Mittelman:

> The smuggling operations would not be possible . . . without the involvement of powerful and wealthy criminals, who have the resources to corrupt state officials. The corruption of political authorities is the crucible in which customs officers, police, and tax

inspectors assist in alien smuggling, but also drug smuggling, intellectual property counterfeiting, illegal currency transactions, and other black- and gray-market activities. In this web of criminals, the rich, and politicians, the holders of public office provide "legal" protection for their partners. . . . [6]

The state machineries in this case go on to empower the subaltern networks almost to their own peril, which brings us to the second point: indeed, if economic globalization is in the business of weakening the power of the state, the practices of subaltern globalization are no less menacing and destructive to the state. To cite Mittelman again:

> [Criminal] groups are alternative social organizations that, in some respects, challenge the power and authority of the state to impose its standards, codified as law. These groups constitute an alternative system by offering commerce and banking in black and gray markets that operate outside the regulatory framework of the state; buying, selling, and distributing controlled or prohibited commodities, such as narcotics; providing swift and usually discreet dispute resolution and debt collection without resorting to the courts; creating and maintaining cartels when state laws proscribe them; and arranging security for the so-called protection of businesses, as well as sheltering them from competitors, the state and rival criminals.[7]

There is therefore no reason to doubt the destructive potential of subaltern globalization. Even those resisting economic globalization and joining ranks with the subalterns may find themselves at risk if and when the destructive potential of subaltern globalization is played out with full ferocity and demonic intent. A quick look at some of the practices of subaltern globalization would provide credence to our contention.

SUBALTERN GLOBALIZATION IN PRACTICE

The element of subalternity in the resistance movements against economic globalization (and the case could also be stretched to reverse globalization) cannot be denied. The antiglobalization protests in Seattle, Rome, Prague, or Washington all tend to indicate that the subalterns or marginalized forces have been put into a dire situation because of economic globalization. The protests are otherwise meant to highlight the grievances of the subalterns worldwide. Simple as this may sound, there is a complex process informing the subalternity of the resistance movements.

The movements are actually intended to unite the dispersed subaltern groups with precise objectives, mainly to overcome or more appropriately lessen the exploitation of the dominant or hegemonic forces. There is a precise Gramscian understanding of the issue here, particularly in impressing upon the subaltern groups to *organize* in order to overcome or reduce the power of the hegemons.[8] Insofar as the task of organization is involved, the globally staged resistance movements tend to highlight not only the sufferings of the victims of economic globalization but also alternative policies and programs that these subalterns may find useful in their battle against economic globalization. But the universality in the resistance movements cannot be stretched very far.

It is true that the subaltern population of both the developed and developing countries have suffered from economic globalization, but the fact remains that there is less universality when it comes to redressing their conditions. To cite one example; the garment workers of developing economies may be suffering from the postglobalization competition and therefore are likely to plead for more openness of the developed market for exporting their clothings, but the garment workers of the developed economies faced with the cheap labor and relatively cheaper clothing of the developing economies are likely to seek more protection of their domestic market and discourage the import of clothing. Put differently, the workers of both developed and developing countries could be complaining about the impact of economic globalization and even openly protesting against it, but interestingly they are doing so from quite opposite, almost contradictory, positions. The subaltern unity here is more tactical than strategic, and is therefore open to the possibility of the leadership and the campaign being co-opted by the forces of economic globalization with concessions of one type or another. Neoprotectionist measures of the developed economies are indeed of this nature.

The resistance movements, however, in and by themselves do not reproduce the life and living of the subalterns. Mittelman has already indicated that "where poverty is severe, criminal gangs flourish."[9] The link between poverty and criminality is less linear than what is seemingly suggested here. A state of subalternity in fact creates conditions that make people disinterested in the business of reproducing the power of the state. Misgovernance otherwise becomes the (dis)order of the day. People, particularly the subalterns, increasingly start depending on informal, often criminal, means for reproducing their livelihood. Even when requiring business or personal security they fall back on the power of the "godfathers," hired goons, *mastans,* and the like, than on the otherwise inept, often corrupt, governmental machineries. A shadowy network of things and transactions get reproduced and in the process destabilizes not only the power of the state but also the power of the subalterns, making them more vulnerable and disempowered. This further creates grounds for fresh recruits and creative but demonic ventures for organizing and reproducing subaltern globalization.

Smuggling, particularly human trafficking, across nations, regions, and continents is a good indicator of the demonic venture found in subaltern globalization. According to a report filed by the Burmese American Democratic Alliance in March 2002:

> Each year thousands of young girls are recruited from rural Burmese villages to work in the sex industry in neighbouring Thailand. Held for years in debt bondage in illegal Thai brothels, they suffer extreme abuse by pimps, clients, and the police. . . . The trafficking of Burmese girls has soared in recent years as a direct result of political repression in Burma. Human rights abuses, war and ethnic discrimination has displaced hundreds of thousands of families, leaving families with no means of livelihood. An offer of employment in Thailand is a rare chance for many families to escape extreme poverty.
>
> Agents have now established networks reaching into the remote areas of Thailand's neighbours including Burma, Laos, Southern China and Cambodia. The children are mainly brought in through north and northeastern Thailand where they are then taken to other areas within the country. Although there are no exact figures available regarding the numbers of children being trafficked into Thailand for sexual exploitation, estimates nevertheless provide an indicative picture. From Burma, it was estimated in 1994 that as many as 20,000 to 30,000 women and girls had been trafficked primarily into brothels in Thailand, with 10,000 new recruits being added each year.[10]

Although Thailand is believed to be the primary destination of trafficked Burmese women and children, other destinations include China, India, Bangladesh, Taiwan, Pakistan, Malaysia, Singapore, Japan, and countries in the Middle East.[11] If this is the case, then it is quite understandable that, in the context of human trafficking from Burma (that is, Myanmar), a very vibrant regional cum global relations exists and it is being reproduced by none other than the dubious and shadowy forces of subaltern globalization. Indeed, for human trafficking to take place across regions and continents, there must be a demonic, yet creative, relationship among members of various sectors and professions, races and religions, countries and nationalities, almost paralleling the complex networks of economic globalization.

More important, however, poverty, vulnerability, and marginalization are the required conditions for large-scale human trafficking.[12] In fact, the vulnerability of the subalterns itself creates conditions for the latter to become an easy, often consenting, prey of the smugglers, not only in making the subalterns the subject of smuggling but also in making them available in the very operation of smuggling. In this context, it may be pointed out that there is a substantial difference between the *smugglers* and the *smuggling agents*, although both are in the business of criminalizing the society and the world.[13] The former are the owners of capital invested in smuggling, while the latter are mere workers, paid in cash every time they successfully deliver the goodies to their destinations. In fact, it is the smuggling agent that does all the dirty work, including bribing security and other governmental officials at each stage of his/her journey, while the smugglers enjoy the big profit margin of the smuggled goods.[14] Viewed from the standpoint of the smuggling agent, it is just another occupation, somewhat desperately undertaken for a better rate of returns, required no less for reproducing the life and livelihood of the equally desperate subalterns.

Human trafficking, however, goes on to reflect more broadly disorder and misgovernance not only within the state but also in the relationship that goes in the name of interstate commerce. Indeed, such disorder and misgovernance further empower the dubious and shadowy forces of subaltern globalization. They end up with networks and activities that are as menacing to the state and interstate relations as they are to the life and living of the subalterns. Such is the irony of subaltern globalization. The complex structure is somewhat demonically intriguing. I will limit myself to four areas, with particular reference to terrorism.

NARCO-TERRORISM

Narco-production and trading is a lucrative business in this region. In 2001 Myanmar surpassed Afghanistan as the largest producer of illicit opium and heroin in the world. To provide some knowledge of the amount, 865 metric tons of opium was produced in Myanmar in 2001, almost all of which were processed into heroin and sold to the illicit market both within and outside the region.[15] This is more than double the amount of illicit opium that is available in other heroin-producing countries, such as India, Colombia, Mexico, or Laos.[16] It may be mentioned that there exists a vibrant but complex relationship between opium growers and heroin producers, drug dealers and consumers, security and customs officials, high-risk investors and money launderers, not only nationally but also regionally and globally. As the following U.S. Drug Enforcement Agency report suggests:

> Opium poppy cultivation and heroin refining take place in remote, mountainous border regions. Armed ethnic groups such as, the United Wa State Army, the Kokang Chinese, and the Myanmar National Democratic Alliance Army control the cultivation areas, refine opium into heroin, and also produce methamphetamine. Associates of these organizations from other Asian nations have shipped tons of heroin from Burma to the United States within the past decade. The largest single heroin seizure in the United States consisted of 486 kilograms of Burma-produced heroin that the U.S. Customs Service discovered in a containerized shipment of plastic bags from Southeast Asia, via Taiwan, en route to a warehouse in Hayward, California, in May 1991.[17]

But Myanmar, apart from being a member of the infamous "Golden Triangle," is also close to yet another major narco-producing region, the "Golden Crescent." In the smuggling of heroin from Myanmar beyond the region and the continent, both India and Bangladesh are used as transit points.[18] This further exacerbates problems related to narco-terrorism in the region. In fact, one critical problem arising out of the confluence of two major narco-producing and trading regions is the cementing of a diabolic relationship between insurgent groups and narco-terrorism. Such a relationship is quite common in and around Thai-Myanmar, Indo-Myanmar, and Bangladesh-Myanmar borders. Not that all the insurgent groups engage in narco-production or narco-trafficking, but it has been found that almost all of them have regularly taxed and exhorted money from the traffickers while providing protection to the latter for conducting trafficking in drugs. There are several critical implications of this.

First, the transnational narco-networks, now backed by armed insurgents, make anti–narco-production or anti–narco-trafficking drive immensely difficult. And given the terrain (both physical and topographical) in which the insurgents and the traffickers operate, there is now all the more reason to believe that the *nationally organized* military or coercive solutions may not be the correct way of overcoming the menace of narco-terrorism.

Second, weapons, particularly small arms, in the hands of both the insurgents and traffickers become more rampant, indeed, to the point of threatening the law and order situation in the vicinity. A large portion of the money received from taxing and extorting the narco-traffickers goes on to purchase small, at times sophisticated, arms for the insurgents. I will have more to say about this issue later.

Finally, subaltern aspirations get entwined between insurgency and narco-terrorism, almost to the point of blurring the distinction between the two. While this becomes handy for the state machineries in the strategy of depicting the insurgents as narco-traders and winning back the support of the members of the dissenting communities, it often leads them to quick-fix remedies with little or no results. As the World Bank–sponsored study on Indo-Bangladesh border smuggling once pointed out, "Ordinary men, women and even children participate in smuggling as couriers, porters and rickshaw pullers," which only indicates that the subalternity of smuggling or even narco-terrorism is far more complex than what is readily understood.[19] There is therefore no guarantee that the narco-menace would discourage the subalterns from joining the trade.

Money Laundering

Narco-terrorism would not make much headway without the practice of money laundering.[20] It is the latter that provides the required funds for the production and, later on, shipments of the narcotics across regions and continents. The weakness and corruption prevalent in the banking system of the region remain easily susceptible to money laundering. As Kaung maintains:

> Burma's banks are more like a dubious "Ponzi" or pyramid scheme[21] than well-run commercial banks. Between 1962 and 1988, the banks in Burma were all state-owned, and lent primarily to state owned enterprises. After 1988, the declaration of a so-called open market economy made way for private commercial banks, but they were never built on strong capital. These private commercial banks lent money to the newly enlarged private sector and managed to attract some private deposits too. But the performance of

Burma's commercial banks has proved something of a mixed bag. It has been alleged that banks in Burma are money laundering facilities and not real banks. The ruling junta has never revealed the cash reserve ratio that banks legally need to operate, as inflation has continued to soar at around 20 to 25 percent each year.[22]

In Myanmar's case this connivance between the banks, money launderers, and the state goes even deeper, with the narco-traffickers benefiting the most. In fact, it has been alleged that Khun Sa, a notorious drug trafficker, agreed to cease-fire conditions when the government of Myanmar (GOM) allowed Sa to invest his drug profits in the country's infrastructure and legitimate businesses.[23] The drug trafficker cum money launderer, with the connivance of the bank and the state, ended up running legal businesses! When such a structure comes into being it becomes impossible to eradicate narco-trafficking and all the corroborating agencies, including money laundering and terrorism, unless and until the state itself goes through a sustained period of reform and restructuring.

At times certain other structural factors are also responsible in reproducing money laundering, as is the case with the stateless but relatively well off Rohingyas living abroad. As stateless and with few licit areas in which to invest, these Rohingyas have no option but to launder money to various Rohingya nationalist or insurgent groups, mainly to fulfill their subaltern aspirations in the northern Arakan region of Myanmar. That a part of this money would be used in purchasing arms and later on in insurgent or terrorist activities can never be ruled out.

One should not, however, make too much of a case about money laundering and its *ipso facto* relationship with terrorism. This is because the financial cost of contemporary terrorism has not been that great. Take the instance of 9/11, which, while requiring nineteen suicide attackers, had a financial input of only $500,000.[24] But this was enough to kill more than 3,000 civilians and cause a material damage of at least $40 billion, and this is exclusive of the hundreds of billions of dollars lost as a result of the slowing down of global economy immediately after the attack. If routing out terrorism is the objective, I guess a far more creative handling of the phenomenon is required, and this is true nationally, regionally, as well as globally.

Illegal Small Arms

If anything that has empowered the terrorist groups lately it has been the proliferation and use of illegal small arms. In April 1996 the Bangladesh military seized the following weapons from the vessels off Cox's Bazar, a place incidentally not very far from the Bangladesh-Myanmar border:

List of Illegal Small Arms

1.	AK-47 rifles	500
2.	Machine guns	80
3.	Rocket launchers	50
4.	Grenades	2000

Source: Binalakshmi Nepram, *South Asia's Fractured Frontier: Armed Conflict, Narcotics and Small Arms Proliferation in India's North East* (New Delhi: Mittal Publications, 2002), p. 99.

It is difficult to imagine that these weapons, including many in the pipeline, enter Bangladesh without some connivance of the state machineries, particularly police and customs departments. But even the knowledge of possible "helpers" does not provide a clear picture as to who *received* the arms and, more important, who *supplied* them. The best we can do in this kind of circumstances is consult *Jane's Infantry Weapons,* a book of notable distinction, and find out the names of the countries manufacturing these weapons. According to the *Jane's* 1996 edition, the following countries, both developed and developing, were listed as the main producers or suppliers of small arms: Argentina, Austria, Belgium, Brazil, Britain, Chile, China, France, Germany, India, Iran, Iraq, Israel, North Korea, Pakistan, Russia, Singapore, South Africa, South Korea, Spain, Switzerland, Turkey, the United States, Venezuela, and many more.

But this does not help much unless we identify the *birthmark* (i.e., the original manufacturer) of the small arms that are found and used in terrorist activities. But since the public had no access to the seized weapons mentioned above, there was no way to find out the birthmark of these weapons. But then a survey conducted at Dhaka University in 1995–1996, supplemented by various newspaper reports, helped to trace the type, birthmark, and cost of small arms found in the hands of student political cadres and in-campus *mastans* (gangsters):

Small Arms Used by Mastans in Dhaka University

Type	Birthmark/Manufacturer	Price (Taka, in Thousands)
Saddam pistol	India	40–50
9 mm bore pistol	Italy	50–60
22 bore pistol	Spain, Italy, Brazil	30
7.65 mm bore pistol	Italy	60
Chinese rifle	China	80
303 cut rifle	Britain	25
.45 revolver	USA	60

German revolver	Germany	n.a.
.324 revolver	Pakistan	15–22
Pipe gun	Local	3–5
Shutter gun	India	n.a.

Source: Abdullah-al Shams, "Campus Terrorism." Research conducted under the supervision of the author, Department of International Relations, University of Dhaka, September 1996; Neila Husain, "Proliferation of Small Arms and Politics in South Asia: The Case of Bangladesh," *RCSS* (Regional Centre for Strategic Studies, Colombo) *Policy Studies* 7 (May 1999).

The type and birthmark of the small arms indicate that the bulk of them were produced in developed countries, but it does not tell us how they made it to the university. It is unlikely that these weapons were directly shipped or airlifted from the manufacturing countries to their destination in Dhaka. What is more likely is that these weapons entered Bangladesh from various border points (Bangladesh-Myanmar as well as Indo-Bangladesh) via a vibrant subaltern network (both dubious and political) that possibly included at various stages of their shipments members of both developed and developing countries.

On this issue, a national daily of Bangladesh reported:

> Sixteen northern districts of the country, especially the frontier ones are flooded with illegal arms and ammunition, posing a threat to law and order situation. These arms are mostly possessed by political activists, outlawed extremists, terrorists, extortionists and miscreants. The illegal arms include both foreign and local stun gun, SMG, sawed-off rifle, SLR, revolver and pipe gun. Most of the firearms are in the hands of activists of "three political parties" who have separate hideouts in different places in this region including frontiers of Natore, Pabna, Sirajganj and Bogra districts.[25]

The subaltern nature of the network cannot be denied, although the flow of small arms has gone beyond those adhering to some form of subaltern aspirations. In fact, the flow has become so acute and extensive that even the former Indian High Commissioner to Bangladesh, Deb Mukherjee, publicly noted that "It is possible that firearms are among the items *smuggled* from India into Bangladesh."[26] Put differently, without an extensive subaltern network, it is impossible to imagine the flow of small arms, whether Cox's Bazaar or Dhaka University. At times, however, not only the arms flow but also the network could prove deadly. Let me cite an example by quoting Singh:

> A large number of terrorist groups are believed to be in possession of man-portable SAMs now. . . . The whereabouts of the unaccounted 560 Stinger missiles (out of the stock supplied to Afghan Mujahideen) are unknown, and all efforts to recover them have failed so far. A few had appeared in Iran, having been sold by the Mujahideen. Another 312 were reportedly sold in the open market at Landi Kotal (Pakistan) in January 1993. Earlier this year (1995) the LTTE shot down two Sri Lanka Air Force aircraft carrying passengers.[27]

What we have here is a subaltern network consisting of Afghans, Iranians, Pakistanis, and missiles making it to the hands of the Tamil Tigers, Indians, and Sri Lankans. But then, an American-made weapon changing hands in Afghanistan, Iran, Pakistan, India, and finally reaching Sri Lanka can only make everyone culpable when the said weapon is finally used against the Sri Lankans. Similar is the case with the weapons that are used in Bombay, Karachi, Dhaka, Delhi, Colombo, or any other place in South Asia. Indeed, if there is an element of subaltern bonding among the users of small arms, there is also a bonding, albeit more social, among those killed by these weapons. This is because most of the victims turn out to be disempowered, marginalized subalterns!

If we take a critical and holistic stock of narco-terrorism, money laundering, and illegal small arms, it becomes easy to comprehend the changing nature of contemporary terrorism. When it comes to the issue of organizing and reproducing terrorism, the latter has ceased to remain "national" or "statist." Instead, terrorism has now become "transnational," making the best, if not creative, use of globalization, particularly of the subaltern variant. In this light, it is not difficult to see as to why some Rohingyas, lifelong stateless and somewhat perennially disempowered and marginalized, ended up taking arms and even seeking military training from the Taliban in Afghanistan. Put differently, the "low-intensity conflict" of the Rohingyas, while keeping them conflict-prone but in utterly miserable conditions, created a milieu for some to enter the network of subaltern globalization. While the intention possibly was to make a difference to their plight, the entry into the network of subaltern globalization further alienated and stigmatized the stateless Rohingyas. The plight of the latter, however, is multiformed and multilayered, with social, cultural, and political as well as local and global dimensions.

THE PLIGHT OF THE ROHINGYAS

According to *1997 Statistical Yearbook,* published by the Government of Myanmar, the "official" population of the Arakan or Rakhine State, where most Rohingyas reside, numbered around 2.6 million.[28] In addition to this 2.6 million (and this is according to some unofficial estimates made in 1991), another one to two million Rohingyas also reside in the Rakhine State.[29] This would imply that the overall population of the Rakhine State is around four or five million.[30] In government circles, however, the Rakhine State is the home of the officially designated majority—the Buddhist Rakhines.[31] The distinction between "Rohingyas" and "Rakhines" here is a deliberate one, not so much for the sake of semantics as for the reason of the state. Let me explain.

The word "Rohingya" is a taboo in the capital city of Yangon and I would imagine in the rest of Myanmar. In both national (or more appropriately, governmental) and international circles within Myanmar, the word simply does not exist. Even the National Museum of Myanmar in Yangon, which has an excellent collection of materials of all subnationalities (labeled by the government as "national races" and categorized into seven in terms of their language—Shan, Mon, Karen, Kayah, Chin, Kachin, and Rakhine), makes no mention of the Rohingyas nor does it have any collection dedicated to them. Why this taboo? Why this deliberate attempt to shun and silence the Rohingyas? Before attempting to dwell on this issue, let me first reflect on the origins of the Rohingyas in Myanmar.

There are basically two theories. One theory suggests that the Rohingyas are descendents of Moorish, Arab, and Persian traders, including Moghul, Turk, Pathan, and Bengali soldiers cum migrants, who arrived between the ninth and fifteenth centuries, married local women, and settled in the region. Rohingyas are therefore a mixed group of people with many ethnic and racial connections. This position is mainly upheld by the political fronts of the Rohingyas, including most scholars sympathetic to their cause.[32]

The second theory, on the other hand, suggests that the Muslim population of the Rakhine State is mostly Bengali migrants from the erstwhile East Pakistan and now Bangladesh, with some Indians coming during the British period. This theory is further premised on the fact that since most of them speak Bengali with a strong "Chittagong dialect," they cannot but be illegal immigrants from Bangladesh. The government of Myanmar, including the majority Burman-Buddhist population of the country, subscribes to this position.[33]

There is probably an element of truth in both these theories, but before dwelling further on them let me reflect on the nature of identity in the Arakan. I shall begin with the conceptualization of Arakan itself. "Arakan" is a Bengali/Arabic/Portuguese version of the local term "Rakhine," which in turn becomes "Yakhine" in standard Burmese.[34] Critics suspect that the term Arakan/Rakhine has come from the Pali name "Rakkhapura," (in Sanskrit, "Raksapura"), which means "Land of Ogres," a name that was given to the region by Buddhist missionaries, indeed, with some pejorative, racist intent.[35] But the linguistic content had further transformation. In fact, more interestingly, in Chittagong dialect, Rakhine came to be pronounced as "Rohong" or "Rohang" and the people from this land, "Rohingyas."[36] The difference between the various terms or rather the identity arising out of them was not wholly linguistic in nature.

Although for many years the people of Arakan had been referred to as Rakhines and for reason of local dialect some of them later on referred to as Rohingyas, it did not take long for the two identities to be politicized, with the

Arakanese Buddhists calling themselves "Rakhines" and the Arakanese Muslims calling themselves "Rohingyas." Religion alone, however, cannot be blamed for the refuge sought by the Arakanese Muslims in the term "Rohingya." A precise colonial legacy played a critical role in dividing the people of Arakan, contributing to a gradual refuge of the Arakanese Muslims in a newer identity.

The period between 1824 and World War II remained critical in the organization of the Rohingya identity. The former date refers to the annexation of the Arakan by the British, while the latter date refers to the expulsion of the British from the Arakan by the Japanese. In each of these two dates, the Arakanese Muslims played out in a way, which only resulted in an increased alienation between them and the Buddhist population of Arakan. Let me explain.

It has been alleged that the British annexed the Rakhine region in 1824 when the Burman military started pushing the Arakanese Muslims further west well inside the British Raj territories.[37] Whatever may have been the real reason, many of the Arakanese Muslims, particularly those whose parents or grandparents had previously lived in Burma but left the place on the account of the Burmans' conquest of Arakan toward the end of the eighteenth century, returned to the Arakan following its annexation by the British. Put differently, the British annexation of the Arakan encouraged a steady movement of population from the west to the east—that is, from Bengal or India to the Arakan. A testimony of this lies in the fact that the population of Maungdaw Township increased from 18,000 in 1831 to about 100,000 in 1911.

The fate and political position of the Arakanese Muslims otherwise became closely tied up with the British colonial power. Not surprisingly, therefore, when the Japanese occupied Burma in 1942 and expelled the British from the Arakan, a sizeable section of the Arakanese Muslims fled Burma and the Arakan and took shelter in Bengal. Indeed, it was during this period that the political affiliation of the Arakanese became clear, with the Arakanese Buddhists supporting the Japanese while the Arakanese Muslims supported the British. Such political affiliations, however, proved fatal for the Arakanese Muslims, who increasingly sought refuge in a newer identity, Rohingya, not only to distance themselves from the Arakanese Buddhists but also to cement solidarity within their own ranks to overcome their position of vulnerability and despair. The fatal outcome could not be contained.

According to some scholars favorable to the Myanmaran government, the latter cannot be blamed totally for the fate of the Rohingyas. This is because, as it is argued, at the time of Burma's independence, the Rohingyas not only formed their own army but also approached the "Father" of Pakistan, Muhammad Ali Jinnah, "asking him to incorporate Northern Arakan into East Pakistan."[38] The

Rohingyas continued with their demands even in the 1950s. The new state of Burma had no other choice but to consider them as non-Burmese and dissidents who were bent on wrecking the territorial integrity of the country. Apart from subscribing to the argument of "original sin," such a position is ill disposed toward the task of resolving the issue and overcoming the plight of the Rohingyas. But then, that is not all.

With the possible exception of the premilitary days of early 1960s, the government of Myanmar at every stage of governance and national development has systematically denied providing the Rohingyas some kind of recognition, including the right to acquire citizenship. It may be mentioned that at one point of postindependence history the Rohingyas' claim of separate ethnic identity was recognized by the democratic government of Premier U Nu (1948–1958).[39] But subsequent governments denied this and the issue was completely stalled following the military takeover of the country in 1962. The currently practiced Citizenship Law of Myanmar, which incidentally was promulgated in 1982, bears testimony to all this. A quick look at some of the things arising from the provisions of the said law will suffice here.

The entire population of Myanmar is practically color-coded! Actually, following the launching of "Operation *Nagamin*" (Dragon King) in 1977, which continued for over a decade, almost the whole of Myanmar's population was registered and provided with identity cards. These cards are all color-coded, mainly for the easy identification of the citizenship status of the bearer. Those residing lawfully in Myanmar can now be divided into four colors:

Pink: those who are full citizens;
Blue: those who are associate citizens;
Green: those who are naturalized citizens; and last,
White: for the foreigners!

The Rohingyas were quickly told that they do not fall under any of these four colors and that no such cards would be issued to them. Instead, a year after Operation *Nagamin* began (that is, in 1978–1979), a huge number of Rohingyas, totaling around 250,000, was forcibly pushed into Bangladesh. But this was only the first major push in recent times. Another big push of the Rohingyas took place some twelve years later in 1991, when over 260,000 of them were pushed into Bangladesh. Save 21,000 documented camp refugees now,[40] all were made to go back, this time with the support of the UNHCR, although through a controversial mechanism. This refers to the change in the UNHCR policy from one of "individual interviewing" before ascertaining one's repatriation to the promotion of repatriation through "mass registration." Critics have already questioned the principle of voluntariness in such repatriation, including the repatriation of the

Rohingyas.[41] It is not surprising that, given the *involuntary* nature of Rohingya repatriation, many of them are found returning and choosing the life of a refugee or illegal migrant in Bangladesh. Exodus, return, and conflict all are recycled and reproduced once again.

More important, in both these instances—1978 and 1991—the Rohingyas went back *not* as citizens of Myanmar but as "stateless" people. And then, after their return to the Arakan, they once again faced forced labor, lack of freedom of movement, periodic displacement, whimsical arrest and killing, and other forms of human rights violations, including torture and rape.[42] If anything, this only helped to reproduce a dismal state of life for the Rohingyas—within Myanmar as *stateless* and beyond the border as *refugees.*

One critical outcome of protracted statelessness and/or protracted refugee-hood was the dispersion of the Rohingyas to different countries of the world. The following is a breakdown of the dispersed Rohingyas:

Bangladesh:	330,000*
Saudi Arabia:	500,000
Pakistan:	250,000
Gulf States	55,000
Malaysia & Thailand:	43,000
Others:[43]	10,000
Total:	1,188,000

Source: Arakan Historical Society, "Problem and Solution of Rohingya from Arakan," unpublished report, Arakan Historical Society, Chittagong, August 2002, p. 4.

* The figure includes both camp and noncamp refugees, including those who have acquired Bangladeshi citizenship illegally.

In the light of this demographic diffusion, the Rohingyas have often been dubbed as Asia's "new Palestinians,"[44] imbibed with what could be referred to as local-global or *glocalized* identity. Indeed, as stateless and as refugees, within or beyond borders, the Rohingyas are as much local as they are global. There are not too many places for them to go, yet staying at one place puts them at risk if not in a serious state of uncertainty. The *glocalized* identity is of course in addition to their *social, cultural,* and *political* identities, all of which were earned either one way or the other through systematic coercion, alienation and marginalization, within and outside Myanmar. With this precise kind of multiformed, multilayered identity, the stage is now set for some among the more desperate Rohingyas to enter into the network of subaltern globalization, including seeking military training from the Taliban and al-Qaeda.

SUBALTERN GLOBALIZATION AND
THE STATELESS MILITANT ROHINGYAS

Let me at this stage clarify two points. First, if we take that some Rohingyas have ended up in Afghanistan through a complex network of subaltern globalization, there is no need to think that all those Rohingyas were living in a state of impoverishment. In fact, the general state of impoverishment of the community itself could be a cause for some relatively well-off Rohingyas to join the network, not solely for fulfilling the subaltern aspirations of the community but for the reason of profiting from the situation as well. Second once the subaltern struggle at home takes a military or violent turn, it cannot escape from being linked to the various networks of subaltern globalization. This is because in order to sustain the subaltern movement through *military means,* there is a dire need for both cash and arms over and above the committed recruits of fighters. Often the funds as well as the arms come via the network of dubious groups and shadowy activities.

In recent times, more so in the post–Cold War era, this has been the case practically with all the militant groups, including those directly involved in subaltern movements. The Tamil Tigers are a good instance, which, despite having being funded by the Tamil diaspora, did not hesitate to enter into the business of selling heroin and hashish for financing arms purchases.[45] Again, take the case of Kachin Independence Organization, a militant group fighting for the interests of the Kachin people within Myanmar, which with five thousand regular "armed" soldiers remains "heavily involved in the heroin trade." [46] This is not something unexpected in view of the protracted nature of these movements and the cost that is involved in sustaining them.

Even a modest accounting will show that the need for cash is quite substantial. For instance, if we take that a militant group is made up of 3,000 fighters or terrorists and that each is paid a monthly allowance of Rohingyas 5,000, the need for cash just for paying the terrorists every month comes to Rs. 15,000,000 (or USD 319,148 at the current exchange rate), which is quite substantial in local standards.[47] Often the militant groups, for the sake of maintaining their freedom—and this is more so in the aftermath of the Cold War—shy away from a particular source of funding. Instead, they now prefer diversifying fund-raising, which at times includes money from taxing the narco-traders or even joining in the business of selling drugs and arms. The following report is a good indicator of the militant groups' involvement in arms trafficking and making money from it:

> Around 100 AK-47 rifles reached different gangs of criminals in the port city (of Chittagong) and its surrounding areas from the insurgents of Arakan state of Myanmar staying in deep forests across the Bangladesh border. . . . Arakan insurgents sold the ri-

fles and some other sophisticated weapons to these gangs through a clandestine channel of local kingpins of arms dealers and smugglers on various occasions in the past few years.[48]

Things could hardly be different for the militant groups fighting for the subaltern aspirations of the Rohingyas, including the Rohingya Solidarity Organization. One could identify at least three sources from which some form of support (financial as well as material) for the militant Rohingyas could materialize. First is the local network within Bangladesh. In fact, both religion and language (with more *Islam* and less *Bengali*)[49] had been central in organizing a sympathetic posture toward the Rohingya refugees since their arrival into Bangladesh. It got shifted to a considerable extent when the presence of the Rohingya refugees contributed to the polarization and criminalization of civil society,[50] but this shift remained limited within the general population without affecting much the "political forces" otherwise sympathetic to the Rohingya cause. On the latter, the list included mainly the Islamic political groups, namely the Rabita Al Alam Islami, the Jaamat-e-Islam, supporters of the Afghan-based Hizbe-Islami of Gulbuddin Hekmatyer, and the like.[51] It is quite likely that these Islamic groups would come forward and help the cause of the Muslim Rohingyas, including supporting the Rohingya Solidarity Organization and/or the Arakan Rohingya Islamic Front both financially and materially.

The second source is external to the region, including support from the Middle Eastern countries and/or from the Rohingya diaspora. It may be mentioned that Khalid bin Sultan bin Abdul Aziz of Saudi Arabia, after visiting the Rohingya camps in Cox's Bazaar (Bangladesh) in May 1992, remarked:

> The Rohingya tragedy is the darkest chapter in the proud history of the people of Arakan. The United Nations should do in Myanmar what it has done for the liberation of Kuwait.[52]

Aziz's statement corroborated with the sentiments prevailing among the Islamic population, particularly the Rohingyas resident in Pakistan, Malaysia, or some Middle Eastern Islamic countries. The likelihood of the latter in providing funds for the cause of the Rohingyas, although it may be limited to the well being of the refugees, cannot be ruled out. But then funds from the first and second sources could bind the Rohingya groups to some of the more sober demands and political positions of the providers, and this may not go along with the strategy opted by the militant groups in fulfilling the subaltern aspirations of the Rohingyas.

It is in this context that the third source of linking the movement with "dubious groups" and "shadowy activities" worldwide takes a momentum. The third source could indeed provide more freedom to the militant groups in carrying out their strategy of violence and militancy, but then it also has the potential of bringing greater opposition, regionally as well as globally, to the otherwise justified demands of the Rohingyas. The global spotlight on the Rohingya Solidarity Organization is precisely an outcome of short-sighted calculation on the part of the latter. The report filed by Lintner is a telling one:

> Among the more than 60 video tapes that the American cable television network CNN obtained from Al Qaeda's archives in Afghanistan in August this year, one is marked "Burma" (Myanmar), and purports to show Muslim "allies" training in that country. While the group shown, the Rohingya Solidarity Organization (RSO), was founded by Rohingya Muslims from Myanmar's Rakhine State and claims to be fighting for autonomy or independence for its people, the tape was, in fact, shot in Bangladesh. The RSO, and other Rohingya factions, have never had any camps inside Myanmar, only across the border in Bangladesh. The camp in the video is located near the town of Ukhia, southeast of Cox's Bazaar, and not all of the RSO's "fighters" are Rohingyas from Myanmar.[53]

Although the report falls short in identifying the main reason for RSO's militancy—that is, protracted statelessness of the Rohingyas within Myanmar—it raised one issue that merits some attention: *locating the Rohingya militants and the RSO within Bangladesh.* The refutation of the report by the Burmese Muslim dissidents provides further credence to the issue raised here. When asked to react to the allegation of Rohingyas' al Qaeda connection, U Kyaw Hla, chairman of the Muslim Liberation Organization of Burma, commented:

> That is impossible. . . . If the Taliban trained and supported the Rohingya exiles, they would be much stronger and much larger. We know *some Rohingya from Bangladesh,* but we have no special connection to that group (emphasis added).[54]

This is not difficult to understand. The Rohingya refugees residing legally or illegally in Bangladesh suffer doubly, that is, from protracted statelessness as well as protracted refugeehood. It may be mentioned that over a decade has passed but, as indicated earlier, some 21,000 refugees are still living in refugee camps and there is no indication as to when their refugeehood would end. Moreover, another 30,000 to 100,000[55] Rohingyas reside outside the camps as illegal refugees and their plight, mainly for lack of documentation and legality, is even greater. The sense of hopelessness does not end there. Even those who have been repatriated with the support of the UNHCR complain that their repatriation was far from being "voluntary" and that they continue to remain stateless.[56] It is in these circumstances that some of the Rohingya refugees residing in Bangladesh probably found it convenient to join the networks of subaltern globalization and make a difference to their hopeless situation. But this further sealed their fate.

In fact, by joining the more militant networks of subaltern globalization, the Rohingya "fighters" found themselves trapped to the place they were brought in, namely Afghanistan. As Lintner maintains:

Many of the recruits were given the most dangerous tasks in the battlefield, clearing mines and portering. According to Asian intelligence sources, recruits were paid Taka 30,000 ($525) on joining and then Taka 10,000 ($175) per month. The families of recruits killed in action were offered Taka 100,000 ($1750). Recruits were taken mostly via Nepal to Pakistan, where they were trained and sent to military camps in Afghanistan.[57]

More important, however, following the disclosure of RSO's links with the Taliban and al Qaeda networks, the Rohingyas as a whole found themselves stigmatized, and governments of different countries became fearful of their presence irrespective of their position as stateless, refugees, migrants, or honest workers. Even the government that was responsible for their plight went public denouncing the Rohingyas and through its spokesman declared:

> There has been a Muslim separatist armed terrorist group calling themselves Rohinga which issued a unilateral "Declaration of Independence" from the Union of Myanmar. We then subsequently learned that some of these individuals were actually trained by the Taleban in Afghanistan, as well as in the terrorist camps in the Middle East. . . .
>
> The State Peace and Development Council [of Myanmar] would cooperate with the US to annihilate terrorism in Burma and put to rest all threats to national and regional security through its "zero tolerance" policy. While the governments of Myanmar and the U.S. have had differences in years past, we are pragmatically in full agreement that terrorists must be given no sanctuary.[58]

This position almost suggests that far from resolving the problem of statelessness of the Rohingyas, the state of Myanmar is possibly looking for another opportunity to push out the Rohingyas into Bangladesh as it did in 1978 and 1991, maybe this time far more ruthlessly and in greater number! Indeed, the post-9/11 stigmatization of the Rohingyas, apart from reproducing their statelessness and refugeehood, puts them in a more desperate situation. The new sense of plight could make the Rohingyas more committed militants and push them further in the business of creatively but demonically using the networks of subaltern globalization.

WHAT IS TO BE DONE?

The most obvious solution lies in providing *citizenship* to the stateless Rohingyas. But can that stop terrorism in the region and beyond, particularly the ones involving the Rohingyas? There is no simple answer to that, although a point can be made that much of the solution lies in *delinking* the Rohingyas from the networks of subaltern globalization, and providing citizenship in this context would go a long way in doing precisely that. But then, any delinking with subaltern globalization would require a far more creative intervention than banging simply on the issue of providing citizenship to the stateless. After all, we have numerous people throughout the world with proper citizenship engaged actively in the organization and reproduction of subaltern globalization. Moreover, providing citizenship to the stateless is more easily said than done. Any move toward enfranchising the Rohingyas could also set a violent reaction from the mainstream political groups and even the citizens, and that itself could create a space for the forces of subaltern globalization to enter and profit from it. What is required therefore is nurturing of options that would be acceptable as much to the stateless Rohingyas as to the state of Myanmar. In this context, let me highlight four areas where such acceptance on the part of the state and the stateless could materialize and create the necessary grounds for delinking subaltern globalization with the stateless Rohingyas. Needless to say, this would make fresh Rohingya recruits to dubious groups and shadowy activities not only unattractive but also devoid of relevance.

REINVENTING NATIONALITY LAWS

There is an element of truth in Mahatma Gandhi's remark that "Law is but the convenience of the powerful." Nationality laws, for that matter, are tilted toward those having citizenship and frown upon those that are circumstantially or structurally marginalized. Even countries that allow "dual citizenship," like Bangladesh, Pakistan, and now India, do so selectively, limiting the option to those residing in the "developed" countries. No such option is available to those residing in underdeveloped or less developed countries. Indeed, if there were such a thing between Bangladesh and Myanmar, the Rohingya issue could be resolved within the framework of dual citizenship. The option, although politically unsaleable at this stage, is worth meriting some consideration in the future.

Moreover, when forces of localization and globalization are increasingly and inextricably intertwined and when the power of national sovereignty has receded considerably in recent times, the identification of "nationality" with "citizenship" has become less meaningful and practical. That is, if we take "nationality" to mean *membership of the nation* and therefore a member of civil society, and "citizenship" to mean *membership of the state* and therefore a member of political society, there exists the possibility of nurturing the former without necessarily having the latter. Mexico is a good instance in this respect, as Gribbin pointed out:

> Mexicans keep, or can regain, "nationality," which bestows property rights and other benefits but withholds the right to vote. Mexico distinguishes between "citizenship" and "nationality." Voting there is a prerogative of citizenship.[59]

Stateless persons can definitely settle for a "nationality" that bestows property rights, the right to work, and other benefits, without however having the right to vote. But this must not mean that they will remain nonvoters forever and be barred from acquiring "citizenship" of the state. People falling under this category, if they so desire, can change their status in several ways. Completing a stipulated number of years as resident and duly submitting tax returns could be one. The second could be buying one's citizenship. If the resident is without a vote and is keen to vote, s/he might as well spend some money. This is quite common in some developed countries, particularly in getting migration certificates. Some countries even openly sell "citizenship." Belize, for instance, sells citizenship for $25,000 per person, while the islands of St. Kitts and Nevis charge $200,000 per person.[60] A price could easily be calculated for Myanmar and updated annually in the light of its economic performance and overall development. Donors could also come forward and provide funds to those unable to pay for their citizenship.

REUSING NATIONAL BORDERS

Imaginative interventions are required in border areas. The illegal flow of people will continue if one side of the border remains weak and poor while the other side remains relatively better off. It is important, therefore, that identical socioeconomic, environmental, and even educational projects are undertaken on both sides of the border to meet the demands of the people residing there. Binational or joint border development schemes could prove helpful. On this matter, nongovernmental organizations on both sides of the border must participate freely, for the chances of their success are more than those of the highly structured governmental interventions.

Moreover, a system of "dual voting," particularly in local elections, can be arranged for those living in the border districts with family and tax obligations on both sides of the border. This is basically to acknowledge the reality that is otherwise present in the context of population movement in the border areas. Moreover, the practice of those having dual citizenship voting in two countries is already there. In fact, in Bangladesh there is already a demand for enrolling the Bangladeshis living abroad as voters under a "separate category of residency."[61] The Dominican Republic has gone even further. It is presently debating the feasibility of allotting two seats in its legislature for representatives of New York's Dominican-American population. If this is the trend worldwide, of redefining constituency and residency of the people, there is no reason why newer approaches cannot be devised with respect to the stateless Rohingyas living within the proximity of Bangladesh-Myanmar border.

DEMOCRATIZING THE SENSES

Set to reproduce the power of nations and nationalities, modern education tends to reproduce violence and conflicts, even considering them acceptable so long as they are directed against *alien* communities, cultures or even countries. Much of the problem, apart from illiteracy, lies with the kind of education that we have been providing to our children in schools, colleges, and universities. In fact, children of this region are literally brought up as "nationalist," *tutored* to fall in love only with their own nation while disliking or even hating the nonconforming others. The task therefore is to come up with an education that will be less alienating and communal or sectarian.

The stateless are even more dismally placed for they are structurally outside the very imagination of the state. Moreover, "national curriculum," to the extent it tends to reproduce the power of majoritarianism and the nation, remains intrinsically statist and consequently apathetic of the stateless. Generation after generation is brought up with concrete knowledge of the state but little or no knowledge of the stateless. Indeed, very little can be expected from such schooling because when the time comes to delegate official responsibilities, the disciplined pupils tend to see more of the state and less of the stateless. It is this state of schooling that needs to be changed in favor of the one that remains sensitive to the making and remaking of the stateless. The earlier the children are exposed to this problem the greater is the chance of them participating and rectifying the things as adults.

Furthermore, "national curriculum" and the system of schooling are not only statist but also highly *governmentalized*—that is, organized, shaped, and reproduced by the government. Unless the sphere of schooling is thoroughly *degovernmentalized* and the age-old role of civil society in this sector clearly restored, there is little likelihood of statelessness being researched and deliberated upon, particularly on the scale that is required. A modest beginning could be made by commissioning newer textbooks and training materials on the issue of statelessness and then delivering them at various levels of schooling, all under the active participation of civil society.

DEPOLICING GLOBAL RESPONSIBILITY

Global responsibility has thus far been limited to the task of *policing* the refugees and the stateless, often to the point of confining them or shunning them off as criminals and terrorists. Similar has been the case with many of the victims of women trafficking, narco-consumption, or even those who have been engaged in informal financial transactions in the wake of inefficient and corrupt formal banking system. And lately terrorism itself has become priority number one in the list of global responsibilities, controlled and delivered by none other than the coercive forces of the state. Such policing of things and people have far reaching implications insofar as the task of overcoming protracted refugeehood/statelessness or even suppressing the terrorists is concerned. Two could easily be identified.

First, in the wake of policing the refugees and the terrorists, the bulk of the people become alienated from those carrying out the task of policing—namely, the government and the security forces. Since the issues get translated into "law and order" situations, the common people in the street become less interested in getting themselves involved in resolving problems related to refugees and terrorists. Often this becomes ideal for the latter to hide and work among the apathetic, alienated people.

Second, policing requires resources, but often in the name of policing the refugees and the terrorists there takes place a systematic drainage of resources. When this is done on a global scale it tends to further impoverish the life and livelihood of the people nationally, regionally, and globally, which is a welcome situation for those engaged in the reproduction of subaltern globalization. Policing otherwise helps create conditions against which it is policing. Such is the irony.

Global responsibility otherwise needs to be *depoliced*—that is, rescued from the hands of the police and the state. A globalized network of civil bodies, engaged in the task of both *conflict prevention* and *postconflict resolution,* has the potential of being more relevant and useful in resolving issues related to protracted statelessness/refugeehood and dismantling the dubious networks of subaltern globalization. Save creative thought and action, nothing can now change the fate of the Rohingyas. The only fear is that postponing the change could make the world fated as well.

THE JEWISH QUESTION:
THE OLD AND THE NEW*

YOSSI SHAIN

The last few years have thrown into sharp relief the fact that the "Jewish question" is still alive and relevant. Indeed, in many world conflicts and dilemmas, Israel and the Jews were inserted and became a focal point of controversy in civilizational issues and discord. The eruption of the Jewish question into the international arena is even more dramatic, after a decade during which there was a growing sense that Jews had achieved a certain degree of normalization, in Israel and the Diaspora.

In the 1990s, the years of the Oslo peace process and the concomitant Israeli drive for normalization, the premier question among Jews, inside and outside Israel, became the content of Jewish identity. Israeli Jews confronted mainly cleavages over growing trends of fundamentalist Jewish religious identity vs. the universal pressures of globalization. Internal debates over religious values and definitions, the challenges of peace, post-Zionism, relations between the homeland and the Diaspora, and so on, prevailed over traditional questions of security vis-à-vis the world at large. During the Oslo years many Israelis and Diaspora Jews believed that comprehensive Middle East peace would alter fundamentally both Israel's Jewish character and the relations between the sovereign Jewish state and Jewish communities in the West. Peace would have enabled Israel to achieve a level of normalization that would have loosened the bonds of involvement with and responsibility for the Diaspora, while releasing the Diaspora from burdensome entanglements with Israeli security issues that had overshadowed their lives in their countries of domicile for over a generation.

Until very recently many observers remarked upon the process of growing detachment between Israel and the Diaspora in the West. This redefinition of relations between the two communities was indeed most noticeable where links between Israeli security and the Diaspora had been the strongest in terms of identity formation and community mobilization: in the United States, whose political system facilitates ethnic involvement in foreign policy.[1] Jewish Americans clearly have the strongest voice among U.S.-based diasporas. In the West European context, Jews expected peace to produce a further decline in anti-Semitism and improve relations with the European Union's growing Muslim population, confirming Jews' successful integration in European society.

The al-Aqsa *intifada* of the autumn 2000 and the ensuing war of attrition between Israelis and Palestinians as well as the September 11 attacks on the United States ended what many have seen as one of the most "extraordinary times in Jewish history." American Jewish Committee's director David Harris wrote that Jews "got mugged in 2000." "It wasn't that everything that happened in the 90's vanished—far from it. It's just that we were reminded that life as a Jew is a bit more complicated, and that progress is not necessarily as linear as we lulled ourselves into believing during the golden decade." [2]

The Middle East violence, the events of 9/11 and their ripple effects brought back to center of Jewish agenda (worldwide) the sense urgency, some will say panic, regarding Jewish security and indeed survival. [3] After 9/11 in particular, the concern for Jewish security within and outside Israel reached its apex. An anti-Semitic wave in the Muslim world and in Europe demonstrated the inextricable link between anti-Israel and anti-Semitic activity and the ties between anti-Semitism and anti-Americanism.

The sense of Jewish vulnerability went far beyond the new threats to Israel that led *Newsweek* magazine to dedicate its April 1, 2002, issue to the question "Will Israel survive?" With synagogues in France and Belgium being set on fire and Jews encountering increased anti-Semitism elsewhere, among many Jews there was a growing sense that as one observer noted, "whenever the world goes crazy, Jews pay the price." [4] The 2002 Seder suicide bombing, perhaps more than any other event, evoked an obvious historical reference to Jewish historical vulnerability. One newspaper headline echoed the Passover Hagada's message "in every generation, they rise up against us to destroy us." Even many of those who had not seen their Jewish identity as a relevant factor in their day-to-day lives were standing up to be counted. Jewish political antennae—intuitive threat perceptions—have remained sharp despite years of apparent absence of danger. Harvard President Lawrence Summers, who describes himself as "Jewish . . . but hardly devout," [5] declared in a speech earlier that he could no longer remain complacent in the face of the virulent anti-Semitism that had manifested itself not only in the Middle East and Western Europe but even on American college campuses, including his own. [6] Jonathan Rosen wrote in the *New York Times Magazine* after the 9/11 attacks of a similar awakening as a secular, integrated Jewish American to the present dangers of anti-Semitism, a phenomenon he had previously associated with a different continent and a different era, Europe of the 1930s and '40s. [7] Jewish vulnerability was dramatically driven home to Americans in the grisly killing of Daniel Pearl. Jewish head—the source of evil. "My father was a Jew, My mother was a Jew, I am a Jew. . . ."

Attempts at delegitimizing Israel, Jewish nationalism as a concept, and Jewish political participation in western democracies, particularly the United States as harmful to transatlantic relations and indeed the future of western civilization drove the Jewish question back on the international agenda. In the year 2002 we have witnessed a German defense minister[8] and a French foreign minister deploring the pernicious and belligerent influence of Jews on U.S. foreign policy,[9] and failed U.S. presidential candidate Pat Buchanan claiming that the American conservative movement has been "hijacked" by predominantly Jewish neoconservatives.[10] At the same time, many in the Islamic world continue to blame Israel and the Jews for the 9/11 terror attacks. They see "Israelis and Jews as interchangeable emblems of cosmic evil";[11] puppet-masters pulling the strings behind the gathering U.S. campaign against Iraq.[12] Indeed, even in the U.S. where Israel is favored in public opinion surveys over the Palestinians by large margins many are leery about the tendency to accuse leading Jewish members of the Bush team, who have been advocating a war with Iraq, for being the mouthpiece of Israel and, by extension, invoking the toxic charges of dual loyalty.[13] Commentator David Frum wrote in October 2002 that "the certainty that American policy is controlled by what one British magazine called 'kosher conspiracy' was the single most widely held opinion I heard in the course of [my] visit to Britain."[14]

To be sure, in many parts of the globe there is a general sense that Israel and the Jews are at the crux of today's major international (indeed, civilizational) conflicts, a heavy burden of responsibility that carries a great deal of danger. Moreover, a view is widely held that the United States will not be able contain anti-American Muslim rage or to successfully fight against terror and the proliferation of weapons of mass destruction, unless it forces on Israel a peace deal with the Palestinians.[15]

The "Jewish condition" today is therefore dominated first and foremost by a self-credibility gap. On the one hand, Jews are often perceived a source of great power—in the Middle East and in the United States—that undermines world stability. One the other hand, Jews themselves, inside and outside Israel, feel and express existential anxieties and prophesies of doomsday scenarios.[16]

What are the seeds of this "New Jewish question"? How is it different from the Old one? To what extent does the new Jewish question redefine homeland-Diaspora relations? And, how does the credibility gap—i.e., the perception and reality of "Jewish Power" (self and other)—impact on world events?

THE OLD JEWISH QUESTION

The Jewish question of the nineteenth and twentieth centuries was intertwined with the economic and political forces that gave rise to modern nationalism in Europe. Demographic explosion pushed millions of Jews to leave the pale for economic reasons while the Tsarist anti-Semitic assault on Jewish autonomy in the east and the more subtle threat to Jewish life by the modern civic state in the West, gave Zionism a strong impetus and urgency. Indeed, the Enlightenment (and its Jewish version the *Haskala*) and European nationalism, whether exclusionary or liberal in nature, did not provide a solution to hatred of Jews. They were always perceived as an alien force culturally and nationally. By the late nineteenth century anti-Semitism was on the rise across the Western world.

Premodern/exilic Jewish identity was ambivalent about power and the use of force in human relations. Contrary to biblical time when power was stressed and chronicled in key figures like Moses and King David, for almost two millennia the Rabbinical Jewish ethos was of quietism and the morality of Jewish responses to oppression was turning the other cheek. "This ethos is already apparent in the Talmudic image of David: the warrior of the biblical narrative has been transformed into the scholar king." [17] Alan Dowty has written that, "Given their insecure status in societies where they comprised the most obviously different group . . . Jewish history generated . . . a psychology characterized by 'the hypervigilance of the haunted, the alert scanning of the insecure, and the continued suspiciousness of the vulnerable.' " This "*gevalt* syndrome," or doomsday mentality, expresses as well as anything the deep-seated pessimism and anxiety rooted in the vicissitudes of Jewish history." [18]

The responses to modernity and anti-Semitism in Europe were either immigration to the new promised land, the United States, further ghettoization by the ultra-Orthodox community, or joining the universal vision of socialism, including the distinctive Jewish socialism of the Bund. Each of these responses was closely related to the environment in which it was created. For the Zionists, the only possible solution was away from the *galut*, diasporic life. Herzl argued that even if Jews were tolerated, they would never be able to live in peace for a long time. In *The Jewish State*, he wrote, "For a little period they manage to tolerate us, and then their hostility breaks out again and again." Herzl didn't deal much with the content of Jewishness, conceiving of Jewish peoplehood primarily as a reaction to anti-Semitism. "We are one people—our enemies have made us one despite, as repeatedly happens in history, distress binds us together and, thus united, we suddenly discover our strength." [19]

Herzl was not a mere nationalist. In many ways he was a visionary of modernity who thought to mobilize the Jews in this project of modernity within the only available structure, the nation-state. He wished to Westernize Jews, make them an integral part of western civilization, which he considered to be a modernizing enterprise. For Herzl, power was necessary, not as a national mission. In the face of the Nazi threat Albert Einstein echoed this sense of Zionism's purpose when he wrote: ". . . [Zionism] is a nationalism whose aim is not power but dignity and health."[20] All and all, the multiple solutions to the Jewish question were driven not only by circumstances in countries of domicile, but also from Jews' self-perception. Indeed, many Jews internalized "the world view of their enemies and persuaded themselves that such violent hatred must, indeed, have had a rational source in their own behavior."[21] Therefore, the solutions to the Jewish question were not only geographic, they were also existential, in terms of redefining Jewishness and the Jewish person. They spoke of authenticity that must necessarily include assertion of Jewish power. For socialist Zionists, the national project was about the recreation of the Jews as a *homo faber*.

For the practical Zionists, the new Jew was based on a new conception of power that negated the weakness of the Diaspora. The new Jew would look healthy and strong and authentic in his relations to nature and physical labor, and unyielding in his defense of himself. This vision selectively borrowed heroic examples from the preexilic past, and utilized the Hebrew Bible as a national literary narrative of heroism, including figure such as the Macabees. The adjective *ivri* (hebrew) was introduced by the Zionists to emphasize the connection of the new generation to an old heroic past and to dissociate from the exilic concept of the *yehudi* (Jewish).[22] This Zionist version became Israel's "civic religion." It allowed for an alliance between secular and Orthodox Jews who spoke about the Jewish right to the land of Israel as a biblical decree. To be sure, many Orthodox Jews initially considered Zionism to be a sanctuary in the face of radical modernism that threatened their tribal life in Europe—refusing to see that Zionism possesses its own version of modernity. These Orthodox became Zionist detractors when realizing that Zionism will not stop at nationalism but will radically transform Judaism.[23] By contrast, in the liberal American arena, assimilation and/or Americanization of the Jewish religion should have recreated the Jew as an indistinguishable part of white America.

After the Holocaust and the creation of the state of Israel, the Jewish question centered mainly around security in the ancestral homeland. This issue was tied to the saving of Jews from all around the world, many of whom were under duress in second and third world countries, while in the West, Jews benefited from the increased public unacceptability of racism and progressed into the highest levels of citizenship. The idea of Jewish power inside and outside the homeland seemed essential for securing Jewish continuity. The 1967 victory catalyzed a Jewish diasporic reawakening, and the vulnerabilities revealed by the 1973 war and the 1991 Gulf War ensured that Jewish security remained a key issue for Jewish American (and European) organizational mobilization. Zionism connected Jewish security with the *aliyah* (migration) of Jews to Israel—anti-Semitism abroad ensured greater Jewish security in the homeland by increasing Jewish numbers there. The large migration from the former Soviet Union since the early 1990s is seen as key to Jewish survival, because of the increase in Israeli Jewish numbers and because the newcomers would at last have the opportunity to express and develop their Jewish identity.[24]

Notwithstanding Orthodox Jewry's misgivings about the secular culture prevailing in Israel, and despite concerns by the Orthodox regarding the Jewish "credentials" of many of the new arrivals, from the early days of Zionism there was a perception among leading Orthodox figures that Israel had made Judaism self-aware and visible, counteracting the assimilationist tendencies of Diaspora Jewry. The famous Orthodox rabbi Joseph Soloveitchik articulated this vision, when he wrote that Israel's creation is the most significant historical contribution to the strengthening of Jewish identity, and the renewal of Jewish history. Indeed, Israel became the focus of the Jewish people. David Hartman has written recently, "In spite of their rejection of many of the values and institutions which traditional Jews regard as sacred and their radically secular interpretation of Jewish history, secular Israelis continue to participate in the body politic of the Jewish people. They have revived the sacred Hebrew language into a living language of everyday life and literature, and they share many of the traditional texts, symbols, and festivals that are essential features of the Jewish tradition."[25]

JEWISH EMPOWERMENT

After its establishment, Israel took on the role of spokesperson for the Jewish people, primarily but not exclusively in international affairs, with other contenders being relegated to a more local status. As Jewish kinship and peoplehood concentrated on the subject of the state of Israel, diasporic institutions, particularly in the United States and the rest of the Western world, became auxiliaries or supporters for the state, and at the same time drew vicarious sustenance for their own identity through their participation in the Zionist endeavor. In the last two decades, and especially after the collapse of the Soviet Union and the ensuing "interwar period" between the Cold War and the New War, there was a resurgence of Jewish identity and a general perception that Jews have arrived, that the Jewish

question was receding, and Jews worldwide could live normal lives while celebrating their identity. All of these perceptions were fed by the Middle East peace
process, the ending of the Cold War, the dominance of the United States as the
world's only superpower, with Jews being very prominent in the United States,
and the desire of many countries in Eastern Europe to forge better ties with Jews.
Another indicator of the new Jewish era was the revival of Jewish communities in
Europe and in the former USSR, amid growing legitimation of diapsoric life
alongside Israeli life.[26]

In the United States, Jewish resurgence benefited from the breakdown of public and private racial barriers brought about by the civil rights movement, and
manifested itself in a new assertion of Jewish culture, the building of new synagogues, religiosity replacing ethnicity, the proliferation of Jewish schools, and
empowerment in all aspects of American politics and society, coexisting with a
fear of loss of Jewish identity due to assimilation. Jewish American organizations
structured their growth around support for Israel, further enhancing Jewish
American cohesion and public visibility. In 1991, Alan Dershowitz wrote, "The
byword of past generations of Jewish Americans has been *shande*—fear of em-
barrassment in front of our hosts. The byword of the next generation should be
chutzpah—assertive insistence on first-class status among our peers."[27] Indeed,
Jews became less and less inhibited in expressing themselves as Jews, with a Jewish agenda, drawing renewed criticism of "Jewish power," the illegitimate exercise
of influence, and even the stifling of the political and social aspirations of other
minorities in the West, including Arabs, blacks, and Muslims. There were even
those who argued that Jews exaggerated and manipulated the Holocaust in an attempt to capture the moral high ground and to excuse Israeli misdeeds, twisting
American foreign policy by placing the Holocaust and anti-Semitism at the center of the American consciousness; that Jewish influence over the Reagan administration was responsible for a manufactured fear of Islamic terrorism against the
United States, coming at the expense of concerns for human rights issues; and
that the Jewish and Israeli lobby prevented the integration of Muslims in America, by developing the myth of a Judeo-Christian ethos that deliberately excluded
American Muslims.[28]

The perception of Jewish power by others links the old and the new Jewish
questions. The Jewish question of European history dealt with a people with virtually no political power who were nevertheless perceived as powerful and, in relations between nations and empires, potentially decisive. In his book *A People
Apart*, a brilliant examination of Jewish life in Europe from the Enlightenment to
the Second World War, David Vital remarks on such perceptions, in the following
case during World War I:

. . . the international power of the Jews' was an odd notion. . . . The Jews . . . had no "international power" whatever that curious term might be held to mean. They had, that is to say, no means—and (the Zionists apart) little desire—to come together to wield autonomous power in their own collective interest. Nor . . . did they have the means of ascertaining in just what their collective interest might consist. The steady flow to Paris, London, and Petrograd of reports on Jacob Schiff, the Rothschilds, and other Jewish notables, their view and their loyalties, real or alleged, left their cumulative impact on all three governments. But it was the predisposition to read more into them than the evidence could actually bear that was decisive and remains, in retrospect, question-begging.[29]

THE NEW JEWISH QUESTION

Today's Jewish question deals with a people that has attained a position of inclusion, state power, respect, and indeed impact in international politics. Yet even today, perceptions of this power far outstrip the reality. As much as they possess global-wide influence, their power is qualified. Sobriety tests constantly remind the Jews of their limitations and vulnerability. In other words, what drives the manifestations of the current Jewish question is a combination of Jewish power in Israel, perceptions of overwhelming Jewish power in the United States, and views on the legitimacy or otherwise of the exercise of that power—inside and outside Israel. Is this power durable or is it ephemeral? To what extent does Israeli-Jewish power vis-à-vis the Palestinians (and its uncertainty) and the perception of Jewish power in the Diaspora propel the Jewish question among Jews and others? Obviously, there are many internal and external manifestations of this question, but here we will deal with the external manifestations. Five corollary (external) manifestations of today's Jewish question may be identified:

First is the acute security dilemma of Israel, and continuous questioning of the legitimacy and very existence of the state even more than fifty years after its establishment. This point is closely linked with the parallel, perhaps reverse, perception of Israeli dominating power that causes injustices to the Palestinians. This vision (or condemnation) also stresses the notion of American complicity with Israeli alleged inflexibility and therefore exposes the United States to global hatreds.

Second is the proliferation and aggravation of anti-Semitism in the Arabic and Muslim world, a world that sees itself under threat from sources that they perceive to be Jewish influenced. To some degree, these expressions of anti-Semitism are politically convenient constructions of Arab and Muslim politicians, but the sentiments run so deep that they deserve discrete attention.

Third, Israel and the Jews are on the fault line of conflict between two much larger international forces, Western civilization and Islam, and the struggle between them tends to implicate the Jews, particularly when they are called upon to make a choice of some kind. This fault line is also expressed in the division between the United States, as the chief exponent of Western values, and those societies that see Western values and power as their principal antagonists. Jews are also associated with the destructive power of brute capitalism, globalization, and its domination over less developed societies.

Fourth is the attempt to isolate the Jewish state and Jews internationally, by a coalition of Arab and Muslim countries, and those whose ideological beliefs motivate them to portray Zionism and Jewish power especially in the United States as a source of evil in the world, or at the very least a prominent barrier to the so-called progress of peace, human rights, ethics, and morality in the world. The Palestinian cause is the link, nurturing both wings—Arab and Western.

Fifth, in the context of Europe, Jews are often perceived as relatively risk-free and appropriate targets for venting frustration regarding European states' relations with their growing Muslim populations, and for the influence they allegedly exercise over U.S. foreign policy in the Middle East, an influence that damages U.S.-European relations and that stymies European efforts at rapprochement with the Islamic world, through the advocacy of U.S. favoritism toward Israel and an aggressive posture towards Muslim countries. Each of these issues requires some elaboration.

As we examine these perceptions, it is important to note that even within the Jewish community itself, deep divisions exist as to how to contend with these challenges and perceptions. In all of Jewish history, Jews have always been divided not only amongst themselves but also on the major questions of their relations with the outside world. All of the above should explain the Jewish self-creditability gap.

On the *first* point, the collapse of the Oslo peace process and the confluence of external pressures and challenges—a complex of regional and world events and developments after 9/11—have revived and centralized the traditional Jewish preoccupation with security and survival. As noted above, the broad Jewish confidence and sense of revival of the 1990s has given way to personal and widespread fears for Jewish security. This situation impacts upon the Jewish question in a way nothing else does. With the collapse of central authority in the West Bank and Gaza, boundaries are uncertain and unable to prevent armed confrontation and the entry of terrorists. Jewish settlements are considered illegitimate by most in the world, and many Israelis also challenge their legitimacy. Not only has the peace process deteriorated into full-scale war, internal strife with Arab Israelis, many of whose leaders express complete solidarity with the goals and the means of the Palestinians, has reached unprecedented levels.[30] Moreover,

Israel's economy has been battered severely by the violence, and outside investment has declined sharply. Iran, Hezbollah, and other enemies call openly for Israel's destruction and work to obtain the means necessary to accomplish it. The months leading to the American war in Iraq were dominated by an impending threat of an Iraqi attack against Israeli cities by non-conventional weapons. The old sense of Jewish doomsday reached new heights. Jeffrey Goldberg has written that anti-Jewish rhetoric in the Middle East "is repellent, but in the past it did not quite touch the malignancy of genocidal anti-Semitism."[31] All of this undermines the very idea of Zionism as the guarantor of Jewish security. In fact, Israel is in many ways perceived to be the source of Jewish insecurity worldwide.

Second, Arab and Muslim anti-Semitism, which initially owed much of its content to European anti-Semitism, had been an undercurrent in Middle East and world politics for at least a century. Its greatest impetus was the Arab defeat in 1948. As some writers at the time claimed, for Muslims it was bad enough to be defeated by Christian, Western imperial powers, but to be defeated by a small population of "lesser" Jews was an unbearable blow to their dignity and honor.[32] With the rise of political Islam after the Iranian Revolution, this animosity toward Jews and Israel, "the little Satan," took on a strong religious dimension. At the same time, realpolitik recognition of Israel occurred in some places. Israelis, who hoped that the advancement of bilateral relations with Arab and Muslim countries would inevitably take care of the problem, had mostly downplayed this hatred of Jews. Both Begin and later Barak asked Anti-Defamation League chief Abraham Foxman to temper his criticism of Arab and Muslim anti-Semitism, in the interests of Israeli bilateral relations.

The failure of the Arab regimes to defeat the Jewish army in 1948 and 1967 resulted in distrust and contempt by the Arab people for their leaders, turning criticism of Israel into a way for Arabs to criticize their own regimes. Bernard Lewis wrote, ". . . resentment of Israel is the only grievance that can be freely and safely expressed in those Muslim countries where the media are either wholly owned or strictly overseen by the government. Indeed, Israel serves as a useful stand-in for complaints about the economic privation and political repression under which most Muslim people live, and as a way of deflecting the resulting anger."[33] U.S. administration officials who had been directly involved in the Middle East peace process now acknowledge their mistakes in minimizing the importance of Arab expressions of hostility to Jews, propaganda and incitement that is spread continuously not only through the traditional government-controlled official and semiofficial media, but through new media such as the widely watched al-Jazeera Arab news satellite network. In Europe, radical Islamic clerics preach incitement and hatred of Jews and of western values. With the outbreak of the second *in-*

tifada, and even more strongly after 9/11, these attacks on Jews proliferated with impunity. Jews were accused of plotting and executing the attacks on America, as many Arabs and Muslims claimed that only Jews could have succeeded in such an undertaking. This hearkens back to the traditional anti-Semitic motif of the Jew as simultaneously debased and contemptible yet possessed of superhuman abilities and power.[34]

The perception that Jews are evil, which grows out of anti-Zionism, became a worldwide blueprint for the isolation of Israel internationally, as was demonstrated at the 2001 UN Conference on Racism in Durban where Israel and Zionism overshadowed all other issues. On the one hand, Arabs, Muslims, and other detractors of Israel have long tried to separate criticism of Israel and Zionism from anti-Semitism. Yet, the very idea of denying Jewish self-determination, while accepting Arab and Palestinian nationalist aspirations, quickly flowed over into unabashed anti-Semitism. This undermines the credibility of those attacking Israel, makes many Europeans uncomfortable, and ensures North Americans' complete rejection. This in turn further feeds the notion of Jewish power and its symbiosis with American power, the idea that American power is in fact held captive by the Jews.

The question remains as to whether perceptions of Zionism as racism and Jews as a problem are endemic to Muslim countries and theology or whether it is something that would change with the successful conclusion of Middle East peace negotiations, which inevitably brings acquiescence to Zionism as a permanent fact. Regardless, such a development is potentially conducive to an improved image of the United States as well. Salman Rushdie wrote recently that ". . . those elements in the Arab and Muslim world who blame America for their own feelings of political impotence are feeling more impotent than ever. As always, anti-American radicalism feeds off widespread anger over the plight of the Palestinians, and it remains true that nothing would undermine the fanatics' propaganda more completely than an acceptable settlement in the Middle East."[35]

This brings us to the *third* and corollary point, the uncomfortable position of Israel and the Jews astride the divide between Western Christianity and Islam, and between the United States and its detractors in the Middle East and other regions. On the fault line between Islam and Christianity, we have recently witnessed how Israel and the Jews can suddenly find themselves implicated, because of relations among the faiths in the holy land. Vatican officials pressured Israel successfully to retract permission for the building of a mosque next to the Church of the Nativity in Nazareth, threatening that the issue "would not merely affect Israel's relations with the Vatican, but would also prejudice the relations of the entire Jewish people with the Christian world." A Vatican official noted that it was Israel that had first defined itself as the representative of the Jewish people as a whole: When it negotiated the establishment of relations with the Vatican in 1992–93, he said, Israel had insisted that the agreement explicitly stated that it had been signed "in the context of the reconciliation between the Jewish people and the Catholic Church." [36]

Tony Judt noted after the 9/11 attacks that "Anti-Americanism and anti-Semitism are closely interwoven historically." Not because there are so many Jews here—there weren't always—but because both are in part about fear of openness, rootlessness, change, the modern atomic world: "Jews as a placeless people, America as a history-less land. [37] In addition, Jews are credited or faulted by many with decisive influence over American foreign policy, particularly in the Middle East. Wariness of America and Jews is inextricably linked with discontent over globalization and the backlash against western economic and cultural domination. The connection of Jews with globalization is not new. Jews were long seen as rootless, international cosmopolitans who worship money above all other values, as Marx claimed. "In the final analysis, the *emancipation* of the Jews is the emancipation of mankind from *Judaism*." [38] Walter Russell Mead has observed that in France, one of the most durable elements of anti-Americanism is the deep belief that Jews control the American financial system. According to him many French "grew up thinking of Uncle Sam as Uncle Shylock. [39] Indeed, there has been a revival of neo-Marxist criticism of capitalism, however this time, including non-Europeans. [40]

The *fourth* point is the prevailing perception among Jews (even the most liberal) that international institutions have been again hijacked by rabid anti-Semites and enemies of the state of Israel, who control the rhetoric and institutions of international legitimacy and justice that single out Israel and by extension the Jewish people as the emblem of all immorality. By the 1990s and the Oslo Peace process, there was a widespread sense that earlier manifestations of such sentiments, most dramatically encompassed in the 1970s in the UN's "Zionism is racism" resolution, were overcome. Recent events, however, have demonstrated once again the resilience and re-emergence of such positions. Jeremy Rabkin, a scholar of International Law at Cornell University observes that the United Nations Human Rights Commission condemned Israel six times in the year 2001 and eight times in the year 2002, when no other state was condemned more than once in any year. He has written "To judge by international authorities . . . Israel is not just a country with some faults but it is world's most odious regime." [41] Irwin Cotler, chair of the Canadian Parliamentarians for Global Action who participated in the UN's notorious World Conference against

Racism in Durban, notes that Israel is often demonized as the "repository of all of the evils of the world," akin to medieval anti-Semitic notions. He writes: ". . . in a world in which human rights has emerged as the new secular religion of our time, the portrayal of Israel as the metaphor for a human rights violator is an indictment of Israel as the "new anti-Christ"—as the "poisoner of international wells" encompassing all the "teaching of contempt" for the "Jew among the Nations," this new anti-Semitism implies.[42] Many Jews also see the recent indictment of Prime Minister Ariel Sharon by Belgium's appeals court (that a genocide lawsuit against Ariel Sharon could go ahead once his term as prime minister of Israel ends) in a similar light, given the appropriation of universal jurisdiction by a national government coupled with the lack of judicial action against any other individuals or states in the Middle East.[43]

The *fifth* point refers to the European context, in which the modern Jewish question was the most acute, and which encapsulates many of the dilemmas enumerated previously. This is why it requires more detailed attention. Since World War II, the Jewish question has reemerged in Europe primarily, but not exclusively, around relations with Israel. Until 1967, West Europeans mainly exhibited sympathy to Israel and its struggles, and anti-Semitism was held to be in bad taste. Germany in particular charted its way back into Western civilization by building relations with Israel and with the Jewish people, though its reconciliation with American Jewry came much later. Israel's temporary love affair with France in the 1950s and '60s came to an abrupt end when De Gaulle unleashed his famous and bizarre denunciation of Jews and Israel. The 1967 war converted French Jews to Zionism and prompted a considerable number to move to Israel. In the 1970s, Western Europe became a "surrogate battlefield" for the Middle East conflict, with terrorists attacking Jewish targets from schools and restaurants to the Israeli Olympic team in Munich. The growing alliance between left-wing Europeans and Palestinians sought to delegitimize Israel, but thereby also endangered the personal security of European Jews. Israel's counterattacks against terror in Europe and Israeli policies towards Palestinians in the West Bank and Gaza were also condemned by Europeans. In West European capitals, Israel is regarded in many ways as a strategic complication, a recurrent irritant in relations with the Arab world, and increasingly as deviant from "Western" values, especially human rights. The "Jewish lobby" in West European states was far from being the conduit to national policy-makers that it was in the United States, and west European public opinion was increasingly hostile to Israel.

The current revival of the Jewish question in Western Europe, whose essence was captured by the infamous dinnertime denunciation by France's ambassador to London of Israel as "that shitty little state," has deep historical roots but is based on more immediate considerations such as European interests in the Middle East and the efforts of western European countries, separately and collectively, to challenge American domination of the global arena. Many political figures in the European Union recognize that the European Union cannot match the United States militarily in the near term, staking their vision of it on a self-professed role as the leading promoter of international policies based on ethics, norms, and morality. The not so quiet implication is that a European Union dedicated to peace, human rights, and justice must serve as a counterweight to an America that asserts its interests through the naked use of power. Many West European commentators, echoing in a more restrained fashion other detractors of American foreign policy, claim that Jewish influence on U.S. policy encourages a more aggressive posture toward Muslim countries, in a region vital to west European security and with which the European Union seeks a rapprochement—not just because of external concerns but more importantly, perhaps, due to Western Europe's difficulties in integrating its burgeoning Muslim population. John O'Sullivan, editor-in-chief of United Press International, notes that anti-Semitic incidents in Europe are not a problem posed by Europe "but largely the work of citizens of North African or Arab origin who reject the notion of being British, French, Belgian, etc. They draw inspiration not from a European anti-Semitism, but from anti-Zionist literature published in the Middle East and propagated in some European mosques." [44]

All and all, recent calls by Israeli spokespeople for the Jews of Austria, France, and other European countries to abandon allegedly "anti-Semitic" Europe in favor of the security theoretically offered by Zionist immigration, is a stinging insult to Europe and the self-image it embraces. This is true not on its own terms, but also in comparison with the United States, whose Jewish community Israelis have largely come to accept as a safe, permanent center of Jewish peoplehood, legitimate and equal in status to the Israeli Jewish community. Indeed, the last point is often a bone of contention between Israel and European Jewry, as both sides assess the risks of anti-Semitism.

The first days of the second *intifada* unleashed an outburst of European hostility to Israel, later exacerbated by the delionization of Prime Minister Sharon, and after 9/11, European fears of the repercussions of the higher U.S. military profile in the Middle East and neighboring regions. West European Jews who express support for Israel are now frequently criticized by their non-Jewish compatriots for backing the "racist" and even "fascist" behavior of the Jewish state. Indeed, there are many Jews in the European "New Left" who join in the criticism, asserting their credentials as good Europeans by attacking Israel. Those West European Jews who seek to continue supporting Israel yet assert a strong

Jewish voice on affairs at home are offered little comfort by Israeli leaders, with Prime Minister Sharon on the right calling on European Jews to solve their problems by immigrating to Israel, while Foreign Minister Shimon Peres on the left tells them that their problems are not as bad as they imagine. Indeed, many European Jews consider Israel's interventions, even when they are supportive, as unwarranted and irrelevant to their reality. A January 22, 2002, editorial in *Ha'aretz* newspaper went so far as to call on European Jews to stay quiet:

> Just as Israel must take these communities into consideration, so must the Diaspora community's leaders take care with their own actions and statements, ensuring that their rhetoric remains restrained and sagacious. The Diaspora leadership has no historic mission to foment religious war against Islam or to lead a clash of civilizations between it and Judaism. The state of Israel, rightly, has taken care during all the years of its political-territorial conflict with its Arab neighbors not to allow that conflict to become a religious war. European Jewry should adopt the state's approach on that sensitive issue.

REDEFINING HOMELAND-DIASPORA RELATIONS

The events of the last two years and their consequences deeply affected the thinking and organizational efforts of the Jewish Diaspora and its relations with Israel. The new posture in which Israel and the Jews found themselves was broadened beyond the seemingly manageable proportions of a national dispute largely about borders to one encompassing religion and fundamentals of Jewish national identity. The growing tendency of Arabs and Muslims to broaden their political language to express hostility to Jews (not just to Israel) that was intensified after 9/11 produced greater Jewish unity and the revival of a new Zionist vision. This unity manifested itself in political mobilization on Israel's behalf and greater emphasis of Jewish organizations and the Israeli government on anti-Semitism as a core issue of the conflict. Indeed, mobilization on this scale, involving national and international informational, lobbying, and solidarity campaigns had not been seen in many years. The new found unity around the issue of "Jewish security" and the rise of anti-Semitism was used by Israel and Diaspora organizations as a unique opportunity to reverse the tide toward a schism between Jewish communities on such issues as "Who is a Jew?" and to undo Israel's apparent retreat from Zionism and Jewish identity into "post-Zionism."[45] This process also included, in Israel, basic rethinking of the relationship between Israel and the Diaspora in terms of legitimacy, status, and identity.

Over the years Israeli-Diaspora relations underwent a shift from the early Zionist vision that put the Israeli state at the center of Jewish existence while negating diasporic existence as illusive and even immoral. This vision that called for the return "home" of all Jews changed to a less ideological/emotional approach that recognizes Jewish life (including of former Israelis) outside the state as legitimate, perhaps even beneficial to the state.[46] This shift manifested itself, among other things, in semantic changes in Jewish discourse, with terms such as the negative *galut* (exile) and later the neutral *tfuzot* (diaspora) being replaced by references to partnership with *ha'am hayehudi* (the Jewish people), regardless of their residence abroad. In the face of the new wave of violence, key players in Israel's political and military establishment went as far as encouraging the redefinition of security concerns along kinship-community lines as opposed to strictly state lines. Such a partnership, particularly with American Jews was articulated by Prime Minister Ariel Sharon when he addressed a large gathering at the annual meeting of the American Israel Public Affairs Committee (AIPAC) on March 2001. He announced that, he considered himself "first and foremost as a Jew" and that he sees himself as having given a mandate to unify not only Israel but "Jews worldwide." He further declared, "The future of Israel is not just a matter for Israelis who live there. Israel belongs to the entire Jewish people. And Israel would not be what it is today if it were not for the efforts of all Jews worldwide." Obviously such a vision runs counter to the Zionist fundamental concept that only a Jewish state can provide a safe haven for Jewish security. It also negates the Israeli desire to act as a normal state whose primary interest is the health of bilateral relations with other countries. Indeed, when "the state founded to solve the age-old problem of Jewish insecurity has itself been plagued by chronic insecurity,"[47] considers American Jews as a "strategic asset" and invite them to take an active part in "Jewish security" it signals a partial reversal in the homeland-Diaspora relations by confirming diasporic power and influence.

For Jewish Americans, the changes in their ties with Israel have potentially significant impacts. Taking on additional consultative duties is a commitment that exposes them to possible risks domestically, such as being accused of becoming Israeli auxiliaries and of undermining U.S. Middle East policy. The presence of American Jewish representatives at the Israeli security decision-making table makes American Jews "culpable" even if they oppose certain decisions in private. Consultation implies obligation and a share in the responsibility for actions taken as a result. Yet it also puts on Israel the onus of listening to Diaspora voices who always wish to simonize their commitment to the ancient homeland with their ultimate loyalty to the United States. This was reflected in the November 2002 memo sent to Israel by a group American Jewish organizations and individual donors that asked Israel to refrain from retaliating in the event of an Iraqi attack on Israel, because it could undermine the U.S. efforts to unseat Saddam Hussein.[48]

Undoubtedly, as much as speaking on behalf of Jewish security outside Israel is a natural kinship responsibility, one must remember that, when it comes to issues of sovereignty or peace and war in the Middle East, the Diaspora, including that part of it based in the United States, will always remain secondary to Israeli decision makers. Thus the Israeli security establishment remains very cautious as to the limits of potential empowerment of American Jews. Indeed, the Israeli desire for an enhanced American diasporic role may pass as quickly as it emerged, as identity issues and conflict rapidly evolve. American Jewish organizations are taking a middle way in some respects on the concept of Jewish national security, pursuing a more vocal and assertive campaign against Arab and Islamic (and more recently European) anti-Semitism, a subject that they had long followed but had been more circumspect about publicizing during the hopeful Oslo years. This, in turn, brings anti-Semitism to a higher position on the Israeli agenda, including within security circles, whose upper echelons are now more disposed to understand the conflict in more Jewish terms. A July 2001 conference organized by Israeli security institutions directly addressed this topic, in cooperation with the U.S.-based Anti-Defamation League.

For West European Jews, like their American counterparts, renewed unity around Israeli security matters may help them contend with their fears for Israel's safety, and by extension their own, and meets certain Jewish organizational needs. However, assertive support for Israeli security policies carries the risk of being assigned responsibility for those policies. The West European Jewish community also remains alert to the potential negative consequences of stressing its vulnerability and of being identified primarily with the issue of anti-Semitism, particularly at a time when it is working towards attaining a greater voice in European affairs as it reaches an advanced stage of integration in Europe. Throughout 2002 European governments and the French government in particular became more aggressive in confronting anti-Semitism. Yet the Jewish community remains on the edge. By 2003 with the war with Iraq approaching and the rift between France and the United States reaching new lows, anxieties of renewed anti-Semitic attacks increased. With demonstrators in Paris and the French media denouncing Bush and Sharon in tandem as the most dangerous world leaders it became evident that the Jewish question in France and French relations with the United States are tied with the new European realities. Indeed when it comes to the French position in the Middle East and vis-à-vis the United States "unable to be spoken is the worry that the estimated 5 million North Africans living in France will retaliate violently against French authorities [and the Jews]." [49]

All and all, European Jewish insecurity is now another component in raising anti-Semitism as a factor in Israeli security thinking and rhetoric. Whereas the resourceful Jewish American community is sought by the Israeli state as a security partner in a way that compromised the original Zionist vision, west European Jews' vulnerability is seen as reaffirmation of the central Zionist tenet that only a strong sovereign Jewish state could ensure refuge and security for world Jewry.

BETWEEN JEWISH POWER AND THE *GEVALT* SYNDROME

The Jewish question continues to resonate, and it is tied to the Jewish and the world reality. These two realities are intertwined and not yet fully consolidated. And therefore they are continuously changing and sensitive to the orbit of threats and challenges, which has shifted eastward in the world. For generations, Jewish acquiescence in others' power came from a realistic recognition of the endemic limits of their political situation. Max Weber has written that the notion of *dina demalchuta dina* ("the law of the land is THE law"), was a Jewish way of making a virtue out of reality, "as a fate apparently desired by God." [50]

In the nineteenth- and early-twentieth centuries, Jews were perceived to form a substantial international base of power, which of course was devoid of real-world content. Even after the Holocaust, the idea of international Jewish power did not recede. Jews were scapegoated and accused of conspiracies throughout the world, for example in the Soviet Union, where Jewish doctors were put on trial, and even American politicians were anxious over Jewish influence on the American system. Certainly, even paranoids have enemies. All and all, Jewish *gevalt* was never far detached from reality. Nevertheless, it is important to acknowledge that in the last few decades, Jewish kinship and peoplehood are more cohesive than ever before, and are not devoid of real power. This power is concentrated mainly in Israel and the United States. In fact, there is a discussion that has developed over the last few decades regarding whether the "powerless people" have become arrogant in their use of power. On the one hand, in the context of Israel, the 1973 war raised questions over the arrogant sense of invincibility that the state had gained in the Six-Day War. This discussion was the launching pad for later debates over the direction Israel should take vis-à-vis its future, continued reliance on military power or a focus on diplomatic means. The second point was related more to the fear of the abuse of power. During the war in Lebanon and the first intifada, even conservative Jewish observers like Abe Rosenthal remarked that "Jews should not break bones." The debate had much to do with the self-perception of the Diaspora, which as much as it felt since 1967 that Jews finally did have power, now realized that such power may reflect badly on itself. There is another prominent stream which runs counter to this: military power and particularistic values based the religious conception of the Jewish right to the land of Israel, a vision that refuses to unilaterally accept humanistic categories of the liberals, on principle, and maintains that the constant threat to Israel and the Jews, almost a given by God, requires total commitment to land and power.

In the last decade the idea of Jewish power derived from the strength of Israel, which began to emerge as a prominent international actor on the road to peace and normalization, and compounded with the Jewish political stature in the United States, which was more forceful and unapologetic. Some Swiss and other detractors have seen in the American Jewish campaigns for Holocaust restitution an excessive thirst for power and control over the American system. In 1996, J.J. Goldberg wrote in his book *Jewish Power,* "From the Vatican to the Kremlin, from the White House to Capitol Hill, the world's movers and shakers view American Jewry as a force to be reckoned with. The New York offices of the Jewish American Committee and the Anti-Defamation League have become obligatory stops for presidents and prime ministers visiting the United Nations or passing through en route to Washington." [51]

The sense of Jewish power and kinship, however, always remains susceptible to fluctuations as a function of endangerment, and a constant sense of identity crisis, inside and outside Israel. The cycle of acute threats followed by relaxation and the rise of internal identity issues, can move very abruptly, confusing perceptions of Jewish power and vulnerability. The question is always present, how much can power serve or endanger the Jews? Doomsday scenarios and visions of salvation and messianic redemption are never far away. Certainly, the Jewish mentality, which springs back to life even after colossal tragedies, tends to forget the threats, and then returns to them rapidly when they emerge. This dimension impacts greatly on Jewish behavior, Jewish internal politics, and Israeli and Zionist diplomacy. There are those who say we are too quick to forget the danger, and those who say Jews dwell on threats too much. During the Oslo period, many said that it was impossible to live in a ghetto of power, and wanted to free Israeli society from the culture of power. Critics of Oslo, however, argued that the Oslo architects injected an "exilic" mentality into Jewish politics and security by focusing on the limitations and the excesses of power. Conservative scholar Ruth Wisse of Harvard University expressed concern about the Jewish tendency to shy away from power after achieving it, and forgetting how Jews longed for sovereign power for so many generations.[52] Israeli writer Aaron Meged considers the latest apologies issued by Israeli intellectuals to Palestinians ("even as Israel is facing the most brutal attacks against its civilian population") as ("HITRAPSUT") as remnants of exilic mentality of groveling before the tormentors.[53] Yossi Klein

Halevi, who was long associated with the Israeli left, captured the general sense of Jewish dilemma of power when he wrote:

> The Palestinians presented us with an unbearable dilemma, forcing us to choose between the two nonnegotiable demands of Jewish history: not to be oppressors and not to be naïve about our enemy's intentions. The very weakness of the Palestinians has been their strength: Precisely because of their vulnerability, we minimized their malevolence, going so far as to create and even arm Arafat's Authority. Now, though, the Palestinian war of national suicide has removed our guilt and squeamishness.[54]

Finally, it is possible to consider the Jewish conundrum as similar to the American one. Indeed the United States, at the apex of its hegemonic power, expresses fears of an ultimate threat, just as it appeared to be virtually invulnerable.

THE IMPACT OF THE SEPTEMBER 11 ATTACKS ON ARAB AND MUSLIM COMMUNITIES IN THE UNITED STATES*

LOUISE CAINKAR

The United States government implemented a wide range of domestic legislative, administrative, and judicial measures in the name of national security and the war on terrorism after the terror attacks of September 11. Most of them were designed and have been carried out by the executive branch of government, with little a priori public discussion or debate. These measures have included mass arrests, secret and indefinite detentions, prolonged detention of "material witnesses," closed hearings and use of secret evidence, government eavesdropping on attorney-client conversations, FBI home and work visits, wiretapping, seizures of property, removals of aliens with technical visa violations, and mandatory special registration. At least 100,000 Arabs and Muslims living in the United States have personally experienced one of these measures.[1] Indeed, of thirty-seven known U.S. government security initiatives implemented since the September 11 attacks, twenty-five either explicitly or implicitly target Arabs and Muslims in the United States.[2] This treacherous legal and political context is augmented by continued public backlash—hate crimes, hate speech, and job discrimination—sensationalized media portrayals of Muslims, and strong anti-Muslim/anti-Islamic rhetoric from the political right. Arab and Muslim American communities feel they have been marginalized as "the other" in American society and continue to have serious concerns about their civil rights and safety.[3] Instead of helping to weave Muslims into the fabric of the nation and garner their support in its antiterrorism efforts, and in spite of public pronouncements to the contrary, government policies have singled them out *as a group* that is dangerous and potentially subversive.

The legislative branch of government, the U.S. Congress, took steps that threaten the civil rights of all Americans when it passed the executive branch–crafted USA Patriot Act (Uniting and Strengthening America by Providing Appropriate Tools Required to Intercept and Obstruct Terrorism Act) in October 2001. Theoretically expressing the will of democratically elected representatives, the act was quickly passed in Congress through the circumvention of normal Congressional procedures by a body of persons who had never read the entire piece of legislation.[4] The USA Patriot Act expands the power of the U.S. government to use surveillance and wiretapping without first showing probable cause, permits secret searches and access to private records by government agents without oversight, authorizes the detention of immigrants on alleged suspicions, denies admission to the United States based on a person's spoken words, and expands the concept of guilt by association, among other things. Comparing the government's response to the events of September 11 to the 1919 Palmer Raids, the World War II internment of persons of Japanese descent, and Cold War McCarthyism, legal scholar David Cole notes they share in common the targeting of immigrants and vulnerable groups; a focus on political speech, political activity, and group identity; and a reliance on broad sweeps instead of focused, objective investigations into the behavior of individuals. These types of far-reaching measures have in the past led to "misguided enforcement directed at political dissidents rather than criminals," according to Cole.[5]

First to be caught in the post-9/11 "investigation dragnet" were some 1,200 citizens and noncitizens, overwhelmingly Arab or Muslim, who were arrested and detained under high security conditions immediately after the attacks.[6] Little is known of the identities of the detainees and their individual fates because the federal government has refused to release detailed information about them. Most of them have been released or deported, including more than 500 persons who were picked up for known technical visa violations (such as overstaying the period granted, not for connections to terrorism, for which they were affirmatively cleared) and subsequently removed from the United States. Also in the immediate post-9/11 period, Arabs and Muslims experienced humiliation at U.S. airports brought about by special security checks and their removal from airplanes, which caused many members of these communities to halt domestic air travel, refusing to endure the degradation of "flying while Arab" (also the title of an article in the February 2002 issue of *Arab-American Business* magazine). While the mass arrests and airline profiling began decreasing in mid-2002, Arabs and Muslims continue to feel under siege from the federal government because of its ongoing home and business raids, property seizures, interviews, arrests, spying, and wiretapping.[7]

The national security benefit of all these measures is questionable. Less than fifty persons have been charged nationwide with connections to terrorism (but not to the perpetrators of the 9/11 attack). Few of these cases have been openly heard, but those for which the outcome is known show the government's case to be weak, based on hearsay and circumstantial evidence. Defendants frequently pled guilty to lesser charges, unrelated to terrorism.[8] All of the more than 200,000

Arab and Muslim men who underwent special registration (discussed later) were affirmatively cleared of terrorism, including the 13,424 residing in the United States who were placed in removal proceedings, some of whom have already been deported.

Overall, these federal government policies, most of which were never subject to a congressional vote, have targeted millions of innocent people on the basis of their religion, country of birth, or ethnicity, in response to the actions of a small number of people who share their ascribed characteristics. It is important to note that the 9/11 perpetrators were not Arab or Muslim Americans nor members of these communities. They were visitors to the United States with an agenda.

The federal government's actions since 9/11 have led the American civil rights community to claim that the government has overstepped its legitimate power in its mission to secure the United States and its borders.[9] Legal experts say the government has engaged in measures that are "unnecessary, unconstitutional, and counterproductive."[10] Many question whether selling "a vulnerable minority's rights . . . in the name of security," has made the country safer.[11] Members of the Arab and Muslim communities in the United States feel they are under intensive scrutiny, their everyday life and formerly taken-for-granted routines disrupted, in the process of the federal government's search for a needle in a haystack—a strategy it has premised on the assumption that these communities are a threat instead of a loyal asset to the investigation of the attacks and to the country.

In many ways, this attitude marks the past thirty-year history of the federal government's relationship to the U.S. Arab community, as nonviolent political activists have been spied on and threatened with deportation and Arab American views on world events have been silenced.[12] In the process, the U.S. intelligence community's attention has been diverted from persons who pose real threats to those who lawfully challenge U.S. foreign policies. As the federal government's post-9/11 initiatives continue to unfold, careful attention should be paid to the actual targets, the veracity of the charges against them, and the impact of more hounding on America's Arab and Muslim communities.

SPECIAL REGISTRATION

One broad and discriminatory federal policy on which we have substantial public information is the U.S. government's "special registration" program also known as the National Security Entry and Exit Registry System (NSEERS). On September 11, 2002, the Immigration and Naturalization Service (INS), then in the Department of Justice, implemented this program, requiring "certain nonimmigrant aliens"[13] to register with the U.S. immigration authorities, be fingerprinted and photographed, respond to questioning, and submit to routine reporting. The targeted aliens were male visitors aged sixteen to sixty-four from twenty-three Muslim-majority countries, plus heavily Muslim Eritrea and North Korea. Special registration was required both of persons already in the United States (call–in registration) and of those newly entering (port–of–entry registration). The purpose of the program was to facilitate the "monitoring" of these aliens because their residence in the United States warranted it "in the interest of national security."[14] INS flyers produced to advertise the domestic call-in part of the program had THIS NOTICE IS FOR YOU splayed across the top, reminiscent of the call-in notices posted for Japanese living in the western United States during World War II. After stating for months that the program was not discriminatory because it would be eventually expanded to include all visiting aliens, the U.S. government announced the phasing out of the domestic call-in part of the program in May 2003. During the program's tenure, its scope was never expanded beyond Arabs and Muslims (plus North Koreans). On December 1, 2003, as special registrants began to comply with mandatory annual re-registration, the Department of Homeland Security announced the cancellation of this part of the program.[15] Attorneys and immigration advocates had feared a new wave of deportations, and claiming that registrants had not been adequately informed of the need to re-register annually.

Government authorities never clearly specified why persons from these countries were selected for the program, although they were often asked. At times they stated that these countries (whose citizens and nationals were required to register) were selected because of the presence of al Qaeda there, although countries with no known al Qaeda presence were included, and countries with proven al Qaeda presence, such as Germany and England, were excluded. In a May 19, 2003, press statement, the Department of Homeland Security, which took over immigration functions from the INS, referred to special registration as a "pilot project focusing on a smaller segment of the nonimmigrant alien population deemed to be of risk to national security."[16] Explicit in this statement is a view that Muslims—or, more specifically, non-U.S.-born Muslim males from Asia, the Middle East, and North Africa—are a security risk for the United States. This assumption lies at the foundation of many Bush administration programs, including ones that affect Muslims who are U.S. citizens, such as FBI Director Robert Mueller's initiative, announced in late January 2003, to tie FBI field office goals for wiretapping and undercover activities to the number of mosques in the field area.[17]

The special registration program's numerical impact was quite profound. According to the Department of Homeland Security, 82,880 persons living in the United States had been "specially" registered by June 1, 2003, through call-in registration. Of these, 13,434 were placed in removal (deportation) proceedings for visa violations, although they were affirmatively cleared of connections to terrorism.[18] Another 127,694 persons were registered at their U.S. port of entry.[19] Out of more than 200,000 persons registered, eleven face security-related charges, cases for which the outcome is not yet known, and none were charged with terrorism.

Visiting citizens and nationals of Iran, Iraq, Libya, Syria, and the Sudan were the first group required to comply with the special registration program. When some 800 voluntary registrants were arrested and detained during this period in Southern California, nationwide protest was sparked. Persons seeking to comply with the rules were handcuffed and led off to jail for visa violations, some reporting verbal abuse and body cavity searches. Most of these detainees were Iranian professionals and their family members, who had not returned to Iran after the Islamic revolution. They were working taxpayers with families who had otherwise lived lawfully (except for their visa status) in the United States for decades. Quite a few had pending applications for permanent residency.[20] Knowing that their visa status was problematic, they sought to register anyhow to show their willingness to cooperate with government. Eventually, most of these detainees were released on bail and placed in removal proceedings by the INS. The director of the Southern California chapter of the American Civil Liberties Union (ACLU) said the arrests were "reminiscent of the internment of Japanese Americans during World War II."[21]

When faced with the charge that the special registration program was a form of racial profiling, Attorney General John Ashcroft stated that designating "specific countries, the nationals and citizens of which are subject to special registration" is "not new." He referenced the actions of attorneys general Janet Reno and Richard Thornburg, who also targeted Arabs and Muslims.[22] The area of immigration, Ashcroft said, has always "drawn distinctions on the basis of nationality." Citing case law in an attempt to refute racial profiling charges, he spoke of the "inevitable process of line drawing" and noted, "Congress regularly makes rules that would be unacceptable if applied to citizens."[23] INS fact sheets tried to clarify the matter by stating, "registration is based solely on nationality and citizenship, not on ethnicity and religion."[24] Nonetheless, it was clear to members of the public that the special registration program was tied to religion. "U.S. Ends Muslim Registry" announced the headline of the December 2, 2003, *Chicago Tribune*.

Although the government has ended the domestic "call-in" part of NSEERS, the program is still quite alive for the thousands placed in removal proceedings and for their families, and for the unknown number who did not register. Willful noncompliers may be criminally charged, fined, and removed from the United

States, and may not be able obtain immigration benefits in the future, even upon marriage to a U.S. citizen. Persons later found to have lied about any material or immaterial fact may be deported, even if they subsequently became U.S. citizens. Registrants allowed to stay in the United States must undergo Port of Entry exit registration. Attorney General Ashcroft amended the Code of Federal Regulations (CFR), declaring willful failure to register and provide full and truthful disclosure of information a failure to maintain nonimmigrant status, a deportable offense.[25] He also amended the CFR by declaring that failure to register upon departure from the United States is an unlawful activity that makes a person presumed to be inadmissible to the United States later because he or she "can reasonably be seen as attempting to reenter for purpose of engaging in an unlawful activity."[26] Ashcroft thereby made noncompliance with the special registration program a bar to immigration, although only Congress has the right to establish such categories of inadmissibility. Special registration may also have denied Arabs and Muslims the right to benefit from any future amnesty or legalization program.

As already mentioned, special registration was not a program mandated by Congress. It was crafted by members of the executive branch of government. Ashcroft cited legislative authority for the program that has a history going back to the 1798 Alien and Sedition Acts, which were primarily aimed at restraining and deporting aliens living in the United States who were considered subversive. Ashcroft specifically cites the 1940 Smith Act, formally known as the 1940 Alien Registration Act, which was passed to strengthen national defense in response to fears of communist and anarchist influences in the United States.[27] The Smith Act was built on 1919 legislation making past and present membership in "proscribed organizations and subversive classes" grounds for exclusion and deportation.

The Smith Act was not only aimed at foreigners. It also prohibited American citizens from advocating or belonging to a group that advocated or taught the "duty, necessity desirability, or propriety" of overthrowing any level of government by "force or violence," and was the first peacetime federal sedition law since 1798. As such, the special registration program lies within the family of policies that permit the government to monitor, restrain, and remove persons whose political beliefs and ideologies it perceives as a threat.

Because the special registration program targeted persons by their country of birth (citizens and nationals) and not their beliefs, it also shared features of the family of U.S. policies based on ideas about race (beginning with slavery and Indian removal), such as the 1790 Naturalization Law, which denied naturalized citizenship to nonwhites (repealed in 1952); the 1882 Chinese Exclusion Act (repealed in 1943); and the Asia Barred Zone and immigration quotas (enacted in 1921, revised in 1924 and 1952). When the latter were abolished in 1965, it signaled the end of an era in which U.S. immigration policies were based principally on race. Thereafter, it was considered against liberal democratic principles to blatantly discriminate by country of birth.

In 1981, however, the regulation of persons from certain "foreign states" reemerged in immigration legislation. The 1981 immigration law was aimed at streamlining procedures and eliminated many reporting requirements for aliens. At the same time, it allowed the attorney general to require "natives of any one or more foreign states, or any class of group thereof" to provide address and other information upon ten days' notice. Attorney General Ashcroft used this law to authorize domestic call-in special registration.[28] Interestingly, the Iran crisis of 1980 was specifically mentioned in the House Judiciary Committee report submitted for the 1981 law, which declared "immediate access to records of nonimmigrants may be vital to our nation's security," contextualizing the authority to implement discriminatory immigration procedures tied to country of birth within the history of Islamic revival and the Iranian Islamic revolution.[29]

Prior to special registration, more Arabs and Muslims (none accused of terrorist connections) had been removed from the United States in the fallout from the September 11 attacks than the number of foreign nationals deported for their political beliefs following the infamous 1919 Palmer Raids.[30] The Department of Justice Inspector General's report confirms that at least 565 persons were removed for visa violations from among those swept up immediately after the 9/11 attacks.[31] As of this writing, more than 13,000 Arabs and Muslims have been placed in removal proceedings for visa violations through the special registration program, although they comprise less than 1 percent of the estimated three million persons who are "out of status" and the eight million undocumented in the United States.[32] History will show that the special registration program was a massive roundup of out-of-status Arabs, Asians, and North Africans from predominantly Muslim countries that is without historical precedent.[33]

NONIMMIGRANT VISAS

Another area in which Arabs and Muslims were broadly impacted by post-9/11 policies is in the issuance of nonimmigrant visas. In October 2001, the State Department issued a classified cable imposing a mandatory twenty-day hold on all nonimmigrant visa applications submitted by men aged eighteen to forty-five from twenty-six countries, subjecting them to special security clearance. Applications from males in most of these countries eventually required approval in

Washington, with no time limit imposed on the response. The impact of this policy on students attempting to return to school, visiting professors and researchers, Fulbright Scholars, medical and chemotherapy patients, artists, and musicians, and businessmen received substantial media attention. The following table shows decreases in fiscal year 2002 nonimmigrant visas awarded for *all* special registration countries except Eritrea, and an overall 39 percent decrease. Decreases are also evident in other areas of the world, but to a lesser extent. Europeans experienced a 15 percent decrease, Asians (excluding special registration countries) experienced a 24 percent decrease, and Africans, a 23 percent decrease.[32] Increased reluctance to visit the United States in the post-9/11 climate also explains in part these decreases.

Visitor Visas Approved, FY 2002 and FY 2001, and % Change for Countries Selected for Special Registration*

Registry Group	Country	Visas Issued, 2001	Visas Issued, 2002	% Decrease	Rank, % Decrease	Rank (No. Visas, FY 2002)
1	Iran	20,268	12,284	39%	12	9
1	Iraq	3,071	1,837	40%	11	18
1	Libya	449	343	24%	19	24
1	Sudan	4,576	2,258	51%	7	17
1	Syria	14,399	8,529	41%	10	11
2	Afghanistan	1,983	1,178	41%	10	22
2	Algeria	7,516	5,084	32%	16	13
2	Bahrain	4,671	2,279	51%	7	16
2	Eritrea	1,590	1,574	1%	21	20
2	Lebanon	32,321	21,741	33%	15	6
2	Morocco	26,159	22,775	13%	20	4
3	Oman	3,963	2,312	42%	9	15
3	Qatar	3,769	1,826	52%	6	19
3	Somalia	1,003	429	57%	3	23
3	Tunisia	9,161	4,269	53%	5	14
3	U.A.E.	17,247	6,090	65%	2	12
3	Yemen	2,875	1,304	55%	4	21
4	Pakistan	95,595	61,538	36%	14	2
4	Saudi Arabia	66,721	22,245	67%	1	5
5	Bangladesh	21,107	15,556	26%	18	8
5	Egypt	61,828	37,381	40%	11	3

5	Indonesia	96,961	68,478	29%	17	1
5	Jordan	33,548	21,043	37%	13	7
5	Kuwait	19,756	11,242	43%	8	10
	Total	550,537	333,595	39%		
	North and South Korea	841,863	802,552	5%*		

Source: INS

*Note: While only North Korea was part of special registration, the INS provided these data with North and South Korea combined. Adding the large numbers for this group (they exceed all other countries added together) into the calculations distorts the outcome.

FY 2002 runs from October 1, 2001 and September 30, 2002 and FY 2001 from October 1, 2000 and September 30, 2001.

Special registration and other national security programs implemented by the federal authorities since the September 11 attacks have yet to prove their value for domestic security. Globally, the special registration program evoked protests from the governments and citizens of the countries whose nationals were affected. The State Department actually thought it an ill-advised program because it would strain important political relationships. Nonetheless, the Justice Department and Homeland Security went ahead with it. Thus, much of the sympathy the United States attracted because of the 9/11 attacks has been squandered by these undemocratic policies and a perception that the country is acting with global arrogance in foreign affairs.[35]

While special registration and visa policies focus on immigrants, their impact is on ethnic communities, which are composed of citizens and noncitizens alike. While we have much less quantitative and qualitative data on the government's implementation of other domestic security programs, research shows they are having significant community impacts, as discussed later in this chapter.

HATE CRIMES

Arab and Muslim American communities have experienced a large volume of negative reprisals from sectors of the American public in the form of hate crimes, defamatory speech, and job discrimination. In the first seven days following September 11, Arabs and South Asians reported 645 "bias incidents and hate crimes" to the Council on American-Islamic Relations (CAIR).[36] At end of six months the figure rose to 1,717, then declined to 325 reported incidents in the second six-month period.[37] CAIR characterized the post-9/11 anti-Muslim attacks as more violent than those of prior years and noted that they included a number of murders. In 2002, CAIR documented a decrease in hate crimes but increasing reports of discrimination, particularly in the workplace and by government agents conducting raids, interrogations, searches, and property seizures.[38] In 2003, the hate attacks continued. For example, on October 5, 2003, a Muslim woman wearing a *hijab* (head scarf) was attacked from behind in a Kmart parking lot in Springfield, Virginia. The white male teenaged attacker allegedly shouted, "You terrorist pig," before running away. The woman was treated for a two-to-three-inch-deep wound on her lower back at a local hospital and released. In September 2003 an arsonist attacked a Georgia mosque.

In Chicago, more than one hundred hate crimes against Arabs and Muslims, as well as against persons mistaken for them, were reported to the Chicago Commission on Human Relations by the end of December 2001. In addition, Arab and Muslim institutions have been attacked. On September 12, 2001, a mob of hundreds of angry suburban whites, some shouting "Kill the Arabs," some wielding weapons, commenced a march to the largest predominantly Arab mosque in metro Chicago. More than 125 suburban police officers were called in to keep the mob from storming the mosque and the primarily Muslim residential community surrounding it. The following night, a similar march occurred and once again the police were called in. For three nights, the police formed a human barricade around the neighborhood. Concerned over the safety of members of this community, the police encouraged Muslims to close the schools affiliated with the mosque and to not attend Friday prayers. The schools were closed for one week, but prayer at the mosque continued.

An Assyrian church on the north side of Chicago and an Arab community center on the southwest side were damaged by arson in the late fall of 2001. The rebuilt community center was again vandalized in March 2002. A mosque in suburban Villa Park was vandalized in the spring of 2003. In the months immediately following the September 11 attacks, Muslim women in Chicago repeatedly reported having their head scarves yanked off or being spit at on the street. These incidents still occur, although with less frequency, and fear still reigns within the community, as will be shown later.

Many community leaders blame the U.S. government's sweeping and unfocused actions in their communities and the media's sensational coverage of them for encouraging anti-Arab and anti-Muslim sentiments. CAIR's executive director, Nihad Awad, connects the continuing attacks on Muslims to "the ongoing right-wing campaign to demonize Muslims and Islam," which is "having an impact on those in our society vulnerable to the siren song of hatred and prejudice."[39] CAIR continues to repeat its request for elected officials and opinion leaders to speak out against all forms of religious intolerance. Arab and Muslim concerns about profiling, intolerance, and the long-term effects of discrimination are increasing.[40]

PUBLIC OPINION AND ISLAMAPHOBIA

Shortly after the attacks of 9/11, public opinion polls showed widespread support for the special treatment of Arabs in America. A poll conducted on September 14 and 15, 2001, found fully half of the respondents in support of requiring all Arabs in the United States, including American citizens, to carry special identity cards.[41] Two late September 2001 Gallup polls found that a majority of Americans favored profiling of Arabs, including those who are American citizens, and subjecting them to special security checks before boarding planes.[42] A December 2001 poll by the Institute for Public Affairs at the University of Illinois found that some 70 percent of Illinois residents were willing to sacrifice their civil rights to fight terrorism, and more than one-quarter of respondents said Arab Americans should surrender more rights than others.[43] A March 5, 2002, CNN/Gallup/*USA Today* poll found that nearly 60 percent of Americans favored reducing the number of admissions to the United States of immigrants from Muslim countries, and an August 8, 2002, Gallup poll found that a majority of the American public said that there are "too many" immigrants from Arab countries.[44] Finally, two ABC News/Beliefnet surveys conducted among a random sample of American adults found that the percentage with an unfavorable view of Islam rose from 24 percent in January 2002 to 33 percent in October, 2002 and that the percentage of American adults who say that Islam "doesn't teach respect for other faiths" rose from 22 percent to 35 percent.[45]

Certain neoconservative and Christian-right spokespersons routinely express displeasure with the idea of American society embracing the Muslim community. They describe Islam as a religion outside the pale of human values while some have labeled Muslims as "worse than Nazis."[46] A booklet authored by William Lind and Paul M. Weyrich, entitled *Why Islam Is a Threat to America and the West,* argues that Muslims "should be encouraged to leave. They are a fifth column in this country."[47] Similarly, televangelist Pat Robertson referred to believers of Islam as potential killers on his *700 Club* program.[48] It is no comfort to Muslims that Franklin Graham, who has called Islam an "evil and wicked religion," was invited to deliver the 2002 Good Friday homily at the Pentagon.[49]

Indeed, members of the Arab and Muslim communities feel uneasy about the close alliance among members of the Bush administration, the anti-Muslim Christian right, and other well-known critics of Islam, such as Campus Watch founder Daniel Pipes. Attorney General Ashcroft, for example, stated in an interview with Tribune Media Services columnist Cal Thomas that "Islam is a religion in which God requires you to send your son to die for him. Christianity is a faith in which God sends his son to die for you." [50] In April 2003 President Bush nominated Pipes to the board of the U.S. Institute of Peace, a government think tank and funder of scholars—an odd choice since Pipes has been repeatedly criticized in the mainstream American press and by scholars for low standards of data collection and unscholarly work.[51] Pipes, who has said that Islam "would seem to have nothing functional to offer," claims that the majority of Muslims are troublesome, violent, terrorists, or terrorist-supporters.[52] Despite being rejected by Congress, Bush made a recess appointment of Pipes to the Institute Board in August 2003.

IMPACT ON THE ARAB AND MUSLIM COMMUNITY

The federal government's policies and actions following the 9/11 attacks, as well as the hate crimes, hate speech, discrimination, and Islamaphobia emitting from sections of the American public, have had substantial negative impact on the American Arab and immigrant-origin Muslim communities.[53] Community members characterize themselves as a "targeted minority." Many feel they are living in a state of siege fully two years after the attacks. While this overall view is shared widely, different subsections—by social class, gender, immigrant generation, and/or country of origin—of these communities may respond in different ways to this status. This part of this chapter looks at data available from interviews with young, college-educated, middle-class Arab American women, who are part of a larger sample in an ongoing study of 9/11 impact on the Muslim and Arab community in metropolitan Chicago, funded by the Russell Sage Foundation. This group was selected because it is the subgroup for which sufficient data currently exist to conduct analysis. The findings reflect the experiences and views of young women (between age twenty-five and thirty-five) who are American citizens and were raised in the United States. They are the second-generation children of Arab immigrants, raised in families in which at least one parent has a postgraduate university education. One could say they are among the privileged in their communities, and since they are themselves college-educated, one would expect their responses to reflect reason, analysis, and critique. While all of the women interviewed are Muslims, some are practicing and some are not. Some of them wear a *hijab* and some do not. The *hijab* has become a key symbol of Islam in American society, although an often misunderstood and misinterpreted one.

As these women testify, wearing it makes one an instant target, although not wearing one does not bring immunity from public disdain.

All of the women interviewed said their lives were changed by the events of 9/11. First, they were shocked by the attacks and that they were perpetrated by Muslims. Then, they were afraid. These sentiments are perhaps best expressed in a poem entitled "first writing since" by Arab American poet and New Yorker Suheir Hammad. An excerpt from the poem follows:

> fire in the city air and i feared for my sister's life in a way
> never before. and then, and now, i fear for the rest of us.
>
> first, please god, let it be a mistake, the pilot's heart failed,
> the plane's engine died.
> then please god, let it be a nightmare, wake me now.
> please god, after the second plane, please, don't let it be anyone
> who looks like my brothers.

In metro Chicago, the backlash began almost immediately, first with verbal attacks on persons assumed to be Arab, and then with physical attacks, phone threats, and burning of Arab institutions. For three days after the attacks, the large mosque and surrounding Arab residential community in Bridgeview (a predominantly white, working- and middle-class suburb southwest of Chicago with a large Arab residential and commercial population) were threatened by mobs of angry whites. More than 125 local police officers were called in to "keep the peace." On Friday, the Muslim day of prayer, the mosque was surrounded by scores of non-Arabs and non-Muslims who were acting in support of the Muslim Arab community and its right to safety and security.

These countervailing trends remain two years after the attacks. While Arabs and Muslims still face discrimination, especially on the job and from government agents, as well as attacks and slurs from some members of the American public, their circle of supporters has been enlarged and they have built and strengthened many relationships with non-Muslim and non-Arab institutions in American civil society. While post-9/11 events have alienated many members of these communities from American society, they have also forged the institutional integration of Muslims into American society. The full political integration of Muslims may require deeper changes in American policies abroad.

SAFETY

All of the educated Arab American women interviewed for this Russell Sage study reported either being the victim of a hate action (physical or verbal) or knowing someone closely who was. Shortly after the 9/11 attacks, one woman wearing a *hijab* was shouted at by the woman in the car next to her: "If I had a gun I'd shoot you now!" Other women interviewed reported their veils being ripped off their heads. Women who wear the *hijab* reported that "the stares, the refusal to look me in the face, and the verbal insults" persisted to the day they were interviewed. Nearly all of them, *muhajibaat* (veiled) or not, still experienced fear for their safety, especially when they were in places that are not ethnically diverse or areas that are all white. One woman said, "You won't find me in a park or a forest preserve"; another said, "Soccer moms scare me the most." All agreed that Muslim women who wear the *hijab* are the most vulnerable to assault in American society because they are so easily spotted and targeted. Women who do not wear the *hijab* profess great respect for these women, whose beliefs and values provide them with the strength to continue wearing it despite the current American climate. Many women who wear the *hijab* were told by family members not to leave the home in the first few weeks following the attacks. Some women were asked to stop wearing it altogether and some complied. Many women considered the mosque a place of safety, but many others considered it unsafe due to the number of attacks and threats on mosques that have occurred in the Chicago area.

Feeling unsafe is not limited to the public sphere. The federal government's pattern of interrogations, arrests, home invasions, and computer and property confiscations may appear strategic to its agents, but they appear random, unfocused, and discriminatory to members of the Arab and Muslim communities. The government's use of secret evidence and closed hearings, the absence of charges and trials, disappearances and eventual releases without charge, the eavesdropping on attorneys, and special registration of Arabs and Muslims have not built community confidence in the government, or in the claim that its target is terrorists and people who support them. In consequence, nearly everyone in the community feels vulnerable to a certain degree, even in their own homes.

Thus, while some women in the study said they felt safest in their homes, others said they felt the hidden eyes of surveillance, assumed their phones were tapped and computers monitored, and were concerned that government agents could enter their homes at any time without permission or leaving a trace. Many respondents reported receiving in the early post-9/11 days threatening phone calls—telling them to "go back where they came from," calling them terrorists, or saying their fathers had been arrested. While untrue, because in fact the government does not call in such cases, these latter calls evoked panic in the family.

The frightful context in which Arabs and Muslims in America lived in the first year after the 9/11 attacks was reported worldwide and prompted the relatives of many living overseas to call and check on the safety of their loved ones in the

United States. Normally considered a place to which people migrate for freedom and safety, another side of America was showing its face. This other side is perhaps most sharply represented by the hundreds of Pakistani families who fled the United States to seek asylum in Canada when the special registration program was launched.

Fearing humiliation if they attempted to board an airplane, most of the women interviewed for the Russell Sage study who used to travel domestically changed their travel patterns after the attacks. They either stopped traveling or chose to drive to their destinations. One *muhajiba* (veiled) woman told of sitting on an airplane next to a man "who fidgeted and moved" the entire flight. It appears that being removed from an airplane for one's appearance or ethnicity, which happened frequently in 2001–2002, was largely but not solely a male experience. Some of these women had since returned to their normal travel patterns, while others remained afraid. According to the Council on American-Islamic Relations, Arab and Muslim complaints of profiling by U.S. airlines decreased substantially in 2002.[54]

RACE

Officially considered Caucasian (white), many Arabs have for a long time rejected this designation because of their treatment in American society and/or because of their physical characteristics. As long as they remain officially white, they are ineligible for the benefits that accrue to members of recognized minority groups and remain hidden to those concerned with the status of minorities. The post-9/11 Arab experience appears to have crystallized the sense among Arabs that they are nonwhites in American society. We are the "other," many women in the study said, the "targeted other." While some had thought Arabs and Muslims were on the path to being accepted as part of the fabric of American society, post-9/11 events changed all that. The questions nearly all have been asked, "Where are you from?" and "Are you a terrorist?" and the comments, telling American Arab women to "go back where you came from," revealed to them the borders between whiteness and otherness.

Most striking, however, is the overwhelming consistency of responses indicating that Arab American women do not feel safe among whites, and do not feel fear among nonwhites. While the post-9/11 backlash is ordinarily described as an ugly side of American society, from the perspective of these women it is a phenomenon of white America. Its purpose, as they see it, is to clarify that Arabs and Muslims will not be granted the same rights and privileges that accrue to members of white society, including the privilege against profiling and guilt by association. Federal government actions only serve to reinforce this idea. One often hears community members remark that after the Oklahoma City bombings, neither all Christians nor all Irish became suspect citizens. The privileged are sorted through with precision, the nonprivileged are profiled and guilt is a collective status.

MEDIA

Arabs and Muslims hold the mainstream American media largely responsible for the public's perceptions of them. It is the mediator of information and messages for the American public. They say the media sensationalize events that put Arabs and Muslims in a bad light, and treat government allegations about them as if they were fact, not applying the same degree of objectivity they might in other matters. Negative media portrayals are rarely balanced by positive ones, except in the few documentaries on Islam or on the post-9/11 backlash that have been aired on public television and some cable stations. They also point to a disjuncture between what the government says and what it does. One woman in the Russell Sage study said: "President Bush says Muslims are part of our society and welcome. But the media show us as violent and terrorist and government actions promote this view."

These allegations against the American media are not new in the Arab community, they have been documented for at least three decades.[55] Former Southern Illinois University professor and media consultant Jack Shaheen, who has done the most work on the negative media stereotyping of Arabs, called them the only group that it was socially acceptable to publicly denigrate in the post-civil rights era. Arab American women say the mainstream American media humiliates Arabs and Muslims; watching or reading it makes them depressed, if not angry.

As a consequence of this alienation or repulsion from mainstream media sources, a majority of Arabs, including Arab American women, choose to use alternate news sources. Cable news shows especially on Fox, MSNBC, and CNN, are seen as the worst and National Public Radio is considered the best of the mainstream American media. Some whose Arabic language is good enough watch Arabic satellite stations, such as Al-Jazeera and ART, which are portrayed by woman in the study as either "more balanced" or showing "the other side that is not shown in the U.S." Others listen to the BBC or watch "Democracy Now" on American satellite television. By far the most common source of news for this educated and computer-savvy group was the Internet and e-mail. The U.S. invasion of Iraq, a prominent feature of the post-9/11 environment, was interpreted by all of the women interviewed in the study as yet another attack on Arabs and Muslims not justified by evidence. Many felt the American media covered it as if it were a sporting event, something they found profoundly offensive and painful; it played into the dehumanization they feel in the United States. The war on Iraq also stimulated a sense of exasperation with the American political system among a majority of Arab American women. Many concluded that voting has little meaning in the United States, and that power and lobbies determine the outcome of events.

CIVIC PARTICIPATION

On the other hand, study respondents reported a number of positive outcomes of the post-9/11 period, the most common being an increase in the civic participation of Arabs and Muslims and their organizations. Mosques and Muslim organizations were forced to come out of the isolation in which they lived and build bridges with other sectors of American society. "If we had not been so isolated, it would not be possible to attack our community on this level," said one woman, echoing the views of others. This is not to say that Muslims are totally at fault for their lack of integration. "We have been stereotyped for years as terrorists. Our issues have been ignored and twisted by the media. Organizations did not want to work with us. We have never been welcome here as Arabs and Muslims, so we have found safety and dignity in our own institutions." While the immediate multiethnic, interfaith response to the siege of the Bridgeview mosque revealed that the Arab and Muslim communities had some degree of ties and support in wider society, leaders of Muslim and non-Muslim civic institutions realized that further protection required much more work in a broader venue.

The Arab and Muslim communities in metropolitan Chicago responded vigorously to the new demands placed on them for civic integration. They opened their institutions to the public, explained their religion, and affirmed their membership in American society by condemning the attacks and repeating this condemnation through annual 9/11 memorials. In metro Chicago, non-Muslim civil institutions—especially those focused on civil rights, legal, religious, immigrant, and ethnic issues—aggressively opened their doors to Arabs and Muslims by sponsoring public educational forums. The most common topics of these forums were civil rights, Islam, federal laws and policies and their impact (such as the USA Patriot Act and special registration), women in Islam, and the war in Iraq. The Arab and Muslim speakers were usually immigrant men and American-born women, although they were more often women than men. Recent unprecedented meetings between Chicago mayor Richard Daley, members of the

Arab Advisory Council of the Chicago Commission on Human Relations, and members of the South Asian Muslim community indicate further progress in Arab and Muslim civic integration.

When asked in the Russell Sage study which community institutions are most important these days, Arab American Muslim women identified the mosque and civil rights institutions. Most respondents felt mosques can and should do a lot more and that they need to be more proactive. Many felt Islamic religious institutions and their members were not adequately prepared for this role and that they needed training in leadership development, advocacy, and civic participation. Some felt mosques should provide more social services and outreach to the poor as a means to establish their roots in the society. However, because Muslim community organizations had to use their resources on self-defense (resources that have been substantially depleted by community fears and government closures of charitable institutions) programs focused on community building have been sacrificed—not unlike the resource drain caused by the federal government's targeting of civil rights activists in the 1960s.

ORGANIZATIONAL IMPACTS: MOSQUES, COMMUNITY-BASED ORGANIZATIONS, AND CIVIL SOCIETY INSTITUTIONS

The findings of interviews conducted by the author for the Russell Sage study and a parallel study for the Annie E. Casey Foundation in the Spring of 2003 with the religious and executive leaders of mosques in the metropolitan Chicago area support the views of the Arab American women. A majority of mosque leaders specifically cited anti-Muslim, anti-Arab sentiments after September 11 as the major challenge their communities face in American society. One leader said: "We are in a desperate situation. We were isolated from others and we need to build bridges."

All of the leaders said the role of mosques and Islamic centers has changed in American society since 9/11. Of those who said it had changed, about half felt the changes were for the better and half felt the changes were negative. Positive changes included more outreach to non-Muslim communities and organizations and more interfaith dialogues and activities—providing non-Muslims with a better understanding of Islam and encouraging greater levels of Muslim civic participation, more critical thinking, and greater cohesion among the congregation of Muslims. Negative changes included redirection of institutional resources toward providing legal counsel and civil rights education, cancellation of programs (in 2001) for women and girls for fear of attacks on them due to their religious dress, and shrinking financial resources as community members became afraid to contribute to mosques in light of new government programs, policies, and activities.

All religious leaders agreed that the relationship between Muslims and non-Muslims has changed since 9/11 and that these changes were largely positive. The Muslim community as a whole has developed more relationships with other faith communities—especially Christian and Jewish—realizing it cannot be isolated during these difficult times, and has found a good deal of support from these communities. Muslims have become more civically active and have been invited to join a broad range of committees, task forces, and boards of directors. They are solicited for participation in local public political activities.

Nonetheless, the feeling of being stereotyped as terrorists by large sectors of the public persist. Religious leaders report widespread community fears of the federal government, lack of trust of persons unknown, feelings of being watched and followed, reduction in charitable giving, experiences with threats and verbal assaults, greater levels of stress, absence from community prayer services, and the permanent departure of families from the United States. The Bush administration's special registration program for visitors to the United States from predominantly Muslim countries was specifically cited as an offensive program that targeted Muslims.[56]

Nearly all mosque leaders said these changes have negatively affected the capacity of Muslim institutions to assist families in financial need and facing sociopsychological stress. The reduction in institutional funds brought about by community reluctance to donate to anything Islamic for fear the federal government will arrest, imprison, or deport them, and the diversion of funds to community defense and civil rights activities, has drained service resources. The positive outcome is the greater level of outreach to non-Muslim organizations that this emergency situation has stimulated, opening the potential for better collaborative programs and projects and a higher level of civic integration.

Representatives of secular community-based organizations reported similar experiences. The vast majority said prejudice, discrimination, misunderstanding of Islam, fear, and government threats were special challenges facing the Muslim community since 9/11. They also said their organizations were doing more civil rights, educational, and legal advocacy work than prior to this time, and were responding to an increased need for trauma counseling due to increased levels of fear and trauma among community members, especially among women who wear the *hijab,* as well as higher levels of discrimination experienced by community members at, for example, public agencies, in hospitals, and in the job market. As at mosques, the post-9/11 period has witnessed a surge in requests for secular groups' participation in coalitions, collaborations, and educational and bridge-building events. Foundations have been largely responsive to these needs by providing the necessary emergency funding.

Until the Bush administration's recent "faith-based initiative," mosques and Muslim organizations were largely excluded from receiving public and private funds, placing them in serious financial stress. It remains to be seen if this initiative will help to promote the important social service, leadership development, and bridge-building work that is being demanded of mosques in the post-9/11 era, work which mosques are anxious to undertake.

One impact of the Muslim-focused multicountry special registration program was that it helped forge a sense of commonality of status among Asian, Arab, and North African Muslim communities in the United States. Targeting Muslims of diverse ethnicities and countries of birth, the program forced these communities to develop shared resources. Special registration was implemented without clear national guidelines, leading to widespread confusion about who needed to register and what could be expected once they did. To clarify and advise, local Muslim communities across the United States held ongoing informational meetings. While the audiences for these meetings generally emerged from preexisting community formations, the experts and advisors were a mix of Arabs, Africans, Asians, and others, as were the subjects of the cases brought for illustration. In Chicago, Muslim women were key organizers and speakers at many of these events, often as attorneys and sometimes as civil rights activists.

Local and national civil rights and legal advocacy organizations within and outside the Arab and Muslim communities stepped up their activities during the special registration period. The American Immigration Law Association, National Immigration Forum, American Arab Anti-Discrimination Committee, and American Immigration Law Foundation teamed up to develop a web-based special registration questionnaire to document people's experiences with the process. Local organizations handed out flyers at INS offices, asking people to call and report their experiences. The Iranian American Bar Association asked everyone with firsthand knowledge of detentions and allegations of misconduct against Iranian nationals to call a toll-free number and share their information for an independent special report. Some local branches of the Council for American-Islamic Relations (CAIR) assembled support teams to provide on-site pre-registration check-in services, offering free legal advice and refreshments, and to track persons detained. CAIR–New York, in a coalition with other organizations, set up an Emergency Family Fund to assist families of "uncharged" detainees. Other local groups, including the Muslim Public Affairs Council in Southern

California, trained volunteers to serve as human rights monitors near INS offices. In an action mirrored in other U.S. cities, during the last week of call-in registration, the Arab American Action Network in Chicago assembled teams of multiethnic, religiously diverse volunteers to advise and support registrants and their families. The ACLU was also a prominent actor in opposing special registration policies and in taking actions to stem abuses.

In the post-9/11 period, despite all of the negative events affecting Muslim and Arab communities in the United States, Muslim civic participation in American society appears to be ascending. Muslims are actively working in civil rights and participating in and convening public discourses about Islam so as to not leave its definition to members of the Bush administration, hostile groups, and the media. Mainstream American civic organizations are taking concrete steps to have Muslim voices at their events, something that occurred only occasionally in pre-9/11 times. These and other indicators show that Islam is being acknowledged by large sectors of the American public as an American religion and that Muslim organizations are emerging from their social isolation.[57]

GENDER

Post-9/11 events have hoisted American Muslim women into the American spotlight. As noted earlier, the attention has largely been negative, as Muslim women who are visibly identifiable by their head scarves continue to face verbal assaults in public. Muslim women are also notably absent in the mainstream American media except in uninformed discussions about them, but so are Muslim men not accused of anti-American activities. On a local level, however, Muslim women are quite prominent in civic activities. They are frequent participants in cross-cultural and interfaith events and are visible activists in civil rights and educational activities. In metro Chicago, social service and other nonprofit agencies are more aggressively seeking Muslim women as staff members. This effort is not always driven solely by deep empathy or concern, however. In the post-9/11 era, many funders expect agencies to show not only staff diversity, but also specific sensitivity to Muslim concerns and needs. Whether driven by pure compassion or partial greed, this outcome is another positive one for Muslims in American society.

Arab American Muslim women, especially those more active in public life, say they find themselves repeatedly asked to explain the role of women in Islam, to defend the idea that they are not oppressed, and to explain the purpose of the *hijab*. This situation forced many of them through a deep soul-searching about their religion and its meaning in their lives (see next section). Some of the more secular women, who could better protect their safety by maintaining silence, questioned how much they were going to stand up for their religion and what it really meant in their lives. The outcome of this soul-searching brought clarity to their lives. Other women, especially religious women, argued that women are not oppressed in Islam, while "at the end of the day, acknowledging that some women are oppressed due to cultural patterns." These women felt that immigrant Muslim women, who are more isolated than both Arab American Muslim women and immigrant men, must find themselves in a far more stressful position vis-à-vis members of American society. While immigrant women lead a public life in which they are visibly Muslim and must endure stares and slurs, they have few opportunities and/or limited language capacity to communicate with the world around them.

THE SHOCK OF 9/11 AND PERSONAL INTROSPECTION

Perhaps one of the most interesting findings of the Russell Sage study of the impact of the September 11 attacks and their aftermath was the deep personal introspection so many Arab American Muslim women reported experiencing. Comments such as "my system got reworked," "it shook me up," and "I went through deep exploration" were common. A key component of this process, whether the individual was secular or religious, was an examination of her religious beliefs. Each woman asked herself what she believed in spiritually and whether and what she was willing to publicly defend. They critically examined and sorted out the essentials of Islamic principles and values as expressed in the Quran and Hadith and separated them from what they saw as proscriptions added by humans. As a result of this process, many religious women reported being more open-minded and less critical of other Muslims on issues that they saw as being of minor importance. The overarching values and principles of Islam (equity, compassion, generosity, and humility) rose to the surface, unabstracted by details of minor behaviors and modes of dress. Women who did not consider themselves religious came to terms with their way of life and choices. All of the women who experienced this critical self-examination said they came out of it stronger and better able to manage the task ahead of them as Muslim women in America.

Another outcome of the introspection was the strong assertion that "I am American." So many women were told to go back where they came from, were treated as foreigners in their native land, or felt unwelcome in public space that they had to examine who they were. Looking at their immigrant parents, fellow community members, friends, values, and upbringing, it became evidently clear that they were Americans. This meant they had every right to freely exercise their religious and political beliefs, to take public stands, and to participate in American social life.

All of these are positions of vulnerability in post-9/11 America. For one *muhajiba* (veiled) woman, participating fully in American social life meant joining a suburban cooking class, much to the shock of her classmates. While it may be difficult for white Americans to imagine her situation and the courage that joining the class required, people of color, especially African Americans, can identify with this brave move. "We will never establish ourselves here until we assert our right to be here," said another women, who felt the United States had regressed decades, to pre–civil rights days.

There are other women, however, whose personal strength has been zapped by post-9/11 events. As one woman said, "While I know inside I am American, when I am asked where I came from I am afraid, and so I say Chicago and want to run and hide." Others say they are Greek, Puerto Rican, or mixed race. By the same token, use of public space and assertion of political and religious beliefs are not yet safe activities for Muslims in post-9/11 America. As noted earlier, many Arab American Muslim women (veiled or not) still fear for their safety in public parks and other areas lacking ethnic and racial diversity. The politically active fear the long tentacles of the federal government, concerned that they may be next, picked up for their championing of issues that challenge the federal government's foreign policies in their homelands, or publicly accused of supporting terrorism.

POLITICAL PARTICIPATION

At risk in the post-9/11 era is a clear, unambiguous distinction between actions that constitute support for terrorism and those that constitute lawful challenges to U.S. foreign policies in Arab and Muslim countries. The actions of the federal government in this regard will be put to the test. Will its agents focus on real threats to American national security, or will they take measures whose main outcome is stifling political debate, thereby blocking the structural integration of Arabs and Muslims into American society? Full political integration of Arabs and Muslims may require opening up the debate on U.S. foreign policies and allowing persons who lawfully oppose these policies more social and media space to voice their arguments, without fear of government harassment and humiliation.

In the study, Arab American Muslim women reported feeling that they are part of a community that is locked out of having any real influence on the American body politic with regard to U.S. foreign policy. The mainstream American media insure this position, they said, by dehumanizing their people, dismissing their legitimate concerns, and portraying them as almost exclusively mobs of America-haters or people who oppose American values. One woman said, "When the media begin to show both sides of the real world, we can play a very positive role in this country."

Women informed about their community's past experiences in America say their silencing by the media and the government is not new. With regard to the U.S. government, they point to thirty-five years of legislation and actions taken against Arab and Muslim community leaders and activists that have stifled their voices in American political debate but done little to prevent terrorism. Included in this discussion are references to Operation Boulder, commenced after the 1967 Arab-Israeli war—during which the FBI spied on Arab Americans and their organizations, interviewed their families, friends, neighbors, and employers, and developed profiles of community activists—and the 1987 Los Angeles 8 case (LA8), in which one Kenyan and seven Palestinian activists were arrested on charges of being "alien terrorists" in the service of the (now largely defunct) Popular Front for the Liberation of Palestine. The eight were taken from their homes in handcuffs and imprisoned under high-security conditions before being released by a judge for lack of evidence. Fifteen years and numerous appeals later, still lacking evidence of support for terrorism, the U.S. government is reopening the case under the provisions of the USA Patriot Act, which shifts the burden of proof onto the defendant. Shortly after the LA8 arrests, the *Los Angeles Times* uncovered an INS-FBI Contingency Plan to detain alien Arabs and Muslims in America *en masse* in a camp in Oakdale, Louisiana. Arab American Muslim women also pointed to repeated INS attempts to deport Palestinian activists who were naturalized U.S. citizens, to consecutive pieces of antiterrorism legislation that replaced anticommunist laws with laws that mainly targeted Arabs, and to the historic exclusion of Arabs from political campaigns, including the return of Arab American campaign donations.

These federal government actions are perceived by many Arab and Muslim Americans as ways to ensure that they are politically voiceless in the United States.[58] The strong support shown by organized Muslims for George W. Bush's first presidential campaign reflects the importance of global issues to Muslim Americans; Bush was perceived as more capable of evenhandedness in Middle East policy than Al Gore and the Democrats. However, the Bush administration's domestic activities since September 11 have all but destroyed this support.[59]

The widely popular appeal to Arab American Muslims of global Islamic revival since the early 1990s is one outcome of years of feeling excluded and denigrated in American society. Linking their civic exclusion, political voicelessness, and persistent negative stereotyping to U.S. foreign policies that put American strategic interests before the human and democratic rights of people in their homelands, Arab Americans shared a sense of powerlessness with many across the globe, who found faith in God the only hope for change.

In the current era of global communication and swift international travel, immigrants are now more able to maintain strong ties to their homelands. Their knowledge of events occurring overseas and concerns for the safety and security of family members left behind are therefore likely to be stronger than among previous immigrant generations. Using the importance to American Jews of U.S. government support for Israel as an indicator of both the strength of these ties in modern times and the relevance of foreign policy concerns to a group's political integration, it would appear to be the case that the full integration into American society of U.S.-based Arabs and Muslims estimated to be some 6 million persons will require opening up the political debates on policies of concern to them and a parallel shift in media coverage of Arabs, Muslims, and events in their homelands. Criminalizing these concerns, and labeling them as "support for terrorism," is counterproductive for American national security.

The post-9/11 period for Arabs and Muslim in America is a paradoxical historical moment. Their communities are experiencing government repression and social outcasting at the same time as their institutions are experiencing enhanced civic inclusion, facilitating their integration into American society. Secretary of State Colin Powell stated in September 2003 interview on public television's *Charlie Rose Show*—while talking about Washington's vision of the future Iraqi government—that he expected it to be "an Islamic country by faith, just as we are a Judeo-Christian . . . Well, it's hard to tell any more, but we are a country of many faiths now."[60] Secretary Powell recognized that the United States must begin to redefine itself as larger than a Judeo-Christian society. Its demographic composition has changed as millions of new immigrants bearing new religions, cultures, and homeland concerns have arrived. The negative stereotyping of Arabs and Muslims emerges in part from their newness and lack of social and political integration in American society. The post-9/11 profiling of them as the "suspected other" or as a fifth column poses a serious challenge to their inclusion. At the same time as the federal government must rationally re-think its war on terrorism, the institutions of American society must open up the issues for public debate and expand their concept of who are the "we" in "In God We Trust."

IR THEORY AND EPOCHAL EVENTS: BETWEEN PARADIGM SHIFTS AND BUSINESS-AS-USUAL*

JEFFREY T. CHECKEL

INTRODUCTION

The events of September 11, 2001, and their aftermath have left indelible imprints on many aspects of American and global society and policy. Of course, real world happenings have implications for scholars as well—in this case, theorists of international relations (IR). However, the challenge is to come to agreement on what those implications might be and then to sketch constructive avenues for future research.

This chapter answers that twofold challenge by advocating a robust, theoretically driven and empirically informed middle ground. In particular, IR theorists do not need a radical paradigm shift to explore migration as a security issue or (dramatically?) changed understandings of sovereignty. Rather, the central challenge is one of better cross-fertilization across existing research programs and subfields. Indeed, the time is ripe for a long-overdue conversation between IR and migration studies (see also Tirman, this volume)[1] and—yes, yet again—for redoubled efforts to minimize the boundaries separating international and domestic politics.

The remainder of the chapter is organized as follows. I begin by placing September 11 in context by examining how IR theorists have responded to other epochal events—most notably, the unexpected and peaceful end of the Cold War. In doing this, I do not minimize the gravity of what has transpired; rather, the (pedagogic) purpose is to distill lessons for scholars as they respond to these more recent events. The table thus set, the chapter next considers how IR and migration theorists, in the wake of 9/11, might benefit from more systematic attention to each other's work. In particular, migration researchers seem well placed to help IR better explore domestic political context, while IR can help migration theory conceptualize better cross-level interactions and the role of the state.

In a third section, I address two central challenges for IR in the wake of September 11—looking at the dark side of transnational politics and rethinking yet again our understanding of sovereignty, a term whose meaning and operation is constitutive for the system at large. I close by offering several cautions and caveats as theorists attempt to grapple with the post-9/11 world.

IR THEORY AND EPOCHAL EVENTS—A CAUTIONARY TALE

It is rather obvious, to be expected, and important that scholars, as well as policy-makers, journalists, and the public at large, respond to large-scale, history-changing events. In this regard, September 11 is no exception. In its wake, key organizations like the Social Science Research Council have sponsored web publications and organized new book series (of which this volume is a part),[2] while leading international relations[3] and security journals[4] have organized article symposia.

Along with this outpouring of scholarship have come embarrassing questions. "Which of your models and theories should I turn to now? What do you academics have to say about September 11? You are supposed to be the scholars and students of international affairs—Why did it happen? What should be done?"[5]

For this writer, such reactions and comments evoke an eerie sense of déjà vu. "Been there, done this," I mutter, referring to another epochal event to which the IR community felt a need to respond—the unexpected and peaceful end of the Cold War. I will not review the now-extensive debate over this question.[6] Instead, it is more important for this volume's purposes to highlight the good and bad about this earlier round of IR soul searching, seeking to derive lessons for new debates post-9/11.

The exemplary good from that post-1989 debate was to push mainstream (American) IR scholarship to broaden its disciplinary foundations. Reaching well beyond economics and microeconomics, scholars began to problematize key concepts and behaviors—interests, sovereignty, consequentialist action—that had previously been taken for granted in security studies and IR. They did this by turning to sociology, organizational sociology, and continental political theory, among others.[7] The result was to broaden our understanding of the social dynamics underpinning the Cold War endgame,[8] and of key security institutions such as NATO[9]—to take just two examples.

Unfortunately, there is no such thing as a free lunch—even in IR scholarship. This innovative theoretical turn was accompanied by problematic developments. For one, there was a tendency to think in either/or terms, especially in the first wave of scholarship. For example, some argued that the Cold War's end was attributable solely to ideational factors,[10] while others suggested that logics of appropriateness were the main drivers of human and state behavior.[11] In addition, theoretical and disciplinary innovation came at the partial expense of operationalized empirical research, where the latter would place greater emphasis on design and method. As a result, it was often unclear just what the ideational/sociological turn was explaining in relation to its nearest competitors; the value-added question loomed large.[12]

For sure, recent studies have moved to correct these problems, with scholars advancing nuanced both/and arguments stressing the roles of ideational *and* material factors; of appropriate *and* consequentialist behavior.[13] Issues of design and method are now getting more attention as well.[14] Still, if these theoretical and methodological moves had been made earlier, unnecessary debates and false starts might have been avoided.

To sum up, IR's encounter with its last epochal event suggests two lessons for theorists contemplating a post-9/11 world. First, be it post–Cold War security studies or the securitization of migration, theoretically innovative and empirically sound arguments will likely involve both material and ideational factors, with differing theories of action (logic of consequences, cost/benefit calculations, self-interested, instrumental behavior *along with* logics of appropriateness, rule-governed, other regarding behavior) at play under different conditions—temporal or substantive.[15]

Second, this exercise in integration is hard to pull off in practice. As scholars, we all have sunk costs, with much training and research invested in particular approaches; it is not easy to reach out to the other side and give its arguments a fair hearing. Still, this would be easier to accomplish if more attention were paid to design and methods at an early stage.[16]

IR AND MIGRATION THEORIES— MAKING NEW CONNECTIONS

The migration literature is rich, varied and multidisciplinary.[17] Elements of this scholarship seem particularly well placed to help IR scholars as they begin to problematize the international-politics/migration nexus.[18]

One can start with an obvious but fundamental fact. Migration is about the movement of people. O.K., but movement into *what?* When borders are crossed, individuals and groups are moving from a transnational to a domestic and national context. Indeed, migration hits home when it shows up on the doorstep, so to speak. At this level, migration scholars can help IR better theorize domestic political context.[19]

Consider the work of Yasmin Soysal on migrants and identity in postwar Europe.[20] This imaginative book actually has a two-part argument—one about the global diffusion of new norms of migrant's rights and one on how domestic institutions reshape immigrant identities in their adopted country. Not surprisingly, IR researchers—being IR types—have focused most on the global/systemic part of Soysal's framework. Yet, it is the domestic part that offers real value added for IR, where the author advances a compelling argument about the constitutive role of domestic institutions in reshaping immigrant identities. Not only does this provide IR researchers with a carefully argued thesis on the importance of domestic politics in understanding the movement of peoples, it also expands the social-theoretic foundations of their analyses. While much recent scholarship has theorized the role of domestic politics and institutions from a rationalist[21] or rational choice institutionalist[22] perspective, Soysal theorizes them from a more sociological orientation.[23]

A second example comes from the work of Gary Freeman. In a clever and counterintuitive argument, Freeman has developed an interest group explanation firmly grounded in pluralist, rational-choice traditions for why immigration restrictions in liberal states—despite the rise of anti-immigrant parties and rhetoric—tend to weaken over time.[24]

The work of Soysal or Freeman in the migration literature does not offer paradigm-shaking insights to IR scholars. Rather, it should simply remind the latter that well developed tool kits from comparative politics await them when and if they theorize the domestic context of the migration/IR nexus.[25]

Of course, cross-fertilization should affect both sides, which suggests that IR has something to offer students of migration as well. Here, I highlight three contributions. First, migration theorists seem particularly wedded to analytic frameworks that focus on either domestic or international factors. Indeed, one recent and comprehensive survey of the migration literature identifies six families of migration theories, all of which operate at either the national—segmented labor market theory, for example—or systemic levels—world systems approaches, say.[26] Yet, if there ever was a topic that cried out for cross-level analysis, it is migration. On this topic, IR has much to offer, from Putnam's[27] notion of two-level games to more recent efforts to theorize the complex interaction among various transnational forces and domestic politics.[28]

Second, many migration theories, by focusing on the individual decision calculus of migrants, the structure of the global (capitalist) economy, or social networks (Adamson, this volume), effectively read the state out of their analyses. This seems odd.[29] At the end of the day, migration policy must still be channeled through and thus effected by the state and its decision makers. In contrast, within IR, the state has always played a central role. Drawing upon this rich tradition, migration theorists might more systematically explore how the (material) structure of state institutions shapes policymaking (so called domestic structures approaches)[30] or, at a deeper level, how the (social) constitution of states[31] and individual decision makers within them[32] affects policy outcomes.

Third, on my reading, all too many theorists of migration build their arguments on a rather limited set of social-theoretic foundations.[33] In particular, the causal motors driving their stories are often material goods (say, a migrant's desire to improve his/her material well being) and cost/benefit calculations by individual actors.[34] In principle, nothing is wrong with such an approach. However, a more social ontology coupled to alternative theories of action might open the analysis to a broader set of explanatory factors influencing migration. As constructivists in IR theory make precisely the latter analytic move, their insights could be valuable for migration theorists. For example, how do social structures and norms shape the migration policies of states?[35] What role do arguing and persuasion (as opposed to strategic calculation) play in shaping contemporary immigration policy?[36]

CENTRAL THEORETICAL CHALLENGES

Among the many challenges for IR raised by September 11, this volume highlights two issues as particularly worthy of attention because of their combined theory/policy relevance—rethinking the nature of transnationalism and of sovereignty. In keeping with this essay's theme, however, this rethink should not involve a conceptual start from the scratch, but an expansion of existing research and theorizing.

TERROR AND TRANSNATIONALISM.

The past decade has seen a revitalization of work on transnationalism and transnational politics.[37] In contrast to earlier studies,[38] recent research is more theoretically and methodologically self-conscious. It has also moved away from the opposition central to early work—transnational organizations *or* state actors—to frameworks stressing the interactions among transnational actors, the state, and domestic social movements.[39]

Yet, in an important sense, these newer works share a common bias in that they explore mainly the "good side" of transnationalism. Indeed, we have numerous studies on how transnational actors have helped promote progressive change in a variety of policy areas, including human rights,[40] security policy,[41] and migrant rights.[42] For sure, there has always been a more IPE-ish strand of this literature, one exploring the role and sometimes deleterious impact of multinational corporations—and especially the social costs of their activities in the developing world. Even here, though, the recent trend is toward studies exploring multinationals' good sides—for example, why more and more of them incorporate human rights and sustainable development into their core mission statements.[43]

There are at least two reasons for this state of affairs. For one, many of these scholars share a normative conviction that IR can and should study those forces promoting progressive change in world politics. However, there is an equally important practical issue. The typical design for most examinations of transnational politics is to conduct one or more qualitative case studies, which then reconstruct transnational influence through detailed process tracing. The data often include internal, semi-confidential documents as well as interviews. Needless to say, there are real challenges in extending such methods and data sources to studies of transnationalism's darker sides—transnational organized crime (Russia-Afghanistan-Columbia) or transnational terrorist networks (al Qaeda).

If nothing else, however, the causes and aftermath of September 11 should remind students of transnationalism that their research program does need to be extended to these darker sides. Contributors to this volume begin to address this challenge by exploring: the role of diasporas in transnational cycles of political violence;[44] the linkages between transnational terror networks and subaltern globalization;[45] and the complex ways in which transnational terror connects to and—somewhat paradoxically—reempowers the state.[46]

A logical next step would be to examine how key concepts in the transnationalism literature—norms, values, advocacy networks, social movements, political community—need to be extended, revised or perhaps discarded when confronted by these darker sides of transnationalism. Consider work on advocacy networks, which often explores the ability of individual agents—political entrepreneurs—to mobilize broader networks. Referred to as norm or moral entrepreneurs[47] these agents persuade, argue, and cajole in the service of some larger good—say, the promotion of women's rights or the banning of sweatshop labor. Yet, as Adamson and Ho (both this volume) note, entrepreneurs can equally use their powers to darker ends, for example, inculcating strategies of violence in diaspora communities.

A similar story can be told about notions of political community. As employed by students of transnationalism and international institutions, community denotes some degree of collective identification among actors (usually states). In addition—and this is key—such identification is positive in that it mitigates violence or other forms of conflict. Recent work on security communities conceptualizes political communities in precisely this manner.[48] Of course, the problem—or, better said, limitation—here is that community and collective identification can in equal measure lead to bad things. For example, recent and innovative work on transnational organized criminal networks views them less as businesses out to maximize profit and more as communities of like-minded actors held together by more than calculations of cost and benefit.[49]

In both these examples, important analytic categories from the transnationalism literature have been applied in new contexts and in ways that apparently did little violence to their core meanings; they traveled well. In itself, this is an important finding, but one possible only because scholars are beginning to explore these darker sides of transnational politics.

Beyond these analytic considerations, the practical challenge of conducting such research can be minimized by drawing upon the growing body of policy-oriented work that explores precisely these nastier sides of transnationalism. For example, Phil Williams of the University of Pittsburgh has developed a robust, policy-oriented research program on various aspects of transnational organized crime.[50] He is also the founding editor of *Transnational Organized Crime,* a peer-reviewed journal published by Frank Cass that is now in its eighth year. A quick glance at its contents suggests rich opportunities for students of the good side of transnational politics to extend and refine both their data sets and central concepts.[51]

SOVEREIGNTY—TIME TO BRING THE STATE BACK IN?

If one shouts the word sovereignty to a roomful of IR scholars, there is likely to be a competition to see who can most quickly modify the term. Is it penetrated? Compromised? Or maybe just plain hollowed out? This adjectival-attachment exercise reflects a simple fact: States are no longer sovereign within their borders. While some would argue that nations have never been as sovereign as we tend to think,[52] virtually all agree that the status of the concept is currently in flux.[53]

Consider a few examples. Students of transnational social movements have shown the profound degree to which networks of non-state actors can challenge and redefine core state prerogatives.[54] Theorists of international institutions regularly document how states—especially in contemporary Europe—have constitutive features of their domestic polities (supremacy of national law, policies on citizenship and ethnic minorities, and the like) changed or imposed from without by regional organizations like the European Union.[55] Finally, students of globalization, while often overstating their case, have demonstrated states' decreasing room for maneuver in a series of policy areas.[56]

None of this is new and, indeed, all these trends were at work prior to 9/11. What, then, is different? Possibly, it is the agents driving the transformations. In the preceding paragraph, sovereignty was being redefined and challenged by nonstate and suprastate actors and forces. However, this may be changing, at least if we take the Bush doctrine at face value. As Richard Haass at the State Department argues:

> Sovereignty entails obligations. One is not to massacre your own people. Another is not to support terrorism in any way. If a government fails to meet these obligations, then it forfeits some of the normal advantages of sovereignty, including the right to be left alone inside your own territory. Other governments, including the United States, gain the right to intervene.[57]

While the policy implications of such views are immense, my concern here is what it means for how IR scholars study sovereignty. Instead of seeking new insights from different disciplines, we might now best be served by looking back to earlier traditions (classical realism) and historical periods (Europe prior to 1900). Such a theoretical and historical look back suggests that students of sovereignty will need "to bring the state back in" to their analyses—not as a penetrated, passive, and reactive unit, but as a powerful and active one reshaping both precedent and international law.[58]

Yet, it is not the simply the Bush doctrine and the unilateral assertion of American power that are currently changing our understanding of sovereignty. Other events, both before and after September 11, have played a less direct but nonetheless important role, revitalizing the ontological status of the state in ways thought highly unlikely in the post–Cold War, globalized 1990s. A key factor here has been the reappearance and growth of threatening forms of non-state activity, at first in the guise of transnational criminal networks and, more recently, via bin Laden-like terror networks.[59]

The response by states has been twofold. At the national level and in a largely uncoordinated way,[60] they have reacted to such threats by strengthening policing and covert-operations units (in Asia and Central Asia—Ahmed and Newberg, respectively, this volume) or by tightening immigration procedures (in Canada).[61] In the process, the coercive apparatus of the state has been strengthened and revitalized.

A second response has been multilateral. Working through the United Nations and other international institutions, there has been a coordinated effort to counter terrorist financing. In the late 1990s, a UN convention that targeted terrorist finances was adopted; post-9/11, the UN's Counter Terrorism Committee was given new powers to fight this problem. As Biersteker's analysis in this volume shows, these multilateral efforts are beginning to pay off—for example, in better national-level reporting and in the elaboration of best-practice procedures in this policy area.

One thus sees an element of reregulation and the reassertion of state prerogatives in what is traditionally viewed as *the* most globalized part of the international economy: finance. While Biersteker is careful not to overstate his case, the analytic implications of his tentative empirical findings are significant.

Simply put, are we witnessing a "return of the state"? While it is too early to tell, the above recounting of unilateral and multilateral responses both before and after September 11 suggests that the sovereign state is not yet as hollowed out as some might suggest. For students of international relations, however, the challenge is not to declare the sovereign state to be dead (hyperglobalists) or alive and thriving (realism). The analytic puzzle is actually much more complex. Clearly, the past half century has seen a radical transformation of the state and state sovereignty, a process which has continued and been accelerated post-9/11 (albeit, perhaps in unexpected ways; see earlier).

Analytically, the most interesting questions, then, are not of an either/or form (the state remains sovereign or it is hollowed out). Rather, in revisiting state sovereignty, we should be charting the agents of change in the historical evolution of sovereignty, the processes through which it occurs, and the implications of such dynamics for national policy and global governance.[62]

Here, students of IR might do well to draw upon the work of Europeanists. These scholars study an institution and entity—the European Union and the emerging European polity—that go well beyond traditional Westphalian notions of sovereign state authority. Indeed, the entire Europeanization literature, while using slightly different language, addresses precisely the dynamic and changing nature of state sovereignty, and the implications of the latter for democratic and legitimate supranational governance.[63]

CONCLUSIONS AND CAUTIONS

In the wake of September 11, scholars of international relations should avoid the dual temptations of radical change ("Why couldn't your theories predict that event") or do-nothingism ("Well, after all, that was just one data point"). Instead, they should seek a middle ground and do so keeping two points in mind.

First, any new theory building exercise—on the securitization of migration, the spread of transnational terror networks and the like—needs to be modest in aspirations. The goal should be contingent, bounded, middle-range explanations,[64] where theory is constructed and refined through the creative interplay of analytic hunches and empirical reality (so-called grounded theory). Such approaches, which typically have a strong emphasis on actors, the institutions in which they operate, and process not only minimize the agent-structure problem that so bedevils social theorists. More important, they create theories closer to the reality of what policymakers perceive and experience on a daily basis.

Yet, this stress on middle-range frameworks again highlights the importance of design and method. Middle-range arguments are typically complex, exploring the interplay among several factors to produce a given outcome. Often, the challenge is to figure out which of these factors is really doing the heavy lifting and which are more secondary. Put differently, the outcome may be overdetermined. While this problem can never be completely eliminated, careful attention to design—by allowing one to control for the effects of various factors—can minimize it.[65]

As an example, let us return to Soysal's argument about how domestic institutions have constitutive, identity-shaping effects on migrants. Whether or not this is true is important for a whole host of reasons. If Soysal is correct, the likelihood of immigrant integration in his/her adopted homeland is higher, which, in turn, lowers the likelihood of alienation, which, in turn, may . . . reduce the number of possible recruits for transnational terrorist networks? But *is* Soysal correct? The ideal follow-on study would seek to isolate the role of domestic institutions by looking cross-nationally at cases where such institutions are historically rooted and strong (the West European countries studied by Soysal) and also at instances where they are nascent and fragile (for example, in a "new" state like Ukraine). *Ceteris paribus,* one would expect the latter—because of the newness of domestic institutions—to have weaker effects on immigrant identities.

Second, everything post-9/11 is not novel.[66] International relations—as both a theoretical enterprise and as a source of policy-relevant knowledge—can make its strongest contribution to interpreting and explaining the renewed (again note: I did not write "new") links among migration, security, violence, and identity by consolidating and building upon the gains of the past decade. For sure, new dimensions need to be explored (the dark side of transnationalism) and new theoretical linkages made (between migration and security; between state practice and sovereignty). However, the raw material for such exercises is already mostly there.

This may sound like a conservative stance, one that legitimates and justifies orthodoxy. However, this misreads my intention. The concern here is to generate theoretically grounded, empirically rich, and policy-relevant knowledge. The fastest way to do this—and time *is* of some essence—would be to avoid another round of great debate and/or interdisciplinary confusion and instead get on with the practical task of developing modest and testable arguments.

NOTES

Introduction

1. Mark J. Miller, "A durable international migration and security nexus: The problem of the Islamic periphery in transatlantic ties," in *Migration, Globalization and Human Security* eds. David T. Graham and Nana K. Poku, (London: Routledge, 2000).

2. Fiona Terry, *Condemned to Repeat? The Paradox of Humanitarian Action* (Ithaca, N.Y.: Cornell University Press, 2002), esp. Chapter 1.

3. Myron Weiner, ed., *International Migration and Security* (Boulder, Colo.: Westview Press, 1993). See also, mainly for the human security dimension, Ole Waever et al., eds., *Identity, Migration and the New Security Agenda in Europe* (London: Pinter, 1993); David T. Graham and Nana K. Poku, eds., *Redefining Security: National Security and Population Movements* (Westport, Conn.: Praeger, 1998); and Graham and Poku, *Migration, Globalization and Human Security.*

4. "The Clash of Globalizations," *Foreign Affairs,* July/August 2002: 108.

5. Phil Williams, "Transnational Criminal Networks," in *Networks and Netwars: The Future of Terror, Crime, and Militancy,* John Arquilla and David Ronfeldt, eds., (RAND, 2001), p. 65.

6. "Terrorism: September 11, 2001," *Migration News,* vol. 8, no. 10 (October 2001).

7. George J. Borjas, "An Evaluation of the Foreign Student Program," *Center for Immigration Studies Backgrounder,* June 2002.

8. Christopher Rudolph, *Security and the Political Economy of International Migration* (Berkeley, Calif.: Institute of Governmental Studies, 2002), pp. 34, 36.

9. Douglas S. Massey, "Why Does Immigration Occur? A Theoretical Synthesis," in *The Handbook of International Migration: The American Experience* Charles Hirschman, Philip Kasinitz, and Josh DeWind, eds., (New York: Russell Sage Foundation, 1999), p. 48.

10. Massey's article is in the impressive *The Handbook of International Migration,* which scarcely mentions security in any of its twenty-four chapters; a noteworthy parallel, *The Handbook of International Relations,* also published by Russell Sage and equally useful, returns the favor: migration is scarcely mentioned.

11. "Guarding the Gates," in Craig Calhoun, Paul Price, and Ashley Timmer, eds., *Understanding September 11* (New York: The New Press, 2002), p. 298.

Empire Through Diasporic Eyes: A View from the Other Boat

*This essay first acquired its present form in lectures delivered at the Social Science Research Council's Global Security and Co-operation program, for which I thank Itty Abraham and John Tirman; and at the Harvard Academy for International and Area Studies, for which I thank Samuel Huntington. A somewhat different version of this chapter has been published in *Comparative Studies in Society and History* (April 2004), and can be obtained from the publisher,

Cambridge University Press. Audiences at the following venues have been generous and stimulating: Harvard anthropology department and Middle East anthropology workshop; Department of Social Anthropology, University of Edinburgh, and the Edinburgh Institute for the Advanced Study of Islam and the Middle East; Schumann Centre for Advanced Studies, European University Institute, Florence. For comments and pointed criticisms, I am grateful to Fiona Adamson, Talal Asad, Vince Brown, Diogo Curto, Kathleen Donohue, Paul Dresch, Bernard Haykel, Cernal Kafadar, Yuen Foong Khong, Alexander Knysh, Peggy Levitt, Saba Mahmood, Tamara Neuman, Sue Roff, William Roff, Andrew Shryock, and Thomas Trautmann.

1. J. R Seeley, *The Expansion of England* (Boston: Roberts Brothers, 1883).

2. Donald Rumsfeld, "On Tomorrow's Armed Forces," *Foreign Affairs* 81, no. 3, (2002): 20–32.

3. Eric Wolf, *Europe and the People Without History* (Berkeley: University of California Press, 1982).

4. The Dutch scholar J. C. van Leur was a solitary figure who sought out this larger story, which he understood as a competitive dynamic of expansion between Islam and Christianity across the region. He died prematurely on a ship sunk by a Japanese torpedo off Java. His writings were collected posthumously in J. C. van Leur, *Indonesian Trade and Society* (The Hague: W. Van Hoeve, 1955).

5. Talal Asad, ed., *Anthropology and the Colonial Encounter* (Amherst, N.Y.: Prometheus Books, 1973).

6. Some of them were also imperial powers, such as Britain and France, while others, such as Belgium, were not. Connections among colonies and metropolises within an empire—such as labor migrations of Indians to Burma; imperial preferential trade tariffs; specialized, geographically restricted botanical inputs into industrial processes (such as *gutta perca* from Malayan jungles, uniquely suitable for sheathing the underwater telegraph cables constituting the empire's nervous system); circulation of military units of Ghurkas among colonies; trade-union agitation by stevedores along a chain of imperial ports—were not anthropological topics when Asad launched his critique. Empire-wide phenomena were not an anthropological level of analysis, so the identification of anthropology's isolated field sites as colonies was already enough of a can of worms to deal with.

7. The idea of foreignness often remains unremarked in these contexts, but is key. Hawaii is no longer considered a colony or imperial outpost because the foreign U.S. government assimilated Hawaii's native, Asian, and creole populations into its constitutional structure by fiat, thus making itself not foreign. In contrast, creole Eurasian populations of *burgers* and *Indos* could not brush off the taint of foreignness in independent Sri Lanka and Indonesia, and mostly left after decolonization despite centuries of local residence and intermarriage. Whether or not cultural identity and historical process matter are often incredibly simple decisions of state.

8. Here is an exchange of three letters, to give a sense of the correspondence.

(1) In a Foreign Office file from 1916 archived at the British Public Records Office (FO371/2781) entitled "Hadramawt Arabs Proceeding from Batavia [in the Dutch East Indies] to Mukalla [in Hadramawt, Yemen]," Mr. Beckett, the British consul at Batavia, writes to his superiors at the Foreign Office, London: "Agent Netherlands Steamship Co. here enquires whether Arabs wishing [to] proceed [to] Mukalla can be landed there or at Aden in batches of 100 up to maximum of 600 and what if any formalities are required regarding conveyance of these nominally Turkish subjects. Intercourse between bonafide Mukalla Arabs there and their native place should I think be encouraged and I could if necessary control bonafides." This note is forwarded by the secretary of state in London to the viceroy in India, asking for an opinion.

(2) The British Resident of Aden, the "man on the spot" administratively in India, comments on the Batavia inquiry: "The reason for this sudden exodus from Batavia is unknown, and this precludes my doing justice to the query. Prima facie not advisable to allow direct communication between Batavia and Makalla by foreign steamship qua possible landing of contraband. Hadramawt people not nominally Turkish subjects, and if they claim to be so their passage at this time into country within our sphere is objectionable. Makalla Sultan would certainly like to check entry of these people into Makalla, as he is closely engaged in coping with sedition fostered by Turkish agents and their advent would hamper him."

(3) A decision is issued by the India Office in London (responsible for India, Aden, Mukalla) and communicated to the Foreign Office (responsible for Batavia consul): "I am to suggest that Mr. Beckett should be informed that the inhabitants of the Hadramawt are not Turkish subjects, and that all Arabs desiring to proceed from Java to that region must land at Aden first. He might at the same time be asked whether he can explain the sudden desire of these men to return to Arabia. Viscount Grey is aware that the Turkish commander at Lahej, Said Pasha, has been intriguing actively in the Hadramawt and that there is much pan-Islamic propaganda in the Dutch East Indies."

9. Osama's father Muhammad bin Laden started off sitting close to the king at his audience and being attentive to royal needs. He built a special external ramp for a debilitated King Abd al-Aziz up to his bedroom, and was entrusted with the construction of royal palaces. Royal favor led to huge contracts for rebuilding the major religious sites of Mecca, Medina, and Jerusalem, and the Bin Laden Group became the largest construction company in the country on the back of the oil boom. Muhammad underwrote government salaries for a few months when King Faysal ascended the throne under difficult circumstances, and a number of Saudi princes got their start in business under bin Laden tutelage. The bin Ladens are part of a broader phenomenon of Hadramis who reached the pinnacle of Saudi society and from there consorted with Texan politician-businessmen-oil elites in companies such as Arbusto, Harken, and Carlyle, extending the Saudi princely treatment to their sons (cf. references in the following footnote).

10. "Feds Investigate Entrepreneur Allegedly Tied to Saudis," *Houston Chronicle,* June 4, 1992; "Bin Laden Family Could Profit from a Jump in Defense Spending Due to Ties to U.S. Bank," *Wall Street Journal* September 27, 2001; "Bush y Bin Laden, socios en los negocios y amigos íntimos," *Sodepaz* 29, September 2001; "A Strange Intersection of Bushes, bin Ladens," *Cleveland Plain Dealer,* November 12, 2001; "Republican-Controlled Carlyle Group Poses Serious Ethical Questions for Bush Presidents," *Baltimore Chronicle,* October 1, 2001.

11. Interview with Zbigniew Brzezinski in *Le Nouvel Observateur* (France), January 15–21, 1998, p. 76. Revising official U.S. accounts of Soviet aggression, the former national security advisor to then-president Carter now claims to have lured the Soviets into Afghanistan and directly caused their demise through imperial overreach. For this, the resulting creation of an armed Islamist movement like the Taliban is a small price to pay, he says.

12. Bernard Cohn once called the imperial point of view the "view from the boat." There were other boats as well.

13. See "diaspora" entry in the *American Heritage Dictionary* (William Morris, ed., *The American Heritage Dictionary of the English Language* [Boston: Houghton Mifflin, 1980]).

14. I adopt this definitional schematism here because I am interested not in the question of origins nor in a narrow conception of ethnicity, but in outcomes, wherever they lead. Erich Auerbach, for example, argues that a particularly Jewish tradition was made universally embraceable as Christianity in the hands of St. Paul (Erich Auerbach, *Scenes from the Drama of European Literature* [New York: Meridian, 1959]).

15. David Armitage, *The Ideological Origins of the British Empire* (Cambridge: Cambridge University Press, 2000).

16. Linda Colley, *Britons: Forging the Nation, 1707–1837* (New Haven: Yale University Press, 1992).

17. Hannah Arendt, *The Origins of Totalitarianism* (San Diego: Harcourt Brace, 1979); Seeley, *The Expansion of England.*

18. New positions proposing minority-group rights are being carved out in liberal philosophy, which is traditionally individualist. Led by Canada-based philosophers such as Charles Taylor and Will Kymlicka, they are vigorously discussed in other Anglo colonies such as Australia and the United States and are part of the ongoing "multicultural" deracination of those countries and their dominant British diasporas. Liberalism as a unified political and economic doctrine finds its classic formulation in Adam Smith as an expressly anti-imperialist position. Free men and free trade would create the wealth of nations on more secure and moral foundations than the un-free men (slavery) and un-free trade (mercantilism) of the first British empire of the Americas. Thought of as an antimonopolist position in politics and economics, liberalism's contemporary extension into culture, such as Taylor's politics of cultural recognition, is not an impossible stretch. It marks a late transformation of the expansive British diaspora into a universalizing constitutionalism, now embracing all cultural comers. While phenotypic commitment is no longer a barrier to this universalization, linguistic commitment remains one.

19. K. N. Chaudhuri, *Asia Before Europe: Economy and Civilisation of the Indian Ocean from the Rise of Islam to 1750* (Cambridge: Cambridge University Press, 1990); Stephen Frederic Dale, *Islamic Society on the South Asian Frontier: The Mappilas of Malabar, 1498–1922* (Oxford: Clarendon Press, 1980); Engseng Ho, "Le don précieux de la généalogie," in *Emirs et présidents: Figures de la parenté et du politique en Islam,* eds. P. Bonte, E. Conte, and P. Dresch (Paris: CNRS éditions, 2001); Engseng Ho, "Before Parochialization: Diasporic Arabs Cast in Creole Waters," in *Transcending Borders: Arabs, Politics, Trade and Islam in Southeast Asia,* eds. Huub de Jonge and Nico Kaptein (Leiden, Netherlands: KITLV Press, 2002); George Fadlo Hourani, *Arab Seafaring in the Indian Ocean in Ancient and Early Medieval Times* (Princeton, N.J.: Princeton University Press, 1951); G. R. Tibbetts, *Arab Navigation in the Indian Ocean Before the Coming of the Portuguese,* vol. 42 of *Oriental Translation Fund, New Series* (London: Royal Asiatic Society of Great Britain and Ireland, 1981).

20. As recorded in the literature, although there were exceptions (see Ahmad Abd Allah al-Saqqaf, *Fatat Qarut* [n.d]; Engseng Ho, "Hadramis Abroad in Hadramawt: The Muwalladin," in *Hadrami Traders, Scholars and Statesmen in the Indian Ocean, 1750s–1960s,* eds. U. Freitag and W. G. Clarence-Smith [Leiden, Netherlands: E. J. Brill, 1997]).

21. The depth and breadth of this indigenization is reflected in attempts at tracking it, giving rise to encyclopedic works in Hadrami literature: massive genealogies (Abd al-Rahman al-Mashhur, bin Muhammad, bin Husayn, ed., *Shams al-zahira fi nasab ahl al-bayt min Bani Alawi furu' Fatima al-zahra' wa-Amir al-Mu'minin 'Ali radiya Allah 'anhu,* vol. 1 [Jidda: Alam al-Ma'rifa, 1984]), a four-volume compendium of diasporic families (Ba Matraf 1984), a five-volume one of poets Alawī al-Ḥaddād, bin Ṭāhir bin Abd Allāh al-Hadār, *al-Madkhal ilā ata'rīkh al-Islām bi-l-sharq al-aqṣā* (al-Qāhira: Dār al-Fikr al-Ḥadīth, printed at the expense of Mu'assasat al-Muḥḍār al-Taḍāmuniyya, 1971); Muḥammad bin Shihāb al-Alawī al-Ḥaḍramī, bin Abd al-Raḥmān, "Supplement to Ḥāḍir al-Ālam al-Islāmī," in *Ḥāḍir al-Ālam Islāmī,* vol. 3, ed., Lothrop Stoddard (Bayrūt: Dār al-Fikr, 1971).

22. Ho, "Hadramis Abroad in Hadramawt: The Muwalladin."

23. Ho, "Le don précieux de la généalogie."

24. Ho, "Before Parochialization: Diasporic Arabs Cast in Creole Waters."

25. Dean Acheson, *Present at the Creation: My Years in the State Department* (New York/London: Norton, 1969), p. 7.

26. C. R. Boxer, *The Portuguese Seaborne Empire, 1415–1825* (New York: Knopf, 1969); Andre Gunder Frank, *ReOrient: Global Economy in the Asian Age* (Berkeley: University of California Press, 1998).

27. Janet Abu-Lughod, *Before European Hegemony: The World System A.D. 1250–1350* (New York: Oxford University Press, 1989); Chaudhuri, *Asia Before Europe: Economy and Civilisation of the Indian Ocean from the Rise of Islam to 1750;* Hourani, *Arab Seafaring in the Indian Ocean in Ancient and Early Medieval Times;* Tibbetts, *Arab Navigation in the Indian Ocean Before the Coming of the Portuguese.*

28. C. Raymond Beazley, *Prince Henry the Navigator, Hero of Portugal and of Modern Discovery, 1394–1460 A.D.* (New York: G.P. Putnam's Sons, 1904); Boxer, *The Portuguese Seaborne Empire, 1415–1825;* Elaine Sanceau, *The Land of Prester John, a Chronicle of Portuguese Exploration* (New York: Knopf, 1944); Sanjay Subrahmanyam, *The Portuguese Empire in Asia, 1500–1700* (London/New York: Longman, 1993); Sanjay Subrahmanyam, *The Career and Legend of Vasco da Gama* (Cambridge: Cambridge University Press, 1997). Before embarking on his great maritime enterprise, Prince Henry had attacked and taken Ceuta as a young man. This was the first Iberian push into the Maghreb, then part of an anticolonial movement, and Ceuta remains under Spanish sovereignty today, a fifteenth-century Crusader border on the North African coast. The Portuguese understood their Indian Ocean enterprise as a continuation of the Crusades, and targeted Muslim interests accordingly. Yet religion is not everything, for the Portuguese were, with the Genoese, seeking to break a joint Venetian-Egyptian hold on Malabar pepper through the Mediterranean and the Red Seas.

29. The international dimensions of this contest are seldom recognized. With minimal communications, Portuguese sailors fought with high morale far from home because they were assured of reinforcements without letup; the Portuguese naval enterprise was well supported by capital from Antwerp. On the other side, two large Turkish/Egyptian fleets with cannon and over a thousand sailors briefly fought alongside Cambay and Calicut ships, mindful of their joint long-distance interests. The outcome was mixed, with the Turks garrisoning Aden, Cambay, and Calicut, retaining their port cities and local naval presence, while the Portuguese commanded main channels on the high seas for the next century.

30. K. M. Pannikar, *Asia and Western Dominance; A Survey of the Vasco da Gama Epoch of Asian History, 1498–1945* (1953; reprint, London: Allen & Unwin, 1993).

31. Abd al-Rahman al-Zahir, whom I discuss below, cut his teeth trading as supercargo on his wealthy father's ship between India and Arabia. His long journeys undertaken in conducting resistance against the Dutch were aboard European steamers. Osama bin Laden's wealthy father Muhammad Awad, flying in his private airplane, claimed distinction as the first Muslim since the prophet Muhammad to have prayed in Jerusalem, Medina, and Mecca in the space of a day. He had bought the plane while executing exclusive contracts for rebuilding some of the holiest sites of Islam. When he crashed and died, the Saudi king Faysal took the family under his wing and banned them from flying for a decade. Osama's brother Salim, an avid pilot, also died in a plane crash, in Texas in 1988. Salim's family still owns the Houston Gulf Airport, bought on the recommendation of his U.S. trustee James Bath, an erstwhile friend of George W. Bush who invested in Bush's early oil ventures. They met while pilots in the Air National Guard. The use of airplanes and satellite TV against the United States in recent events needs no reiteration here. In the sixteenth century, Zayn al-Din al-Malibari's argument for jihad against the Portuguese cited their unjust actions throughout the Indian Ocean region, where Hadrami scholars maintained correspondence with each other.

32. James Duncan Phillips, *Pepper and Pirates: Adventures in the Sumatra Pepper Trade of Salem* (Boston: Houghton Mifflin, 1949).

33. I draw on a number of sources here (al-Mashhur, *Shams al-zahira fi nasab ahl al-bayt min Bani Alawi furu' Fatima al-zahra' wa-AmIr al-Mu'minin Ali radiya Allah anhu;* C. Snouck Hurgronje, *The Achehnese,* trans. A. W. S. O'Sullivan [Leiden, Netherlands: E. J. Brill, 1906]; Anthony Reid, *The Contest for North Sumatra: Atjeh, the Netherlands, and Britain, 1858–1898* [Kuala Lumpur: Oxford University Press, 1969]; Anthony Reid, "Habib Abdur-Rahman A-Zahir (1833–1896)," *Indonesia* 13 [April 1972]: 37–59; H. Mohammad Said, *Aceh Sepanjang Abad* [Medan, Indonesia: Waspada, 1981]). Reid and Said locate the biography within an analytical narrative of Acehnese history. It is important to note that al-Zahir was not *sui generis,* but one in a long line of diasporic Hadramis from Arabia, Gujarat, Malabar, and Penang who became sultans, saints, innovative scholars, and Sufis in Aceh. These may be found in the preceding references, as well as in Azyumardi Azra, *The Transmission of Islamic Reformism to Indonesia: Networks of Middle Eastern and Malay-Indonesian "Ulama" in the Seventeenth and Eighteenth Centuries* (Ph.D. thesis, Columbia University, 1992).

34. Muhammad Abd al-Karim 'Akasha, *Qiyam al-saltana al-Qa'aytiyya wa-l-taghalghul al-isti'-mari fi hadramawt, 1839–1918* (Amman, al-Urdun: Dar Ibn Rushd, 1985).

35. There was a history of Acehnese declarations of Ottoman overlordship, such as in 1515 and 1850 under the Acehnese sultans Sayid Firman Syah and Alaudin Mansur Syah, confirmed by the Ottoman sultans Salim I and Abd al-Majid. Further documentation and examples are given in Reid (*The Contest for North Sumatra,* pp. 3, 83–84, 259) and Azmi Ozcan, *Pan-Islamism: Indian Muslims, the Ottomans and Britain, 1877–1924* (Leiden, Netherlands: Brill, 1997), p. 27. Assertions of Ottoman suzerainty were also declared in Hadramawt at similar times, against Portuguese and English claims (Salah Abd al-Qadir al-Bakri al-Yaf'i, *Ta'rikh hadramawt al-siyasi,* vol. 1. [Cairo: Mustafa al-Babi al-Halabi, 1956]; see also note 12.

36. Anthony Reid, "Habib Abdur-Rahman A-Zahir (1833–1896)," p. 39.

37. Zayn al-Din al-Ma'bari, bin Abd al'Aziz al-Mu'izz, *Tuhfat al-Mujahidin fi ba'd akhbar al-burtughaliyyin* (Tripoli, Libya: Kuliyyat al-Da wa al-Islamiyya, 1987).

38. His legal commentary *Fath al-Mu'in* (Zayn al-Din al-Malibari, Abd al'Aziz, *Fath al-mu'in bi-sharh qurrat al'ayn* [Semarang, Indonesia: Maktabat wa-matba'at Taha Putra, n.d., composed 1574 C.E.]) continues to be published in Indonesia and used in Yemen today, and is itself commented on by Indonesia scholars (Muhammad Nawawi Banteni, bin Umar, *Nihayat al-zayn fi irshad al-mubtadi'in* [Misr: Mustafa al-Babi al-Halabi, 1938]).

39. Muhammad Ba Faqih, bin Umar, *Tarikh al-Shihr wa-akhbar al-qarn al-'ashir,* ed. Abd Allah Muhammad al-Hibshi, (Sana'a: Maktabat al-Irshad, 1999).

40. A major Muslim state in the Deccan, the Adil Shahi sultanate, extended patronage to itinerant Muslim scholars (Richard Maxwell Eaton, *The Sufis of Bijapur, 1300–1700: Social Roles of Sufism in Medieval India* [Princeton, N.J.: Princeton University Press, 1978]). A few decades after the composition of al-Malibari's book, the Hadrami Sayyid Shaykh bin Abd Allah al-'Aydarus cured Sultan Ibrahim Adil Shah of a chronic disease and wielded great influence on him, successfully enjoining him to wear Arab dress (Muhammad al-Shilli, bin Abi Bakr, *al-Mashra' al-Rawi,* 2 vols. (1901), pp. 117–119).

41. Zayn al-Din al-Ma'bari, *Tuhfat al-Mujahidin fi ba'd akhbar al-burtughaliyyin,* p. 47.

42. al-Ma'bari, *Tuhfat al-Mujahidin fi ba'd akhbar al-burtughaliyyin,* p. 69–75.

43. Earliest Portuguese accounts of Cheraman Perumal correlate with al-Malibari's in many respects, as they do with his observations on caste practices (Duarte Barbosa, *The Book of Duarte*

Barbosa, second series, no. XLIV, vol. 1, trans. Mansel Longworth Dames [1518; reprint, London: The Hakluyt Society, 1918], pp. 3–5).

44. al-Maʿbari, *Tuhfat al-Mujahidin fi baʾd akhbar al-burtughaliyyin,* pp. 109–110.

45. One of the leading authorities on the Mappilas is Dale, whom I draw upon here (Stephen Frederic Dale, *The Hadhrami Diaspora in South-Western India: The Role of the Sayyids of the Malabar Coast,* in *Hadrami Traders, Scholars, and Statesmen in the Indian Ocean, 1750s–1960s,* eds. U. Freitag and W. G. Clarence-Smith [Leiden, Netherlands: Brill, 1997]; Stephen Frederic Dale, *Islamic Society on the South Asian Frontier: The Mappilas of Malabar, 1498–1922* [Oxford: Clarendon Press, 1980]). Hadrami sources include al-Mashhur (*Shams al-zahira fi nasab ahl al-bayt min Bani ʿAlawi furuʿ Fatima al-zahraʾ wa-AmIr al-Muʾminin Ali radiya Allah anhu*) and Saʿid Awad Ba Wazir, *safahat min al-taʾrikh al-Hadrami* (n.d.; reprint, Adan: Maktabat al-thaqafa, 1954). Dale has shown the way by drawing parallels among the anti-European Muslim movements in Malabar, Aceh, and the Philippines. While he views these areas as transformed into frontiers by European militarization, following Witteck on Anatolia, my argument rests on seeing them as a connected, domestic realm in which a diaspora is at home.

46. Selim Deringil, *The Well-Protected Domains: Ideology and the Legitimation of Power in the Ottoman Empire, 1876–1909* (London/New York: I.B. Tauris, 1998); Nikki Keddie, *An Islamic Response to Imperialism: Political and Religious Writings of Sayyid Jamal ad-Din "al-Afghani"* (Berkeley/Los Angeles: University of California Press, 1968); Ozcan, *Pan-Islamism.*

47. Dale, *Islamic Society on the South Asian Frontier,* pp. 207–208.

48. Anthony Pagden, *Lords of All the World* (New Haven/London: Yale University Press, 1995).

49. Niccolo Machiavelli, *The Discourses* (London: Penguin, 1983), 291–93, vol. 2, p. 6.

50. The earlier American empires saw more European-to-native marriages and the adoption of nativized identities by their creole/mestizo descendants such as in Mexico. Such boundary crossings were reined in in the second European empires. Racial difference was now thrown up as a high wall and kept the empires' expatriates in closer contact with the homeland.

51. See Adam Smith, *An Inquiry into the Nature and Causes of the Wealth of Nations* (Indianapolis: Liberty Fund, 1981), pp. 591–641. It is not surprising that in leading figures such as Condorcet, Montesquieu, and Smith, the antiimperialist Enlightenment flourished in France and Scotland. The long eighteenth century of worldwide Anglo-French imperial rivalry through foreign wars in the West and East Indies was creating the characteristic modern centralized state in France and England, with its standing army and huge war debts (England's went from under a million pounds to 840 million pounds by 1817), bonds, and a central bank to pay for them (Seeley, *The Expansion of England,* pp. 17–36). The apparent paradox explored by Uday Singh Mehta (*Liberalism and Empire: A Study in Nineteenth-Century British Liberal Thought* [Chicago: University of Chicago Press, 1999] of an anti-Enlightenment conservative such as Edmund Burke being against empire and a liberal such as J. S. Mill being for it, can be resolved by situating Burke with Smith as eighteenth-century thinkers (and from the Irish and Scottish margins) rather than Smith with Mill as British liberals. Eighteenth-century critiques were aimed at the first European empires and the corrupting effects of colonial monopolies on the metropolis, while the nineteenth-century second-empire imperialists J. S. Mill and Macaulay thought their liberal progressivism and paternalism to be enlightened solutions to the problems of the first empires.

52. Anthony Pagden writes: "The languages in which the nineteenth-century empires sought to frame themselves were transfigured products of the early-modern forbears. They were the transfiguration, however, not of the languages of empire but instead of the critique which the enemies of imperialism had levelled against them in the closing years of the eighteenth century. This had insisted that the inescapable legacy of all forms of colonialism could only be human and mate-

rial waste followed by moral degeneracy. Empire's relationship with the non-European world should, in future, be limited to a programme of harmonious exchange" (Pagden, *Lords of All the World*, p. 10).

53. The sight of non-Europeans—the Japanese—puncturing Britain's vaunted invincibility in Malaya and Burma, and America's in the Philippines and Hawaii, was a major step in the decolonization of the mind.

54. That rare moment did not last long, as independence movements, such as in French Vietnam, Dutch Indonesia, and British Malaya, were infected with communism. Decolonization without communism proved a delicate operation with relatively peaceful results in Malaya, belatedly violent ones in Indonesia, and absolutely violent ones in Vietnam, which found the United States supporting, then supplanting, France's imperial role. This is a period of history which has been much neglected, overlooked on account of the modern teleology of national independence (Eric Hobsbawm, *Nations and Nationalism Since 1780* [Cambridge: Cambridge University Press, 1990]; (William Roger Louis, *Imperialism at Bay: The United States and the Decolonization of the British Empire, 1941–1945* [Oxford: Clarendon Press, 1977]). Among anthropologists, Kelly and Kaplan have begun to scrutinize the period and identify the contemporary world of nation-states as a U.S. creation (John D. Kelly and Martha Kaplan, *Represented Communities: Fiji and World Decolonization* [Chicago: University of Chicago Press, 2001]). Amitav Ghosh's *Glass Palace* is an imaginative attempt at understanding the moment of decolonization, and other scholars now revisiting this moment include the historian C. A. Bayly (Burma and Malaya) and the anthropologist Mary Steedly (Sumatra). The classic statement from the horse's mouth is then U.S. secretary of state Dean Acheson's work, *Present at the Creation.* There is a small but active school of British political historians pleased to demonstrate that it was the British, such as Keynes, who tutored the Americans in the delicate art of imperial indirect rule— suzerainty over sovereigns rather than satrapies.

55. Kelly and Kaplan, *Represented Communities,* pp. 1–26.

56. Acheson, *Present at the Creation: My Years in the State Department.*

57. J.G.A. Pocock, *The Machiavellian Moment: Florentine Political Thought and the Atlantic Republican Tradition* (Princeton, NJ: Princeton University Press, 1975), pp. 509–510; Seeley, *The Expansion of England,* pp. 25–30.

58. Stephen Conway, "Britain and the Revolutionary Crisis, 1763–1791," in *The Oxford History of the British Empire, Volume II: The Eighteenth Century,* ed. P.J. Marshall (Oxford: Oxford University Press, 1998); Jack Greene, *Peripheries and Center: Constitutional Development in the Extended Polities of the British Empire and the United States, 1607–1788* (New York/London: Norton, 1987); Bruce P. Lenman, "Colonial Wars and Imperial Instability, 1688–1793," in *The Oxford History of the British Empire, Volume II: The Eighteenth Century,* ed. P.J. Marshall (Oxford: Oxford University Press, 1998).

59. Bernard Bailyn, *The Ideological Origins of the American Revolution* (Cambridge, Mass.: Belknap Press, 1967), pp. 144–159; Gordon Wood, *The Creation of the American Republic* (Chapel Hill: University of North Carolina Press, 1969), p. 39.

60. Wood, *The Creation of the American Republic,* pp. 28–36.

61. Pocock, *The Machiavellian Moment,* p. 510.

62. Pauline Maier, *From Resistance to Revolution: Colonial Radicals and the Development of American Opposition to Britain, 1765–1776* (New York: Vintage Books, 1974).

63. Lenman, "Colonial Wars and Imperial Instability, 1688–1793."

64. Pocock, *The Machiavellian Moment,* p. 523.

65. An apparently noncolonial outcome was achieved over Native American populations by making them invisible and thus beyond representation through physical extermination, cultural genocide, and banishment to miniscule, isolated reservations. As these were sovereign entities, they were therefore foreign and had no claim to constitutional cover. The treatment of Indians with savage violence, extraconstitutionality, and invisibility was to remain a major characteristic of United States behavior abroad toward non-Europeans in the twentieth century, beginning in the Philippines with what has been called "the first genocide of the twentieth century" in sources such as the *Brittanica Student Encyclopedia* (http://www.search.eb.com/ebi/article?eu=299291 &query=spanish%20american%20war). The earliest U.S. Army governors of the Philippines, such as Maj. Gen. Elwell S. Otis and Maj. Gen. Adna R. Chaffee, had distinguished themselves in the American Indian campaigns (Brian McAllister Linn, *The U.S. Army and Counterinsurgency in the Philippine War, 1899–1902,* [Chapel Hill: University of North Carolina Press, 1989], pp. 10, 26). Counterinsurgency methods discovered in those campaigns against "savages," such as crop destruction and population reconcentration, were to be developed in the Philippines and Vietnam.

66. Whitney Perkins, *Denial of Empire: The United States and Its Dependencies* (Leyden: A.W. Sythoff, 1962).

67. "Judge Rebuffs Detainees at Guantanamo," *New York Times,* August 1, 2002.

68. Quoted in Perkins, *Denial of Empire,* p. 28.

69. The sociologist Jeffrey Goldfarb, who runs annual democracy courses in Cracow and Cape Town, recently expressed alarm that his students, committed democrats all, have reached a consensus that ". . . American democracy requires the repression of democracy in the rest of the world. . . . Suddenly the rights of Muslims in the Philippines and Malaysia . . . are not important to the Bush administration." ("Losing Our Best Allies in the War on Terror," *New York Times,* August 20, 2002).

70. James Harrington, *The Commonwealth of Oceana and A System of Politics,* ed. J.G.A. Pocock (1656 and 1700; reprint, Cambridge: Cambridge University Press, 1992).

71. The precedent here is Louisiana, where the expanding United States came upon a large, settled, non-Anglo-Saxon population. For the first time, no bill of rights was granted initially. Such a bill was a specific possession of English people, who had presented William of Orange with one before allowing him into England during the 1688 "Glorious Revolution."

72. "U.S. Bodyguards Buy Time for Afghan Leader," *New York Times,* July 29, 2002.

73. Concubinage, classically the triple exploitation of racial, gender, and political inequalities, takes literal form in U.S.-Korean relations as prostitution, organized jointly by both governments for U.S. troops (see Katharine Moon, *Sex Among Allies: Military Prostitution in U.S.-Korea Relations* [New York: Columbia University Press, 1997]). Invisible in the United States but not Korea, this blight on Korean national honor, conjoining as it does imperial-national concubinage with individual prostitution, has been somewhat relieved by the substitution of non-Korean women.

74. Chalmers Johnson, *Blowback: The Costs and Consequences of American Empire* (New York: Metropolitan Books, 2000), p. 43.

75. C.A. Bayly, *Empire and Information* (Cambridge: Cambridge University Press, 1999), pp. 346–351.

76. Cohn, "Representing Authority in Victorian India," p. 658. In *An Anthropologist Among the Historians and Other Essays* (Delhi: Oxford University Press, 1987).

77. David Cannadine has taken this argument further, tying the ritual performance of hierarchy in empire abroad to the class hierarchies of metropolitan Britain, rendering "imperialism as or-

namentalism" a "remarkable transoceanic construct of substance and sentiment" (Cannadine, *Ornamentalism,* 122).

78. "In Powell's Tour, Brevity As the Soul of Diplomacy," *New York Times,* August 1, 2002.

79. Charles Hirschkind and Saba Mahmood, "Feminism, the Taliban, and the Politics of Counter-Insurgency," *Anthropological Quarterly* 75, no. 2(2002): 331–338.

80. Bin Laden ended his video response to the bombing of Afghanistan with this same demand: "As for America, I say to her people just a few words: I swear by the Great God who lofted the skies with no pillars, that America—and those who live in it—will not dream of security before Palestinians live it in reality, and before all the armies of the infidel have quitted the land of Muhammad" ("Bin Ladin: No Security for America before Security for Palestine," *al-Hayat,* Oct. 9, 2001).

81. Report on U.S. Defense Secretary Donald Rumsfeld's interview on Al Jazeera TV: "When asked whether Mr. Bin Laden and his network, Al Qaeda, attacked the United States because Washington has troops based in Saudi Arabia, Mr. Rumsfeld said American troops were present only in nations where they were welcome. 'We're nowhere where we're not wanted,' he said. 'Where we are is where people who live there have decided they would like to have us for their protection' ("Rumsfeld to Appeal to Arab Public on Mideast TV Network," *New York Times,* October 16, 2001).

82. "Bin Ladin: No Security for America before Security for Palestine," *al-Hayat,* October 9, 2001; translation mine.

83. Pocock, *The Machiavellian Moment,* p. 543.

84. The dénouement on the larger Arabian peninsula was even more galling. Bin Laden and his "Afghan Arabs" repatriated from Afghanistan were then playing a frontline role in destroying the ruling socialist party in South Yemen, his homeland, through assassinations. Throughout the Cold War, the Soviet air base at al-'Anad near Aden had been the largest on the peninsula, dwarfing the U.S. presence there. The final defeat of the socialists in the 1994 Yemen civil war eradicated that threat to U.S. interests in Arabia. For bin Laden and his associates, to then have the United States profit from their domestic victories in Yemen by boosting aerial presence in Saudi Arabia and naval presence at Aden was too much. The bombing of the USS *Cole* was only one in a string of responses.

85. T-shirts sporting bin Laden next to Che Guevara have been popular in Latin America, and Thierry Meyssan's theory of a U.S. conspiracy elaborated in his book *L'Effroyable Imposture* (France: Editions Carnot, 2002) has been "a phenomenon," selling 100,000 copies a week in France ("La Grande Délusion," *Guardian,* April 3, 2002).

86. Turkey's declaration of war on the German side in November 1914 was also formally promulgated as a jihad by the highest national religious authority, the *Shaykh al-Islam* (Snouck Hurgronje, *The Holy War "Made in Germany"* [New York/London: Putnam's Sons, 1915]). Fatwas were issued enjoining Muslims to commit life and property against Russia, England, and France. As these were the powers with dominion over large Muslim populations, the move mirrors the fifteenth-century Portuguese search for Prester John, the mythical Christian king in the Indies or Asia who would help them defeat the Muslims from behind enemy lines. Current European and American anxieties over their immigrant Muslim populations echo Russian, English, and French fears of a fifth column, which the Turkish jihad fatwas sought to exploit.

87. al-Ma'bari, bin 'Abd al-'Aziz al-Mu'izz, *Tuhfat al-Mujahidin fi ba'd akhbar al-burtughaliyyin,* pp. 46–47.

88. Dale, *Islamic Society on the South Asian Frontier,* p. 59; Cesar Adib Majul, *Muslims in the Philippines,* 2nd ed. (Quezon City, the Philippines: University of the Philippines Press, 1973), p. 356.

89. Ozcan, *Pan-Islamism.*

90. Gail Minault, *The Khilafat Movement: Religious Symbolism and Political Mobilization in India* (New York: Columbia University Press, 1982).

91. Commenting on the current U.S. adventure in Muslim Philippines, Andrew Bacevich notes that almost a century ago, in 1906, U.S. troops "drifted toward what came to resemble a strategy of extermination" in the same place. The war had dragged on because ". . . above all, the Moro warrior's perverse willingness to die offset the overwhelming U.S. edge in technology and fire-power" (Andrew J. Bacevich, "We've Sent GIs to the Philippines Before—With Disastrous Results," *Los Angeles Times,* January 22, 2002). Given the textual evidence we have seen, that apparent perversity was in fact a practical corollary of "just war" theories in the face of imperialist aggression and overwhelming odds.

92. See http://news.bbc.co.uk/hi/english/world/south_asia/newsid_1623000/1623281.stm (28 October 2001).

93. Chalmers Johnson has one of the most convincing analyses on these issues, integrating economic and political explanations under the concept of empire. "Blowback" is his name for the messes created by empires—unintended consequences of imperial actions which rebound on empires. In his view, the United States accumulated blowback during the Cold War, and accumulated more in the decade after it ended. His prescription thus calls for the scaling back of the Cold War structures of imperialist rivalry. This is a comprehensive and detailed vision for multilateralization and demilitarization (Johnson, *Blowback,* 228). While his proposals, such as U.S. support for an international criminal court, are shared worldwide, they are far from mainstream U.S. consensus and are little debated internally. Exceptionalism is the prerogative of empire, and history unfortunately provides no precedence of an empire unilaterally retiring while at the top of its game.

94. Lord Cromer, British consul general to Egypt (1883–1907) and actual ruler of the country, remained keenly aware of the contradictions inherent in indirect rule, which could ". . . be justified [only] if we are able to keep before our eyes the possibility of evacuation. . . . If that possibility becomes so remote . . . it would be better for us . . . that we should take over the government of the country, guarantee its debt, etc." (Arendt, *The Origins of Totalitarianism,* p. 213). For Arendt, Cromer ". . . embodies the turning point from the older colonial to imperialist services." Colonization of Egypt was not wholehearted but merely a means to the security of India, held for imperial reasons of state.

95. Patrick Buchanan, *A Republic, Not an Empire: Reclaiming America's Destiny* (Washington, D.C.: Regnery, 1999).

96. Robert Kagan and William Kristol, "Toward a Neo-Reaganite Foreign Policy," *Foreign Affairs* (July/August 1996). Dean Acheson opens his memoirs with precisely such a split in the United States in September 1939, between the isolationist America First Committee and the Committee to Defend America by Aiding the Allies (Acheson, *Present at the Creation,* p. 3). Taking a leaf from his book, specialists on the military today have expressed impatience with the question of whether the United States is an empire or not. They see instead an urgent task ahead: to acknowledge the reality of the imperial burden and to move along with the serious business of how to do it best (Bacevich, "We've Sent GIs to the Philippines Before"; Thomas Donnelly, "The Past as Prologue: An Imperial Manual," *Foreign Affairs* [July/August 2002]; Stephen Peter Rosen, "The Future of War and the American Military: Demography, Technology, and the Politics of Modern Empire," *Harvard Magazine,* May 2002). The burdens of hegemony as understood by Richard Perle (chair, Defense Policy Board) and Paul Wolfowitz (deputy secretary of defense) of the current U.S. administration are articulated in their contributions to the volume *Present*

Dangers (Robert Kagan and William Kristol, eds., *Present Dangers: Crisis and Opportunity in American Foreign and Defense Policy* [San Francisco: Encounter, 2000]).

97. For a study of the combined use of unmanned aerial vehicles and special operations forces, see Stephen Howard, "Special Operations Forces and Unmanned Aerial Vehicles: Sooner or Later?" Thesis. Air University, Maxwell Air Force Base, 1995

98. Bacevich, "We've Sent GIs to the Philippines Before."

99. Gary Leupp, "The 'War on Terrorism' in Yemen," *CounterPunch*, May 20, 2002.

100. With the disappearance of empire-sized rivals like the Soviet Union, U.S. instincts for an anticolonial empire—i.e. for invisible modalities of military power—underwent massive development in the 1990s. In addition to the large, visible, industrial, conventional arms of missiles and warships counterposed to the Soviets, a new "Special Operations Command" was created in the 1986 Goldwater-Nichols restructuring of the Department of Defense. "Special Operations Forces" (SOF) are ethnographically inspired and given an extremely broad mandate throughout all situations: peacetime, major warfare, low-intensity conflict. "They are also warrior-diplomats capable of influencing, advising, training, and conducting operations with foreign forces, officials, and populations" (Special Operations.com 2002). Like anthropologists, they have specialized regional skills in language, culture, and geography. But more, they embody a liberal arts ideal of straddling the cultural divide between arts and sciences; when "reliably data-linked" to "real-time video furnished around-the-clock by unmanned aerial vehicles" (Howard 1995), they become an unmatched mobile meld of man and machine, a total social fact of virtual warfare easily insinuated into any situation. This combination qualifies them as a small, multi-purpose, clandestine force for use on the spot to train and assist foreign military and paramilitary forces; engage in counterterrorism, psychological operations, information collection; spot targets, "unconventional warfare;" liaison with civilian populations, etc. They were used behind Iraqi lines during the first Gulf War and assumed a major role in the Afghanistan war. Through the Joint Combined Exchange Training (JCET) program, they operated with their own budget in 101 countries in 1997, linking directly to the militaries there. They are a new, empire-wide channel of direct influence, and their aggrandizement as "warrior-diplomats" acknowledges their usurpation of civilian functions in the conduct of foreign policy. They cross borders without passports.

101. While Pannikar demonstrated the importance of an imperial framing, he too succumbed to the anticolonial obsession with land, writing as he did in the first flush of Indian independence and the euphoria of territorial sovereignty: "The final failure of the European effort to conquer and hold Asia is an example of the limitation of sea power and has lessons which no one can overlook. . . . In the final and decisive main duels of history the party which begins with high sea power is defeated by land power. . . . Ultimately in Asia also, the land masses asserted themselves against the power based on the sea, and the withdrawal of European power from Asia is in effect a reassertion of the power of land empires shaking themselves free from the shackles of maritime mercantilism" (Pannikar, *Asia and Western Dominance*, p. 16).

102. The nationalist's nation is a strangely anthropomorphic thing, with an animal will to self-determination and a soul sensitive to disloyalty. I suspect that antiabsolutist theories of the self as sovereign, such as Locke's, in turn later enabled one to think of the sovereign state as a self. Thought of in these terms, the postcolonial nation-state is merely the continuation of the regime of private property widely instituted under colonialism, with new selves now highly and irrevocably invested in the idea of owning de-communalized objects truly liberated to the market under conditions of democratic access. While postcolonial elites now have the land, imperial strategies continue to find value in other parts of a portfolio larger and lighter than real estate and its fruits. Locke's individual, sovereign over self and property, was of course congenitally suited to the merchant classes, with their portable wealth, rather than the landed aristocracy.

103. The concept of the plural society, associated with colonialism since Furnivall (J. S. Furnivall, *Colonial Policy and Practice: A Comparative Study of Burma and Netherlands India* [London: Cambridge University Press, 1948]), is more correctly an imperialist phenomenon. Colonizers move themselves to new land. Imperialists move others. The plural society, though experienced as social compartmentalization, was a product of motion—populations shunted about to work within the large internal space of imperial economies.

104. Wilfred Blythe, *The Impact of Chinese Secret Societies in Malaysia: A Historical Study* (London/Kuala Lumpur: Oxford University Press, 1969).

105. W.E.B. DuBois, *Dark Princess: A Romance* (Jackson: University Press of Mississippi, 1995).

106. This has changed since the early 1990s. September 11, 2001, has made real and believable the possibility of an internal Saudi collapse. This thought makes it urgent for the United States to now have direct presence in Iraq, to preempt its being sealed out of the whole Gulf region in such an eventuality or its having to fight Iraq, Iran, and a post–Saudi Arabia all at once.

107. In contrast, despite the U.S. media-government obsession with unearthing new links between al-Qaeda and Islamist movements everywhere, most contemporary movements of political Islam, such as the Algerian FIS, Palestinian Hamas, and Egyptian Muslim Brotherhood, have settled into national containers, parting ways with the anti-imperial nineteenth-century legacy of the perpetual exile Jamal al-Din al-Afghani. Another notable exception is the *harakat al-Tahrir*, which has long championed the cause of the caliphate.

Displacement, Diaspora Mobilization, and Transnational Cycles of Political Violence

1. Paul Collier, "Economic Causes of Civil Conflict and Their Implications for Policy," World Bank Working Paper, June 15, 2000, p. 6.

2. Daniel Byman, Peter Chalk, Bruce Hoffman, William Rosenau, and David Brannan, *Trends in Outside Support for Insurgent Movements* (Santa Monica, Calif.: Rand, 2001).

3. Benedict Anderson, "Long-Distance Nationalism," in *The Spectre of Comparisons: Nationalism, Southeast Asia and the World* (London: Verso, 1998), p. 74.

4. Independent International Commission on Kosovo, *The Kosovo Report: Conflict, International Response, Lessons Learned* (Oxford: Oxford University Press, 2000), p. 45. See also Mary Kaldor, *New and Old Wars: Organized Violence in a Global Era* (Stanford: Stanford University Press, 1999).

5. Robin Cohen, *Global Diasporas: An Introduction* (London: UCL Press, 1997), pp. 1–55; and William Safran, "Diasporas in Modern Societies: Myths of Homeland and Return," *Diaspora: A Journal of Transnational Studies* 1, no. 1 (Spring 1991): 83–99.

6. James Clifford, "Diasporas," *Cultural Anthropology* 9, no. 3 (1994): 302–338; Myron Weiner, "Labor Migrations as Incipient Diasporas," in *Modern Diasporas in International Politics*, ed. Gabriel Sheffer (London: Croom Helm, 1986), pp. 47–75. See also the discussion in Cohen, *Global Diasporas*, pp. 127–176.

7. For discussions of the difficulties in disentangling the political and economic factors that contribute to producing migration flows, see Aristide Zolberg, Astri Suhrke, and Sergio Aguayo, *Escape From Violence: Conflict and the Refugee Crisis in the Developing World* (New York: Oxford University Press, 1989), pp. 30–33; and Saskia Sassen, *The Mobility of Labor and Capital: A Study in International Investment and Labor Flows* (Cambridge: Cambridge University Press, 1988).

8. Fiona B. Adamson, *Mobilizing at the Margins of the System: The Dynamics and Security Impacts*

of Transnational Mobilization by Non-State Actors, Ph.D. thesis, Columbia University, 2002, pp. 136–171.

9. Brian Axel, *The Nation's Tortured Body: Violence, Representation and the Formation of a Sikh Diaspora* (Durham, N.C.: Duke University Press, 2000).

10. See John Kenny, "Fenians in America: The Local Production of a Transnational Social Movement," unpublished paper, University of Chicago, 1999.

11. Nevzat Soguk, *States and Strangers: Refugees and Displacements of Statecraft* (Minneapolis: University of Minnesota Press, 1999).

12. Michael Mann, *The Sources of Social Power: Volume 1—A History of Power From the Beginning to A.D. 1760* (Cambridge: Cambridge University Press, 1993), p. 21.

13. Edward Said, "Intellectual Exile: Expatriates and Marginals," in *Representations of the Intellectual: The 1993 Reith Lectures* (New York: Pantheon, 1994).

14. Charles Tilly, *From Mobilization to Revolution* (Reading, Mass.: Addison-Wesley, 1978), p. 69. On the process of framing more generally, see Erving Goffman, *Frame Analysis: An Essay on the Organization of Experience* (Cambridge, Mass.: Harvard University Press, 1974).

15. Benedict Anderson, *Imagined Communities: Reflections on the Origins and Spread of Nationalism* (London: Verso, 1983), p. 4.

16. Eric Hobsbawm, *The Age of Empire, 1875–1914* (New York: Vantage, 1989), pp. 154–155.

17. See, for example, Barnett R. Rubin, "Afghanistan: Political Exiles in Search of a State," in *Governments-in-Exile in Contemporary World Politics*, ed. Yossi Shain (New York: Routledge, 1991), pp. 70–91.

18. See Mark Juergensmeyer, *The New Cold War? Religious Nationalism Confronts the Secular State* (Berkeley: University of California, 1993); or Samuel P. Huntington, *The Clash of Civilizations and the Remaking of World Order* (New York: Simon and Schuster, 1996).

19. See Tilly, *From Mobilization to Revolution*, pp. 62–63.

20. See Byman et al., *Trends in Outside Support for Insurgent Movements;* Collier, "Economic Causes of Civil Conflict and Their Implications for Policy."

21. Kerby A. Miller, "Class, Culture, and Immigrant Group Identity in the United States: The Case of Irish-American Ethnicity," in *Immigration Reconsidered*, ed. Virginia Yans-McLaughlin (New York: Oxford University Press, 1990), pp. 96–129.

22. James Adams, *The Financing of Terror* (London: New English Library, 1986), pp. 131–155; Raymond James Raymond, "The United States and Terrorism in Ireland, 1969–1981," in *Terrorism in Ireland*, eds. Yonah Alexander and Alan O'Day (New York: St. Martin's Press, 1984).

23. Byman et al., *Trends in Outside Support for Insurgent Movements*, pp. 48–49.

24. Philip Martin, "International Migration and Trade," HCO dissemination notes, no. 29 (Washington, D.C.: World Bank, 1994).

25. Nicholas van Hear, *New Diasporas: The Mass Exodus, Dispersal and Regrouping of Migrant Communities* (London: UCL Press, 1998), pp. 167–169.

26. See Khalid Medani, "Funding Fundamentalism: The Political Economy of an Islamist State," in *Political Islam: Essays From the Middle East Report*, eds. Joel Beinin and Joe Stork (Berkeley: University of California Press, 1996).

27. Cited in Manuel Castells, *End of the Millennium* (Cambridge, Mass.: Blackwell, 1998), p. 169.

28. Fiona Carruthers, "Escape at Any Price," *Time Magazine*, June 7, 1999.

29. Castells 1998, pp. 166–205; James H. Mittelman and Robert Johnston, "The Globalization of

Organized Crime, the Courtesan State, and the Corruption of Civil Society," *Global Governance* 5, no. 1 (January–March 1999): pp. 103–126.

30. Collier, "Economic Causes of Civil Conflict and Their Implications for Policy"; Byman et al., *Trends in Outside Support for Insurgent Movements*.

31. Janet MacGaffey and Rémy Bazenguissa-Ganga, *Congo-Paris: Transnational Traders on the Margins of the Law* (Bloomington, Ind.: Indiana University Press, 2000), p. 3.

32. See, for example, Margaret E. Keck and Kathryn Sikkink, *Activists Beyond Borders: Advocacy Networks in International Politics* (Ithaca, N.Y.: Cornell University Press, 1998) and Thomas Risse-Kappen, *Bringing Transnational Actors Back In: Non-State Actors, Domestic Structures, and International Institutions* (New York: Cambridge University Press, 1995).

33. See Clifford Bob, "Marketing Rebellion: Insurgent Groups, International Media and NGO Support," *International Politics* 38, no. 3 (September 2001): 311–33. On the concept of sites of power in the international system, see David Held, *Democracy and the Global Order: From the Modern State to Cosmopolitan Governance* (Stanford: Stanford University Press, 1995), pp. 176–188.

34. Brigitte Nacos, *Terrorism and the Media: From the Iran Hostage Crisis to the Oklahoma City Bombing* (New York: Columbia University Press, 1994).

35. Bruce Hoffman, *Inside Terrorism* (New York: Columbia University Press, 1998), p. 4.

36. See Yossi Shain, *The Frontier of Loyalty: Political Exiles in the Age of the Nation-State* (Middletown, Conn.: Wesleyan University Press, 1989) for a discussion regarding competing claims of legitimacy by dissident exiles and governments.

37. Byman et al., *Trends in Outside Support for Insurgent Movements;* Collier, "Economic Causes of Civil Conflict and Their Implications for Policy"; David C. Rapoport, "The Four Waves of Rebel Terror and September 11," in *The New Global Terrorism: Characteristics, Causes, Controls,* ed. Charles W. Kegley, Jr. (Upper Saddle River, N.J.: Prentice Hall, 2003), pp. 36–59.

38. See Adamson, *Mobilizing at the Margins of the System.*

39. John Kenny, "Diaspora Nationalism and the Political Incorporation of Immigrants: Evidence from 19th Century America," paper prepared for presentation at the annual meeting of the American Political Science Association, Atlanta, Ga., September 2–5, 1999.

40. Collier, "Economic Causes of Civil Conflict and Their Implications for Policy."

Return of the State?

*In addition to the research assistance of Peter Romaniuk, I would like to acknowledge the work of the other members of the Watson Institute's Targeting Terrorist Finances research group, Sue Eckert, Jesse Finkelstein, Elizabeth Goodfriend, and Aaron Halegua, for their ongoing collaboration on this project.

1. Harold Lasswell, "The Garrison State," *American Journal of Sociology* 45 (1940): 455–468.

2. Stephen D. Krasner, "State Power and the Structure of International Trade," *World Politics* XXVIII, no. 3 (1976): 317.

3. Stephen E. Flynn, "America the Vulnerable," *Foreign Affairs* 81, no. 1 (January/February 2002): 62.

4. Bob Woodward, *Bush at War* (New York: Simon & Schuster, 2002), p. 73.

5. Curtis A. Ward, "Building Capacity to Combat International Terrorism: The Role of the United Nations Security Council," unpublished manuscript, p. 3.

6. Targeted financial sanctions entail the use of financial controls to apply coercive pressure on government officials, elites who support them, or members of nongovernmental entities in an effort to change or restrict their behavior. Since the sanctions apply only to a subset of the population, they are "targeted" and therefore hold the potential of minimizing negative impact on innocent civilian populations. The use of targeted financial sanctions by the international community increased substantially during the 1990s. The United Nations Security Council first experimented with them against the Haitian regime of Raoul Cedras in 1994, but the frequency of use of the instrument has grown in the past few years. Targeted financial sanctions have been employed by the UN against UNITA in Angola (1998), the Taliban regime in Afghanistan (1999, 2000, 2001), and RUF members fighting within Liberia (2001). The European Union imposed targeted financial sanctions on the Milosevic regime in Serbia in 1999. For more information, see *Targeted Financial Sanctions: A Manual for Design and Implementation—Contributions from the Interlaken Process*, published by the Watson Institute for International Studies, Brown University, and available at www.watsoninstitute.org and at www.smartsanctions.ch/interlaken _manual.htm.

7. Ward, "Building Capacity to Combat International Terrorism," p. 4.

8. See especially points 3 and 5 in the Annex to the letter dated January 15, 2002 from the chairman of the Security Council committee established pursuant to resolution 1373.

9. See especially the CTC web site at www.un.org/terrorism.

10. Stockholm Process on Implementing Targeted Sanctions, Final Report, *Making Targeted Sanctions Effective: Guidelines for the Implementation of UN Policy Options*, eds. Peter Wallensteen, Carina Staibano, and Mikael Eriksson, 2003 paragraph 127, pp. 56–57; available at www.smartsanctions.se.

11. See especially the FATF web site at www.oecd.org/fatf.

12. Development Committee of the Joint Ministerial Committee of the Boards of Governors of the Bank and the Fund on the Transfer of Real Resources to Developing Countries, *Intensified Work on Anti-Money Laundering and Combating Financing of Terrorism (AML/CFT) Joint Progress Report on the Work of the World Bank and the IMF*, DC2002-0022, September 25, 2002.

13. The chair of the CTC, U.K. Ambassador Sir Jeremy Greenstock, told the UN Security Council on October 4, 2002: "Sixteen Member States have not yet filed a report with the CTC. Of these, seven have not made any kind of written contact; they are: Chad, Dominica, Equatorial Guinea, Guinea-Bissau, Liberia, Swaziland and Tonga." By the summer of 2003, all 191 member states of the UN had submitted reports.

14. Walter Gehr, "Recurrent Issues" (briefing for member states), April 4, 2002; available at www.un.org/Docs/sc/committees/1373/rc.htm.

15. Ward, "Building Capacity to Combat International Terrorism," p. 10.

16. Gehr, "Recurrent Issues," p. 2.

17. Ward, "Building Capacity to Combat International Terrorism," p. 11.

18. Ibid., p. 12.

19. Security Council committee established pursuant to resolution 1267 (1999), "Guidelines of the Committee for the Conduct of Its Work," adopted November 7, 2002, pp. 2–3.

20. Bonn International Center for Conversion, *Design and Implementation of Arms Embargoes and Travel and Aviation Related Sanctions: Results of the Bonn-Berlin Process* (Bonn: BICC, 2001), pp. 56–58.

21. *Terrorist Financing*, report of an independent task force sponsored by the Council on Foreign

Relations, Maurice Greenberg, chair, William F. Wechsler and Lee S. Wolosky, project co-directors, October 2002, p. 32.

22. *Making Targeted Sanctions Effective,* eds. Wallensteen, Staibano, and Eriksson; see especially paragraphs 223–243, pp. 81–86.

23. *Terrorist Financing,* p. 8.

9/11: Insinuating Constitutional and International Norms

*An earlier version of this paper was presented at a roundtable on antiterrorism law sponsored by the Program in Law and Public Affairs at Princeton University in May 2002. This analysis reflects events as of late 2002.

1. See David Cole, "Enemy Aliens," *Stanford Law Review* 54 (2002): 953, 960–65.

2. See "Detention, Treatment, and Trial of Certain Non-Citizens in the War Against Terrorism," 66 Federal Register 57833 (November 13, 2002), an executive order authorizing the convening of military commissions to try noncitizen alleged terrorists.

3. See "Uniting and Strengthening America by Providing Appropriate Tools Required to Intercept and Obstruct Terrorism Act of 2001," §§ 411–412, Pub. L. no. 107–56, 115 Stat. 272 (2001).

4. See USA Patriot Act, § 412(a). As of July 2002, the attorney general had not resorted to the seven-day detention power in any cases. See "Questions Submitted to the House Judiciary Committee to the Attorney General on USA Patriot Act Implementation," at 17, appended to "Letter from Assistant Attorney General Daniel J. Bryant to Senator F. James Sensenbrenner Jr." (July 26, 2002), available at http://www.fas.org/irp/news/2002/10/doj101702.pdf.

5. See ibid. at 16 (reporting that as of July 2002, only a single alien had been denied admission to the United States under the expanded definition).

6. See e.g., William Glaberson, "War on Terrorism Stirs Memory of Internment," *New York Times,* September 24, 2001, p. A18; David Cole, "Liberties in a Time of Fear," *New York Times,* September 25, 2001, p. A29.

7. Jack Goldsmith and Cass Sunstein make a similar argument in contrasting reactions to the use of military tribunals in World War II (leading up the the Supreme Court's decision in *Ex parte Quirin*) and in the wake of September 11. See Jack Goldsmith and Cass R. Sunstein, "Military Tribunals and Legal Culture: What a Difference Sixty Years Make," *Constitutional Commentary* 19 (2002): 261, 280–81.

8. See, e.g., Neil A. Lewis, "Lawmakers Tap Brakes on Bush's Hurtling Antiterrorism Measure," *New York Times,* September 25, 2001, p. B7, reporting constitutional objections to the Bush administration antiterrorism proposals.

9. See, e.g., Jeffrey Rosen, "Civil Right," *New Republic,* October 21, 2002, p. 14.

10. See, e.g., Cass R. Sunstein, *The Partial Constitution* (Cambridge: Harvard University Press, 1993), arguing that the aspirations of the Constitution can be ascertained not only from judicial interpretation, but also from broad public deliberation; Mark Tushnet, *Taking the Constitution Away From the Courts* (Princeton: Princeton University Press, 1999), framing a populist view of constitutional law; Lawrence Gene Sager, "Fair Measure: The Legal Status of Underenforced Constitutional Norms," *Harvard Law Review* 91 (1978):1212, asserting full validity of constitutional norms even in the face of judicial underenforcement. See also William E. Forbath, "Caste, Class, and Equal Citizenship," *Michigan Law Review* 98 (1999):1, describing scholarship focused on constitutional development outside the courts.

11. See Peter J. Spiro, "Treaties, Executive Agreements, and Constitutional Method," *Texas Law Review* 79 (2001): 961.

12. On the plenary power doctrine, see e.g., Gerald L. Neuman, *Strangers to the Constitution: Immigrants, Borders, and Fundamental Law* (Princeton: Princeton University Press: 1996), 118–38; Louis H. Henkin, "The Constitution and United States Sovereignty: A Century of Chinese Exclusion and Its Progeny," *Harvard Law Review* 100:853 (1987). For a nonacademic treatment, see Jeffrey Rosen, "Holding Pattern," *New Republic,* December 10, 2001, p. 16 ("Over the last 50 years the Supreme Court has imposed few constitutional constraints on the ability of Congress and the president to detain, exclude, and deport aliens in ways that would be grossly unconstitutional if applied to citizens.").

13. See *Nguyen* v. *INS,* 533 U.S. 53 (2001) (while upholding gender discriminatory provision in naturalization provision, applying ordinary domestic equal protection framework); *Zadvydas* v. *Davis,* 533 U.S. 678 (2001) (finding government to lack statutory authority to detain removable aliens on indefinite basis on grounds that indefinite detention would raise "serious constitutional doubts"); see also Peter J. Spiro, "Explaining the End of Plenary Power," *Georgetown Immigration Law Journal* 16 (2001): 339.

14. Most notably in the *Zadvydas* decision, which bracketed the application of its constraints on detention in terrorism cases. See *Zadvydas,* 533 U.S. at 696 ("Neither do we consider terrorism or other special circumstances where special arguments might be made for forms of preventive detention and for heightened deference to the judgments of the political branches with respect to matters of national security.").

15. See Dan Eggen and Mary Beth Sheridan, "Justice Drafts New Rules for Deportation; Terrorist Suspects Would Be Removed," *Washington Post,* September 19, 2001, p. A1, describing legislation proposed by Department of Justice in immediate wake of September 11.

16. The circuit courts have split on the issue of whether deportation hearings can be conducted in secrecy, paving the way for consideration of the issue by the Supreme Court. Compare *North Jersey Media Group* v. *Ashcroft,* 2002 U.S. App. Lexis 21032 (3d Cir. September 17, 2002), finding press and public to have no First Amendment right to open deportation hearings, with *Detroit Free Press* v. *Ashcroft,* 303 F.3d 681 (6th Cir. 2002), finding closed removal hearings to violate First Amendment. On the detentions and secret proceedings, see generally Cole, supra note 1, at 960–65. More significant civil liberties decisions are likely to emerge in the context of citizens detained without charge as "enemy belligerents," as the plenary power over aliens will not pose a threshold barrier in those cases. The most significant decision to date upheld the government's power to hold a citizen captured on the battlefield. See *Hamdi* v. *Rumsfeld,* 2003 U.S. App. Lexis 198 (4th Cir. 2003). That decision would not by itself support the detention, as an enemy belligerent, of José Padilla, who was apprehended at Chicago's O'Hare airport; as an interim opinion of the same court had observed, in the absence of "meaningful judicial review, any American citizen alleged to be an enemy combatant could be detained indefinitely without charges or counsel on the government's say-so" in such cases. See *Hamdi* v. *Rumsfeld,* 296 F. 3d 278 (4th Cir. 2002). The Padilla case comprises the only use of the enemy belligerent designation outside the theater of military operations. One might wonder whether the government will use this approach in future cases, even if the Hamdi and Padilla detentions withstand court challenges. If not, the question further demonstrates the thesis suggested here, that enforcement authorities find themselves restrained by extrajudicial dynamics.

17. Others would contest this conclusion. See, e.g, Lawyers Committee for Human Rights, "A Year of Loss: Reexamining Civil Liberties since September 11" (2002), at 1 ("Since September 11, the United States has lost something essential and defining: some of the cherished principles on which this country is founded have been eroded or disregarded"). Two responses: First, to the extent that we have witnessed civil liberties reversals in the wake of September 11, even significant ones, they have not been nearly as severe as initially feared. Isolating restraining agents thus becomes a useful undertaking. Second, the mere fact of such characterizations, and of mobilized

advocacy against rights-infringing responses, is itself constitutionally consequential and evidentiary, especially when set in historical relief. See Goldsmith and Sunstein, supra, at 267–70 (describing complete lack of opposition to trial by military commission of Nazi saboteurs during World War II). Such constitutionally grounded opposition to antiterrorism measures reflects a constitutional discourse in which security concerns no longer represent a constitutional trump.

18. See, e.g., Michael Hirsh, "Bush and the World," *Foreign Affairs* 81, no. 5 (September/October 2002): 18.

19. See, e.g., Harold Honju Koh, "The Case Against Military Commissions," *American Journal of International Law* 96 (2002): 337.

20. See U.S. Department of Defense, Military Commission Order No. 1 (March 21, 2002), available at http://www.defenselink.mil/news/Mar2002/d20020321ord.pdf.

21. See, e.g., George Lardner Jr., "Democrats Blast Order on Tribunals: Senators Told Military Trials Fall Under President's Power," *Washington Post*, November 29, 2001, p. A22.

22. See, e.g., "A Travesty of Justice," *New York Times*, November 16, 2001, p. A24, condemning tribunal prospect as "a dangerous idea [involving] a crude and unaccountable system that any dictator would admire"; "Military Justice (Continued)," *Washington Post*, November 26, 2001, p. A24; "An Un-American Secrecy," *Los Angeles Times*, November 17, 2001, p. 24 (to same effect).

23. The tribunal option enjoys support from key Democratic legislators. See, e.g., Joseph I. Lieberman, "No Excuse for Second-Class Justice," *Washington Post*, January 2, 2002, p. A13. Indeed, Lieberman and colleague Carl Levin brought the administration to task for not deploying the tribunal option in the Moussaoui prosecution. See Walter Pincus, "Senators Ask: Why No Tribunal for Suspect? Democrats Surprise Pentagon Officials," *Washington Post*, December 13, 2001, p. A14.

24. See Laurence H. Tribe, "Trial by Fury: Why Congress Must Curb Bush's Military Courts," *New Republic*, December 10, 2001, p. 18; while criticizing administration failure to consult Congress on tribunals as well as elements of the framework for the tribunals, Tribe asserts "the core of the executive order [authorizing the tribunals], its gratuitous branches pruned, is consistent with the Constitution."

25. See Ruth Wedgwood, "The Rules of War Can't Protect Al Qaeda," *New York Times*, December 31, 2001; Ruth Wedgwood, "The Case for Military Tribunals," *Wall Street Journal*, December 3, 2001, p. A18. Wedgwood was consulted by Defense Department lawyers with respect to the formulation of procedural rules adopted for the tribunals.

26. See also, e.g., Kenneth Anderson, "What to Do with Bin Laden and Al Qaeda Terrorists? A Qualified Defense of Military Commissions and United States Policy on Detainees at Guantanamo Bay Naval Base," *Harvard Journal of Law and Public Policy* 25 (2002): 591; and Curtis Bradley and Jack Goldsmith, "The Constitutional Validity of Military Commissions," *Green Bag* 2d 5 (2002): 249, asserting the tribunal's constitutionality. Other academics, of course, have strongly condemned the tribunals. See, e.g., George Fletcher, "War and the Constitution: Bush's Military Tribunals Haven't Got a Legal Leg to Stand On," *American Prospect*, January 1, 2002, p. 26; and David Cole, "National Security State," *The Nation*, December 17, 2001, p. 4.

27. 317 U.S. 1 (1942), upholding trial of Nazi saboteurs by military commission.

28. In the immediate wake of President Bush's executive order authorizing the use of tribunals, a survey found the American public overwhelmingly in support of their use against noncitizens, whether captured inside or outside the United States (supported by a 64 to 26 percent margin for those captured outside the United States, and a 64 to 27 percent margin for those inside the

United States). See NPR/Kaiser/Kennedy School Poll on Civil Liberties: Military Tribunals, available at www.npr.org/news/specials/civillibertiespoll/civilliberties_supplement.html.

29. Including, for instance, so liberal a columnist as Anthony Lewis. See Anthony Lewis, "Wake Up, America," *New York Times,* November 30, 2001, p. A27 ("I do not doubt that leaders of Al Qaeda could properly be tried by a military tribunal," under procedures more narrowly drafted than the initial Bush executive order).

30. On this score, I think Goldsmith and Sunstein exaggerate the magnitude of domestic opposition to the tribunals. See Goldsmith and Sunstein, supra, at 271–74. No doubt they have been more skeptically received than were the military commissions of *Ex parte Quirin,* as they amply demonstrate, but there has been significant support, however qualified, from unexpected mainstream quarters on the question.

31. On European public opinion relating to the treatment of the Guantanamo detainees, see "A Transatlantic Rift," *Economist,* January 19, 2002, reporting that in Europe, "the prisoner's fate dominates airwaves and parliaments."

32. See, e.g., Amnesty International, Memorandum to the U.S. Government on the Rights of People in U.S. Custody in Afghanistan and Guantanamo Bay (April 2002); Richard Goldstone, "Prosecuting Al Qaeda: September 11 and its Aftermath," Crimes of War Project, December 7, 2001, available at http://www.crimesofwar.org/expert/a1.

33. See Barbara Crossette, "Effort by U.N. To Cut Traffic in Arms Meets a U.S. Rebuff," *New York Times,* July 9, 2001, p. A8.

34. See *Soering* v. *United Kingdom,* 161 Eur. Ct. H.R. (ser. A) (1989).

35. Keith B. Richburg and T.R. Reid, "France Cautions U.S. Over Sept. 11 Defendant," *Washington Post,* December 13, 2001, p. A13; highlights European opposition to capital punishment in 9/11 context, reporting that France, Britain, Germany, Italy, Belgium, and Spain are holding people allegedly linked to the al Qaeda network or suspected of involvement in other terrorist plots against European targets or American targets in Europe; T.R. Reid, "Europeans Reluctant to Send Terror Suspects to U.S.; Allies Oppose Death Penalty and Bush's Plan for Secret Military Tribunals," *Washington Post,* November 29, 2001, p. A23.

36. See Sam Dillon and Donald G. McNeil Jr., "Spain Sets Hurdle for Extraditions," *New York Times,* November 24, 2001, p. A1.

37. See, e.g., James Orenstein, "Rooting Out Terrorists Just Became Harder," *New York Times,* December 6, 2001, p. A35; in the wake of authorization of military tribunals, he observes that cooperation in the global fight against terrorism "is imperiled when foreign governments don't trust us to respect the basic rights of the people we ask them to send us."

38. See, e.g., Cole, supra note 1, at 958; Laura A. Dickerson, "Using Legal Process to Fight Terrorism: Detentions, Military Commissions, International Tribunals, and the Rule of Law," *Southern California Law Review* 75: 1407, 1465 (2002).

39. For a case study of the consequentiality of NGOs in international lawmaking, see Anne Marie Clark, *Diplomacy of Conscience: Amnesty International and Changing Human Rights Norms* (Princeton: Princeton University Press, 2001).

40. See Amnesty International, supra, at 44–57; Human Rights Watch, "Commission Rules Meet Some, Not All, Rights Concerns" (March 21, 2002); "Lawyer's Group Voices Concern about Post–September 11 Measures," *Agence France Presse,* September 11, 2002, reporting views of International Commission of Jurists.

41. See Jess Bravin, "U.S. Prepares Tribunal System to Prosecute Alleged Terrorists," *Wall Street Journal,* December 2, 2002, p. A8.

42. The Human Rights Committee, charged with interpreting the International Covenant on

Civil Rights, accepted the legitimacy of military tribunals in exceptional circumstances in an opinion issued in 1984. See Human Rights Committee, General Comment 13/21, para. 4 (April 12, 1984).

43. See Katharine Seelye, "Guantanamo Bay Faces Sentence of Life as Permanent U.S. Prison," *New York Times*, September 16, 2002, p. A1.

44. See, e.g., "European Parliament Presses U.S. Over Guantanamo Detainees," *Agence France Presse*, January 30, 2003; Nikki Tait, "Judges Attack U.S. Treatment of Guantanamo Bay Detainees," *Financial Times*, November 7, 2002, p. 5, reporting Court of Appeals decision expressing "concern that in apparent contravention of fundamental principles of law [a British citizen in detention at Guantanamo] may be subject to indefinite detention in territory over which the United States has exclusive control, with no opportunity to challenge the legitimacy of his detention before any court or tribunal" while refusing to mandate intervention of British authorities with United States on the matter; Julia Preston, "Departing Rights Commissioner Faults U.S.," *New York Times*, September 12, 2002, p. B22. Editorial comment on Guantanamo was stepped up at the anniversary of the opening of Camp X-Ray. See, e.g., Geoffrey Bindman, "It's Time to Charge These Men—or Set Them Free," *Times* (London), December 3, 2002, p. 5; "Perpetual Limbo: U.S. Must Clarify the Fate of Guantanamo Detainees," *Financial Times*, December 4, 2002, p. 18.

45. U.S. courts are unlikely to find jurisdiction over constitutional challenges to the Guantanamo detentions, on the grounds that U.S. government conduct on Guantanamo is not subject to ordinary constitutional constraint. See *Rasul v. Bush*, 215 F. Supp. 2d 55 (D.D.C. 2001), rejecting a challenge to Guantanamo detentions on this jurisdictional basis. Congress has shown little interest in the issue, nor have other domestic actors, with the sometime exception of editorialists. See, e.g., John Mintz, "Delegations Praise Detainees' Treatment," *Washington Post*, January 26, 2002, p. A15.

The Immigrant As Threat to American Security

1. Oscar Handlin, *The Uprooted: The Epic Story of the Great Migrations that Made the American People* (New York: Grosset and Dunlap, 1951), p. 3.

2. Wald, Powell, and Reuther were the children of immigrants, not immigrants themselves.

3. On the Irish, see Oscar Handlin, *Boston's Immigrants, 1790–1865: A Study in Acculturation* (Cambridge: Harvard University Press, 1941); on the Chinese, see Andrew Gyory, *Closing the Gate: Race, Politics, and the Chinese Exclusion Act* (Chapel Hill: University of North Carolina Press, 1998), and Erika Lee, *At America's Gates: Chinese Immigration During the Exclusion Era, 1882–1943* (Chapel Hill: University of North Carolina Press, 2003); on the Germans during World War I, see Frederick C. Luebke, *Bonds of Loyalty: German-Americans and World War I* (De Kalb: Northern Illinois University, 1974); on eastern and southern Europeans in the 1920s, see John Higham, *Strangers in the Land: Patterns of American Nativism, 1860–1925* (1992; New Brunswick: Rutgers University Press, 1955), and Gary Gerstle, *American Crucible: Race and Nation in the Twentieth Century* (Princeton: Princeton University Press, 2001); on Mexicans in the 1930s, see Abraham Hoffman, *Unwanted Mexican Americans in the Great Depression: Repatriation Pressures, 1929–1939* (Tucson: University of Arizona Press, 1974), and Mae Ngai, *Impossible Subjects: Illegal Aliens and the Making of Modern America* (Princeton: Princeton University Press, 2004); on Japanese internment, see Roger Daniels, *Concentration Camps USA: Japanese Americans and World War II* (New York: Holt, Rinehart, and Winston, 1971).

4. One of the oldest and still one of the best efforts of this sort is Higham, *Strangers in the Land*; for a more recent effort, see David H. Bennett, *The Party of Fear: From Nativist Movements to the New Right in American History* (Chapel Hill: University of North Carolina Press, 1988).

5. For a history of this country's anti-Catholic origins, see Higham, *Strangers in the Land,* pp. 4–7, and Bennett, *Party of Fear,* Part I, passim.

6. Handlin, *Boston's Immigrants;* Bennett; *Party of Fear;* Tyler G. Anbinder, *Nativism and Slavery: The Northern Know-Nothings and the Politics of the 1850s* (New York: Oxford University Press, 1992); David R. Roediger, *The Wages of Whiteness: Race and the Making of the American Working Class* (London: Verso, 1991).

7. Bennett, *Party of Fear,* pp. 233–37, 319–321.

8. On the importance and meaning of republicanism to American political culture in the nineteenth century, see Sean Wilentz, *Chants Democratic: New York City and the Rise of an American Working Class* (New York: Oxford University Press, 1984). On its troubling implications for immigrants and others thought to lack the necessary political independence and virtue, see Gary Gerstle, "Ideas of the American Labor Movement," in *Ideas, Ideologies, and Social Movements: The U.S. Experience Since 1800,* eds. Stuart Bruchey and Peter Coclanis (Charleston: University of South Carolina Press, 1999), pp. 72–89; Matthew Frye Jacobson, *Whiteness of a Different Color: European Immigrants and the Alchemy of Race* (Cambridge: Harvard University Press, 1998).

9. Higham, *Strangers in the Land,* pp. 54–58. The fear of what radicalism and revolution would do to the American republic can best be grasped by reading what politicians such as Theodore Roosevelt wrote and said in reaction to Haymarket, the strikes of the 1890s, and the assassination of William McKinley. See, for example, Theodore Roosevelt, "American Ideals," in *The Works of Theodore Roosevelt,* vol. 13, National Edition, ed. Herman Hagedorn (New York: Scribner's Sons, 1926), p. 7; Howard L. Hurwitz, *Theodore Roosevelt and Labor in New York State, 1880–1900* (New York: Columbia University Press, 1943), pp. 11, 181, 283.

10. Gary Gerstle, "Immigration and Ethnicity in the American Century," in *Making Sense of the Twentieth Century,* ed. Harvard Sitkoff (New York: Oxford University Press, 2000), pp. 275–95.

11. Gerstle, *American Crucible,* pp. 4–5; Jacobson, *Whiteness of a Different Color;* Reginald Horsman, *Race and Manifest Destiny: The Origins of American Racial Anglo-Saxonism* (Cambridge: Harvard University Press, 1981).

12. Richard Hofstadter, *Social Darwinism in American Thought* (Boston: Beacon Press, 1955); Jacobson, *Whiteness of a Different Color;* Roediger, *Wages of Whiteness;* James R. Barrett and David Roediger, "In Between Peoples: Race, Nationality, and the 'New Immigrant' Working Class," *Journal of American Ethnic History* 16 (Spring 1997): 3–44.

13. Gyory, *Closing the Gate;* Lee, *At America's Gates;* Alexander Saxton, *The Rise and Fall of the White Republic: Class Politics and Mass Culture in Nineteenth-Century America* (London: Verso, 1990).

14. Couldn't Americans legitimately argue that the preservation of German traditions might include an admiration for the German kaiser and thus constitute a threat to republicanism? Most German immigrants addressed this problem by insisting that their cultural affection for Germany entailed no political loyalty. To the contrary, they insisted, Germans were committed to American political traditions. They were German only in culture, not in politics. This argument persuaded most Americans—until World War I. Luebke, *Bonds of Loyalty;* Russell A. Kazal, *Becoming Old Stock: The Paradox of German-American Identity* (Princeton: Princeton University Press, 2004).

15. David Kennedy, *Over Here! The First World War and American Society* (New York: Oxford University Press, 1982); Gerstle, *American Crucible,* chapter 3; Higham, *Strangers in the Land,* pp. 194–263.

16. The situation of the Germans was made more precarious by the long period of official neutrality—two and a half years (August 1914–April 1917)—that preceded America's entry

into war. For most of that time, the American government insisted that it would not take sides in the conflict, and that it would continue to maintain trade and other kinds of relations with both the Triple Entente and Central Powers. German Americans interpreted this neutrality to be genuine, meaning that they were free to express their neutrality, their belief (if they were socialists) that the working people had nothing to gain from this war, their continued love of German culture, their suspicions of England, and, in some cases, their sympathies with Germany's war aims. But America's neutrality was never as evenhanded as the Germans immigrants interpreted it to be. Owing to a large volume of trade between the United States and England and a common cultural and political inheritance, a majority of Americans felt closer to England than to Germany. In 1915 and 1916, public and official opinion in America moved steadily in the direction of England and the Triple Entente and against Germany and its allies. Luebke, *Bonds of Loyalty*.

17. This paragraph and the ones on the German American experience that follow it are largely based on these sources: Ibid.; H.C. Peterson, *Propaganda for War: The War against American Neutrality* (Norman: University of Oklahoma Press, 1939); George Sylvester Viereck, *Spreading Germs of Hate* (New York: H. Liveright, 1930); Christopher Gildemeister, "My Four Years in Germany: Progressivism, Propaganda and American Film in World War I (unpublished seminar paper, Catholic University of America, 1994); Kennedy, *Over Here!*; Ronald Schaeffer, *America in the Great War: The Rise of the War Welfare State* (New York: Oxford University Press, 1991); Higham, *Strangers in the Land;* Kazal, *Becoming Old Stock*.

18. Kazal, *Becoming Old Stock*.

19. Robert K. Murray, *Red Scare: A Study in National Hysteria, 1919–1920* (Minneapolis: University of Minnesota Press, 1955); William Preston Jr., *Aliens and Dissenters: Federal Suppression of Radicals, 1903–1933* (Cambridge: Harvard University Press, 1963); Higham, *Strangers in the Land*, pp. 194–263; Gerstle, *American Crucible*, pp. 81–127; David Montgomery, *The Fall of the House of Labor: The Workplace, the State, and American Labor Activism, 1865–1925* (New York: Cambridge University Press, 1987); Joseph A. McCartin, *Labor's Great War: The Struggle for Industrial Democracy and the Origins of Modern American Labor Relations, 1912–1921* (Chapel Hill: University of North Carolina Press, 1997); Nell Irvin Painter, *Standing at Armageddon: The United States, 1877–1919* (New York: W.W. Norton, 1987); Steven Fraser, *Labor Will Rule: Sidney Hillman and the Rise of American Labor* (New York: Free Press, 1991); H.C. Peterson and Gilbert C. Fite, *Opponents of War, 1917–1918* (Madison: University of Wisconsin Press, 1957).

20. Murray, *Red Scare*, p. 79.

21. The best work on the history of anarchism in the United States has been done by Paul Avrich. See, in particular, *The Haymarket Tragedy* (Princeton: Princeton University Press, 1984), and *Sacco and Vanzetti: The Anarchist Background* (Princeton: Princeton University Press, 1991).

22. Higham, *Strangers in the Land;* Gerstle, *American Crucible*.

23. Murray, *Red Scare*.

24. This refusal made it impossible for federal law enforcement agencies to target citizens and explains why most of those arrested and virtually all of those deported were immigrants, who were vulnerable to the antisedition provisions of the Alien Act of 1918.

25. Murray, *Red Scare*, pp. 239–262; Stanley Coben, *A. Mitchell Palmer: Politician* (New York: Columbia University Press, 1963).

26. Murray, *Red Scare*, p. 276.

27. Avrich, *Sacco and Vanzetti*.

28. Gerstle, *American Crucible*, pp. 95–104.

29. Ibid., pp. 95–109.

30. *Congressional Record*, March 17, 1924, p. 4389; April 8, 1924, pp. 5868–69; April 5, 1924, p. 5693.

31. This account of Japanese internment is based on the following: Daniels, *Concentration Camps, USA;* Roger Daniels, *Prisoners Without Trial: Japanese Americans in World War II* (New York: Hill and Wang, 1993); Peter Irons, ed., *Justice Delayed: The Record of the Japanese Internment Cases* (Middletown, Conn.: Wesleyan University Press, 1989); Jacobus tenBroek, Edward N. Barnhart, and Floyd W. Matson, *Prejudice, War and the Constitution: Japanese American Evacuation and Resettlement* (Berkeley: University of California Press, 1958); Dillon S. Myer, *Uprooted Americans: The Japanese Americans and the War Relocation Authority during World War II* (Tucson: University of Arizona Press, 1971); Gary Y. Okihiro and Joan Myers, *Whispered Silences: Japanese Americans and World War II* (Seattle: University of Washington Press, 1996); Alice Yang Murray, ed., *What Did the Internment of Japanese Americans Mean?* (Boston: Bedford Books, 2000); Greg Robinson, *By Order of the President: FDR and the Internment of Japanese Americans* (Cambridge: Harvard University Press, 2001).

32. Alice Yang Murray, "The Internment of Japanese Americans," in Murray, ed., *What Did the Internment of Japanese Americans Mean?*, p. 3.

33. Stephen Fox, *The Unknown Internment: An Oral History of Italian Americans during World War II* (Boston: Twayne Publishers, 1990), pp. 151, 163–64.

34. In addition to the sources listed in the previous notes, see also John Dower, *War Without Mercy: Race and Power in the Pacific War* (New York: Pantheon, 1986).

35. Yuji Ichioka, *The Issei: The World of First Generation Japanese Immigrants, 1880–1924* (New York: Free Press, 1988); Gerstle, *American Crucible*, pp. 60–62, 109–113.

36. *Report of the Commission on Wartime Relocation and Internment of Civilians*, Personal Justice Denied 66 (CLPEF 1997); Lt. Gen. J.L. DeWitt, U.S. Army, *Final Report: Japanese Evacuation from the West Coast, 1942* (Washington D.C.: Govt. Printing Office, 1943), p. 97.

37. Western Defense Command, under General DeWitt's control, did draw up plans for mass expulsion and internment of West Coast Italians and Germans, but these proposals never attracted the kind of support from Western politicians, Western public opinion, or Washington bureaucrats that Japanese internment did.

38. In 1942, the Germans landed eight soldiers disguised as American civilians on Long Island, New York, with instructions to blow up key U.S. military installations. They were captured before they could do any harm and tried and executed under military law. Louis Fisher, *Nazi Saboteurs on Trial: A Military Tribunal and American Law* (Lawrence, Kansas: University Press of Kansas, 2003).

39. Peter Irons, "Gordon Hirabayashi v. United States: 'A Jap's a Jap,' " in *The Courage of their Convictions,* Irons, ed. (New York: Free Press, 1988), pp. 37–62.

40. Though the effects of internment on the Japanese American population are beyond the purview of this essay, it should be said that those effects, in terms of loss of wealth, status, freedom, family integrity, and culture, were extreme and would not be overcome for two generations. The disgraceful episode would finally elicit from the U.S. government a formal apology in 1990.

41. I examine more fully the experience of Muslims and Arabs in the United States since September 11, 2001, in "Pluralism and the War on Terror," *Dissent* (Spring 2003), 31–38.

42. An additional reason why the Red Scare of 1919–1920 declined more quickly than the Radical Islamicist Scare of today lies in the changing foreign policy of the Soviet Union in the early 1920s. The Soviet Union stopped making international revolution its chief priority, choosing instead to consolidate its power within the confines of the nation and empire it had wrested from

the czars. This change made other countries fear the Soviet Union and communism less than they had and diminished what these other countries had construed as a campaign of international terror. The Soviet Union had become more of a conventional nation-state and easier to negotiate with through traditional diplomatic channels. This has not happened, of course, with al Qaeda.

Governance, Immigration Policy, and Security

1. A. J. Bacevich, *American Empire: The Realities and Consequences of U.S. Diplomacy* (Cambridge: Harvard University Press, 2002), p. 225.

2. Thomas Faist defined transnationalism as the "sustained ties of persons, networks and organizations across the borders of multiple nation-states." (Thomas Faist, *The Volume and Dynamics of International Migration and Transnational Social Spaces* [Oxford: Oxford University Press, 2000], p. 2). Transnationalism is the increased tendency of immigrants to simultaneously maintain multifaceted attachments to their country of birth, country of resettlement, and even other countries to which their compatriots have migrated, or to regional and global nonstate entities. Transnationalism is especially esteemed in Canada. The October 2002 Throne Speech to the Canadian Parliament stated that "Canada has a unique model of citizenship, based simultaneously on diversity and mutual responsibility. This model requires deliberate efforts to connect Canadians across their differences, to link them to their history and to enable their diverse voices to participate in choosing the Canada we want."

3. *Siskin's Immigration Bulletin* (Memphis, Tenn.: Siskind, Susser, Haas & Devine, December 22, 2000).

4. Doris Meissner, *After the Attacks: Protecting Borders and Liberties* (Washington, D.C.: Carnegie Endowment for International Peace, 2001), p. 1.

5. Quoted in *Globe and Mail,* October 30, 2001, p. 1. Campbell Clark, Bush's spokesperson, said that Bush aimed to tighten the continent's borders, not the borders with Canada, and that the United States wanted to put the heat on prime minister Chretien to harmonize immigration and customs.

6. Allan Thompson, *Toronto Star,* October 31, 2001, p. A7. Allan Thompson headed the Ottawa Bureau of the newspaper; see also Richard Brennan, "$9M Security Plan for Ontario," *The Toronto Star,* October 31, 2001, pg A6.

7. Americans have an enormous capacity for collecting intelligence information abroad. Canada has virtually none. If the security clearance of refugees was harmonized, security clearances would largely be relegated to an American determination.

8. Audrey Macklin, a law professor at the University of Toronto after examining the issue, concluded that the "security perimeter" was not a real option but served as a discursive security blanket, "one that furnished comfort by conjuring up a visual image around which people can deposit their anxieties." "Borderline Security," in *The Security of Freedom: Essays on Canada's Anti-Terrorism Bill,* eds. Ronald J. Daniels, Patrick Macklem and Ken Roach (Toronto: University of Toronto Press, 2001), 386.

9. Cambell Clark, "Canada Urged to Do More About Security" *Globe and Mail,* November 1, 2001, p. A10.

10. In an interview with Allan Thompson of the *Toronto Star* (November 12, 2002, p. A7), Paul Cellucci argued that his idea for a joining screening and a common border perimeter (the earlier language of harmonizing immigration and refugee policy had been totally displaced) was now dubbed a "zone of confidence." If developed, he argued, it would avoid all the cross-border hassles.

11. Cf. the *National Post* headline story by Sheldon Alberts, "Tighten Ties to America: Committee," December 2, 2002, p. A1.

12. There is a widespread belief, in Canada as well as the United States, that terrorists posing as refugees come to Canada in order to access entry into the United States. James Bissett, a former Canadian ambassador and deputy minister in the Department of Immigration from 1985 to 1990, wrote an article entitled, "Canada's Asylum System: A Threat to American Security," and served on an expert panel assessing immigration and intelligence findings at the National Press Club in Washington, D.C., on August 22, 2002 under the auspices of the anti-immigration Center for Immigration Studies. He helped to legitimize the belief that Canada's allegedly lax procedures on asylum allowed fifty terrorist organizations to become established in Canada (http://www.cis.org/articles/2002/back402.html).

13. Governance deals with the exercise of power among the different segments of society and the formal and informal institutional structures within and among governments and other social sectors to foster civic freedoms, commerce, and the arts. Governance goes beyond the realm of formal decision-making structures and players to include the plurality of actors who guide public opinion and choices.

14. According to the documents registered in Canada, the agreement benefited that country. "By designating the United States as a country that complies with Article 33 of the Refugee Convention and Article 3 of the Convention Against Torture, persons seeking protection in Canada can be returned to the United States for assessment of their claims. This will reduce the number of refugee claims made by persons arriving from the United States." *Canada Gazette* 136, no. 43 (Saturday, October 26, 2002), http://canadagazette.gc.ca/partI/2002/20021026/html/regle-e. html-36.

15. According to statistics from Citizenship and Immigration Canada (CIC), the numbers of refugee claims made between January and September 2001 initially totaled 31,251, but the figures were subsequently adjusted to 33,374. In 2002, from January to mid-September, there were 22,145 claims, roughly two-thirds of the number of claims the previous year. Part of the decline in numbers was attributed to the imposition of a visa requirement on Hungary and Zimbabwe; there were 147 claims from Hungary in 2002 compared to 1,034 in 2001, and 57 claims from Zimbabwe in 2002 compared to 359 in 2001.

16. The Immigration Refugee Board (IRB) had been faced with a mounting number of claims growing from 22,714 in 1997 to 34,253 in 2000. The IRB expected to reach 47,000 claims in 2002. In fact, in the first 3 months of 2002, there were only 6,754 refugees compared to 10,130 claims made in Canada in 2001. That meant that, without the Safe Third Country provisions, Canada was expected to receive 25,000 claims. Since approximately half the claims came into Canada by land from the United States, and making provision for those who would still be allowed to cross because of exceptions in the act—for example, that they had relatives in Canada—the Canadian intake was expected to decline by 10,000 who would then make their claims in the United States.

17. However, it was also expected that many of those who would normally cross by land would divert to entry by air (not covered in the agreement) or enter Canada (perhaps illegally) and make an inland claim. On October 10, 2002, National Public Radio reporter Bill Frelick said, "Here you have an official charged with enforcing immigration laws in the United States who's telling us that he is one of the architects of an agreement that will create a higher degree of illegality."

18. For example, Ottawa businessman and Canadian citizen Maher Arar was arrested while transiting through the United States. He was deported to Syria, where he remains in prison as of this writing. Prominent Indo-Canadian author Rohinton Mistry cancelled his book tour in the United States because of the "unbearable humiliation" he and his wife faced at American airports. Many such stories made front-page news in Canadian newspapers.

19. In October 2002, the Canadian government issued a travel advisory warning Canadian citizens born in five countries (Iran, Iraq, Libya, Syria, and Sudan) that they may want to rethink plans to travel to the United States for fear that they would come under undue scrutiny at United States airports. On Wednesday, October 30, 2002, Foreign Affairs Minister Bill Graham called a U.S. photo and fingerprint law that targets selected foreign visitors "unconstitutional." On November 11, 2002, the Canadian Islamic Congress Council issued a travel advisory warning Muslims in Canada that travel to the United States may subject them to significant delays and very intrusive procedures. "The United States is not safe for Muslims right now."

20. Cf. Campbell Clark, "PM Shrugs off Immigrants Travel Trouble," *Globe and Mail,* November 6, 2002, p. A1.

21. "Woman Tells of Humiliation by U.S. Officials," *Globe and Mail,* November 6, 2002, p. A7. In another case, a Canadian citizen of Indian origin returning from India after visiting her parents was delayed at Chicago's O'Hare airport, had her Canadian passport mutilated by an INS officer, and was deported back to Yemen. No one checked her Canadian status or allowed her to consult with Canadian officials.

22. Cf. Peter Small and Christian Cotroneo, "We Don't Welcome You Anymore," *Toronto Star,* November 7, 2002. See also the article by Paul Sperry, "Homeland Insecurity: Screening of Arab-Canadians Continues. Despite Minister's Claims, Security Policy Remains in Force," WorldNet-Daily.com, November 3, 2002: "A new immigration-security policy to screen Canadian citizens born in the Middle East remains in force, INS inspectors said today, despite claims to the contrary by Canadian officials" (http://www.worldnetdaily.com/news/article.asp?ARTICLE_ID= 29525).

23. The content of these rules were, in fact, first published in WorldNetDaily.com on September 19, 2002 as part of the National Security Entry-Exit Registration System, or NSEERS, authorized under the USA Patriot Act passed in response to 9/11. The applicable rule reads: "A case that might warrant discretionary registration could be: A non-immigrant alien who is a dual national and is applying for admission as a national of a country that is not subject to special registration, but the alien's other nationality would subject him or her to special registration." Even as the Americans withdrew the automatic application of the rule to Canadian citizens born abroad in specific countries, the United States still insisted on applying the rule at its discretion to Canadian citizens of such countries of origin. A statement released through the U.S. embassy in Ottawa stated that, "Place of birth by itself will not automatically trigger registration." But the statement continued: "U.S. immigration officials reserve the right to register any aliens, including Canadians, whom they believe pose a threat to the United States" (November 1, 2002).

24. The 1996 census recorded 1.4 million landed immigrants in Canada who had been granted permanent resident status but had not become citizens. On November 3, 2002, the U.S. publicized its intent to toughen border rules for most Commonwealth citizens. Washington was preparing new regulations that would make it harder for citizens of most Commonwealth countries to get into the United States. Under the proposed rules, any Commonwealth citizen who lives in Canada but who is not a Canadian citizen will need valid travel documents to enter the United States.

25. Mary Vallis, *National Post,* November 4, 2002, p. 6.

26. *Canadian Press* wire story, November 7, 2002.

27. President George Bush announced a plan to create a new border security agency in which the Border Patrol, which had been part of the immigration service, would be merged with the Customs Service, now a part of the Treasury Department, and both placed under the Justice Department. Merging the beleaguered U.S. Immigration and Naturalization Service and the Customs Service into a single agency was intended to tighten border security in response to the Sept. 11

attacks. The initial plan had called for consolidation to make it easier for the federal government to oversee the nation's borders, limit border crossings in response to specific threats, and cut out bureaucratic hurdles and wasteful spending by federal agencies with overlapping functions. The clear victory of the Republicans in the midterm elections allowed Bush to have his way.

28. John Manley was the cabinet member who persuaded his colleagues, in the interests of the Canadian economy as well as joint security concerns, to be flexible and allow American border guards in Canada to carry guns in order for the planned joint customs inspection system to proceed.

29. Cf. Jennifer Loven, "Ridge Assures Canadian Official that Border Security Won't Damage Relations," *Associated Press*, December 6, 2002.

30. CTV News, December 6, 2002.

31. The *National Post* (December 6, 2002) quoted Tom Ridge, the newly nominated U.S. Homeland Security Director, as follows: "Despite Canadian reservations, the United States is going to stick with its plan to toughen border security because it is worried about terrorists coming south from Canada" (http://www.nationalpost.com/utilities/story.html/id).

32. In contrast, reports even by Canadian news services based in Washington noted that Canadians were balking at these measures at enhanced border security that would exhaustively scrutinize every Canadian who crosses into the United States (http://cnews.canoe.ca/CNEWS/World/2002/12/04/6439-cp.html).

33. The Foreign Affairs and International Trade Committee of the House of Commons drafted a report entitled "Partners in North America: Advancing Canada's Relations with the United States and Mexico," suggesting efforts in the past have been reactive rather than proactive and incoherent rather than coherent. The report advocated establishing a North American security perimeter and customs union both to recover from Canada's diminished diplomatic status and to enhance Canadian/American diplomatic, trade, and security integration. (Cf. the *National Post* headline story by Sheldon Alberts, "Tighten Ties to America: Committee," December 2, 2002, p. A1.)

34. In response to American pressure, Project Identity was initiated as an effort by Citizenship and Immigration Canada to detain unidentified new arrivals, most of them refugee claimants, whose identities are uncertain and who lack credibility, are evasive and uncooperative with immigration officers, or who have destroyed or concealed papers, such as passports or other forms of identity. (Cf. Estanislao Oziewicz, "Canada Plans to Identify Unidentified New Arrivals." *Globe and Mail*, November 28, 2002, print edition, p. A8.)

35. *Hands* uses the term partnerships to avoid worries that Canada was selling out its sovereignty on the altar of harmonization and security fears.

36. This fact did not inhibit the *Toronto Star* from totally misinterpreting the report with a headline "MPs Urge Crackdown on Refugees" (December 7, 2001, p. A7).

37. *Toronto Star,* November 23, 2001.

38. These few cases hardly substantiate the widespread charges made by civil libertarians and spokespersons for the Arab community in Canada that Arab men were being held simply because they were Arab or that Muslim organizations were being selectively oppressed.

39. Jack Donnelly (Graduate School of International Studies at the University of Denver), in his November 2, 2001, presentation at the Denver Roundtable, "New Directions in U.S. Foreign Policy," differentiated between abuses at the policy and the program levels. For Donnelly, there is a disconnect between policy statements/initiatives and programming. Raising issues of human rights violations falls under policy statements, while in programming, the Bush administration

is not particularly concerned about human rights and relies to a large degree on the bureaucracy. "When foreign policy becomes ordered around an ideological goal, it is likely that human rights, both domestic and international, will be trampled on."

40. The inclusion of tiny island states may seem odd as a link to any threat to Canadian security. The inclusion seems to have been motivated by the fact that one of them is the island state where Australia deposited the "refugees" from the boat it intercepted on the high seas. In another case, the island was allegedly a place being set up to be used by criminals to buy passports and even citizenships so the island could be used as a transit point for these "refugees" to move onto Canada or the United States.

41. Hungary, with 2,759 refugees, was, in fact, first both nationally and in Ontario; Zimbabwe, with 1,652, ranked fifth nationally, and fourth in Ontario.

42. Ward Elcock, director of CSIS, testified as long ago as the summer of 1998 before a Canadian Senate Committee that an "infrastructure has been established here to support a terrorist act in Canada."

43. On November 2, 2001, the Bush administration placed Hamas on its official list of terrorist groups even though the so-called Izz al-Din al-Qassam Brigade utilizes only 10 percent of the Hamas budget and 90 percent of its estimated $70 million annual budget is devoted to an extensive social services network, including schools, orphanages, mosques, health-care clinics, soup kitchens, and sports leagues. "Approximately 90 percent of its work is in social, welfare, cultural, and educational activities," according to Reuven Paz, a well-known counterterrorism expert and director of the International Policy Institute for Counter Terrorism in Herzilya. (Cf. "Experts: Hamas Has Reasons to Refrain from Terror Attacks," *Jerusalem Post,* February 18, 2000 (http://www.jpost.com/Editions/2000/02/18/News/News.2873.html). In December 2001, the Bush administration seized the assets of the Holy Land Foundation, the largest Muslim charity in the United States, for allegedly funding Hamas. It took a further year for Canada to follow suit.

44. Agents of the Canadian Security Intelligence Service (CSIS) interviewed Mohammed Hussein al-Husseini as long ago as 1993. Al-Husseini evidently reported that Hezbollah used Canada for fund-raising, a safe haven, and recruitment. The cells across Canada had been surveying important buildings in Canada and providing planning and logistical support for terrorist attacks in the United States. The Saudi national Hani Abdel Rahim al-Sayegh was accused of belonging to Hezbollah and taking part in the June 25, 1996, terrorist bombing of a military complex in Dhahran, Saudi Arabia, that killed 19 U.S. servicemen. (Cf. Steve Macko, *ENN Daily Intelligence Report,* May 8, 1997, 3:128, "Hezbollah Terrorist Operations in Canada.") In the October 31, 2002, *National Post,* Stewart Bell recapitulated how Canada had been used by Hezbollah as an "offshore base" for raising (and laundering) money, and purchasing blasting devices, night-vision goggles, powerful computers, and camera equipment used to record attacks against Israeli forces. Canadian banks had already been authorized to seize the assets of Hezbollah's military wing. Bill Graham repeatedly insisted, however, that he would not outlaw Hezbollah in its entirety because it was involved in social and political work in Lebanon.

45. Martin Rudner, director of the new Canadian Centre for Intelligence and Security Studies (CCISS) at Carleton University's Norman Patterson School of International Affairs, dubbed Imad Mugniyah as a "key Hezbollah operations commander." (Cf. Stewart Bell, "Leading Terror Suspect Tied to Canadian Cell: Imad Mugniyah," *National Post,* November 12, 2002.)

46. Ibid., A6.

47. Allan Thompson, "U.S. Envoy Urges Joint Screening," *Toronto Star,* November 12, 2002, p. A18.

48. For a more systematic analysis of these fears concerning infringement on civil liberties, see

the vast majority of essays in *The Security of Freedom: Essays on Canada's Anti-Terrorism Bill,* Daniels et al., 2001, cited earlier.

49. This may be true in the United States as well. Cf. Peter J. Spiro, "Insinuating Constitutional and International Norms" in this volume.

50. *Suresh, Appellant,* v *The Minister of Citizenship and Immigration and the Attorney General of Canada, Respondents,* File No.: 27790.

51. *Ahani* v. *Minister of Citizenship and Immigration,* 2002 SCC 2 File No.: 27792.

52. D.L. Brown conjoined the refugee and security issue in his article, "Attacks Force Canadians to Face Their Own Threat," in the *Washington Post,* September 23, 2001, p. A36. J. Bagole et al. echoed the same perception in the *Wall Street Journal* on September 24, 2001. In Canada, many media reports shared the same sentiments. Stewart Bell wrote an article in the *National Post* entitled, "A Conduit for Terrorists" (September 13, 2001). See also Diane Francis, "Our Neighbour's Upset Over Our Loose Refugee System," *Financial Post,* September 22, 2001.

53. The 2002 Canadian Government Throne Speech in October ignored the issue of immigrants and refugees in the context of the new Smart Border Doctrine and, instead, put the entire emphasis on the free movement of goods and services. "The Canada-U.S. Smart Border Declaration contributes to both our national security and the free flow of people, goods and commerce across our shared border. The government will build on this work and increase its consular presence to expand fair and secure trade and commerce, and to brand Canada in the United States. It will continue to work bilaterally and multilaterally to resolve trade disputes over softwood lumber and agriculture."

54. Tu Thanh Na, "Fugitive in Terror Case is Arrested in Canada," *Globe and Mail,* October 17, 2001, p. 1.

55. Julian West, "Taliban Has Massive Spy Network," *National Post,* October 29, 2001, p. 7.

56. The most bizarre incident occurred when a Canadian who only spoke French drove ten meters (not miles) into the Maine section of a border town to fill his truck with gasoline without checking in with immigration. This had been the traditional practice for people living in the border-straddling town. The Canadian was arrested, held in an American prison for thirty-five days, and finally released on bail after being charged with illegal entry into the United States.

57. Globalization is not only a phenomenon of our time; it is also an object of widespread criticism. There are three types of critics of globalization. For economic dissidents of both the nationalist and the egalitarian utopian variety, globalization is equated with the exploitation of the majority of the world's population by the few rich countries using capitalist markets under the control of multilateral corporations and aided and abetted by complicit international organizations. For cultural dissidents, globalization is the effort to impose Western culture and secularization on the world's non-Western peoples and undermine established religions, profoundly held cultural values, traditional communities, and tribal ways—peoples for whom identity is sacred and rooted in a particular place and a specific history. For grotian dissidents, globalization is a radical and revolutionary change in the human condition whereby all the peoples of the world become interdependent economically, environmentally, in terms of disease control, etc., in a regime that requires an international legal and political regime to manage the situation.

58. The enlightenment promised to marry the private sphere of reason of the self-legislating autonomous individual to the public realm of rational debate as the center of the political process so that coercion would not determine any outcome. However, uncovering the contradiction rather than the coherence in the political landscape made room for an ideal alternative developed as a pure transcendental idea, a wish, a dream, an illusion or a utopia—whatever one may wish to label it, but *not* one that was a product of reasoning within the bounds of understanding,

but the product of a leap of faith. So rather than wedding internal rational thought to public debate, ideal dreams were to take advantage of social contradictions. And in the name of utopian ideals, coercive power—the very nemesis of reason and intellectual influence—prevailed both in the challenge to the new world order and in the response.

59. As an example of fragmentation in the United States after 9/11, the American INS issued visas to 105 foreign nationals in spite of the fact that their names appeared on government lists of suspected terrorists and even though a security system created in November 2001—Visas Condor—was created precisely to prevent this happening. Why? Because responsibility for intercepting such approvals shifted between the Justice Department and the FBI, the CIA, the State Department, and the multiagency Foreign Terrorist Tracking Task Force formed by President Bush in October 2001 that assumed control of the system in April 2002. Of the 38,000 "Condor" applications processed through August 1, 2002, about 280 names turned up on the antiterrorism lists. Though the State Department was given a refusal recommendation for the 200 visa applicants, the rejections arrived after the 30-day hold had expired; the visas had already been issued.

60. This was also my interpretation in the autumn of 2001. Cf. Howard Adelman, "Refugees and Border Security Post–September 11," *Refuge* 4, (August 20, 2002): 5–14; Howard Adelman, "Canadian Borders and Immigration Post-9/11," *International Migration Review* 36 no. 1 (Spring 2002): 15–28. Subsequent events have only confirmed this interpretation and allowed me to put the developments into a larger historical and theoretical context.

Praetorian Passages

1. *The Baburnama: Memoirs of Babur, Prince and Emperor,* translated, edited, and annotated by Wheeler M. Thackston. (Washington, D.C.: Smithsonian Institution Press, and New York: Oxford University Press, 1996), p. 58.

2. Kate Mallinson, "The World in 2003: The Devil's Cauldron," *Economist,* January 2003: 48.

3. See Paula R. Newberg, "The Political Economy and Displacement and Recovery: Regional Approaches to Reconstruction in Afghanistan" (Washington, D.C.: Migration Policy Institute, 2003).

4. See Rene Grousset, *The Empire of the Steppes: A History of Central Asia,* trans. Naomi Walford (New Brunswick: Rutgers University Press, 1970); David Christian, *A History of Russia, Central Asia and Mongolia,* vol. 1 of *Inner Eurasia from Prehistory to the Mongol Empire* (Oxford: Blackwell Publishers, 1998); Morris Rossabi, "The Mongols and Their Legacy," in *The Legacy of Genghis Khan: Courtly Art and Culture in Western Asia, 1256–1353,* eds. Linda Komaroff and Stefano Carboni (New York: Metropolitan Museum of Art, and New Haven: Yale University Press); Ira M. Lapidus, *A History of Islamic Societies* (Cambridge: Cambridge University Press, 1988); Beatrice Forbes Manz, *The Rise and Rule of Tamerlane* (Cambridge: Cambridge University Press, 1989); Thomas W. Lentz and Glenn D. Lowry, *Timur and the Princely Vision: Persian Art and Culture in the Fifteenth Century,* chapter 5 (Washington, D.C.: Smithsonian Institute Press, 1989); Jos L. Gommans, *The Rise of the Indo-Afghan Empire, c. 1710–1780* (Delhi: Oxford University Press, 1999, republished from E.J. Brill, 1995); Stephen Frederic Dale, *Indian Merchants and Eurasian Trade, 1600–1750* (Cambridge: Cambridge University Press, 1994); K.N. Chaudhuri, *Asia Before Europe: Economy and Civilization of the Indian Ocean from the Rise of Islam to 1750* (Cambridge: Cambridge University Press, 1990).

5. See, for example, Karl Ernest Meyer and Shareen Blair Brysac, *Tournament of Shadows: The Great Game and the Race for Empire in Central Asia* (New York: Counterpoint Press, 2000).

6. For a relatively early lament about this pattern of interaction, see Arnold J. Toynbee, *Between Oxus and Jumna,* chapter 45 (New York: Oxford University Press, 1961); Ayesha Jalal, *The State of Martial Rule: The Origins of Pakistan's Political Economy of Defence* (Cambridge: Cambridge

University Press, 1990); Hasan-Askari Rizvi, *The Military and Politics in Pakistan, 1947–88* (Lahore: Progressive Publishers, 1986).

7. See Colonel Algernon Durand, *The Making of a Frontier* (republished by Indus Publications, Karachi, 1977); on the northern boundaries, see *Imperial Gazetteer of India: A Gazetteer of Afghanistan and Nepal* (Calcutta, 1908). The Durand Line officially expired in the 1990s and adherence to the original demarcation remains thus far a matter of habitual practice.

8. Zbigniew Brzezinski, *Game Plan: How to Conduct the U.S.-Soviet Contest* (Boston: Atlantic Monthly Press, 1986).

9. See Raja Anwar, *The Tragedy of Afghanistan: A First-Hand Account* (London: Verso, 1988); Anthony Hyman, *Afghanistan Under Soviet Domination, 1964–81* (New York: St. Martin's Press, 1982); Barnett Rubin, *The Fragmentation of Afghanistan* (New Haven: Yale University Press, 1992); Riaz M. Khan, *Untying the Afghan Knot: Negotiating Soviet Withdrawal* (Durham: Duke University Press, 1991).

10. Peter Marsden, *The Taliban: War, Religion and the New Order in Afghanistan* (London: Zed Books, 1998); Ahmed Rashid, *Taliban: Militant Islam, Oil, and Fundamentalism in Central Asia* (New Haven: Yale University Press, 2000); William Maley, ed., *Fundamentalism Reborn? Afghanistan and the Taliban* (London: Hurst and Company, 1998).

11. Paula R. Newberg, "Missing the Point: Human Rights in U.S.-Pakistan Relations," (Washington, D.C.: United States Institute of Peace, 2002).

12. Regular reporting from the United Nations Drug Control Program, the U.S. Department of State, and international human rights organizations arrived at similar conclusions, albeit through vastly different analyses.

13. Brzezinski, *Game Plan*.

Migration and Security As an Issue in U.S.-European Relations

1. Christopher Bennett, "Aiding America," *NATO Review* (Winter 2001–2002).

2. The Euro-Atlantic Partnership Council (nineteen allied- and twenty-seven partner-countries) on September 12 unconditionally condemned the attacks as brutal atrocity and a threat against the associated countries' shared values. In the next few days a similar statement came from the NATO-Russia Permanent Joint Council and from the parallel NATO-Ukraine Commission.

3. For the data, see the U.S. Office of Homeland Security, *National Strategy for Homeland Security* (Washington, D.C.: Government Printing Office, July 2002).

4. United Nations, International Organization for Migration, *World Migration Report* (New York: United Nations Publications, 2000), p. 6.

5. Ibid.

6. Eurostat, *Demographic Statistics, 1999* (Brussels: 2000).

7. Organization for Economic Cooperation and Development, *Trends in International Migration. SOPEMI Annual Report* (Paris: OECD, 1998).

8. See, for instance, a number of papers in the series "Balkan Crisis Report"; F. Debie, "Balkans: une criminalité (presque) sans mafias?" *Critique internationale,* no. 12 (July 2001); D. Hobbs, "Going Down to the Global: The Local Context of Organized Crime," *The Howard Journal* 37, no. 4 (November 1998); and different chapters in P.C. Van Duyne, V. Ruggiero, M. Scheinost, V. Valkenburg, eds., *Cross-border Crime in a Changing Europe* (Tilberg, the Netherlands: Tilburg University, 2000).

9. UN International Organization for Migration, *World Migration Report,* pp. 197–200.

10. See F. Pastore and G. Sciortino, "Immigration and European Immigration Policies," in *Extending the Area of Freedom, Justice and Security Through Enlargement: Challenges for the European Union,* ed. J. Apap (forthcoming).

11. Oliver Roy, *L'Islam mondialisé* (Paris: Editions du Seuil, 2002), p. 197.

12. Roy, *L'Islam mondialisé.*

13. Michael Scott Doran, "Somebody Else's Civil War," *Foreign Affairs* 81, no. 1 (January/February 2002).

14. Such results were also in the nonpartisan survey by the Chicago Council on Foreign Relations (with the German Marshall Fund of the United States), *Worldviews 2002,* published in early September 2002.

15. For the doubts about the connection between Iraq and al Qaeda, see, for instance, Don Van Natta Jr. and David Johnston, "Portrait of a Terror Suspect: Is He the Qaeda Link to Iraq?" *International Herald Tribune,* February 10, 2003.

16. Brian Whitmore, "Bosnia Becoming a Terror-War Asset," *Boston Globe,* February 3, 2002.

War Against Havens for Terrorism

1. Nicholas Lemann, "The Next World Order," *The New Yorker,* April 1, 2002.

2. *New York Times,* February 25, 2002; Michael Klare, "Endless Military Superiority," *The Nation,* July 15, 2002, pp. 12–16; William Hartung, Frida Berrigan, and Michelle Ciarrocca, "Operation Endless Deployment," *The Nation,* October 21, 2002, pp. 21–24.

3. Ibid.

4. Herbert Butterfield, *Christianity and History* (New York: Fontana Paperback, 1957), p. 137.

5. Michael Duffey, "Does Might Make Right?" *Time,* September 30, 2002, p. 39.

6. Nicholas Lemann, "The Next World Order," *The New Yorker,* April 1, 2002.

7. Condoleezza Rice, "Life After the Cold War," *Foreign Affairs,* January/February 2000.

8. Editorial, "The Greater Nuclear Danger," *New York Times,* September 27, 2002, p. 30.

9. Bill Keller, "A Beautiful Friendship," *New York Times,* May 18, 2002.

10. John Ikenberry, "America's Imperial Ambition," *Foreign Affairs* 81, no. 5 (September/October 2002); Hendrik Hertzberg, "Manifesto," *The New Yorker,* October 14–21, 2002, pp. 63–66; William Pfaff, "The Temptation of Hegemony: Geopolitics Have Changed For The Worse," *International Herald Tribune,* September 11, 2002.

11. Ikenberry, "American's Imperial Ambition."

12. Simon Schama, "The Nation: Mourning in America; A Whiff of Dread for the Land of Hope," *New York Times,* September 15, 2002.

Globalization, Low-Intensity Conflict, and Protracted Statelessness/Refugeehood

1. Bertil Lintner, "Bangladesh: Championing Islamist Extremism," *South Asia Intelligence Review: Weekly Assessments and Briefings* 1, no. 15 (September 16, 2002); Bertil Lintner, "Is religious extremism on the rise in Bangladesh?" *Jane's Intelligence Review,* May 2002.

2. I have used "stateless people" and "refugees" somewhat synonymously, not because I find the legal distinction weak and lifeless (see Imtiaz Ahmed, "Globalization, State and Political Process in South Asia," in *Globalization and Non-Traditional Security in South Asia,* ed. Abdur Rob Khan

[Dhaka: Academic Press, 2001]) but to highlight that in most cases one leads to the other, with the bulk of the stateless and refugees living in constant fear, uncertainty, and immense poverty.

3. Jeremy Brecher, Tim Costello, and Brendan Smith, *Globalization From Below: The Power of Solidarity* (Cambridge, Mass: South End Press, 2000), Ahmed, "Globalization, State and Political Process in South Asia."

4. Nirad C. Chaudhuri, *The East Is East And the West Is West* (Calcutta: Mitra & Ghosh, 1996), pp. 1, 5.

5. Brecher, *Globalization From Below*, 10.

6. James H. Mittelman, *The Globalization Syndrome: Transformation and Resistance* (Princeton, N.J.: Princeton University Press, 2000), p. 208.

7. Ibid., p. 214.

8. Antonio Gramsci, *Selections from the Prison Notebooks* (New York: International Publishers, 1971); Imtiaz Ahmed, *State & Foreign Policy: India's Role in South Asia* (New Delhi: Vikas Publishing House, 1993).

9. Mittelman, *The Globalization Syndrome*, p. 209.

10. Burma-American Democratic Alliance, "Burma: 40 Years of Dictatorship," leaflet, 2002, p. 2, http://www.badasf.org/2002BHRD-flyer.htm.

11. Bureau of Democracy, Human Rights, and Labor, U.S. State Department, "Country Reports on Human Rights Practices—2001," (Washington D.C.: Government Printing Office, March 4, 2001), p. 60.

12. Burma-American Democratic Alliance, "Burma: 40 Years of Dictatorship"; Louise Brown, *Sex Slaves: The Trafficking of Women in Asia* (London: Virago, 2000).

13. Ahmed, Imtiaz, "Travails of Refugees across Bangladesh-India Border," in *Regional Security in South Asia: The Ethno-Sectarian Dimensions,* ed. Nancy Jetly (New Delhi: Lancers Books, 1999), p. 439.

14. Christina Fink, *Living Silence: Burma under Military Rule* (Dhaka: University Press Limited, 2001), p. 137.

15. DEA Intelligence Division, Office of International Intelligence, Europe, Asia Africa Strategic Unit, *Burma Country Brief,* Drug Intelligence Brief, Washington D.C., May 2002, p. 1.

16. Ibid., p. 2.

17. DEA Intelligence Division, *Burma Country Brief,* 1; Shwe Lu Maung, *Burma: Nationalism and Ideology* (Dhaka: University Press Limited, 1989).

18. Ibid., p. 4.

19. Chandan Nandy, "World Bank Study Indicts BSF, Customs," *The Telegraph,* January 21, 1995.

20. Money laundering here is understood as changing the form and ownership of monies generated from illegal sources. For a detailed exposition, see Giri Raj Shah, *Encyclopedia of Narcotic Drugs & Psychotropic Substances* 2 (New Delhi: Gyan Publishing House, 1998), pp. 491–511.

21. This refers to the notorious scheme of Charles Ponzi, an Italian migrant, who promised U.S. investors on the East Coast that he could double their money in just ninety days. This attracted 40,000 investors and a great deal of excitement, but soon it was found that it was a farce. The investors in the process lost millions of dollars. See Kyi May Kaung, "Bank Crisis Reeks of a Ponzi Scheme," *Irrawaddy,* February 26, 2003.

22. Kaung, "Bank Crisis Reeks of a Ponzi Scheme."

23. DEA Intelligence Division, *Burma Country Brief,* p. 11.

24. Georg Witschel, "Global Terrorism: Trends and Response," *RCSS* (Regional Centre for Strategic Studies, Colombo) *Newsletter* 9, no. 1 (January 2003): p. 2.

25. *Daily Star* (Beirut), October 19, 2000, p. 10.

26. *Daily Star,* p. 12; Husain, "Armed & Dangerous: Small Arms and Explosives Trafficking in Bangladesh."

27. Jasgit Singh, "Light Weapons and Conflict in Southern Asia," in *Light Weapons and International Security* ed. Jasgit Singh (Delhi: Indian Pugwash Society, 1995), p. 59.

28. This is, however, an estimated figure. See Ministry of National Planning and Economic Development, the Government of the Union of Myanmar, *1997 Statistical Yearbook* (Yangon: Central Statistical Organization, 1997), p. 22.

29. Martin Smith, *Burma: Insurgency and the Politics of Ethnicity* (London: Zed Books and Dhaka: University Press Limited, 1991), p. 30.

30. Abdur Razzaque and Mahfuzul Haque, *A Tale of Refugees: Rohingyas in Bangladesh* (Dhaka: Centre for Human Rights, 1995), p. 14; Maung, *Burma: Nationalism and Ideology,* p. 4.

31. Smith, *Burma.*

32. Razzaque and Haque, *A Tale of Refugees;* Tessa Piper, "Myanmar: Muslims from Rakhine State: Exit and Return," *WRITENET,* Practical Management (U.K.), (December 1993): p. 2.

33. As one governmental press release noted (U Ohn Gyaw, "Press Release," Ministry of Foreign Affairs, Government of Myanmar, Yangon, February 21, 1992):

> In actual fact, although there are 135 national races in Myanmar today, the so-called Rohingya people are not one of them. Historically, there has never been a "Rohingya" race in Myanmar. Since the first Anglo-American War in 1824, people of Muslim faith from the adjacent country illegally entered Myanmar Naing-Ngan, particularly Rakhine State. Being illegal immigrants they do not hold immigration papers like other nationals of the country.

34. Joe Cummings and Tony Wheeler, *Myanmar: A Lonely Planet Travel Survival Kit* (Hawthorn, Victoria: Lonely Planet Publications, 1996), p. 364.

35. Ibid.

36. Razzaque and Haque, *A Tale of Refugees,* p. 14.

37. Cummings and Wheeler, *Myanmar,* p. 365.

38. Smith, *Burma,* p. 41.

39. A radio program in "Rohingya language" was also conducted during this period, but after the 1962 military coup it was stopped. This information is based on the author's discussion with some "researchers" in Yangon (Myanmar).

40. There are also a large number of undocumented illegal refugees living outside the camps in the Cox's Bazaar area of Bangladesh. No official statistics are found, although unofficially some put the figure between 30,000 to 100,000. For the lower figure of 30,000, see Amnesty International, "Myanmar/Bangladesh: Rohingyas—The Search for Safety," International Secretariat, London, September 1997. The higher figure was cited to the author by an UNHCR official who wanted to remain anonymous.

41. Medecins Sans Frontieres, for instance, noted (see "MSF's concerns on the repatriation of Rohingya refugees from Bangladesh to Burma," MSF, Amsterdam/Paris, 1 May 1995, pp. 2–5):

> In June 1994 the GOB gave permission to the UNHCR to start interviewing in all the camps. UNHCR found out in one test-run camp that 23% of the refugees wanted to be repatriated. In July 1994, UNHCR suddenly changed its policy. The agency changed from information sessions to promotion of repatriation, stating that the situation in Burma is "conducive for return." The willingness to repatriate allegedly increased to

about 95%. UNHCR also abandoned the system of private interviewing and implemented a system of mass registration for voluntary repatriation. . . .

MSF believes that the repatriation of Rohingyas is not voluntary and that the procedures set by the UNHCR do not guarantee that the refugees are able to take a decision out of free will. MSF is concerned that the UNHCR is trying out a new repatriation policy for countries *where a fundamental change of circumstances has not taken place.* MSF questions if this policy fits the statutory UNHCR-mandate of voluntary repatriation" (emphasis added).

42. Kirsten Young, "Mission Report—Bangladesh/Myanmar," UNHCR (United Nations High Commissioner for Refugees), in-house Circulation, March 19–28, 1995; Imtiaz Ahmed, "Refugees and Security: The Experience of Bangladesh" in *Refugees and Regional Security in South Asia,* eds. S.D. Muni and L.R. Baral, (New Delhi: Konark Publishers, 1996); Amnesty International, "Myanmar/Bangladesh: Rohingyas—The Search for Safety," International Secretariat, London, September 1997.

43. In other parts of the world, either with nationality of another or host country or simply as illegal migrant.

44. Smith, *Burma,* p. 241.

45. Giri Raj Shah, *Encyclopaedia of Narcotic Drugs & Psychotropic Substances* 2 (New Delhi: Gyan Publishing House, 1998), p. 515.

46. Federation of American Scientists, "Burmese Terrorist Groups," 2003. www.fas.org.

47. Praveen Swami, "APHC: The Nexus with Terror," *South Asia Intelligence Review: Weekly Assessments and Briefings* 1, no. 31 (February 17, 2003): p. 7.

48. *Daily Star* (Beirut), November 30, 2002, p. 12.

49. It could not forge Bengali nationalism based on language mainly because the Rohingyas speak Bengali with a strong Chittagonian dialect. The Bengali language that is central to the *bhadrasantan* or the bourgeois tongue and Bengali nationalism is relatively elitist and markedly different from the Chittagonian dialect.

50. Imtiaz Ahmed, "Limits of Civil Society: Rohingya Refugees, Locals and the Passage to Unsettlement, *South Asian Refugee Watch* (Colombo and Dhaka) 1, no. 1, July 1999.

51. *Daily Star* (Beirut), February 7, 1992; *Daily Ajker Kagoj* (Dhaka), August 25, 1992; *India Today* (New Dheli), September 12, 1992.

52. *Pakistan Times,* May 22, 1992.

53. Lintner, "Bangladesh: Championing Islamist Extremism."

54. Naw Seng, "Exiled Muslims Deny Taliban Connections," *Irrawaddy,* August 9, 2002.

55. See note 40.

56. Medecins Sans Frontieres, "MSF's concerns on the repatriation of Rohingya refugees from Bangladesh to Burma."

57. Lintner, "Is religious extremism on the rise in Bangladesh?"

58. Myanmar Information Committee, "Burma Committed to Work with ASEAN, US on All Forms of Terrorism," August 9, 2002 www.burmanet.org; Seng, "Exiled Muslims Deny Taliban Connections."

59. August Gribbin, *Washington Times,* November 14, 1999.

60. Ibid.

61. Imtiaz Ahmed, "Electoral Process in Bangladesh: Rationales for Reforms," in *Comparative*

Electoral Processes in South Asia, eds. Devendra Raj Panday, et al. (Kathmandu: Nepal South Asia Centre, 1999): p. 24.

The Jewish Question

* Prepared for a workshop on The Migrations of Threat: National Security After September 11, Social Science Research Council, Washington, D.C., November 16, 2002. An earlier draft of the paper was presented as the 2002 Goldman Lecture at Georgetown University, April 17, 2002. A second draft was crafted with Barry Bristman as part of the project "who speaks for the Jews and with what authority."

1. See Yossi Shain, "American Jews and the Construction of Israel's Jewish Identity," *Diaspora* 9, no. 2 (Fall 2000): pp. 163–202.

2. David Harris, "Letter from One Jew to Another," October 29, 2002, www.ajc.org.

3. Clyde Haberman, "Among Jews, Urge to Panic is Premature," *New York Times,* June 18, 2002, p. 21.

4. This quote was related to journalist Daniel Ben-Simon.

5. Summers's speech is available online at http://president.harvard.edu/speeches/2002/morningprayers.html.

6. See Marcella Bombardieri, "On Campuses, Critics of Israel Fend off a Label," *Boston Globe,* September 21, 2002. Also see Elli Wohlgelertner, "Take Back the University," *Jerusalem Post,* August 9, 2002.

7. The Uncomfortable Question of Anti-Semitism," *New York Times Magazine,* 4 November 2001.

8. William Safire, "The German Problem," *New York Times,* September 19, 2002.

9. Herb Keinon, "French FM: US Jewry more 'intransigent' than Israel, *Jerusalem Post,* April 25, 2002.

10. Jennifer Harper, "Buchanan's new magazine aims to rescue 'hijacked' right," *Washington Times,* September 25, 2002.

11. Rosen, "The Uncomfortable Question of Anti-Semitism," *New York Times Magazine,* 4 November 2001, p. 48.

12. See Michael Slackman, "Arab Forum Assails Jews, 9/11 'Propaganda'," *Los Angeles Times,* August 31, 2002. See also "The Big Lie," downloaded September 6, 2002 from CBS.com at www.cbsnews.com/stories/2002/09/04/60II/printable520768.shtml.

13. See Lawrence F. Kaplan, "Toxic Talk on War," *Washington Post,* February 18, 2003.

14. *Daily Telegraph* (London), October 21, 2002.

15. See Michael Ignatieff, "The Burden" *New York Times Magazine,* pp. 26–27.

16. For survey data that shows the widespread feeling of vulnerability among American Jews, see Steven M. Cohen, "The more Jewish, the more vulnerable," *Ha'aretz* (Jerusalem), February 2, 2002.

17. Haym Soloveitcik, "Migration, Acculturation and the New Role of Texts in the Haredi World," in *Accounting For Fundamentalism: The Dynamic Character of Movements,* eds. Martin E. Marty and R. Scott Appleby, (Chicago: University of Chicago Press, 1994), p. 221.

18. Alan Dowty, *The Jewish State: A Century Later* (San Francisco: Californian University Press, 1999), p. 25.

19. Theodor Herzl, "The Jewish State," in *Nationalism Reader,* ed. Omar Dahbour and Micheline Ishay, (New Jersey: Humanities Press International, Inc, 1995).

20. Albert Einstein, *Ideas and Opinions,* (New York: Bonanza Books, 1954), p. 172.

21. Bernard Wasserstein, "Anti-Semitism and Anti-Americanism," *Chronicle of Higher Education,* Review, September 28, 2001.

22. Yael Zrubavel, *Recovered Roots, Collective Memory and the Making of Israeli National Tradition,* (Chicago: Chicago University Press, 1995), pp. 25–26.

23. Yigal Elam, *The End of Judaism: The religion-Nation and the Realm* (Hebrew) (Tel Aviv: Yidiotsfarim, 2000).

24. This vision was well articulated by historian Jacob Talmon in the 1960s, well before the Russian immigration came to pass.

25. David Hartman, *Israelis and the Jewish Tradition: An Ancient People Debating Its Future,* (New Haven: Yale University Press, 2000), pp. 151–52.

26. See Larry Tye, *Home Lands: Portraits of the New Jewish Diaspora* (New York: Henry Holt & Company, 2001). German Foreign Minister Joschka Fischer called the rebuilding of a Jewish community in Germany and the reaction of Germans to it as his country's "second chance." Incredibly, Berlin is the fastest growing Jewish community in Europe. Jewish life was becoming normalized within the new structures of Europe and globalization. Mark Shlyak, a Ukrainian Jew, comments, "I like the Jewish state and think the return of Jews to their historical model is a big step and a great step. But the strength and influence of the Jewish people today is mainly expressed by the fact that they live across the world and that they are influencing the way other countries believe and live. The task of helping the diaspora, of creating the conditions in the diaspora that will let communities like this flower again, is not any less important than Jews emigrating to Israel."

27. Allen Dershowitz, *Chutzpah,* (Boston: Little &, Brown, 1991), p. 9.

28. See Yvonne Yazbeck Haddad, "American Foreign Policy in the Middle east and Its Impact on the Identity of Arab Muslims in the United State," in *The Muslims of America,* ed. Yvonne Yazbeck Haddad, (New York: Oxford University Press, 1991), pp. 217–35.

29. David Vital, *A People Apart, A Political History of the Jews in Europe: 1789–1939* (Oxford: Oxford University Press, 1999), pp. 662.

30. On this development see Dan Schufeftan, "Voice of Palestine: The New Ideology of Israeli Arabs," *Azure* 14 (Winter 2003): pp. 73–106.

31. Jeffrey Goldberg, "In the Party of God," *The New Yorker,* October 14 and 21, 2002, pp. 190–191.

32. Bernard Lewis, *What Went Wrong: Western Impact and Middle Eastern Response* (Oxford: Oxford University Press, 2001), p. 154.

33. *The New Yorker,* November 19, 2001, p. 56.

34. In a series of articles published in December 2002 in Egypt's semiofficial Al-Ahram newspaper, Osama el-Baz, the Egyptian president's political adviser, criticized the anti-Jewish sentiment being expressed in the Arab world. El-Baz wrote that Arab writers have enough evidence to support the Palestinian cause without resorting to racist-like attacks against Jews and "reviving old, negative European myths such as . . . describing Jews as sons of monkeys and pigs." "We have to understand that whenever we hurt Jews, we are committing a fatal mistake as attacking them reflects a racist tendency [in Arab societies] that may harm both our national interests and the Palestinian cause," *Associated Press,* December 31, 2002.

35. *New York Times,* op-ed, February 4, 2002.

36. Ori Nir, *Ha'aretz* (Jerusalem), February 14, 2002.

37. Bryan Appleyard, *London Sunday Times,* Sept 23, 2001.

38. Karl Marx, "On the Jewish Question," in *The Marx-Engels Reader,* 2nd edition, ed. Robert C. Tucker, (New York: W.W. Norton and Co., 1978), p. 49.

39. Walter Russell Mead, "Review Essay: Why Do They Hate Us?" *Foreign Affairs* 82, no. 2 (March/April 2003): p. 141.

40. During the Asian economic downturn of a few years ago, Malaysian Prime Minister Mahatir Mohamed accused international financier George Soros, a Hungarian Jew, with deliberately causing the crisis as a means of keeping Asians and Muslims down. In the current reality, even Israel's vision of a New Middle East was quickly interpreted as a Jewish attempt to dominate the Arab-Muslim world. Interestingly enough, the Middle Eastern backlash against globalization, which Islamists often articulate as opposition to American/Israeli domination, has also been welcomed by ultra-Orthodox Jews within Israel, who feel threatened by globalization. universalizing cultural and economic forces.

41. Cited in David Hazony, "Rome's New Empire," *Azure* 14 (Winter 2003): p. 19.

42. See Irwin Cotler, "Human Rights and the New Anti-Jewishness: Sounding the Alarm," The Jewish People Policy Planning Institute, Jerusalem, November 2002, p. 3.

43. See Robbie Sabel, "The Cynicism of the Belgians," *Ha'aretz* (Jerusalem), February 20, 2002.

44. From a debate on anti-Semitism, The New Atlantic Initiative, American Enterprise Institute, Washington D.C., October 30, 2002.

45. On this point see Yoram Hazony's, *The Jewish State: The Struggle for Israel's Soul* (New York: Basic Books, 2000).

46. See Steven Gold, *The Israeli Diaspora* (New York: Routledge, 2002).

47. Alan Dowty, "Israel Foreign Policy and the Jewish Question," *MERIA Journal* 3, vol. 1, (March 1999): p. 4.

48. Dana Mibank: "Group Urges Pro-Israel Leaders' Silence on Iraq," *Washington Post,* November 27, 2002, p. A13.

49. Jim Hoagland, "Chirac's Temptation," *Washington Post,* February 27, 2003, p. A27; Also see Daniel Ben Simon, "Uneasy calm on the French Front," *Ha'aretz,* February 28, 2003.

50. Max Weber, *Economy and Society,* (1914), p. 591.

51. J.J. Goldberg, *Jewish Power: Inside the American Jewish Establishment* (Reading, Mass.: Addison-Wesley, 1996), p. 4.

52. Yossi Shain and Barry Bristman, "The Jewish Security Dilemna," *Orbis* 46, vol. 1 (Winter 2002): p. 61.

53. Israeli Radio Reshet B, March 4, 2002, 7:00 PM.

54. *The New Republic,* April 4, 2002.

Impact of September 11 Attacks on Arab and Muslim Communities in the United States

*This article is based on the findings of an ongoing ethnographic study funded by the Russell Sage Foundation of the impact on the events of September 11 on the Muslim and Arab community in metropolitan Chicago.

1. Some 83,000 persons living in the U.S. underwent call-in special registration, according to the Department of Homeland Security. I estimate that at least 20,000 additional Arabs and Muslims

nationwide have been affected by one or more of the numerous Post-9/11 national security initiatives.

2. See Fred Tsao and Rhoda Rae Gutierrez, *Losing Ground* (Chicago: Illinois Coalition for Immigrant and Refugee Rights, 2003) for a list of the thirty–seven initiatives, policy changes, and laws.

3. See, ibid.; Council on American-Islamic Relations, *Guilt by Association* (Washington D.C.: CAIR, 2003); United States Department of Justice, Office of Inspector General, *The September 11 Detainees* (Washington DC: GPO, 2003); American Arab Anti-Discrimination Committee, *Report on Hate Crimes and Discrimination Against Arab Americans: The Post-September 11 Backlash* [September 11, 2001, to October 11, 2002] (Washington D.C.: ADC, 2002); Michael Isikoff, "The FBI Says, Count the Mosques," *Newsweek,* February 3, 2003; Louise Cainkar, "No Longer Invisible: Arab and Muslim Exclusion After September 11," *Middle East Report* 224, fall (Washington D.C.: Middle East Report and Information Project, 2002), available at http://www.merip.org/mer/mer224/224_cainkar.html.

4. David Cole and James Dempsey, *Terrorism and the Constitution* (New York: The New Press, 2002).

5. Ibid., 151.

6. The term "investigation dragnet" is used by the Council on American-Islamic Relations in its 2003 report: *Guilt by Association.*

7. Ibid. CAIR reports a decrease in discrimination complaints associated with airline profiling and an increase in complaints referencing actions of the federal government.

8. See, e.g., Frank Main, "Man Nabbed in 9/11 Probe Gets 8 Months," *Chicago Sun-Times,* September 4, 2002; Laurie Cohen and Kim Barker, "Court Deals U.S. Defeat in Islamic Fund Case" *Chicago Tribune,* February 6, 2003.

9. See, e.g., American Civil Liberties Union, *The ACLU Defends Freedom: Civil Liberties After 9/11. A Historical Perspective on Protecting Liberty in Times of Crisis.* (New York: ACLU, 2002); Ann Beeson and Jameel Jaffer, *Unpatriotic Acts: The FBI's Power to Rifle Through Your Personal Belongings Without Telling You* (New York: American Civil Liberties Union, 2003); American Civil Liberties Union, *Seeking the Truth From Justice. Patriot Propaganda: The Justice Department's Campaign to Mislead the Public About the USA PATRIOT Act* (New York: ACLU, 2003).

10. David Cole and James Dempsey, 2002, *Terrorism and the Constitution.*

11. Ibid.

12. There are volumes of material on this topic. See, e.g., Michael Suleiman, ed., *Arabs in America: Building a New Future* (Philadelphia: Temple University Press, 1999). For a summary, see Louise Cainkar, "No Longer Invisible."

13. "Non-immigrant aliens" includes all immigrants who are inspected by the INS upon entry to the United States who are not US citizens, permanent residents, applicants for permanent residency, or applicants for asylum. The rule for special registration excludes non-immigrants who are diplomats, persons working with international organizations, and a few other narrow categories of non-immigrants (categories A and G).

14. INS memo (undated) HQINS 70/28 from Johnny Williams, Executive Associate Commissioner, Office of Field Operations.

15. The *Washington Post* reported on November 21, 2003, that the Department of Homeland Security was "preparing to abandon" the annual reporting aspect of the program in response to complaints from lawyers and advocates that registrants were not properly informed of this requirement and that it would put into motion another wave of removals for those who do not comply. Dan Eggen, "U.S. Set to Revise How It Tracks Some Visitors/Muslims Have Protested

Use of Registration," *Washington Post*, November 21, 2003. On December 1, 2003, the program was cancelled.

16. U.S. Department of Homeland Security, "Fact Sheet: US-VISIT Program" May 19, 2003.

17. See, e.g., Council on American-Islamic Relations, *Guilt by Association;* United States Department of Justice, *The September 11 Detainees;* Fred Tsao and Rhoda Rae Gutierrez, *Losing Ground;* Michael Isikoff, "The FBI Says, Count the Mosques"; Louise Cainkar, "No Longer Invisible";

18. Personal communication with Carol Hallstrom, Department of Homeland Security, Community Relations, Chicago, June 2003. Also see Richard Swarms, "More than 13,000 May Face Deportation," *New York Times*, June 7, 2003.

19. Personal communication with Carol Hallstrom.

20. Reuters, December 18, 2002. All persons placed in removal proceedings are permitted an administrative hearing.

21. Reuters, December 18, 2002; BBC News Online, December 19, 2002; *Newsday*, December 13, 2002.

22. For a detailed discussion of the special registration program and its historical precedents, see Louise Cainkar, "Special Registration: A Fervor for Muslims," *Journal of Islamic Law and Culture* 7, no. 2, 2003.

23. 67 Federal Register 52585 (Washington D.C.: USGPO).

24. Immigration and Naturalization Service "Special Registration Q&A", December 13, 2002; at www.ins.usdoj.gov.

25. 8 Code of Federal Regulations 214.1. (Washington D.C.: USGPO).

26. 8 Code of Federal Regulations 264.1 (f) (9), (Washington D.C.: USGPO). This presumption can be overcome. Consular officials are initially in charge of making this determination.

27. The Smith Act required that all aliens over the age of thirteen be fingerprinted and registered, and required parents and legal guardians to register those thirteen years of age and younger. In turn, aliens received a numbered Alien Registration Receipt Card from the INS proving registry and were required to carry this card with them at all times. This law is still on the books. This would mean that always carrying one's passport bearing registration information is mandatory, although it is not currently enforced.

28. Public Law 97–116.

29. "Need for Legislation," U.S. House Judiciary Committee Report No. 97-264, October 2, 1981.

30. See Alex Gourevitch, "Detention Disorder," *American Prospect*, January 21, 2003. Five hundred and fifty-six foreign nationals were deported during the Palmer Raids.

31. United States Department of Justice, *The September 11 Detainees*, p. 105.

32. Persons "out of status" are thought to be 40 to 45 percent of the estimated 8 million undocumented persons in the United States. The rest are persons who "entered without inspection." Persons in the latter category are not subject to special registration; it is assumed to contain relatively few Arabs and Muslims.

33. The outcome of the Department of Homeland Security removal hearings remains to be seen. Persons with valid applications for immigration benefits with close dates may be allowed to stay.

34. Data sent by staff at the U.S. Immigration and Naturalization Service (now defunct).

35. See study by the Pew Research Center for the People and the Press, cited in Christopher Marquis, "World's View of U.S. Sours After Iraq War, Poll Finds," *New York Times*, June 3, 2003.

36. Council on American-Islamic Relations, *The Status of Muslim Civil Rights in the United*

States: Stereotypes and Civil Liberties (Washington, D.C. April, 2002); South Asian Leaders of Tomorrow, "American Backlash: Terrorists Bring War Home in More Ways Than One," (Washington, D.C., September 28, 2001).

37. Mohamed Nimer, "Muslims in American After 9-11," *Journal of Islamic Law and Culture* 7, no. 2, 2003.

38. Council on American-Islamic Relations, *Guilt by Association.*

39. Council on American-Islamic Relations press release, October 6, 2003.

40. Arab American Institute Foundation, *Profiling and Pride: Arab American Attitudes and Behavior Since September 11* (Washington, D.C.: July, 2002).

41. Daniel Smith, "When 'For a While' Becomes Forever," *Weekly Defense Monitor,* October 2, 2001.

42. *Chicago Sun-Times,* October 2, 2001.

43. *News Sun* (Ill.), December 20, 2001.

44. Gallup News Service, August 8, 2002.

45. ABCNEWS.com, October 28, 2002, http://www.religioustolerance.org.

46. Mathew Lee, "US Evangelist says Muslims 'Worse Than Nazis,' " *Agence France Press,* November 12, 2002.

47. William Lind and Paul Weyrich, *Why Islam is a Threat to America and The West* (Washington D.C.: Free Congress Foundation, 2002).

48. Mohamed Nimer, "Muslims in American After 9–11."

49. See, e.g., Omeira Helal and Arsalan Iftikhar, "Pipes Nomination a Slap in the Face for Muslims," *San Francisco Chronicle,* May 11, 2003.

50. See Mohamed Nimer, "Muslims in American After 9–11." For more documentation of these types of comments, see American Arab Anti-Discrimination Committee, *Report on Hate Crimes and Discrimination against Arab Americans: The Post September 11 Backlash.*

51. Bill Tammeus, "Let's Not Repeat the Hysteria of McCarthyism," *Kansas City Star,* May 24, 2003; Omeira Helal and Arsalan Iftikhar "Pipes Nomination a Slap in the Face for Muslims."

52. Ibid.

53. I use the term "immigrant-origin Muslim communities" to make a distinction between Muslims whose family roots are in Africa, Asia, and the Middle East and who brought Islam with them upon migration to the United States and the often-called indigenous Muslims, who are mostly African-Americans and Euro-American converts. While affected by post-9/11 events, the latter group has been under less federal government scrutiny than the former, as far as we know.

54. Council on American-Islamic Relations, *Guilt by Association.*

55. See, e.g., Jack Shaheen, *The TV Arab: Arab and Muslim Stereotyping in American Popular Culture* (Bowling Green, Ohio: Bowling Green State University Press, 1984) and Jack Shaheen, *Reel Bad Arabs: How Hollywood Vilifies a People,* (New York, Olive Branch Press, 2001).

56. See Louise Cainkar, "Targeting Muslims, at Ashcroft's Discretion," *Middle East Report On-Line* (Washington D.C.), March 14, 2003, available at http://www.merip.org/mero/mero031403. html; and Louise Cainkar, "A Fervor for Muslims: Special Registration."

57. For other indicators, see Louise Cainkar, "No Longer Invisible."

58. See, e.g., Nabeel Abraham, "Anti-Arab Racism and Violence in the U.S.," in Ernest McCarus, ed., *The Development of Arab American Identity* (Ann Arbor, Mich.: University of Michigan Press, 1994).

59. Council on American-Islamic Relations, "Poll: Majority of Muslims Suffered Post-9/11 Bias," (Washington, D.C.: August 21, 2002).

60. "Powell calls U.S. 'Judeo-Christian,' Then Amends," at *WashingtonPost.com*, September 23, 2003.

IR Theory and Epochal Events

* Thanks to Thomas Biersteker and John Tirman for comments on an earlier version of this chapter.

1. Two recent state-of-the-art handbooks—one for migration (Josh DeWind, Charles Hirschman, and Philip Kasinitz, eds., *The Handbook of International Migration: The American Experience* [New York: Russell Sage, 1999]) and one for IR (Walter Carlsnaes, Thomas Risse, and Beth Simmons, eds., *Handbook of International Relations* [London: Sage Publications, 2002]), largely ignore the potential contributions from the other subfield.

2. See www.ssrc.org for an excellent overview of these various initiatives.

3. "Symposium on September 11," *International Organization, Dialog-IO* (Spring 2002).

4. "The Threat of Terrorism: U.S. Policy after September 11," *International Security* 26 (Winter 2001/2002).

5. Bruce Jentleson, "The Need for Praxis: Bringing Policy Relevance Back In," *International Security* 26 (Spring 2002): 169, citing an unnamed Washington policy maker.

6. For example, see Richard Ned Lebow and Thomas Risse-Kappen, eds., *International Relations Theory and the End of the Cold War* (New York: Columbia University Press, 1995); Robert English, "Power, Ideas and New Evidence on the Cold War's End: A Reply to Brooks and Wohlforth," *International Security* 26 (Spring 2002).

7. While much of this research eventually came to be grouped under the banner of constructivism, it has roots that extend well beyond American IR and well before 1989. For excellent discussions, see Stefano Guzzini, "A Reconstruction of Constructivism in International Relations," *European Journal of International Relations* 6 (June 2000); Emanuel Adler, "Constructivism and International Relations," in *Handbook of International Relations,* eds. Walter Carlsnaes, Thomas Risse, and Beth Simmons (London: Sage Publications, 2002); Ted Hopf, *Social Construction of International Politics: Identities and Foreign Policies, Moscow, 1955 & 1999* (Ithaca, N.Y.: Cornell University Press, 2002), chapter 6; and Maja Zehfuss, *Constructivism in International Relations: The Politics of Reality* (Cambridge: Cambridge University Press, 2002), chapter 1.

8. Jeffrey T. Checkel, *Ideas and International Political Change: Soviet/Russian Behavior and the End of the Cold War* (New Haven: Yale University Press, 1997); Matthew Evangelista, *Unarmed Forces: The Transnational Movement to End the Cold War* (Ithaca, N.Y.: Cornell University Press, 1999), who highlight ideational factors.

9. Alexandra Gheciu, "Security Institutions as Agents of Socialization? NATO and Post–Cold War Central and Eastern Europe," in *International Institutions and Socialization in the "New" Europe,* ed. Jeffrey T. Checkel (book/journal manuscript in preparation, February 2004).

10. Rey Koslowski and Friedrich Kratochwil, "Understanding Change in International Politics: The Soviet Empire's Demise and the International System," *International Organization* 48 (Spring 1994).

11. For a critical discussion, see Hopf, *Social Construction of International Politics,* chapter 1.

12. Stephen Brooks and William Wohlforth, "Power, Globalization and the End of the Cold War: Reevaluating a Landmark Case for Ideas," *International Security* 25 (Winter 2000/2001); Jeffrey T. Checkel and Andrew Moravcsik, "A Constructivist Research Program in EU Studies?" (*Forum*

Debate) *European Union Politics* 2 (June 2001); Margarita Petrova, "The End of the Cold War: A Battle or Bridging Ground between Rational and Ideational Approaches to International Relations (Review Article)," *European Journal of International Relations* 9 (March 2003).

13. Thomas Risse, Stephen Ropp, and Kathryn Sikkink, eds., *The Power of Human Rights: International Norms and Domestic Change* (Cambridge: Cambridge University Press, 1999); Matthew Evangelista, "Norms, Heresthetics, and the End of the Cold War," *Journal of Cold War Studies* 3 (Winter 2001); James Fearon and Alexander Wendt, "Rationalism v. Constructivism: A Skeptical View," in *Handbook of International Relations,* eds. Walter Carlsnaes, Thomas Risse, and Beth Simmons (London: Sage Publications, 2002).

14. Brooks and Wohlforth, *Power, Globalization and the End of the Cold War.*

15. Migration theorists (such as Douglas Massey, "Why Does Immigration Occur? A Theoretical Synthesis," in *The Handbook of International Migration: The American Experience,* eds. Josh DeWind, Charles Hirschman, and Philip Kasinitz [New York: Russell Sage, 1999], pp. 47–50) are now making similar calls for theories that synthesize arguments from several different approaches—in particular, through the use of temporal sequencing.

16. See also Joseph Jupille, James Caporaso, and Jeffrey T. Checkel, "Integrating Institutions: Rationalism, Constructivism and the Study of the European Union—Introduction," *Comparative Political Studies* 36 (February/March 2003).

17. For an overview, see DeWind, Hirschman and Kasinitz, eds., *The Handbook of International Migration.*

18. The comments here and later are a reflection on my own attempts to link IR and migration, in a project exploring the spread of new citizenship/membership norms in contemporary Europe. Jeffrey T. Checkel, "Norms, Institutions and National Identity in Contemporary Europe," *International Studies Quarterly* 43 (March 1999), for example.

19. While international relations scholars have made progress on the latter over the past two decades, much work still remains. Peter Gourevitch, "Domestic Politics and International Relations," in *Handbook of International Relations,* ed. Walter Carlsnaes, Thomas Risse, and Beth Simmons (London: Sage Publications, 2002).

20. Yasmin Soysal, *Limits of Citizenship: Migrants and Postnational Membership in Europe* (Chicago: University of Chicago Press, 1994).

21. Helen Milner, "Rationalizing Politics: The Emerging Synthesis of International, American and Comparative Politics," *International Organization* 52 (Autumn 1998).

22. Lisa Martin and Beth Simmons, "Theories and Empirical Studies of International Institutions," *International Organization* 52 (Autumn 1998).

23. See also John Meyer and David Strang, "Institutional Conditions for Diffusion," *Theory and Society* 22 (August 1993).

24. Gary Freeman, "The Decline of Sovereignty? Politics and Immigration Restriction in Liberal States," in *Challenge to the Nation-State: Immigration in Western Europe and the United States,* ed. Christian Joppke (Oxford: Oxford University Press, 1998).

25. See also Helen Milner, "International Theories of Cooperation Among Nations: Strengths and Weaknesses (Review Article)," *World Politics* 44 (April 1992).

26. Massey, "Why Does Immigration Occur?" pp. 36–47; see also Christian Joppke, "Why Liberal States Accept Unwanted Immigration," *World Politics* 50 (January 1998), pp. 292–93 and passim. Soysal (*Limits of Citizenship*) and Rogers Brubaker (*Nationalism Reframed: Nationhood and the National Question in the New Europe* [Cambridge: Cambridge University Press, 1996]) would be the (partial) exceptions proving the rule.

27. Robert Putnam, "Diplomacy and Domestic Politics: The Logic of Two-Level Games," *International Organization* 42 (Summer 1988).

28. Margaret Keck and Kathryn Sikkink, *Activists Beyond Borders: Advocacy Networks in International Politics* (Ithaca, N.Y.: Cornell University Press, 1998); Risse, Ropp, and Sikkink, eds., *The Power of Human Rights*. On the importance of theorizing such interactions more generally, see Gourevitch, "Domestic Politics and International Relations."

29. Massey, "Why Does Immigration Occur?" pp. 50–51; John Tirman (this volume).

30. Peter Katzenstein, *Small States in World Markets: Industrial Policy in Europe* (Ithaca, N.Y.: Cornell University Press, 1985).

31. Alexander Wendt, *Social Theory of International Politics* (Cambridge: Cambridge University Press, 1999).

32. Alastair Iain Johnston, *Social States: China in International Institutions, 1980–2000* (Princeton: Princeton University Press, forthcoming).

33. For example, Massey, "Why Does Immigration Occur?"

34. More formally, these accounts integrate a materialist ontology with an instrumental, calculative theory of action typically associated with rational choice.

35. Amy Gurowitz, "Mobilizing International Norms: Domestic Actors, Immigrants and the Japanese State," *World Politics* 51 (April 1999): pp. 413–45; see also Soysal, *Limits of Citizenship*. While they use a different language, many students of international law explore similar dynamics. For example, Peter Spiro (this volume) offers a fascinating exploration of how international norms may be affecting U.S. policy on immigration and aliens post-9/11.

36. Jeffrey T Checkel, " 'Going Native' in Europe? Theorizing Social Interaction in European Institutions," *Comparative Political Studies* 36 (February/March 2003).

37. While closely related, this research is conceptually and empirically distinct from the burgeoning literature on globalization. For a good discussion, see Michael Zuern, "From Interdependence to Globalization," in *Handbook of International Relations*, ed. Walter Carlsnaes, Thomas Risse, and Beth Simmons (London: Sage Publications, 2002).

38. For example, Robert Keohane and Joseph Nye, eds., *Transnational Relations and World Politics* (Cambridge, Mass.: Harvard University Press, 1972).

39. Thomas Risse-Kappen, ed., *Bringing Transnational Relations Back In: Non-State Actors, Domestic Structures and International Institutions* (Cambridge: Cambridge University Press, 1995).

40. Daniel Thomas, *The Helsinki Effect: International Norms, Human Rights, and the Demise of Communism* (Princeton: Princeton University Press, 2001).

41. Evangelista, *Unarmed Forces*.

42. Checkel, "Norms, Institutions and National Identity in Contemporary Europe."

43. Thomas Risse, personal communication, October 2002.

44. Fiona Adamson, this volume.

45. Imtiaz Amed, this volume.

46. Tom Biersteker, this volume; Howard Adelman, this volume; Paula Newberg, this volume.

47. Martha Finnemore and Kathryn Sikkink, "International Norm Dynamics and Political Change," *International Organization* 52 (Autumn 1998); see also David Lumsdaine, *Moral Vision in International Politics: The Foreign Aid Regime, 1949–1989* (Princeton: Princeton University Press, 1993).

48. Emanuel Adler and Michael Barnett, eds., *Security Communities* (Cambridge: Cambridge University Press, 1998).

49. Janice Bially-Mattern, "Narratives of Criminal Identity: 'Illicit' Political Communities in World Order," paper presented at the International Studies Association Annual Convention, February 2003.

50. For details, see http://www.gspia.pitt.edu/ridgway.

51. See also Bially-Mattern, "Narratives of Criminal Identity."

52. Stephen Krasner, *Sovereignty: Organized Hypocrisy* (Princeton: Princeton University Press, 1999).

53. See also Biersteker, this volume.

54. Keck and Sikkink, *Activists Beyond Borders.*

55. Judith Kelley, *Institutions and Ethnic Politics* (Princeton: Princeton University Press, forthcoming).

56. Zuern, "From Interdependence to Globalization."

57. As cited in Nicholas Lemann, "The Next World Order," *New Yorker,* 25 March 2002.

58. A key difference between the discussion here and the debate over humanitarian intervention can be summed up in two words: international institutions. The Bush administration seems ready to invoke a role for them, but mainly as after-the-fact covers for decisions made on other grounds. In contrast, most proponents of humanitarian intervention see an up-front role for institutions like the UN in creating new law and precedent regarding sovereignty's limits.

59. Note that I say "reappearance." As the chapters by Gerstle and Ho demonstrate, September 11 was not the first time that America (and other countries) faced compelling threats (real or imagined) from immigrant communities or terror networks. There is a rich and sad history from which both scholars and policymakers should learn.

60. Europe is a partial exception. Even before September 11, a strengthening of common immigration and asylum procedures had been a priority for the European Union. Moreover, multilateral cooperation against terror extends back several decades. Peter Katzenstein, "Coping with Terrorism: Norms and Internal Security in Germany and Japan," in *Ideas & Foreign Policy: Beliefs, Institutions and Political Change,* eds. Judith Goldstein and Robert Keohane (Ithaca, N.Y.: Cornell University Press, 1993).

61. Adelman, this volume.

62. See also the excellent discussion in Thomas Biersteker, "State, Sovereignty and Territory," in *Handbook of International Relations,* eds. Walter Carlsnaes, Thomas Risse and Beth Simmons (London: Sage Publications, 2002).

63. For example, Johan P. Olsen, "The Many Faces of Europeanization," *Journal of Common Market Studies* 40 (December 2002); Erik Oddvar Eriksen and John Fossum, eds., *Democracy in the European Union: Integration through Deliberation?* (London: Routledge, 2000).

64. Alexander George, *Bridging the Gap: Theory and Practice in Foreign Policy,* (Washington, DC: United States Institute of Peace Press, 1993); Bruce Jentleson, "The Need for Praxis: Bringing Policy Relevance Back In," *International Security* 26 (Spring 2002): 173–174.

65. In his review of the migration literature and call for synthetic, middle-range arguments, Massey makes a strikingly similar point. Massey, "Why Does Immigration Occur?" pp. 50–52.

66. Gary Gerstle (this volume) on previous "threats" from immigrant communities in the United States and Ho (this volume) on Bin Laden's historical forerunners superbly contextualize current debates and arguments.

CONTRIBUTORS

Fiona B. Adamson is an assistant professor of international relations and the director of the Program in International Public Policy at the School of Public Policy, University College London. She received her Ph.D. in Political Science from Columbia University, where her dissertation examined the impact of non-state actors on global security and stability.

Howard Adelman has been a professor of philosophy at York in Toronto since 1966 and was the founder and director of the Centre for Refugee Studies at York University and Editor of *Refuge* until the end of 1993. His latest volume is *Humanitarian Intervention in Zaire* (Red Sea Press, 2003).

Imtiaz Ahmed is professor and chair, Department of International Relations, University of Dhaka. His most recent publication is *Water Futures in South Asia, a Special Issue of Futures: the journal of policy, planning and futures studies,* Elsevier Science, Exeter, U.K., October/November 2001 (as guest editor).

Thomas J. Biersteker is Henry R. Luce Professor at Brown University and director of the Watson Institute for International Studies. His most recent book, co-edited with Rodney B. Hall, is *The Emergence of Private Authority in Global Governance* (Cambridge University Press, 2002).

Louise Cainkar is a sociologist and senior research fellow at the University of Illinois at Chicago (UIC), Great Cities Institute. She has been conducting engaged research in U.S. immigrant communities for more than 15 years and has worked as a grantmaker to immigrant community organizations. She is widely published and regarded as a national expert on Arab immigrants, Arab Americans, and immigrant Muslim communities.

Jeffrey T. Checkel is professor of Political Science at the University of Oslo, where he is also a research professor at ARENA. He is editor most recently of *International Institutions and Socialization in the New Europe.*

Gary Gerstle is professor of history at the University of Maryland and author, most recently, of *American Crucible: Race and Nation in the Twentieth Century* (2001).

Engseng Ho is Associate Professor of Anthropology at Harvard University, and Academy Scholar at the Harvard Academy for International and Area Studies. He is interested in how issues of mobility challenge received theories of society and state. He pursues this interest through the study of diasporas and empires, employing ethnographic and historical material. His fieldwork experience is in Yemen and maritime Southeast Asia, among Arab, Chinese, and Malay communities.

Paula Newberg is an international consultant for organizations such as the UN Foundation, and a specialist on Central Asia. Among her works is *Judging the State: Courts and Constitutional Politics in Pakistan* (Cambridge University Press, 1995).

Stephen Schlesinger is director of the World Policy Institute at the New School University in New York City. He is the author of *Act of Creation: The Founding of the United Nations.*

Yossi Shain, who holds a dual appointment as professor of government and diaspora politics at Georgetown and professor of political science at Tel Aviv University, is currently a visiting fellow at the Center of International Studies at Princeton University. His latest book is *Marketing the American Creed Abroad: Diasporas in the U.S. and Their Homelands* (Cambridge University Press, 1999).

Peter J. Spiro is professor of law at Hofstra University Law School.

John Tirman (editor) is a program director at the Social Science Research Council.

Mario Zucconi teaches international relations at the University of Urbino, Italy, and is senior associate with the Center for International Political Studies (CeSPI, Rome). Among his latest publications is *The Impact of Economic Sanctions: The Case of Serbia* (Angeli, Milan, 2001).

INDEX